# From Ellis Island to JFK

# From Ellis Island to JFK

*New York's Two Great Waves of Immigration*

Nancy Foner

Yale University Press, New Haven and London

Russell Sage Foundation, New York

Published with assistance from the foundation established in memory
of Philip Hamilton McMillan of the class of 1894, Yale College.

Designed by Charles Ellertson.
Set in Cycles type by Tseng Information Systems.
Printed in the United States of America by Sheridan Books, Chelsea, Michigan.

Library of Congress Cataloging-in-Publication Data
Foner, Nancy, 1945-
From Ellis Island to JFK : New York's two great waves of immigration / Nancy Foner.
    p.    cm.
Includes bibliographical references and index.
ISBN 0-300-08226-6 (alk. paper)
1. Immigrants—New York (State)—New York—History.   2. New York (N.Y.)—
Emigration and immigration—History.   I. Title.
JV7048 .F65   2000
974.7'1'008691—dc21
                              00-026933

A catalogue record for this book is available from the British Library.

10 9 8 7 6 5 4 3 2 1

*To Peter and Alexis*

# Contents

# Acknowledgments

*I*n the course of writing this book I have had a great deal of help from many people and institutions. I began work on this book as a visiting scholar at the Russell Sage Foundation, a wonderful environment in which to do research and write. I am grateful to Victor Nee, Sarah Mahler, Alex Stepick, and Min Zhou, the other visiting immigration scholars that year, for sharing their unpublished papers and research findings and for providing an informal forum in which to discuss ideas. Cathie Jo Martin and Louise Tilly, also visiting scholars, gave much-appreciated advice. My thanks, too, to staff members at the Russell Sage Foundation for their assistance, particularly Camille Yezzi, Jamie Gray, and Sara Beckman, and to Eric Wanner, president of the foundation, for his support of the project.

While writing this book, I have had the good fortune to be part of a growing community of U.S. immigration scholars. My colleagues on the Social Science Research Council's Committee on International Migration, and in the Working Group on Historical Comparisons, were a source of ideas and insights. The New School University's International Center for Migration, Ethnicity, and Citizenship, run by Aristide Zolberg and Peter Benda, has provided a stimulating environment for New York immigration scholars; the series of talks and research papers that came out of the Immigrant New York program was especially useful.

For careful readings of the entire manuscript, or for their expertise on particular sections, I am indebted to Richard Alba, Hector Cordero-Guzman, Aristide Zolberg, and two anonymous readers for Yale University Press. Luis Guarnizo, Peggy Levitt, Robert Smith, and Khachig Tololyan fielded questions and provided helpful suggestions for the analysis of transnationalism past and present. All errors that remain, of course, are mine.

I owe a special debt to Hector Cordero-Guzman and John Mollenkopf for calculating census data for use in the book. Thanks, as well, to Josh

DeWind, Philip Kasinitz, and Mary Waters for serving as valuable sounding boards along the way.

Charles Grench, my editor at Yale University Press, provided support for the book from the very beginning, when the book was just an outline, and guided the manuscript through the publication process. Karen Gangel was an excellent manuscript editor. At the Russell Sage Foundation, David Haproff and Suzanne Nichols offered helpful advice and support as well.

Portions of Chapter 7 appeared originally as "What's New about Transnationalism: New York Immigrants Today and at the Turn of the Century," in *Diaspora* 6, no. 3 (1997): 355-76. Some of the material in Chapter 5 was published as "Immigrant Women and Work in New York City, Then and Now," in *Journal of American Ethnic History* 18, no. 3 (1999): 95-113, and as "Benefits and Burdens: Immigrant Women and Work in New York City," in *Gender Issues* 16, no. 4 (1998): 5-24, the latter reprinted by permission of Transaction Publishers.

My deepest thanks, as always, go to members of my family. My parents, Anne and Moe Foner, gave encouragement at every stage. Once again, my mother read and commented on various drafts of the manuscript with a keen sociological eye. Alexis, my daughter, has heard more about immigrant New York than she perhaps will ever want to know. Finally, my husband, Peter Swerdloff, spent hours talking over ideas with me, helped me sharpen many of the arguments, and made countless stylistic suggestions. For his love and patience, I am most indebted.

# Introduction

*I*n the history, the very personality, of New York City, few events loom larger than the wave of immigration that peaked in the first decade of the twentieth century. Between 1880 and 1920, close to a million and a half immigrants arrived and settled in the city—so that by 1910 fully 41 percent of all New Yorkers were foreign born. The influx changed the way New Yorkers lived, the shape of their institutions, the flavor of their politics, the very food they ate. The new arrivals, mostly eastern European Jews and southern Italians, left a living legacy as well, since a large and influential part of New York's current citizens are their descendants.

Today, a new wave of immigrants is again changing the face of the city. This time, however, they no longer come predominantly from Europe. Instead, they arrive from the Dominican Republic, from China, from Mexico, from Jamaica. They are Asians, Latin Americans, and West Indians in the main, and they are mostly people of color. Immigrants already constitute over a third of the city's population. More than two and a half million have arrived since 1965, and they are now streaming in at a rate of over one hundred thousand a year.[1]

A reedy, low-lying mud bank in the Upper Bay called Ellis Island grew famous as the port of entry for the last great migration. More than twelve million people passed through its halls between 1892 and 1954, the vast majority landing there in the first three decades of its existence as an immigrant-processing center. The story of these multitudes—the "huddled masses"—was, of course, immortalized in verse and was tied as well to the extraordinary statue in whose shadow they arrived. Today most people coming to the city enter through the more prosaic gates of John F. Kennedy International Airport. And so far, nothing monumental marks their passage.

That does not mean that their arrival is unnoticed. Indeed, there is every indication that the new migration will have as much impact on the city as the old. The new immigrants are already changing the economy. They're affecting the city's institutions—the schools and colleges, the hospitals, the social services, the political landscape. Whole neighborhoods are changing, new cuisines are turning up in restaurants, the driver of your taxi is speaking Urdu on his intercom. And the commentators and analysts, popular and academic, in the press and in the journals, are comparing the new immigration with the old.

This is not surprising. The future of the city and, in fact, the shape of the entire country in the years ahead will be affected by the wave of new arrivals. The relationship between this movement and the influx of a century ago is both a useful and an unavoidable concomitant to any understanding of what's happening now.

Another element makes the comparison essential. An elaborate mythology has grown around immigration at the turn of the century, and perceptions of that earlier migration deeply color how the newest wave is seen.

Memories of the last great immigration are emotional and strongly held. Family lore and stories celebrate the grit and determination that drove European immigrants to make it in America; films and fiction portray their struggles and achievements; they are even honored in a national museum on Ellis Island that draws several million visitors every year.

The literature alone is copious. New York's Italian immigrants have been immortalized in novels like *The Godfather* and *Christ in Concrete*, while the successes—and angst—of Jewish immigrants and their children form the basis for many fictional accounts, from Abraham Cahan's *The Rise of David Levinsky* to Philip Roth's *Portnoy's Complaint*. There is a virtual industry based on recording and analyzing the experiences of New York's Russian Jewish immigrants. *The World of Our Fathers* spawned a counterpart, *The World of Our Mothers;* academic accounts chronicle everything from Jewish involvement in labor unions and vaudeville to tales of Jewish gangsters.[2] Countless memoirs by successful immigrant entrepreneurs, politicians, entertainers, and intellectuals record their humble roots and memories of things past. And library shelves are filled with biographies of such famous immigrants as Rudolph Valentino and Irving Berlin.

In addition, those who comment on and, in some cases, set policies about the newest New Yorkers—politicians, scholars, and writers—are often themselves descendants of the earlier wave. Understandably, they frequently hark back to the triumphs and tribulations of their ancestors when they speak about the latest newcomers.

A process akin to what historians have called the invention of tradition has taken place, a kind of "invention of immigration."[3] A century ago, many native-born Americans viewed newly arrived eastern and southern European immigrants with fear and loathing, as "repulsive creatures" who menaced the very foundations of American civilization.[4] These negative attitudes have long been forgotten in a haze of history, replaced by images that glorify the past. For many present-day New Yorkers, their Jewish and Italian immigrant forebears have become folk heroes of a sort—and represent a baseline against which current arrivals are compared and, unfortunately, often fail to measure up.

A series of strongly held, if often contradictory, images has come to characterize the earlier immigrants: they worked hard; they strove to become assimilated; they pulled themselves up by their own Herculean efforts; they were, in the case of Jews, "the people of the book"; they had strong family values and colorful roots. They were, in short, what made America great.

Against this image of immigrant giants of the past, present-day arrivals often seem a pale imitation. Admittedly, many politicians and public figures praise the newest New Yorkers for their traditional immigrant work ethic, initiative, and drive. At the same time, a common popular fear is that the newcomers will have trouble—indeed, often resist—fitting in; that they are here for government handouts rather than to work; and that their origins in non-Western cultures are poor preparation for American life. Many worry that today's arrivals are undermining American values and changing America's racial makeup—that they will make America, to use Peter Brimelow's phrase, an alien nation.[5]

As is often the case, popular myths and images give a distorted picture of the complex realities that underlie them. Some of the popular beliefs are misleading, others too simplistic. A detailed comparison of immigration at the beginning and end of the twentieth century will show what really happened in both periods and what the lives of immigrants, then and now, have been like.

There is another reason for comparing the two immigrations. Much of the scholarly material on immigration is fairly narrowly drawn, focusing on specific groups of immigrants and specific aspects of their experiences at one point in time. There is virtue in the broad view that a comparison encourages. Widening the focus to include earlier as well as recent immigrants gives a better sense of the impact they have had on New York City over time—and how the immigrants themselves have been transformed in the process.

The comparison also brings into sharper focus particular aspects of today's immigration that might be overlooked or minimized if the latest arrivals were simply considered on their own. As Reinhard Bendix has put it in another context, comparative studies "increase the 'visibility' of one structure by contrasting it with another."[6] Certain contemporary patterns, like improvements in the position of immigrant women and the role of education in immigrant mobility, stand out in sharper relief when set against those of earlier arrivals. And while the differences stand out, a comparison makes clear that there are also many similarities and continuities with the past.

There are other benefits to bringing together the historical and contemporary literature on immigration. So far the two literatures have largely flowed in separate streams, with historians or sociologists often "discovering" what has been acknowledged and treated in the other's discipline for some time.[7] Insights from historical studies—for example, on the reasons for the varying success of different immigrant groups—can enrich our understanding of contemporary immigration. In much the same way, sociological research on such topics as immigrants' incorporation into the labor market can shed light on the past.

The comparison may also be of value from a theoretical point of view. It helps to evaluate whether conceptual frameworks that have been used to understand the turn-of-the-century immigration, like analyses of the process of becoming "white," are useful in understanding the new arrivals. And it raises questions about whether models and concepts elaborated in light of today's immigration, from economic restructuring to transnationalism, are, as they're often presented, unique to our current period or whether they also pertain to the past. Indeed, by setting the present against the past, we can better understand what is really "new" about the new immigration. As the historian David Kennedy puts it, "The only way we can know with certainty as we move along time's path that we have come to a genuinely new place is to know something of where we have been."[8]

As an interpretive synthesis, the book brings together strands from the mass of literature on past and present immigration. It draws on both qualitative and quantitative material. Census data cannot capture the rich texture of the immigrant experience; narratives of particular individuals and families, by the same token, must be placed in the context of wider group patterns. The sources I use are extremely varied. They range from historical accounts of Jews and Italians to contemporary ethnographic studies of the newer arrivals; statistical material, from census reports to surveys collected by social science researchers and governmental bodies; and a broad array of novels, memoirs, and biographies. Along the way, I draw on my

Table 1    Foreign-Born Population of New York City, 1900–98

| Year | Total Population (in thousands) | Foreign-Born Population (in thousands) | Percentage of Foreign Born in New York City | Percentage of All U.S. Foreign Born in New York City |
|------|------|------|------|------|
| 1998 | 7,520.6 | 2,810.6 | 37.4 | 10.7 |
| 1990 | 7,322.6 | 2,082.9 | 28.4 | 10.5 |
| 1980 | 7,071.6 | 1,670.2 | 23.6 | 11.9 |
| 1970 | 7,894.9 | 1,437.1 | 18.2 | 14.9 |
| 1960 | 7,783.3 | 1,558.7 | 20.0 | 16.0 |
| 1950 | 7,892.0 | 1,860.9 | 23.6 | 17.8 |
| 1940 | 7,455.0 | 2,138.7 | 28.7 | 18.3 |
| 1930 | 6,930.4 | 2,358.7 | 34.0 | 16.5 |
| 1920 | 5,620.0 | 2,028.2 | 36.1 | 14.5 |
| 1910 | 4,766.9 | 1,944.4 | 40.8 | 14.3 |
| 1900 | 3,437.2 | 1,270.1 | 37.0 | 12.2 |

*Source:* Kraly 1987: table 2.2; Mollenkopf 1993: appendix, table 2; U.S. Bureau of the Census, March 1998 Current Population Survey, Annual Demographic Supplement, calculated by John Mollenkopf, Center for Urban Research, CUNY Graduate Center; Camarota 1998.

firsthand research on Jamaican immigrants as well as on my study of immigrant health-care workers in New York.[9]

Broad as the book is, it does not, of course, cover everything. In comparing the two immigrations, it focuses on some fundamental aspects of the immigrant experience, from why immigrants come in the first place to where they live and work, the dynamics of race and homeland ties, the nature of migrant women's lives, and the role of education. The book is not meant to be an exhaustive comparison, and in choosing to examine certain topics in depth I have inevitably neglected others. There are, for example, no chapters on immigrants' religious practices, their role in politics and labor unions, or nativist reactions to immigration, all important subjects that deserve careful historical-comparative study by other scholars.[10] As is already clear, the book also limits its focus to New York. New York is the quintessential immigrant city and has long been a main gateway for new arrivals. Since 1900, between 10 and 18 percent of the nation's foreign-born population has lived in New York City, with the figure at 14 percent in 1910 and about 11 percent in 1998 (see table 1). Currently, few cities in the country have a percentage of immigrants as high as New York's—and the same goes for the wider metropolitan area. More than one out of three of New

York City's residents is now foreign born, and the figure is one out of four for the whole metropolitan area.[11]

Of concern here are the two peak periods of immigration to the city. The "old" immigrants in this book refer to those who arrived between 1880 and 1920, and the "new" to those who have come since the mid-1960s. In the earlier era, the focus is on Italians and eastern European Jews. Although they were not the only newcomers of the time, it was the enormous tidal wave of eastern European Jews and southern Italians that defined what was then thought of as the new immigration. The Irish and Germans, who had dominated the immigrant flow to the city since the mid-1800s, were still arriving, but in the last decade of the nineteenth century, their numbers had declined, eclipsed by the newer waves from Italy and Russia.[12] By 1920, nearly half a million foreign-born Russian Jews and about four hundred thousand immigrant Italians lived in the city. With their children, New York City's Italian Americans numbered over eight hundred thousand; the Jewish population had soared to over 1.6 million, or almost 30 percent of the city's population.[13]

No two groups now dominate in this way. Today New York's immigrants include sizable numbers of most Asian, West Indian, and Latin American nationalities and many European groups as well. For this reason, the discussion of the present era ranges over a large number of groups, although there is more attention to the top ten—for example, Dominicans, Chinese, and Jamaicans—who, not surprisingly, have been the subject of a number of studies. Other groups with substantial numbers (and who have also been the focus of scholarly accounts) also come in for examination along the way.

The plan of the book is as follows. Chapter 1 begins the comparison with some basic questions about immigrants in the two eras: Who are they? Why and how have they come? Obviously, today's immigrants come from many different countries and a variety of backgrounds. Does this mean that they come to America for different reasons? Or do some of the same underlying causes of migration still operate? And how do illegal, or undocumented, migrants fit into the picture?

In Chapter 2, I look at immigrant residential patterns now and then. We think of immigrants as inevitably clustering in their own ethnic neighborhoods, and I discuss the extent to which this was, and remains, the case. There are also new features to the settlement process in that some immigrants head straight for middle-class suburbs, while others play a role in reviving New York City neighborhoods that have sunk into decline.

Chapter 3 considers the way immigrants in the two eras have been incorporated into New York's economy. It's a case, in many ways, of déjà vu, as recent arrivals again work in bleak garment sweatshops and set up shop to sell wares to their compatriots. But what difference does it make that turn-of-the-century newcomers came at a time of industrial expansion, whereas today they enter a postindustrial, service-oriented economy? Today's immigrants also arrive with much more educational and occupational variety than their predecessors. In addition, New York is now home to a large native black and Hispanic population, which gives the issue of competition for jobs at the bottom of the occupational ladder a different tone. In Chapter 4, I continue the discussion of work by focusing on immigrant women. Since the beginning of the twentieth century, working daughters have given way to working mothers, and the key question is how this shift has affected immigrant women's lives both inside and outside the home.

Chapter 5 attempts to unravel the complexities of racial perceptions in the two eras. "The swarthy Italian . . . content to live in a pig-sty," Jews with "their unmistakable physiognomy. . . . Money is their God"—these epithets remind us that immigrants a century ago were victims of harsh prejudice and did not seem fully white to many New Yorkers.[14] In the current period, the crucial issue is how the latest immigrants fit into New York's changing racial hierarchy. How does being black affect West Indians? Are Hispanics a race? And have Asians become almost white?

In Chapter 6, I take up the issue of transnationalism—a term coined by contemporary social scientists to characterize the way today's migrants forge ties across national borders. Transnationalism isn't new, even though it often seems as if it was invented yesterday, and I explore continuities as well as differences between past and present migrants' links with their home societies.

Chapter 7 shifts the focus to education. Many New Yorkers look with longing to a time when the public schools taught immigrant children how to become Americans and were the gateway to better jobs and a better life. Such views say more about the frustrations of the current era than the realities of the past. How did immigrants perform in school in the past? How are they doing now? As for notions that the schools have abandoned their assimilating mission in the wake of bilingual programs and multiculturalism, these fears are, I argue, ungrounded. In fact, one of the paradoxes of the current period is that immigrant children who become too American, and shed their immigrant culture and associates in the process, are often at risk of academic failure.

Chapter 8, in conclusion, looks to the future. At issue is whether—and in what ways—the descendants of the latest immigrants will repeat the experiences of their Jewish and Italian predecessors. Will the children of the current immigrants, like second-generation Italians and Jews, progress up the social ladder? Will they become "white" the way Jews and Italians did? Will they cut off ties to their parents' homelands? The past, as the book makes clear, is not a blueprint for the future, yet a look at what happened then is helpful in coming to grips with the contemporary situation—and in assessing what is in store for the children of today's immigrants as they grow up and take their place, as native New Yorkers, in an ever changing New York City.

# CHAPTER 1

# Who They Are and
# Why They Have Come

*E*mma Lazarus was wrong. Or to be more precise, she took a modest amount of poetic license. "Give me your tired, your poor, your huddled masses yearning to breathe free"—the words of her poem, engraved at the base of the Statue of Liberty, have a strong resonance today as America welcomes a new wave of immigrants to its shores. Although immigrants still often come to escape oppressive governments and poor economic conditions, much has changed. Emma Lazarus's characterization of immigrants as "the wretched refuse of your teeming shore" and "the homeless, tempest-tost" was overdrawn for the past. It is even less appropriate today, when so many newcomers are from the ranks of their home country's professional and middle classes.

Obviously, today's arrivals are no longer mainly European, and they come from a much wider array of nations and cultures than their predecessors. But because most immigrants are from relatively poor and developing nations does not mean, as many Americans believe, that the immigrants themselves are uniformly poor and uneducated. Although many now arrive, as before, with little education and few skills, significant numbers of the newest New Yorkers enter with college degrees and technical expertise.

The reasons why millions have left their homelands to come to America are complex and multifaceted. It has always been too simple to see immigration to this country as a quest for liberty and freedom. Nor is the move inevitably an escape from hunger and want, as the occupational backgrounds of many of today's newcomers make clear. An analysis of the underlying causes of immigration shows that the forces historians have identified as important in the last great wave—population growth, persecution, chain migration, and the globalization of capitalism—still operate, although additional factors are also involved. Changes in U.S. immigration policy have affected the magnitude and shape of the latest wave; they have also altered the immigration process itself.

A hundred years ago, immigrants arrived at Ellis Island dirty and bedraggled, after a long ocean journey in steerage; now they emerge from the cabin of a jet plane at John F. Kennedy International Airport, often dressed in designer jeans or fashionable attire. Because of the new barriers to legal entry, many end up living in New York without proper documents. Illegal aliens, of little concern at the turn of the past century, have become a dominant theme in public discourse and debates about the latest wave, although fears about their numbers and threat to society have been vastly overblown.

## Who Has Come

In the years just before and after 1900, New York City's new immigrants were overwhelmingly Russian Jews and Italians. They came two by two, to use Glazer and Moynihan's apt analogy, much like the Irish and Germans who dominated the immigrant flow in the mid-nineteenth century.[1]

In 1880, just before the mass migration began, only 12,000 foreign-born Italians lived in New York City; by 1910, the number had soared to 341,000. The growth of the city's Russian Jewish immigrant population was even more astounding, going from around 14,000 in 1880 to 484,000 in 1910.[2] Bear in mind that New York City was then a much smaller place, with a little under 5 million people in 1910.[3] In that year, Russian Jewish and Italian immigrants together accounted for close to a fifth of the city's population; all the foreign-born made up 41 percent of the citywide total. The heavy concentration of Jews and Italians was a New York phenomenon. According to the 1910 census, a quarter of the Italian-born population and about a third of the Russian-born Jews in the entire country lived in New York City. No other big city came close: the next most popular destination for Italians, Philadelphia, had 45,000 Italian immigrants, while Chicago, the second choice for newly arriving Russians, had 122,000 Russian Jews.[4]

Today no two immigrant groups dominate New York that way, and most immigrants come not from Europe but from Asia, Latin America, and the Caribbean. Never before has the United States received newcomers from so many different countries—all of which seem to be represented in New York. From a nationwide perspective, the city stands out for its remarkable ethnic diversity. In Los Angeles, the nation's other premier immigrant capital, more than half of the post-1965 adult immigrants counted in the 1990 census came from just three countries: Mexico, El Salvador, and Guate-

Table 2    Foreign-Born Residents of New York City, by Country of Birth, 1990

| Country of Birth | Number | Post-1964 Arrivals |
|---|---|---|
| Dominican Republic | 226,560 | 202,102 |
| China[1] | 164,586 | 145,362 |
| Jamaica | 116,100 | 101,580 |
| Italy | 101,651 | 37,557 |
| USSR | 80,333 | 60,110 |
| Guyana | 73,846 | 70,523 |
| Haiti | 70,987 | 65,287 |
| Colombia | 68,787 | 61,383 |
| Poland | 61,634 | 25,490 |
| Ecuador | 60,119 | 54,616 |
| Trinidad | 58,212 | 53,586 |
| Korea | 57,555 | 55,688 |
| India | 42,674 | 41,503 |

*Source:* For total figures, Mollenkopf, Kasinitz, and Lindholm 1995; for post-1964 arrivals, Flores and Ortiz 1997, both based on U.S. Bureau of the Census, 1990, Public Use Microdata Sample.

*Note:* This table lists the top thirteen foreign-born groups in 1990.

[1]Includes Hong Kong and Taiwan.

mala. Miami's immigrant arrivals are overwhelmingly Cuban, Haitian, and Nicaraguan. New York City is a different story. The top three groups in 1990 — Dominicans, Chinese, and Jamaicans — were just under 30 percent of all post-1965 arrivals there. No other foreign country accounted for more than 5 percent, and there were substantial numbers of nearly all European as well as most Asian, West Indian, and Latin American nationalities.[5] Altogether, in 1990, post-1964 immigrants constituted a significant chunk — 22 percent — of the city's 7.3 million residents.[6] That year all of the foreign-born constituted 28 percent of the city's population; by 1998, the Census Bureau estimated that the proportion had gone up to 37 percent — an astounding 2.8 million immigrants.

The Caribbean connection is especially strong. In 1990, one out of every three immigrant New Yorkers was Caribbean born, with Dominicans heading the list (see tables 2 and 3).[7] In fact, they are the largest new immigrant group in the city, accounting for just over 200,000, or about 12 percent, of the post-1964 arrivals tallied in the 1990 census. Their number keeps growing. With increases in annual immigration after the passage of the Immigration Act of 1990, and more visas available to spouses and children of permanent resident aliens, the number of legal Dominican immigrants arriving in New York City went from an annual average of 14,470 in the 1980s

Table 3    Foreign-Born Residents of New York City, by Country of Birth, 1998

| Country of Birth | Number | Country of Birth | Number |
|---|---|---|---|
| Dominican Republic | 412,431 | Jamaica | 137,698 |
| Former Soviet Union | 235,708 | Ecuador | 132,117 |
| Mexico | 198,041 | Haiti | 99,998 |
| China[1] | 192,612 | Italy | 80,897 |
| Guyana | 159,973 | Korea | 80,007 |
| Trinidad | 146,186 | Poland | 74,353 |

Source: U.S. Bureau of the Census, March 1998 Current Population Survey, Annual Demographic Supplement, calculated by John Mollenkopf, Center for Urban Research, CUNY Graduate Center.

Note: This table lists the top twelve foreign-born groups in 1998.

[1] Includes Hong Kong and Taiwan.

to over 22,000 in the 1990–94 period.[8] By 1998, according to the Current Population Survey, some 412,000 foreign-born Dominicans were living in the city.

The city's black population is increasingly West Indian. Almost a third of the non-Hispanic black population is now foreign born. Jamaica is a major source of immigrants, as are Haiti and Trinidad. Guyanese, who were barely noticed in the 1960s, ranked as the city's sixth largest immigrant group by 1990. That year the fourteen Commonwealth Caribbean nationalities, if considered as one category, were the largest group in the city.[9] From a national perspective, what is striking is how heavily Caribbean immigrants are concentrated in New York. Over half of the Haitians, Trinidadians, and Jamaicans and close to three-fourths of the Dominicans and Guyanese who legally entered the United States between 1972 and 1992 settled in the New York urban region.[10]

There has also been a huge Latin American influx. Although New York City is home to only a tiny proportion (3 percent) of the country's Mexican immigrants, they are newly emerging players in the immigration picture. The city's Mexican population grew by a striking 173 percent between 1980 and 1990 and continued to mushroom in the 1990s. By 1998, according to Census Bureau estimates, Mexicans were the third largest immigrant group in New York City. The number of foreign-born Ecuadorians, about sixty thousand at the time of the 1990 census, had more than doubled eight years later.

The days when Hispanic meant Puerto Rican are over. Puerto Ricans first started arriving in large numbers after World War II, the migration to New York peaking in the 1940s and 1950s. (As U.S. citizens by birth,

Puerto Ricans born on the island of Puerto Rico are not classified as immigrants when they move to New York.) Although since 1970 more Puerto Ricans have left than entered the city, they are still one of New York City's largest ethnic groups, accounting for 12 percent of the population in 1990. The growing number of Central and South Americans and Dominicans, however, has dramatically changed the city's Hispanic population. At the time of the 1990 census, 897,000 Puerto Ricans accounted for only about one-half of the city's Hispanics, down from 61 percent in 1980.[11] Their proportion shrunk even further during the 1990s. Dominicans are now the second largest Hispanic group, making up about a quarter of all Hispanic New Yorkers; a combination of Ecuadorians, Colombians, and Mexicans represent about another quarter.

Asians are also a major presence in the new New York; in 1990 they made up close to a quarter of the city's post-1964 foreign-born population. The Chinese lead the list. Indeed, in 1990 New York had the largest Chinese population of any American city.[12] By 1998, an estimated 193,000 foreign-born Chinese (mainly from China but also from Hong Kong and Taiwan) lived in the city, more than twice the number of any other Asian immigrant group.

Yet in New York, Asian does not mean only Chinese, as any visitor to the city knows well. The largest Asian Indian population in the country is now in the New York area. Most Indian immigrants live in the suburbs, but in 1998 a sizable number, close to fifty thousand, resided in the five boroughs. Although New York and its suburbs may not be as popular a destination for Filipinos and Koreans as West Coast cities, the New York region attracts significant numbers of these groups, too. According to the 1998 Current Population Survey, the city was home to about eighty thousand Koreans and thirty-eight thousand Filipinos.

Nor has European migration disappeared. Once more, New York City is home to thousands of Russian immigrants. (Whereas Southeast Asians are the dominant refugee population in many other parts of the country, most refugees in New York are from the former Soviet Union.) In the 1970s, about 35,000 Soviet Jewish refugees moved to the New York metropolitan area, although the number slowed to a trickle when the Soviet Union slashed the number of exit visas in the 1980s. In the 1990s, the immigration picked up again. Average annual immigration from the former Soviet Union rose tenfold from the 1980s to the 1990s, with some 66,000 arriving in New York City between 1990 and 1994 alone. By 1998, immigrants from the former Soviet Union were the second largest foreign group in the city, some 235,000 strong. A special diversity visa program established in 1990 to allow immigration from underrepresented countries benefited Irish and Polish immigrants, whose numbers had also been on the rise in the 1990s. By 1998, about 74,000 Polish immigrants lived in the city. Migration from Italy, by the same token, slowed to a trickle of about 400 a year in the early 1990s; most foreign-born Italian New Yorkers arrived before 1965.

The extraordinary ethnic diversity of today's immigrants is matched by the variety of their occupational and class backgrounds—from poor farmers and factory workers to physicians, engineers, and scientists. There are immigrants like Pradip Menon, born into a wealthy professional family in Poona, India, who arrived in New York with a college degree in engineering from a prestigious university and an M.B.A. from an equally prestigious management school.[13] And there are those like Benjamin Velasquez, a poor farmer in El Salvador who worked on his family's parcel of land growing corn and beans.[14] A century ago, the immigration to New York was not marked by the same extremes—or by anywhere near the current proportion of professionals and executives.

This does not mean that the "old" Jewish and Italian immigrants were from the depths of their societies. An exceptionally high proportion of Jewish immigrants had worked in skilled trades before they emigrated. No other eastern or southern European group came close. Whereas Jews accounted for only 9 percent of all immigrants with work experience who entered the United States in the first decade of the twentieth century, they constituted 29 percent of all skilled immigrants.[15] "Who leaves for America?" went a common saying among Russian Jews. "The tailors, shoemakers, and horse thieves." Fully two-thirds of the Jewish immigrants arriving in the United States between 1899 and 1910 who reported an occupation were skilled workers, the largest group being tailors, followed by carpenters, dressmakers, and shoemakers.[16]

The Italian immigration was strikingly different. It was primarily a peasant migration from the agricultural regions of the south. Only 16 percent of the Italians who came to America between 1899 and 1910 who reported prior work experience were skilled workers. Three-quarters were farm workers or common laborers. Even so, those most likely to leave Italy for America were in the middle and lower-middle levels of the peasantry rather than day laborers with no land at all.[17]

Then, as now, immigrants were positively selected in terms of ambition, determination, and willingness to work and take risks. Immigration, Rubén Rumbaut observes, requires both restlessness and resourcefulness. "On the whole," he writes, "the main reason the richest of the rich and the poorest of the poor do not immigrate is because they are, respectively, unmoved or unable to move." [18]

Although yesterday's newcomers were more skilled than we may recall, professionals were scarce. Of those arriving in America between 1899 and 1910, only 1.3 percent of previously employed Jewish immigrants were professionals, and only .5 percent of the Italian immigrants.

This is a far cry from today. Enormous changes in educational and occupational structures throughout the world have produced growing numbers of professional, technical, and white-collar workers. A substantial number who move to the United States—and New York—are so-called brain-drain immigrants. In the 1980s, 23 percent of working-age male immigrants and 20 percent of female immigrants entering New York City who reported an occupation to the Immigration and Naturalization Service (INS) were professionals, executives, or managers. In the early 1990s, the proportions were even higher: 27 percent for men, 36 percent for women.[19] According to the 1990 census, 10 percent of the working-age immigrants living in New York City were college graduates; an additional 6 percent had a master's degree or more.

Large numbers of professional and highly educated newcomers are a modern-day phenomenon, but huge numbers of low-skilled and poorly educated immigrants also continue to arrive. In 1990, 18 percent of the working-age immigrants in New York City had less than a ninth grade education. Another 22 percent had gone beyond the eighth grade but had not graduated from high school. The disparities in some groups are especially striking. One out of five of the working-age post-1965 Chinese immigrants had a college degree or more, whereas one out of four had less than a ninth grade education.[20]

Just as Italians and Jews had strikingly different occupational backgrounds, so, too, there are marked differences among today's groups. In the current wave, Caribbean and South and Central American arrivals have the lowest proportions with college degrees and experience in professional and managerial positions. At the time of the 1990 census, under 10 percent of New York City's Dominicans, Ecuadorians, Haitians, Guyanese, Trinidadians, and Colombians over the age of twenty-five who had arrived in the 1980s were college graduates. This compares to a third or more from Asia, Africa, the Middle East, and western Europe, who also, not surprisingly, often held high-level jobs before they emigrated; more than 30 percent of the Asian, western European, and African immigrants entering New York City in the 1980s who reported an occupation to the INS were professionals, executives, and managers.[21] Indians, Filipinos, and Taiwanese stand out with extraordinarily high levels of educational attainment: in 1990, about half or more who arrived in the 1980s had college degrees, putting them ahead of non-Hispanic white New Yorkers, for whom the figure was 42 percent.[22] Again, as one would expect, these groups also had high proportions with professional backgrounds.[23]

What about the background of undocumented immigrants? This is a relevant question today, but not for turn-of-the-century European arrivals. A hundred years ago, the nature of immigration restrictions and immigrant travel meant that very few newcomers lived in New York "illegally."

Then, as Alexander Aleinikoff puts it, "a diligent foreigner could sell the family farm and cow, buy steerage tickets to the U.S. and take up residence here (provided he or she was not infected with a contagious disease or offensive foreign political ideology)."[24] Until the 1920s, there were no numerical limits on European immigration—and no immigrant visas or special papers that had to be secured from the United States. Europeans were excluded only on qualitative grounds; criminals, prostitutes, and the physically and mentally ill were prohibited entry, as were those likely to become public charges. In 1917, illiterate immigrants were added to the list with the imposition of a literacy test, basically a simple reading test in the language of the immigrant's choice.[25] Since nearly all newcomers to New York came by boat and were processed through Ellis Island, they had no way to avoid immigration inspections intended to weed out the unhealthy and undesirable. Even before this, steamship companies had their own examinations in the port of origin; immigration legislation of 1891 made these companies responsible for returning deportees to their homeland and for providing food and lodging while they were detained in the United States.

Admittedly, some Italians whom America would not accept for medical or criminal reasons resorted to illegal strategies. According to one account, "There was no document or stamp essential to emigration that could not be expertly forged, including . . . health certificates. In addition, legitimate documents sometimes changed hands repeatedly. . . . For 50 lire one could rent American citizenship papers that had been brought to Italy by repatriated emigrants. Fifteen lire would be refunded if the person returned them after use."[26] A number of Italians were smuggled on ships, like Matteo, who, in 1913, was turned away at the medical screening by the ship's doctor in Palermo because of an injured eye. For the price of eight hundred lire, he soon managed to board a New York–bound cargo ship as a seaman, shoveling coal in the boiler room.[27] New York's small Chinese community was also home to some who had entered illegally, despite the Chinese Exclusion Act of 1882, which banned the immigration of Chinese laborers.[28] The "paper son" strategy, the main illegal route to entry, became common after Supreme Court cases in 1915 and 1916 ruled that foreign-born children of Chinese who were American citizens were entitled to American citizenship. A Chinese American returning from a trip to China would report to the immigration authorities that he and his wife had produced a son during his stay in China. He would then sell the legal papers to someone who wanted to come to America.[29]

The number of these illegal immigrant New Yorkers at the beginning of the twentieth century was minuscule, however. Today, limits on the number of available immigrant visas, combined with the continuing desire of many to move to the United States, have created a climate in which undocumented immigration flourishes. Nevertheless, fears about the numbers involved are exaggerated. Illegal aliens are not flooding the New York area. At any one time, a relatively small proportion of New York City's immigrant population is undocumented. A widely accepted figure from the Immigration and Naturalization Service put the number in New York State at about 540,000 for 1996—an estimated 80 percent of whom live in New York City.[30] California has the lion's share—some 40 percent of the nation's illegal immigrants, compared to 11 percent in the state of New York.

The overwhelming majority of the undocumented in the New York area have not snuck secretly across the border or hidden out in boats. Most enter the United States legally on temporary visas and become illegal immigrants—or visa overstayers, in immigration parlance—by failing to leave when their visas expire. According to INS estimates, nine out of ten of New York State's illegal residents in 1996 had overstayed their visas.[31] The undocumented rarely come from the ranks of the very poorest in their home countries. Available studies show that, like their legal counterparts, unauthorized immigrants are self-selected in terms of ambition and willingness to work. They tend to have above-average levels of education and occupational skills in comparison with their homeland populations.[32]

Indeed, a study of Dominican immigrants in New York City in the early 1980s found that the undocumented held more prestigious jobs before emigrating than did the documented immigrants; they were far more likely to have been professionals and managers in the Dominican Republic.[33] Another survey of some two hundred undocumented immigrants in New York and New Jersey concluded that they often came from lower-middle- and middle-class households in their home countries.[34]

The various scams and schemes to get into the United States described later in the chapter do not come cheap. Getting a tourist visa—the way most undocumented New Yorkers initially enter—requires resources. Applicants have to prove to consulate officials that they have a job and accumulated assets in their home country and have the incentive to return home after a brief visit to the United States. If they do not actually have the assets, it is expensive to purchase false documents to show they do. It helps to have confidence and a sophisticated sense of how bureaucracies work, something often associated with high levels of education. Other schemes, from buying false passports to coming through Puerto Rico or Mexico, can cost thousands of dollars, which means that the undocumented often come from the ranks of the more economically secure or have relatives abroad willing to underwrite their expenses.[35]

## Why They Come

To uproot oneself and move to another country is a major, often traumatic decision. Why did hundreds of thousands move to New York in the past—and why do they keep coming? At first glance, the differences in their reasons are striking. After all, if so many professionals and highly skilled people are coming today, it seems logical to assume that their motivations differ from those of Italian peasants and Jewish artisans a century ago. Indeed, contemporary immigration has a lot to do with America's political and economic penetration worldwide and the diffusion of a modern culture of consumption, a culture out of the reach of most people in developing countries. Also, liberalized U.S. immigration policies in the past few decades have opened America's doors to many groups who were once shut out.

Yet if the causes of immigration in the two eras differ, closer examination also shows many broad underlying similarities. As Douglas Massey and his colleagues put it, in a review of international migration theory, individuals and families emigrate in response to changing circumstances set in motion by political and economic transformations of their societies.[36] Population growth and economic disruptions, attendant upon industrialization, urbanization, and agricultural development, set the stage for large-scale migration from Europe in the past and still operate as underlying causes of migration in many developing countries today.

At the end of the nineteenth century, the incorporation of eastern and southern Europe into the orbit of the expanding capitalist economy had a devastating impact on Russian Jews and southern Italians.[37] A hundred years later, a globalizing market economy set populations in developing regions on the move. In both eras, immigrants have sought to raise their incomes, accumulate capital, and control economic risks by moving to New York, where higher-paying jobs may be had.[38]

But migration is not simply a matter of rational calculations in response to market forces, as neoclassical and new economic theory would suggest.[39] If Russian Jews a century ago were escaping political oppression, so, too, many of today's immigrants are in a flight to freedom. Whatever the initial causes, once set in motion, immigration movements become self-perpetuating, so that today, as in the past, migration can be thought of as a process of progressive network building. "Networks developed by the movement of people back and forth in space," Alejandro Portes and Rubén Rumbaut write, "are at the core of the microstructures that sustain migration over time."[40] Historians use the term chain migration to describe the way past migration encourages present migration: migrants encourage and sponsor friends and relatives to join them. Contemporary social scientists theorize about the role of network connections in lowering the costs, raising the benefits, and reducing the risks of international migration. Among the mechanisms involved in what has been labeled "cumulative causation" is the emergence of a culture of migration; migration becomes integrated into the structure of values and expectations so that it is seen as a part of the normal course of events.[41]

## Going to "LaMerica" and the "Golden Land"

Thomas Archdeacon has observed that at the end of the nineteenth century the pressures of overpopulation, the prospects of economic mobility, and the availability of rapid transportation set people all over the world on the road.[42] Italians were especially likely to move, and most Italians who came to the United States between 1876 and 1930—about 80 percent—were from the regions south of Rome known as the Mezzogiorno.[43]

Dislocations in the nineteenth century caused by rapid population growth and the expansion of capitalist agriculture left southern Italians worse off than before. Although the population of Italy increased by 25 percent between 1871 and 1905, the economy slackened. Population growth put greater pressures on the land, especially in areas where the pattern of inheritance led to fragmentation of holdings. Many peasants, according to one account, were left barely clinging to their fields and hence vulnerable to any agricultural setback.[44]

With the end of feudalism, peasants faced a growing need for money to pay rent on the land they worked or to pay interest on loans extended by landowners and contractors at the beginning of the growing season. Oppressive taxes were an added burden.[45] Making a living, or supplementing the family income, as an artisan or craftsman became less promising as cheaper manufactured goods flooded rural markets.[46] Peasants hungered for land. The breakup of church, state, and communal property meant that land was for sale in many areas, but peasants lacked the cash to buy it. According to one account, emigration rates were higher from regions of small properties, where land was for sale and farmers were in competition, than from regions dominated by large estates that gobbled up the land on the market.[47]

The changing world market for southern Italy's agricultural products brought more troubles. In the 1880s, wheat prices plummeted as cheap American grain entered European markets on a mass scale; the southern Italian citrus industry suffered when the emerging North American citrus industry in Florida and California led to cuts in American imports of Italian fruit. Between 1888 and 1898, a Franco-Italian tariff war reduced the French importation of Italian wines, and the Italian protective tariff on wheat raised bread prices, placing an added burden on peasants. Organizations by peasants in Sicily to agitate for lower rents and higher wages were suppressed in the 1890s. And natural calamities, such as a phylloxera epidemic that destroyed Sicilian grape vines, major earthquakes, and volcanic eruptions of Vesuvius and Etna in the early 1900s, added to the level of human misery.

For eastern European Jews, political and religious persecution aggravated economic hardships.[48] A combination of industrialization, the overcrowding of the cities, and rampant anti-Semitism, including discriminatory laws, created a severe crisis in the already oppressive conditions of Jewish life.[49] By 1880, the number of Russian Jews had risen to about 4 million, up from 1.6 million in 1825. As the century came to a close, the pressure of numbers on a limited range of occupations had become intense.

Russian Jews were confined to the Pale of Settlement, a region stretching from the Baltic to the Black Sea (in what is now Poland, Lithuania, and Ukraine). The May Laws that followed the assassination of Czar Alexander II in 1881 imposed additional constraints. Jews were now prohibited from owning or renting land outside towns and cities of the Pale, and wholesale expulsions of Jews from villages of the Pale, on the grounds of illegal residence, became common.

Even before the May Laws, however, Russian Jews had been moving into industry and trade. The services they traditionally offered peasants, as middlemen and moneylenders, were less in demand owing to improvements in communication and transportation. Plus they faced increasing competition from a growing Christian middle class. As the principal buyers of the peasants' produce and sellers of finished products, Jews were hurt by the peasantry's increasing poverty. With the prohibition of rural residence, the May Laws added to Jews' economic difficulties by cutting them off from their customers, the peasants.[50]

In the cities and towns where Jews now had to live, overcrowding and overcompetition were the rule.[51] As Moses Rischin graphically puts it, "The bulging cities and withered towns rivaled one another in their raw poverty."[52] In the four-year period 1894–98, the number of Jewish paupers increased by almost 30 percent, and large numbers of Jews in many communities depended on charity.[53] Growing up in the town of Polotzk, Mary Antin experienced the overcrowding of occupations and physical confinement typical of many places within the Pale during the last years of the nineteenth century: "It was not easy to live, with such bitter competition as the congestion of the population made inevitable. There were ten times as many stores as there should have been, ten times as many tailors, cobblers, barbers, tinsmiths. A Gentile, if he failed in Polotzk, could go elsewhere, where there was less competition. A Jew could make the circle of the Pale, only to find the same conditions as at home."[54]

In 1891, thousands of Jews were expelled from Moscow, St. Petersburg, and Kiev. In 1897 thousands more were deprived of a livelihood as restaurateurs and innkeepers when the liquor traffic became a government monopoly. The introduction of the "percentage rule" in 1886, which restricted the proportion of Jewish students admitted to secondary schools and universities within the Pale, made it more difficult for Jews to enter the professions.

Worse still was the anti-Semitic violence. The assassination of Alexander II set off a wave of pogroms, massacres of Jews, and destruction of shops and synagogues that was encouraged, and perhaps even organized, by the czarist government. "I remember sitting by the window," Mollie Linker recalled. "When it got dark, you close the shutters, you were afraid. You were actually always in fear because of big pogroms. . . . I remember that scare . . . was in us all the time."[55]

Unwanted and unprotected, Russian Jews saw little hope for improvements in their native land. Indeed, the czarist government pointed to emigration as a solution open to Jews. "The Western borders are open to you Jews," said Count Ignatiev, author of the May Laws. The Russian government relaxed its rigorous rules forbidding emigration, giving Jews the right to leave, under obligation of abandoning Russian citizenship forever.[56]

America, with its expanding industrial economy, job opportunities, and higher wages and standard of living, beckoned to Jews and Italians. For Jews, there was also the promise of a less hostile government, without official anti-Semitic restrictions—and the knowledge that earlier Jewish immigrants, largely from Germany, had found freedom and economic success in the "Golden Land."[57] "I heard so much about America," said Fannie Shapiro, "a free country for the Jews."[58]

By the end of the nineteenth century, travel to America had become quicker and cheaper. Railroads made German ports accessible to the towns of eastern Europe, and steamships penetrated ports deep in the Mediterranean basin.[59] More steamships were now crossing the ocean, and the newer ones were bigger, faster, and safer than before.

Greater speed meant that each ship could make more transatlantic crossings annually; with greater size, as many as two thousand to three thousand people could be crammed into steerage sections, where most immigrants traveled. To recruit immigrants, steamship companies advertised with posters showing the prices and sailing dates. Tickets could be paid for in installments. In 1880 a transatlantic passage in steerage from Naples cost fifteen dollars; by 1899 it was twenty-eight dollars, and the fare from the port of Bremen was between thirty-six and thirty-eight dollars.[60]

Once migration from southern and eastern Europe got under way, it had a self-sustaining, indeed, a cumulative effect. Relatives in New York sent back money and prepaid tickets for the transatlantic voyage so that more and more family members could afford to come. Networks reduced the risks as well as costs of migration; relatives in New York could provide help with housing and getting a job. In one Italian village, a cobbler was nicknamed "Cristoforo Colombo" for being the first to migrate to the New World. When he heard by chance that a worker in New York could earn in a single day what it would take a week to earn in the village, he sailed from Naples. Within a year of landing in New York, he had saved enough money to send for two of his brothers, thereby initiating a chain of migration that eventually brought more than half of the population of his village to the new land.[61]

"America letters" and remittances spread the news of opportunities and inspired prospective emigrants. "The most effective method of distributing immigrant labor in the United States . . . is the [international and domestic] mail service," concluded an early twentieth-century report prepared for the U.S. Bureau of Labor on southern and eastern European unskilled workers in American factories.[62] Mary Antin felt a "stirring, a straining" while reading a letter from her father, who had gone to America ahead of the family. "My father was inspired by a vision. He saw something—he promised us something. It was this 'America.' And 'America' became my dream."[63] In Italy, "birds of passage" who returned from America for a visit or short stay were also important sources of information and inspiration. Returning emigrants were called "americanos," a word meaning "someone who got rich, no one knows how."[64]

Over time, a culture of migration developed as migration became ingrained in the repertoire of people's values and behaviors.[65] "America was in the air," Mary Antin recalled of her home in Russia. "Businessmen talked of it over their accounts; the market women made up their quarrels that they might discuss it from stall to stall; people who had relatives in the famous land went around reading their letters for the enlightenment of less fortunate folk. . . . Children played at emigrating."[66]

In Italy, "America fever" became an epidemic. "Going to America has become so popular recently," wrote the *prefetto* of the province of Cosenza in 1894, "that young men feel almost ashamed if they have not been overseas at least once. Ten years ago America evoked images of danger and distance. Now people feel more confident about going to New York than to Rome."[67] The mayor of one southern community officially greeted visiting dignitaries: "I welcome you in the name of the five thousand inhabitants of this town, three thousand of whom are in America and the other two thousand preparing to go."[68]

## Still the Golden Door

Today, it is towns in the Dominican Republic, Jamaica, and China that are sending masses of people to the city of New York. By 1981, almost four hundred people from Los Pinos, a Dominican village of about one thousand, had migrated to the United States, and nearly every one of them had a neighbor, friend, or relative in New York.[69] Perhaps as many as half a million Jamaicans now live in this country, a fifth of the population of the island itself. A joke along the migrant stream has it that Greater Kingston, Jamaica's major urban center, has added two new postal zones: Miami and New York.[70]

One reason so many immigrants come today is that they can. Government policies, as Alexander Aleinikoff argues, are an important part of the migration story.[71] In the past, the Johnson-Reed Immigration Act of 1924 played a critical role in ending the massive influx of Russian Jews and Italians by establishing very small nationality quotas for southern and eastern European immigrants.[72] After decades of restrictions, America opened its gates in 1965, abandoning the old country-of-origin quotas that favored northern and western Europeans. Instead of allocating visas primarily on the basis of place of birth, family reunification and, to a lesser extent, skills were now emphasized within the context of annual immigration ceilings that, after a series of legislative changes, stood at 675,000 in the mid-1990s.[73] The big winners were Asians, who had been severely restricted from immigration, and natives of the English-speaking Caribbean, who had been subject to small quotas for dependencies. U.S. policies toward refugees also allowed the large-scale admission of certain groups, Soviet Jews and Cubans being especially prominent in the New York area.

In some cases, it was also a question of the countries of origin loosening their exit policies. The world's major communist nations, China and the Soviet Union, allowed few people to leave until the 1970s. Like other independent Latin American countries, the Dominican Republic had been exempt from the national-origins quota system and had no numerical cap on immigration to the United States before 1965; by introducing numerical limits for the Western hemisphere for the first time, the new American law actually made it harder for Latin Americans to enter the United States. But even before the 1965 law, the extremely restrictive emigration policies of the right-wing dictator Rafael Trujillo made it difficult for Dominicans to leave; only after his death, in 1961, did migration to this country become significant.[74]

American immigration law opened the gates to many groups, but there are clearly other reasons for the enormous response—and for the huge backlogs; in the early 1990s the wait for a visa was often between two and nine years, and sometimes even longer.[75] It is hard to generalize about the movement of millions of people from so many different cultures, classes, and countries, yet a number of factors stand out. Economic, demographic, and political disruptions have led people to come here in search of a better life. In the context of a modern culture of consumption, their expectations may be even higher than those of their forebears a century ago.

In the nineteenth century, railroads, steamship lines, state bureaus of immigration, and letters from emigrants spread information about the New World. Since World War II, information about the good life in America has become more plentiful than ever. Television—and imported American programs—reach into even the poorest areas, bringing images of American society and American goods that are reinforced by movies and radio programs.[76] Newspapers, movies, and magazines tell of American events and life. Aspirations are further fueled by letters, phone calls, and visits from migrants as well as by promises of political elites and the expansion of educational opportunities.

Usually, these aspirations cannot be fulfilled at home. American life-styles are not attainable for the overwhelming majority in Third World countries, partly because of demographic pressure as populations have spi-raled upward, and even more because of the inequalities of economic de-velopment. Neither the resource base nor the levels of economic develop-ment in immigrants' home countries are adequate to meet the needs and expectations of the population.

In the English-speaking Caribbean, the legacy of plantation slavery and the distorting effects of colonial rule, as well as continued dependence on world powers, lending institutions, and corporations, have combined to produce economies that cannot deliver the kinds of jobs, lifestyles, and consumption patterns that people want. In Jamaica, as one man I met said, "money is hard." The Jamaican economy cannot provide enough "good" jobs that pay enough to support what people there consider a decent living. In recent years, Jamaican living standards have fallen in the face of the country's crippling foreign debt, the decline in prices for major exports, and soaring inflation. According to one survey, 60 percent of the popula-tion of the island would move to the United States if given the chance.[77]

In nearby Haiti, migration is an alternative employment strategy in an impoverished country with a chronically high unemployment rate, a rav-aged economy, and little opportunity for the middle class to advance.[78] The Dominican Republic, although more prosperous than Haiti, offers a variation on the same themes. The enormous outflow from the Dominican Republic to the United States, two social scientists argue, has been sus-tained by the failure to modernize agriculture, the exclusion of labor from the benefits of increasing industrialization, and the expanding and increas-ingly frustrated middle class.[79]

In general, migration provides the means for small farmers and skilled workers to stabilize their family livelihoods and to meet long-desired aspi-rations for consumption items like domestic appliances, automobiles, and television sets, as well as for additional land and implements. For urban professionals, it offers a way to reach living standards commensurate with their educational achievements.[80]

In many sending countries, like India, Korea, Taiwan, and the Domi-nican Republic, the growth of high-level jobs has not kept pace with the expansion of higher education, so that the well educated often cannot find jobs that match their training. One study speaks of college graduates in Taiwan fiercely competing for jobs requiring only an elementary or junior high school education. Another discusses Indian college graduates spend-ing years in underpaid starting positions or paying enormous bribes just to get a foot in the door.[81] In Brazil, many university graduates have to content themselves with lower-status jobs than they had expected from their training—and lower living standards. Where there is soaring inflation, as in Brazil in the late 1980s and early 1990s, the middle as well as the lower strata find their living standards eroded. By 1994, inflation had reached over 2500 percent annually in Brazil, a rate of 40 percent a month. Prices for many goods bought by average middle-class Brazilians, from a can of Coca-Cola to a pair of Levi's, were far higher than in the United States, while salaries lagged behind.[82] In the Philippines, in the 1980s, the economic crisis meant that even a schoolteacher could afford to buy no more than two chickens a month and only low-quality rice.[83] Haitians in New York from middle-class backgrounds explain that they send home photos showing them in front of a packed refrigerator. "It's something to be very proud of," they say, because relatives in Haiti have trouble keeping food in the refrigerator for fear of losing electric power.[84]

In tandem with basic economic factors, oppressive political conditions have driven many people out of their homelands. Once again, anti-Semitism and government restrictions on educational opportunities, as well as a bleak economic outlook, impel Russian Jews to leave. "Everyone just knew that it had to be better," said one professional who moved to New York in 1983. "Materially, yes, that had something to do with it, but I mean in all senses of the word—to breathe freely, not to have to make all sorts of deals on the black market, not to be afraid."[85]

In the 1970s and 1980s, Haitians fled not only a ravaged economy but the dictatorships of "Papa Doc" and "Baby Doc" Duvalier, and in the early 1990s they were escaping the brutality following the military coup against Jean-Bertrand Aristide. Salvadorans left a country devastated by a long civil war (1979–92), often emigrating under the threat of violence and death.[86] Certainly, a major reason many Chinese leave their homeland is the unpredictable and rigid communist system and the limits on freedom and advancement.[87] Unstable political conditions also have been a factor in the case of Taiwanese, Korean, and Hong Kong immigrants. Indeed, many wealthy Hong Kong Chinese fled with their capital in fear of what would happen in 1997 when the People's Republic of China claimed sovereignty over the British crown colony. Political insecurity played a role in Korean emigration to the United States in the 1970s and early 1980s, although it has been reduced substantially since 1987, when a popular presidential election put an end to the sixteen-year South Korean military dictatorship.[88]

America holds out the promise of political and cultural freedom—and material abundance. The magnet for professionals as well as the less skilled is the chance to earn higher wages and maintain a better standard of living than was possible at home. In 1987, the minimum monthly salary for full-time work in the United States was six times higher than that in the Dominican Republic; by 1991 it was thirteen times higher. Consumer goods that are taken for granted by people at all class levels in the United States, like telephones, refrigerators, and automobiles, are beyond the reach of the Dominican lower class and not a certainty for the middle class either.[89] In Brazil, salaries for professionals and semiprofessionals pale in comparison to what immigrants can make here, even in the most menial jobs. In one week, they can earn as much, if not more, than they would earn in a month back home—though in the 1980s and early 1990s, the cost of living in some Brazilian cities and New York was nearly comparable. A woman who earned two hundred dollars as a head nurse in a large urban hospital in Brazil spoke in wonder of how she made five times more in New York City by working long hours as a babysitter.[90] "In Brazil," said one woman, "if you want a $50 dress, you can only buy it by paying on credit over twelve months. And by the time it's paid for, the dress is worn out. But in the United States, if you want a $50 dress, you just go out and buy it for cash. And, can you imagine, in New York, a TV costs one week's earnings? But in Brazil even a month's wages won't pay for one."[91]

It is not just that wages are better here. Jobs are also available. New York may not be the expanding industrial center it was at the turn of the last century, but it continues, even in years when the economy has flagged, to provide employment opportunities for new immigrants in service jobs, burgeoning-enclave economies, and the much smaller, but still active, manufacturing sector (see Chapter 3).

As before, migration, once begun, has a kind of snowball effect. Immigrants spread the news of the benefits to be had in New York; as one Jamaican woman said, "People telling you all the while, so you say you would like to know New York." In the Dominican village of Los Pinos, migration to New York was the daily and endless subject of discussion. Information about wages, the price of food, and working life in New York was widely circulated in the community. When a teacher asked her first-grade class what they would do with a million dollars, a seven-year-old boy answered that he would buy an airplane and go to New York.[92] Wherever they are from, immigrants in New York encourage and facilitate the migration of relatives and friends by sending back funds to finance the trip, serving as sponsors, helping prospective newcomers meet requirements for entry or immigration, offering accommodations, and showing the ropes to new arrivals.

By allocating most immigrant visas along family lines, United States immigration law reinforces and formalizes the operation of migrant networks.[93] According to one estimate, the immigrant multiplier for each immigrant worker is around 1.2. In other words, for each new immigrant admitted as a laborer rather than as a relative of someone already established here, 1.2 additional immigrants can be expected to arrive within ten years.[94] Another study calculated that for each new Filipino immigrant, one additional family member would arrive in the future; for each Korean immigrant, .5 family members would eventually come.[95]

Networks of friends and relatives serve as financial safety nets for the new arrivals and as sources of all kinds of information about life in New York. And they help the newcomers get jobs. One of the first men to arrive in New York from the village of Los Pinos eventually found union jobs for more than a dozen later arrivals in the large New York hotel where he had worked for fifteen years.[96]

Steamship lines no longer channel immigration into New York, yet the presence of large numbers of friends and relatives continues to attract immigrants to the city and the surrounding region. Once an immigrant community develops, it tends to expand as compatriots are on hand to offer newcomers a sense of security and the prospect of assistance. Immigrants, as Charles Tilly puts it, create "migration machines: sending networks that articulated with particular receiving networks in which new migrants could find jobs, housing, and sociability." Moving to New York, as one Jamaican woman said, "became the thing to do. Most of my friends were here."[97] New York is also appealing because newcomers do not stand out; it has a tradition of immigration, with many different immigrant and racial groups evident in daily life.

The city itself has an image that draws certain immigrant groups. With large numbers of Caribbean people in New York, the city has become, as Bryce-Laporte writes, the special object of their "dream[s], curiosity, sense of achievement, and drive for adventure."[98] To Caribbean immigrants, New York is often synonymous with America. The city is salient in Caribbean immigrants' mental map as a center of North American influence and power and as a logical entry point into the country.[99]

In general, countries with a history of American military, political, and economic involvement and intervention have been sending large numbers to the United States. The entire Caribbean region has known the presence of the United States. During the past hundred years, Puerto Rico, Cuba, the Dominican Republic, Haiti, Nicaragua, Panama, and Grenada have all been under direct U.S. military rule at one time or another. The United States has also exercised overwhelming economic dominance in the Caribbean region.[100] In Asia, the Korean War was followed by American economic and political involvement and military presence in South Korea; and in the Philippines, strong military and business connections and a century of colonial and postcolonial rule have produced a pervasive cultural Americanization of the population—to name but two countries in that region of the world.[101]

## How They Come

For most immigrants today, the journey to New York is shorter and easier than at the turn of the last century. Despite horror stories in the media about dangerous border crossings and shipboard smugglings, the fact is that the vast majority of contemporary immigrants—documented and undocumented alike—spend only a few hours on a plane before arriving at Kennedy airport. A century ago, Jewish and Italian immigrants had to undergo a grueling ocean voyage as well as long, sometimes dangerous trips to their port of departure.

For many Jews and Italians of that time, getting to the port was an ordeal involving travel by train or wagon, or even stretches on foot. For Jews there were legal difficulties as well. Russian Jews often traveled west through Austria-Hungary to German ports. Because most of them probably lacked the necessary papers, they were crossing the borders illegally, although, according to one account, German authorities looked the other way because Jewish emigration was good business for German shipowners.[102] Mary Antin recalled that without the help of two kindly German Jews, the local authorities would have sent her family back to Russia for want of two hundred rubles. En route to Hamburg, the "emigrants were herded at stations, packed in cars, and driven from place to place like cattle."[103] The railroad cars that carried Morris Cohen and his mother to Bremen "might have been cattle cars, for there were no seats. We sat on the floor and slept by reclining our heads on our bundles. In the morning and in the afternoon when the train stopped at stations, mother or I would go out and purchase some hot water which, with the hard bread and a few other things, served as our meals."[104]

Because train schedules were not coordinated with sailing dates, emigrants had to wait days or sometimes weeks at the port for their paperwork to be completed or for their ship to arrive. In the 1880s and 1890s, the port of Genoa "was woefully congested; . . . the sleeping and eating facilities did not provide for more than one-third of those awaiting transport."[105] An emigrant named Tontonno, who arrived in Naples in 1906, described in his diary how he and his *paesani* slept ten to a room and two or more to a bed in a hotel managed by the ship company. In Italian port cities, moreover, emigrants "had to run the gauntlet of a small army of peddlers, thieves, and confidence men . . . all of whom earned their daily bread by extracting every possible penny from their departing conationals."[106]

Arriving in Hamburg in 1892 with her Aunt Masha, after days of travel by wagon and then train from a small village in western Russia, Rose Cohen wrote that "we were all shown (really driven) into a large room where many dirty, narrow cots stood along the walls." Her father, who had gone to New York two years earlier, had sent two prepaid steamship tickets to his family. Now in Hamburg "Aunt Masha shivered as she looked at the cot in which we two were to sleep. . . . The air in the room was so foul and thick that it felt as if it could be touched. From every corner came sounds of groaning and snoring. But worst of all were the insects in the cot. . . . We stayed in Hamburg a week. Every day from ten in the morning until four in the afternoon we stayed in a large, bare hall waiting for our names to be called." After the cholera epidemics of 1892, the German government subjected migrants from eastern Europe to medical exams that included baths and fumigation. Rose Cohen remembers how her little "underwaist, which still had some money in it" was taken to be "steamed." Although the money was not touched, "when I looked at my pretty little slippers I wept bitter tears. They looked old, and wrinkled, and two of the buttons were off."[107] In Hamburg, men and boys had their heads closely cropped and received a chemical shampoo; women and girls had their hair combed with fine-tooth metal combs.[108]

There was questioning, too. In the wake of immigration legislation in the 1890s, each passenger bound for America had to answer a series of twenty-nine questions recorded on the manifest lists, concerning, among other things, physical and mental health, ability to read and write, and whether they had at least thirty dollars. Steamship companies, which now had to bear the cost of returning rejected immigrants, instituted inspections of their own to weed out those with diseases and defects. In 1907, examiners at Italian ports turned away more than 35,000 intending emigrants for medical and other reasons—far more than the 4,707 Italians rejected at Ellis Island in 1904 and 1905.[109]

Then there was the crossing in steerage, quite literally next to the ship's steering equipment below the waterline.[110] Passengers were crammed together in dark, crowded, unsanitary, and foul-smelling quarters on tiers of iron bunks with straw mattresses. A journalist traveling as an immigrant from Naples in 1906 reported: "How can a steerage passenger remember that he is a human being when he must first pick the worms from his food . . . and eat in his stuffy, stinking bunk, or in the hot and fetid atmosphere of a compartment where 150 men sleep, or in juxtaposition to a seasick man?"[111]

In 1908, the Immigration Commission sent an agent disguised as an immigrant to cross the Atlantic in steamship steerage to investigate conditions. The ship's crew, she found, scrubbed and disinfected the lavatories only on the last day of the journey—just in time for the official inspection upon landing. Sleeping compartments were never mopped; receptacles for the seasick appeared only on upper decks. As a result, the air below deck was foul. "During these twelve days in steerage," the immigration official reported, "I lived in a disorder and in surroundings that offended every sense. Only the fresh breeze from the sea overcame the sickening odors."[112] Recalling his own trip across the Atlantic, Samuel Chotzinoff writes of the smell of "ship": "This pervasive, insidious odor, a distillation of bilge and a number of less identifiable putrescences, settled on one's person, clothes, and luggage and stayed there forever, impervious to changes of habitat, clothing, and the cleansing agents available to the poor."[113]

"We were huddled together in steerage literally like cattle—my mother, my sister and I sleeping in the middle tier, people being above us and below us as well as on the same level," Morris Raphael Cohen recalled. "We could not eat the food of the ship, since it was not kosher. We only asked for hot water in which my mother used to put a little brandy and sugar to give it taste. Towards the end of the trip when our bread was beginning to give out we applied to the ship's steward for bread, but the kind he gave us was unbearably soggy."[114] According to the immigration agent investigating steerage conditions in 1908, the meat and fish provided by the steamship company reeked, the vegetables were a "queer, unanalyzable mixture," and the stewed fruit seemed more like the refuse of edible fruit.[115] The open deck space reserved for steerage passengers was usually small and situated in an area most directly affected by dirt from the stacks.

Finally, after about ten days or two weeks, the immigrants arrived in Manhattan, where they were packed on the top decks of barges that took them to Ellis Island. Once there, they had to wait on long lines for medical inspections and questioning, all the while afraid that they might be turned away. At peak times, thousands of persons were processed in a single day. Most went through easily in a day, although some were detained for further inspections. Relatively few were denied entry. In 1905, for example, the first year in which a million immigrants arrived, barely more than 1 percent were deported or excluded.

Today, the actual trip to New York is less harrowing for most newcomers. In the contemporary jet age, time-consuming ocean voyages and land journeys are no longer necessary. It is now fast—and relatively cheap—to travel by airplane to John F. Kennedy International Airport, the "port" of entry for most of New York's latest immigrants. For many bound for New York, the international airport where they board the plane is in their home city; modern transportation by plane, car, bus, or train usually makes getting there fairly easy for those who live far away. Depending on the country of departure, the flight to New York itself takes anywhere from three or four hours up to a day or so. As in earlier times, newcomers worry about passing muster with immigration authorities upon arrival, but the vast majority get through immigration control in a couple of hours at most.[116] Even those who end up staying illegally in New York usually arrive with valid passports and legitimate tourist visas.

The main difficulties involve getting an immigrant visa and "green card" in the first place. The immigration process typically begins in the United States, with a resident family member or employer filing an application with U.S. authorities (about 70 percent of immigrant visas go to family members). Because of long backlogs it can take years to be legally admitted as a permanent resident alien after the approval of the application for entry. In 1997, more than 3.6 million people were waiting for immigrant visas to the United States, 98 percent of whom were on the list for family preference visas. (Mexicans accounted for more than 25 percent of the waiting list; Filipinos, 16 percent; Indians, 7 percent; Chinese, 6 percent; and Dominicans, 4 percent.)[117] Frustrated by the wait, or the inability to get on the list at all, many decide to come in other—illegal—ways.

U.S. consular officials are wise to the strategies of those who abuse tourist visas; the current standard for a tourist visa in major sending countries is guilty until proven innocent, the presumption being that tourist-visa applicants will stay in the United States and work unless they can prove other intentions.[118] Tourist visa applicants have to convince the U.S. consulate in their home country that they will return; this is usually done by showing they have strong ties and sufficient resources to be attracted home again. Acceptable proof includes titles to land, savings passbooks, and deeds to vehicles.[119] If real documents are not available, prospective migrants resort to false ones. Dominicans, for example, pay hefty sums for false titles to landholdings or forged savings passbooks. Maxine Margolis describes Brazilians presenting consular officials with inflated bank statements and tax returns and borrowing large sums of money from friends and relatives that they temporarily deposit in their bank accounts.[120] One enterprising Dominican university graduate, Enrique, who had no permanent job or savings, employed the following strategy: he opened a bank account with money borrowed from three relatives and held the account for a few months in order to receive monthly statements of his balance. He also had an uncle who managed a money-exchange house write a letter stating that Enrique had been an employee for several years and would return to his job after his holiday. Enrique and his wife were granted temporary visas for recreational travel; rather than return after the visas expired, they remained in New York, where they both found work as sales clerks.[121]

Another route is to purchase or borrow someone else's passport that has a valid U.S. tourist visa already stamped on it. The photo of the legitimate owner is replaced with that of the person who is going to travel on the passport; after entering the United States, the passport is returned to the "seller" for use by another customer.[122] In 1997, the going rate for false documents in the Dominican Republic, from passports to visa stamps and marriage certificates, was anywhere from five thousand to eight thousand dollars, depending on what was needed.[123] Once in the United States, fake marriages to a U.S. citizen, typically for a price of several thousand dollars, have been a way to legalize one's status, although various laws to combat marriage fraud and illegal immigration have made this more difficult.

The least desirable, and least common, way for Dominicans to come to New York is through Puerto Rico or Mexico or as stowaways on cargo ships bound for the United States. The border route involves flying to Mexico, taking a bus, assisted by a guide, to the border, crossing into the United States at night with the help of a "coyote," or smuggler, and finally flying to New York. In the 1990s, many Dominicans were paying at least seven hundred dollars each for places on yolas, rickety narrow boats equipped with outboard motors, which made the trip across the hazardous Mona Passage to Puerto Rico carrying up to forty or fifty passengers.[124] Those who succeeded in landing in Puerto Rico, a U.S. Commonwealth, could board a domestic flight to anywhere in the United States with a minimum of documentation that is easily forged back home.[125] For Salvadorans, the price of traveling to the United States under coyote escort through Guatemala and Mexico was up to three thousand dollars in 1995.[126]

The price is much higher for Chinese immigrants who have been smuggled into the United States on freighters and fishing vessels from Asia. These activities came to public attention in June 1993, when the *Golden*

*Venture* ran aground off Queens with nearly three hundred Chinese migrants aboard, ten of whom died as they tried to swim ashore through the frigid waters. Since then, a crackdown on the shipborne smuggling of Chinese into this country has led smugglers to seek new routes through the Caribbean, Central America, and Canada. In the 1990s, for a fee of up to forty thousand dollars, prospective immigrants have been taken to Central America and then smuggled into the United States by plane, by land, or on small boats.[127]

For those few who take such complicated, sometimes dangerous routes, the physical trip to the United States can be the hardest and most frightening part of the immigration process. Peter Kwong describes the appalling conditions that illegal Chinese immigrants experience at the hands of "snakeheads" (smugglers). On one boat that the Coast Guard boarded off Hawaii in 1996, 120 men were "packed into a tight, twenty-by-thirty-foot camouflaged compartment that had been nailed shut. The men were naked and had been held between decks for several weeks without showers or ventilation; they were caged in their own waste and ate in a mass-feeding area where bowls were nailed to the table."[128] Among the travails undocumented Salvadoran migrants face on their thousand-mile-or-more journey to the United States are long treks through desert, with little water or food; the constant threat of detection and deportation in Guatemala and Mexico; the possibility of being strip-searched by thieves, smugglers, and officials who slit open the seams of travelers' clothing looking for hidden money; drownings in rivers they must cross; separation and abandonment; and, for women, rape and other forms of sexual abuse. One woman now living on Long Island told Sarah Mahler, an anthropologist, about her near-death experience: she was left by coyotes inside an airtight trailer (with only one small window) with 150 other Salvadorans, without food or water, for nearly a day.[129]

That such conditions exist today is horrifying. Fortunately, they are the exception rather than the rule. Indeed, for the overwhelming majority of contemporary immigrants, the trip is relatively easy. For most, getting to New York is only the beginning of a much longer and more difficult journey that involves settling in, adjusting, coming to terms with life in a new country, and ultimately deciding whether to make America their permanent home.

In story, film, and family lore, turn-of-the-century immigrants are often recalled as noble sufferers and heroes who weathered hardships in Europe and a traumatic ocean crossing to make it to America. That is a hard act to follow.

Indeed, those who endure the most difficult journey to America today by risking their lives crossing borders or being smuggled on ships are not modern-day heroes in the public eye. As undocumented immigrants, they are stigmatized and unwanted. Illegal entry, as I have shown, was not an issue a hundred years ago for European immigrants. Today, however, it is a major public concern. One reason for the focus on "illegals" in immigration debates is that it is one way that old-time Americans can support the notion that immigration is good and made America great while at the same time distancing themselves, and their ancestors, from contemporary arrivals. My people, the argument goes, came legally in the past—they were the model immigrants; today, too many are illegal and should not be here at all.

But contrary to conventional wisdom, New York is not awash in a sea of illegal immigrants. At any one time, the undocumented are a fairly small proportion of New York's foreign-born. And the evidence suggests that many come with skills and education—and are not inevitably of "lower quality" than their compatriots who arrive legally, green card in hand.

Although many contemporary immigrants, as in the past, have suffered economic difficulties and political oppression in their homelands, they are not the "huddled masses" in modern dress. Even a century ago, immigrants did not come from the very bottom of their societies; now a substantial minority are from the top levels. The Korean greengrocer and the Indian newsstand dealer on the corner may have college and even graduate degrees. The West Indian nanny may have been a clerical worker in her homeland, the Polish beautician, a teacher. Poor farmers, factory workers, and artisans still arrive, of course. But a new kind of professional, middle-class immigrant is also a part of the current stream. Diversity, the buzz word of the 1990s, is an apt description of the newest New Yorkers. In almost every way—economically, educationally, and culturally—they are more diverse than their predecessors a hundred years ago, and this has enormous implications for understanding what happens when they settle in New York. As we shall see, the distinctive characteristics of modern-day immigrants—in combination with the distinctive qualities of late twentieth-century New York—go a long way toward explaining why their experiences and lives differ in so many ways from those of their predecessors in the last great immigration wave.

# CHAPTER 2

# Where They Live

*T*he image and the reality are different—and they are different in unexpected and complex ways. A popular picture of contemporary immigrant life is colored by memories of tenement existence on Manhattan's Lower East Side and in the Little Italys of a hundred years ago. Popular memories have a way of romanticizing the old neighborhoods; today, public images often simplify the residential picture.

When New Yorkers look back on the past, they have a tendency to remember the old ethnic neighborhoods as closely knit communities where their grandparents and great-grandparents struggled to realize the American Dream. Conditions were hard, the story goes, but immigrants were excited about being in America and determined to do well. Often forgotten in a haze of nostalgia are the grim realities of grinding poverty and tenement life. An extreme example is a recent television Christmas special in which Angela Lansbury, playing Mrs. Santa, accidentally lands (with her reindeer, of course) in the Lower East Side at the turn of the century.[1] The room she rents from a Russian Jewish landlady is in a well-furnished, clean, and rather spacious apartment—tenement life turned middle-class for the television audience. Needless to say, this kind of Disneyfied version of immigrant life bears little relation to the actual squalor of the crowded tenements that Jews and Italians were forced to inhabit.

Now, a hundred years later, New York's newcomers are commonly pictured in the public imagination as huddled together in poor ethnic neighborhoods like the immigrants of old. Because so many immigrants today are from Third World countries—and are people of color—old-time New Yorkers often expect the newcomers to live in slum conditions that resemble those of the poorest domestic minorities.

This view is not altogether wrong. Many contemporary immigrants do live in squalid housing—something that has invited comparisons with Jacob Riis's *How the Other Half Lives,* which chronicled the poverty and despair of Manhattan tenement life in the 1890s. When a *New York Times* editorial describes current immigrant living conditions as "steerage style housing," it evokes outrage that not much has changed in the past hundred years. Rat-infested rooms, urine-drenched passageways, illegal apartments carved out of basements and gangways—contemporary journalists are right to call these awful conditions a modern-day scandal. According to a special series on the new New Yorkers in *New York Newsday,* "The conditions many contemporary immigrants are forced to call home would have Jacob Riis turning in his grave."[2]

Maybe so. But Riis would have been astonished by some remarkable changes in the way immigrants live. Unlike past arrivals, many recent ones now start out in decent housing in lower-middle-class neighborhoods that they have helped revive. Although immigrant New Yorkers today, like their predecessors, often cluster in ethnic neighborhoods with their own kind, they are more dispersed residentially than they used to be. Indeed, polyethnic neighborhoods quite unlike anything that existed in the early 1900s are now found scattered throughout the city. And although many immigrants in the past moved outside New York City's boundaries to the surrounding counties, some current arrivals are settling into a new, more affluent suburban existence in the region's bedroom communities.

What has happened is that more immigrants now arrive with skills and resources and find jobs that can support a middle- or lower-middle-class lifestyle right from the start. Not only are today's arrivals diverse in terms of class, but they come from countries all over the globe. Even more important, New York's urban landscape has been transformed almost beyond recognition. It's difficult to look at two groups of people—and compare how they lived—when the living conditions and experiences of all New Yorkers have changed so dramatically over the past hundred years. When Riis was writing in the 1890s, horse-drawn railway cars were still a common sight on New York's streets, over half the city's population lived in tenements, and hot running water and steam heat were luxuries beyond the reach of the immigrant, and native-born, poor. Manhattan was the population center of the city. The borough of Queens was mainly a place of fields, meadows, and woods; contemporary guidebooks encouraged Manhattanites to take day trips there to enjoy the bucolic atmosphere and get away from the hectic pace of city life.[3] If Jacob Riis found himself in late twentieth-century New York, he might think he was on a different planet.

## The Old Ethnic Neighborhoods

When *How the Other Half Lives* was published in 1890, Russian Jewish and Italian immigrants lived out the classic ethnic neighborhood story, concentrated in densely populated ethnic communities that provided cheap accommodations close to where they worked. Mainly, this meant lower Manhattan.

At the turn of the century, much of Queens, Brooklyn, and the Bronx, to say nothing of vast sections of the surrounding suburban counties, was undeveloped and sparsely populated—which is not surprising, since they were hard to reach from the center of the city. In 1890, when the idea for the subway was just being hatched (the subway did not open until 1904), omnibuses, horse railways, cable lines, and elevated railways constituted the city's rapid-transit system. These means of transport were slow and crowded and did not effectively link Manhattan to what would become, after consolidation in 1898, the city's other four boroughs: "Horse railway cars crept through the crowded streets at five or six miles per hour and steam-powered elevated trains traveled at twelve miles per hour. . . . There were 94 miles of elevated railways that skirted the surface congestion and ran from one end of Manhattan Island to the other; there were 265 miles of horse-drawn railways and 137 miles of horse omnibuses that plodded along its traffic-clogged avenues and streets; and there was even a mile-long stretch of cable railway that hauled commuters across the Brooklyn Bridge."[4]

Manhattan was teeming with people, its population soaring at an astounding rate throughout the nineteenth century. By 1910, a record 2,331,542 people lived in Manhattan, about 850,000 more than would reside there in 1990. More people lived on this small twenty-three-square-mile island at the turn of the century than in any of thirty-three of the nation's forty-six states. Within Manhattan itself, most people clustered downtown; in 1910, one-sixth of all New Yorkers lived below Fourteenth Street on one eighty-second of the city's land.

Manhattan far exceeded the other four boroughs in population. In 1900, Manhattan accounted for fifty-four of every one hundred New Yorkers; ninety years later, only twenty out of every one hundred resided there. Many parts of the Bronx, Brooklyn, Queens, and Staten Island were thinly settled. At the turn of the century, the Bronx was home to only 200,507 people, or 6 percent of the city's population; Queens, with a population of 152,999 (4 percent of the city's total) was a rural borough of marshes, meadows, colonial estates, and small villages.

The central business district of the city was below Fourteenth Street—within walking distance of the tenement areas that drew in the latest arrivals. When Russian Jews and Italians started to pour into the city, there were few alternatives to the downtown neighborhoods. The immigrant laborer, Thomas Kessner observes, could not afford the luxury of living on the outskirts. "He had to be close to sources of job supply—the docks, warehouses, factories, and business streets—to take advantage of sudden openings and opportunities. Uncertain employment, long hours, and low wages also made commuting impractical. He had to live where he worked, and slum housing placed him at the industrial-commercial core of the city. The streets were dirty, unsafe, and unhealthy; the style of life was unattractive, but this housing placed him at the pulse of the job market for which he qualified."[5] It also placed immigrants near friends, relatives, and compatriots who spoke the same language, shared the same customs, and helped them to find housing and work and to learn the ropes in New York.

In the early years of the Italian and Jewish influx, newcomers flocked to the lower Manhattan neighborhoods that are still, in the public eye, a symbol of their identity. Manhattan's Lower East Side carried the sobriquet of a private city, "Jewtown," while there were three Little Italys south of Fourteenth Street.[6] In 1890, over half of New York City's Italians lived in just three wards bordering on Canal Street;[7] in the same period, three-quarters of the city's Jews congregated in the Lower East Side, south of Fourteenth Street and east of the Bowery, and the percentage was still as high as 50 percent by 1903.[8]

When the hero of Abraham Cahan's novel *The Rise of David Levinsky* gets off the boat, a New Yorker tells him, "Walk straight ahead. . . . Just keep walking until you see a lot of Jewish people."[9] Practically all Jewish immigrants who came to New York before 1900 initially found their way to the Lower East Side, some steered there by representatives of immigrant aid societies, most joining friends or relatives. The neighborhood was literally bursting at the seams. If at the turn of the century Manhattan was among the most congested urban places in the world, the single most crowded district was the Lower East Side. A report issued in 1895 by the state's Tenement House Committee found that a portion of the Lower East Side had a population density higher than Bombay's. The Tenth Ward exceeded seven hundred people per acre, and some blocks on the Lower East Side in 1895 approached the astounding ratio of one thousand per acre. (By way of comparison, in 1990 the densest census tract in Manhattan, in Washington Heights, had 308 people per acre.)[10] Of the fifty-one blocks in the city in 1906 with over three thousand inhabitants, thirty-seven were on the

Lower East Side. Even more remarkable, most of the buildings there were less than seven stories.[11]

The Lower East Side, from the Bowery to the East River and from Market Street to Fourteenth Street, had become, by the first decade of this century, a Jewish cosmopolis.[12] Riis wrote that the "jargon of the street, the signs of the sidewalk, the manner and dress of the people . . . betray their race at every step. Men with queer skull caps, venerable beards, and the outlandish long-skirted kaftan of the Russian Jews . . . crowded out the Gentiles in the 10th Ward. . . . When the great Jewish holidays come round every year, the public schools in the district have practically to close up."[13] The touchstones of the east European shtetl were all around: synagogues, burial societies, kosher butchers, and Yiddish-language newspapers.[14] A lively Yiddish theater, enacting dramas that resonated with the immigrants' problems, attracted Jews of every rank and persuasion, from the sweatshop woman with her baby and the Russian anarchist to the ghetto rabbi.[15] The Lower East Side became the center of the pushcart trade; whole blocks were lined with high-piled carts selling every conceivable item, from candles, dried fruit, and oilcloth to "big carp, little carp, middle-sized carp, but everywhere carp."[16]

Not far to the west, Italian colonies flourished, leading observers like Louise Odencrantz to characterize them as almost independent of the life of the city.[17] By 1900, Italians had completely taken over the best-known Little Italy in the Fourteenth Ward, where only a scattering of elderly Irish remained.[18] In lower Manhattan's Little Italys, people "speak their own language, trade in stores kept by countrymen, and put their savings into Italian banks. Italian newspapers supply them with the day's news. . . . Italian priests minister to their spiritual needs . . . and societies composed only of Italians are organized for mutual aid and benefit. The stores all bear Italian names, the special bargains and souvenirs of the day are advertised in Italian, and they offer for sale the wines and olive oils, 'pasta,' and other favorite foods of the people."[19] Every Italian enclave had an annual religious festival honoring some favorite patron saint or the Madonna. In lower Manhattan, the largest *festa* honored San Gennaro, the patron saint of Naples.[20] San Gandolfo, patron saint of Polizzi Generoso, in the Sicilian province of Palermo, was honored in September on the Lower East Side with a three-day festival replete with band concerts, a parade, and a grand procession for compatriots and the faithful.[21]

Italians and Jews were rarely close neighbors, however. Research based on 1910 and 1920 census data shows high levels of residential segregation for each group in New York City.[22] In her study of Italian immigrants, the historian Miriam Cohen found that it was extremely difficult to find a Manhattan block in 1905 (and 1925) that was a mixture of Italians and Jews "because most blocks were heavily dominated, if not exclusively populated, by one or the other immigrant group. Moreover, a block that may have been ethnically mixed in 1905 was almost certainly in a transitional stage, soon to be dominated by one group in 1925."[23]

After about 1900, large numbers of Jews and Italians ventured outside the old central quarters to Harlem, Brooklyn, and the Bronx, where they created new ethnic colonies. By 1910, a little under 60 percent of the city's Italian and Russian immigrant population lived in Manhattan—down from about 75 percent ten years earlier. About a third now lived in Brooklyn.[24] Harlem, in 1910, had some seventy-three thousand Italians and about one hundred thousand Jews, leading one scholar to title his book *When Harlem Was Jewish*. Each group settled in and came to dominate particular blocks and sections—Harlem's Little Italy was distinct from streets with a definite Jewish cast.[25]

In moving out of lower Manhattan, some Jewish and Italian immigrants followed the path described by the classic urban sociologists of the Chicago school, leaving the primary immigrant ghettos for a better grade of housing in secondary areas as they improved their social and economic standing. But many unsuccessful immigrants also left downtown, either out of economic necessity or in the hope of making economic progress. And many immigrants bypassed the original areas of settlement altogether as they headed directly to upper Manhattan or Brooklyn neighborhoods as soon as they stepped off the boat.[26] "They did not," writes Thomas Kessner, "come to fresher neighborhoods . . . by way of dispersal from the industrial core, nor had they assimilated or climbed the occupational ladder; they were as 'green' as those immigrants who had previously settled downtown, but nonetheless they settled in 'secondary settlements.' These neighborhoods were often no further along the road to assimilation and occupational progress than the Lower East Side, where schools and settlement houses abounded."[27]

By the turn of the century, the old downtown ethnic neighborhoods were filled to capacity. Slum clearance projects and municipal improvements like parks, schools, and bridge approaches destroyed hundreds of buildings and thousands of apartments at the very moment when the tide of immigration to New York was reaching its peak. The construction of a school, a bridge approach, and a new street after 1901, for example, destroyed fifteen hundred apartments (a quarter of existing housing) in the main Little Italy below Fourteenth Street.[28] Similarly, many thousands of

Jewish immigrants were displaced when hundreds of buildings were condemned to make room for the Willamsburg and Manhattan bridges.[29] The overcrowded Lower East Side staggered under the weight of the new wave of immigrants. At the same time, the building of bridges and subway lines between 1900 and 1910 opened new districts for mass settlement. By 1916, only about a quarter of New York City's Jews still lived on the Lower East Side.

Italians moved north from lower Manhattan in search of work on the city's expanding rapid-transit lines and in the booming construction industry in central Harlem. By 1910, they dominated the east Harlem tenement district lying east of Third Avenue and south of 125th Street. Neapolitans lived between 106th and 108th Streets; immigrants from Basilicata lived from 108th Street to about 115th Street. The streets themselves were predominantly a male domain, a place where men hung out in front of their regional and social clubs, engaged in card games on folding tables set up on sidewalks, played boccie, and socialized.[30] As they settled in Brooklyn, Italians generally moved into run-down tenement areas that had been previously inhabited by the Irish. The early Italian neighborhoods in Brooklyn developed in the Red Hook and Williamsburg districts near waterfront docks, warehouses, and factories.[31]

Russian Jews also changed Harlem's ethnic makeup. By 1910, it was home to the second largest concentration of immigrant eastern European Jews in the nation. Inundated by thousands of Jewish settlers, once-moderately populated sections of East Harlem now had densities of between 480 and 560 people per acre.[32] After the construction of the Williamsburg Bridge in 1903, so many people moved across the East River to the Williamsburg section of Brooklyn that the *New York Tribune* dubbed the new span "Jews' Highway."[33] In a pattern of residential succession, Jews replaced Germans in wards of Williamsburg. Further away, at the western end of Brooklyn, they carved out a new neighborhood in Brownsville, which started up as a kind of Jewish factory town.

In 1886, when Jews first began acquiring property there, Brownsville was a quiet rural area of about four thousand, where one could see farmers plowing their fields and cows and sheep grazing in the meadows. Ten years later, the *New York Tribune* described Brownsville as a "land of sweatshops and whirring sewing machines, of strange Russian baths, of innumerable dirty and tiny shops."[34] In 1905, Brownsville's Jewish population had soared to almost fifty thousand, roughly 80 percent of the neighborhood's residents. The area came close to resembling a modern, densely populated, overly large shtetl, with an open-air peddler's market, at least twenty synagogues, and four Hebrew schools. By 1925, over two hundred thousand lived there, still some 80 percent of the population.[35] It was, writes Alter Landesman, in his study of the community, a completely Jewish world.[36] On the streets, the store signs were in Yiddish, the newsstands displayed the Yiddish dailies and weeklies next to the English newspapers, and street corners were sites of meetings on Jewish issues. The clothing industry dominated the occupational horizon in this working-class area; a large percentage of the community's residents were employed in local garment shops. "We were Brownsville—*brunzvil,* as the old folks said," the critic Alfred Kazin wrote, recalling his childhood, "the dust of the earth to all Jews with money, and notoriously a place that measured all success by our skill in getting away from it."[37]

## Tenement Life

For the overwhelming majority of Jewish and Italian immigrants, home was a tenement apartment, whatever the neighborhood they lived in. In the 1890s, the high-rise apartments going up in Manhattan were mainly for the wealthy; middle-class New Yorkers were still able to afford modest row houses uptown.[38] About three-quarters of Manhattan's residents in 1900 were tenement dwellers—the newest immigrants being the most likely inhabitants. Census data for that year show that the proportion of Russian Jewish and Italian immigrants occupying tenements in lower Manhattan exceeded the average. Over 90 percent of the Jews lived in tenement apartments, and the figure for Italians was only slightly lower.[39] Conditions in the tenements were appalling by standards of the time; to modern-day New Yorkers, they are almost unimaginable. Access to steam heat, hot running water, and private toilets—what we now view as basic necessities—were unknown luxuries to this early wave of immigrant poor.

The least desirable building type was the rear tenement. Found in Little Italy, rear tenements, as the name implies, were accessible only through an alley or the tenement built on the front of the lot. The rooms were small and dark, and toilets were outside, in the yard separating the back building from the front.[40] Somewhat better were railroad flats in barracks-type tenements built between 1850 and 1880, which housed many of Little Italy's residents. The first string of rooms had some light; the back rooms were without any windows. Individual apartments lacked running water, let alone functioning kitchen sinks or bathrooms; residents of a floor had to share a communal hall sink, which was frequently broken, dilapidated, and filthy. Those in upper-story apartments often had to haul water up in buckets from a ground-floor pump.[41] Indeed, in 1884, the Tenement House Committee found that only 30 percent of the tenements examined had any water closets, and almost none had running water above the first floor.[42] In his memoirs, Samuel Chotzinoff describes how a number of outhouses provided sanitation for the residents of the Lower East Side tenement house where his family rented a three-room railroad flat at the turn of the century: "This arrangement did not strike us in any way unusual. The water closets—as they were unflatteringly called (there was no water anywhere around)—were always locked, and each family was given a key. In the summer . . . the children playing on the street would shout for some member of their family to throw the key, wrapped in paper, down on the pavement. More often the request would be multiple: 'Mamma, throw down my beanbag, a piece of bread and butter, and the key to the water closet!' Sometimes, a child could earn a penny by giving his key to a passer-by in distress."[43]

The Jewish Lower East Side became the domain of newer "dumbbell" tenements, built in the wake of 1879 tenement regulations. Only one room in the three- and four-room apartments received direct light and air from the street or rear yard; narrow air shafts were the source of ventilation for the inner rooms and provided some minimal light. Residents had to use hallway toilets located off the air shafts. "To live, a family of eight in three rooms seemed to us quite normal," noted one Jewish resident, "as was being without a bathroom and sharing the toilet with three neighbors."[44] If the family bathed at home, they did so in the kitchen in a large tub of hot water placed in the middle of the room. More often, people used the public baths. "At night large families and families with boarders converted the entire apartment into a bedroom, spreading out mattresses on the parlor floor. In the summer, the roofs and fire escapes provided cooler places to sleep."[45] Samuel Chotzinoff recalls the sleeping arrangements in his family's small apartment when he was a child: "My parents occupied the only bed in the house, in the small windowless and doorless room between the kitchen and the front room. My sisters slept on improvised beds on the floor of the latter, I on four chairs set up each night in the kitchen." In the morning the chairs "would be pulled from under me, one by one, as they were required for breakfast." In the summer, "except when it rained, my youngest sister and I slept on the fire escape."[46]

The construction of "new law" tenements, built after 1901 legislation, brought improvements; according to specifications, each unit in new buildings had to have its own toilet and running water, and each room had to have an exterior window of minimum dimensions.[47] Older buildings had to be renovated, at least to the extent of replacing pit toilets in the yard (known as "school sinks," unattached to the city's sewer system) with sanitary toilet facilities and installing interior windows in walls of windowless rooms in order to permit the flow of air. In her study of Little Italy's Elizabeth Street, Donna Gabaccia found that many landlords of older buildings installed internal windows and either built toilets or supplied water in hallways or apartments. Yet the new law did not require baths, and in 1905 not a single apartment in the tenements on Elizabeth Street, even in the new-law tenements, provided a bath.[48]

A 1911–13 study of Italian wage-earning women in lower Manhattan found that the majority of the more than one thousand women visited at home had no private toilet but used one in common with others in the tenement, "sometimes as many as four families using the one toilet, often filthy, dark, and with plumbing out of order." One household visited had the luxury of hot water three times a week, "but the sole water supply of many, cold at that, was a sink in a public hallway. . . . Each tenant had to supply his own cook stove, and some apartments were not even supplied with gas, dangerous oil lamps being used."[49]

Despite these grim conditions, immigrants often went to great lengths to clean and decorate their apartments, fixing up their parlors with curtains, mirrors, and bric-a-brac. Still, the fight against grime and dirt was endless, and labor-saving devices like washing machines and vacuum cleaners were "millionaire things" out of the reach of immigrant families.[50] During most of the pre–World War I era, only the better-off could afford steam-fitted apartments with hot and cold running water in their bathrooms and with electricity; most used kerosene for light and coal for cooking.[51]

Immigrant quarters were extremely crowded. According to a 1908 census of 250 East Side families, fewer than a quarter of them slept two in a room; about 50 percent slept three or four in a room; and nearly 25 percent, five or more in a room.[52] A description of the apartments in the Orchard Street building that now houses the Lower East Side Tenement Museum brings out just how tiny the rooms were: "The largest room, the living room or parlor located at the front or rear of the floor with windows looking onto the street or yard, measures about 11 feet by 12 feet 5 inches (about 138 square feet), while the inner bedrooms are about 8 feet 6 inches square (about 67 square feet). Each apartment [of three rooms] totaled about 325 square feet."[53] The whole apartment, in other words, was the size of the living room in a contemporary house or apartment. Many southern Italians on Elizabeth Street lived in partner households, with one family subletting a room from the other. The pattern was for each family to remain economically independent and to eat separately as well.[54]

Then there were the boarders. Some Italians and even more Jews took in boarders to help pay the rent.[55] Only the most fortunate boarders had a bedroom to themselves. Boarders slept on makeshift beds, couches, and floors in kitchens, parlors, or hallways, sometimes on a mattress on the floor or on a board placed across two kitchen chairs.[56] When Louis Borgenicht and his wife arrived in New York in 1889, they had a boarder "Jim, whom we met on the boat. [He] didn't mind the darkness of the place, nor the fact that the bathroom was two flights down, and the sink in the hall on the second floor. He was a decent fellow, and starting from scratch like us. When he explained that he could pay us a tiny sum for boarding him temporarily, Regina flung a cover over the couch and Jim had a place to sleep."[57] Unfortunately, Borgenicht's trust in Jim was misplaced; he made off with Borgenicht's silver watch brought from abroad.

The problems associated with boarders, so much a part of the landscape on the Jewish Lower East Side, were a frequent subject of articles and letters in the Yiddish press of the early 1900s. "My wife took in a boarder, a *landsman* who had a wife and three children in Europe," wrote one immigrant, Jacob Rosen, to a Yiddish newspaper in 1903. "Soon he became chummy with my wife. She told me he wanted to buy her a hat and a skirt. At first I couldn't believe my ears, then I became jealous. One morning after I had left the house to go to my laundry, the boarder tried to attack my wife, but she escaped and locked him in the apartment. She came running to the laundry; I was furious but waited till I had calmed down. Then we went home. I took two sticks and we beat him so hard he couldn't go out for eight days. He gave us $80 and made us promise not to write his wife."[58]

Although most reports of tenement life describe apartments in lower Manhattan, housing conditions in the Harlem and Brooklyn immigrant neighborhoods of that time were not much better. Tenement existence there, too, was the rule. Living conditions in the Italian colonies of Red Hook and Williamsburg were described in one account as "often primitive."[59] Brownsville, according to another study, was considered by some to be an even worse ghetto than the Lower East Side, "with an even larger number of sweatshops, tenement hovels, itinerant peddlers, beggars, and gangs of wayward youths."[60] By 1904, 88 percent of the dwelling units in Brownsville were in tenements; three years later, the figure had risen above 96 percent.[61] Indeed, Alfred Kazin recalls Brownsville of the 1920s and 1930s as "New York's rawest, remotest, and cheapest ghetto."[62]

Uptown, in Harlem, affluent Russian Jews settled into comfortable brownstones and apartments, just as successful Lower East Side and Brooklyn Jews lived in better-equipped and more expensive housing. The few rich immigrant Jews at the time could even afford more than one home. By 1913, Louis Borgenicht, the "king of the children's dress trade," had a house in the then Brooklyn suburb of Borough Park as well as a summer estate in the Catskills, complete with stables, gardens, orchards, a tennis court, and swimming pool.[63] For the large numbers of Harlem's working-class Jewish residents, however, dumbbell tenements and densely populated streets reminiscent of those downtown were still the unfortunate reality.[64] In *Mercy of a Rude Stream*, an autobiographical novel, Henry Roth describes how his family moved from the Lower East Side to "Jewish Harlem" just before the outbreak of World War I. "What if they had to use gas light for illumination, and not electricity?" he says of the family's new apartment. "They were used to that on the East Side. What if the bathroom-toilet was not in the house . . . but in the hall, and the bathtub looked like an immense green-painted tin trough set in a wooden coffin of matched boards, and the paint came off and stuck to your bottom in hot water? They had no hot running water anyway, and bathed in warm water from the kettle rarely. Rent was only $12 a month; that was the important thing. Mom had immediate access to a window on the street, Pop a convenient stable for his horse and milk-wagon."[65]

In Italian Harlem, immigrants lived in what Robert Orsi describes as substandard tenement buildings from the first days of the community. As late as the 1930s, bathtubs were an exception; toilets were still often located in the hallway or on the corridor of each floor; and most families relied on coal stoves in the absence of radiators and steam heat.[66]

These primitive conditions were unusual for the time. By the 1930s, living conditions for immigrants and their children in other areas of the city were much better. Indeed, the 1920s have been described as a watershed period for New York's Jews in terms of housing, marking a shift from tenement to apartment building. In the midst of a massive construction boom, thousands of Jews moved into recently built one- and two-family houses and apartment buildings in Brooklyn and the Bronx. The new apartment houses had elevators, the latest plumbing advances, and larger and better-designed units, including hallways that provided privacy for each room.[67] But this gets us ahead of our story, into the movement of a growing number of immigrant New Yorkers into the emerging middle class in the years after the immigration flow had come to a halt. In the period of concern here, before the first World War, the tenement era was still a grim reality for most newcomers—and it would be years before they, or their descendants, could look back on it with nostalgia.[68]

## A New Immigrant Geography

Although the faces are different, New York City's contemporary immigrant enclaves bring back memories of the last great wave. The city now boasts three Chinatowns, a little Odessa-by-the-Sea, Caribbean Brooklyn, and a Dominican colony in Washington Heights.

Where immigrants live continues to be a complex combination of choice and constraint. As before, the new arrivals often gravitate to areas with kinfolk and friends, where they find comfort and security in an environment of familiar languages and institutions; at the same time, they are limited by the availability of affordable housing and by prejudice and sometimes outright discrimination from dominant groups. This sometimes leads them to the same neighborhoods that Italians and Russian Jews inhabited. Indeed, Chinese and Dominican immigrants now inhabit decrepit buildings not far from Manhattan's Tenement Museum on the Lower East Side, where a preserved tenement memorializes the old immigrant experience. Moreover, when immigrants move outside New York City in search of work, they're often dispersing to the same industrial cities in the region that attracted newcomers at the turn of the century.

But today's immigrants are not simply repeating past settlement patterns. The newest arrivals are branching out over a wider terrain, both in the city and in the region as a whole. Most are avoiding long-standing immigrant and minority areas to settle in places that, until recently, were the domain of middle- and lower-middle-class native New Yorkers. In the process, immigrants are often credited with reviving neighborhoods that, in their absence, might well have sunk into severe decline.

Since the last great wave, the contours of the city and its surrounding areas have changed in dramatic ways. Manhattan is no longer the most populous borough—and more people live in the counties that make up the greater metropolitan area than in New York City itself. By 1990, Brooklyn and Queens held close to 60 percent of the city's 7.3 million residents—and two-thirds of the city's immigrants. Manhattan's share of the city's foreign-born was 18 percent, down from 57 percent eighty years earlier. The New York urban region had grown to nearly 20 million: about one out of five were foreign born.[69]

The expansion of New York City's public transportation system, improved highways, and the automobile revolution, among other things, have made the outer boroughs and suburban areas more accessible to downtown districts than they were a hundred years ago. Moreover, manufacturing, as well as the service jobs most available to newcomers, is much less centralized. There are many—and expanding—employment opportunities outside of New York City's old urban core. Although most immigrants work in the county where they live, today they commute longer distances to work than their turn-of-the-century predecessors, who often lived within walking distance.[70] Given the more dispersed settlement patterns and the extreme ethnic and class heterogeneity of the current immigrant population, it's not surprising that the latest arrivals are more likely to begin outside the classic ethnic neighborhood.

## Ethnic Enclaves

Not that immigrants no longer cluster. Indeed, ethnic enclaves are alive and well in New York City. Probably the best-known is Manhattan's Chinatown, which has expanded beyond its original ten-block area to encompass much of what was once the Italian and Jewish Lower East Side. Limited housing and high rents in Chinatown and the enormous growth in New York City's Chinese population have led to the development of satellite Chinatowns in Brooklyn and Queens, where a substantial proportion of the city's Chinese now live.[71] The largest and oldest of the satellite Chinatowns is Flushing, Queens, which is emerging as an alternate finance center to the core Chinatown. Chinese residents call the Eighth Avenue section of Brooklyn's Sunset Park Ba Da Dao ("Avenue of Prosperity"), where, by one account, there are now over 250 Chinese businesses, from vegetable stalls and seafood stores to video shops and travel agencies, as well as some two hundred garment factories.[72] Koreans, too, are creating what Pyong Gap Min calls an overseas Seoul in Flushing, where he estimates about one quarter of New York City's Koreans live. They are heavily concentrated in a dozen blocks, where they can find employment in Korean-owned stores, speak the Korean language, attend Korean churches, and enjoy Korean food.[73]

Dominicans have created a city-within-a-city in northern Manhattan's Washington Heights.[74] Upper Broadway, one journalist writes, "abounds with *bodegas, farmacias* . . . restaurants serving *pollo* and *platanos* and travel agents offering bargain [flights] to the Dominican Republic."[75] With the surge of Dominican immigration in the 1990s, Inwood, to the north of Washington Heights, and Hamilton Heights, to the south, have also taken on an increasingly Dominican character.

Brooklyn's Brighton Beach now smells and tastes increasingly Russian; it was reported in 1995 to have the world's greatest concentration of Soviet émigrés.[76] There's also a growing presence of former Soviets in neighboring Gravesend-Homecrest and Bensonhurst, as well as in the Forest Hills–Kew Gardens area of Queens.[77]

Elsewhere in Brooklyn, in Crown Heights, Flatbush, and East Flatbush, West Indian beauty parlors, restaurants, record stores, groceries, and bakeries dot the landscape, and sounds of Haitian Creole and West Indian accents fill the air. Along Nostrand, Utica, and Church Avenues, many businesses display some Caribbean referent—a flag, a country's name, a few words in dialect, or perhaps just a painted palm tree. "[When I walk] along . . . Nostrand Avenue," the novelist Paule Marshall notes, "I have to remind myself that I'm in Brooklyn and not in the middle of a teeming outdoor market in St. George's, Grenada or Kingston, Jamaica."[78] Several neighborhoods in the northeast Bronx (Williamsbridge and Wakefield) and southeastern Queens (Springfield Gardens and Cambria Heights) have also developed a definite West Indian flavor.

Although many black West Indians prefer to live among their compatriots, those who wish to move beyond the ethnic neighborhood run into difficulties. As Roger Waldinger observes: "Blacks who have succeeded in this quest have found that the limited tolerance of whites for more than a handful of black neighbors has made integration short-lived; part-black areas have been quick to tip to all black, and, thus, the 'old neighborhood' has too often caught up with those who thought they had left it behind."[79] The result is that in New York City, as well as in the suburbs, black immigrants tend to be confined to largely black areas (see Chapter 5). Interestingly, Guyanese and Trinidadian immigrants of East Indian background are developing distinctly Indo-Caribbean neighborhoods apart from their compatriots of African descent, a popular destination being the Richmond Hill section of Queens, a lower-middle-class white area that has drawn Asian and Hispanic, rather than black, immigrants.

*Ethnic Succession*

Although today's immigrants often huddle in ethnic bastions in a timeworn pattern, the neighborhoods they are moving into differ from those that housed the last great wave. It's ethnic succession with a new twist, as the latest arrivals establish themselves in communities that, until recently, were home to middle- and lower-middle-class native whites, themselves descendants of earlier European immigrants.

When Jews and Italians came to New York a century ago, they started out in the city's slums, typically in areas where German and Irish immigrants had lived before. Southern blacks and Puerto Ricans who arrived in the 1940s and 1950s crowded into many of the same neighborhoods on the Lower East Side, Harlem, and Williamsburg, where cheap housing was available and jobs were not far away or hard to get to.[80] Now, most newcomers are bypassing the old ghetto neighborhoods. One might have expected Hispanic immigrants to follow Puerto Ricans' residential path, but on the whole they have not. Nor are West Indians concentrated in the large, long-standing African American neighborhoods of Harlem and Bedford-Stuyvesant.[81]

The old ghetto areas, as Roger Waldinger points out, do not provide much housing for recent arrivals because of accelerated abandonment, on the one hand, and urban renewal and gentrification, on the other.[82] Areas such as Central Harlem and East Harlem, for example, have an abundance of public housing that is already occupied mainly by the native-born and for which there are long waiting lists. Immigrants are moving farther afield to where the jobs are—and to where there is housing. As native young white householders and retirees left New York City for the suburbs and the Sunbelt, and as many aged white ethnic New Yorkers died, they opened up access to reasonably good housing stock in Queens and Brooklyn; the departure of whites from many of the region's other central cities and aging suburbs has had the same effect. In New York City, the white population plummeted by 1.3 million in the 1970s and by about half a million in the 1980s. The white population of the twelve inner counties around the city declined by about 530,000 in the 1980s as well.[83]

Newcomers have been able to take advantage of the housing opportunities that arose, and some have even bought their own homes, for a number of reasons: they began in the middle rather than the lower reaches of the labor market; they often pooled the income of several working family members; or, in some cases, they brought financial capital from abroad. Relatively inexpensive rentals, sometimes in immigrant-owned homes, were available in many places throughout the region, too. Once a group became established in a community, family and ethnic networks tended to draw others in. As immigrants streamed into new areas, their presence caused further flight by native whites. Or as Flores and Salvo put it, the native-born have desired "to maintain some social and spatial distance from the encroaching immigrant population."[84]

Jackson Heights, a Queens neighborhood that has one of the largest immigrant populations in the city, is an example of this new kind of succession. At the time of the last great wave at the beginning of the century, Trains Meadow, as it was then called, was a rolling landscape of fields, meadows, and streams with some two dozen houses and several farms that grew vegetables for city markets. The opening of the subway line in 1917 made the community accessible. The real estate developer Edward MacDougall, who decided on the name Jackson Heights, promoted it as a garden suburb of cooperative apartments and single-family houses for middle-class New Yorkers; Jews were openly excluded as part of the garden suburb ideal. Although Jackson Heights thrived during the 1920s, the Great Depression brought financial difficulties; MacDougall began to divide some of the seven-room flats into cheaper, less luxurious three- and four-room apartments and even offered furnished rooms for rent. To raise more money, he built new apartments that covered the twelve-hole golf course, tennis courts, and community gardens. In its less luxurious incarnation, Jackson Heights, for the next few decades, was home to middle- and lower-middle-class white New Yorkers (although given anti-Semitic restrictions, few Jews lived there before the 1950s). By 1990, the area's residents were mainly Latin American and Asian immigrants; the non-Hispanic white population, which had been 67 percent in 1970, was down to 28 percent.[85] Much the same thing happened in nearby Flushing, which lost 55 percent of its white population between 1970 and 1990. As whites died or moved to the suburbs and other parts of the country, Flushing underwent a process of Asianization as Koreans, Indians, and Chinese streamed in. In 1990, the census counted 19,508 Asians in Flushing, up from only 2,571 twenty years before.[86]

In the wake of the white exodus from New York City, immigrants have played a key role in revitalizing many neighborhoods that had fallen on hard times. Some observers, Mayor Rudolph Giuliani among them, argue that without immigrants many of New York City's neighborhoods would have suffered inexorable decay. As of 1993, immigrants occupied 46 percent of the city's "accessible" housing units—rental housing available for immediate occupancy without the long waiting lists common in public housing. In some neighborhoods, like Jackson Heights and East Flatbush, immigrants occupied more than 75 percent of accessible housing. Without immigrants, it has been said, many of these apartments and houses would have been vulnerable to abandonment.[87]

This kind of scenario is of course highly speculative. What is clear, however, is that the massive number of immigrants arriving in recent years has helped many deteriorating neighborhoods make a comeback. By the 1970s, for example, Brooklyn's Brighton Beach was in decline: apartments stood empty as elderly Jewish residents died off or moved to Florida, and the main commercial avenue turned into a decaying strip of old stores. Since the 1980s, the massive influx of Soviet Jews has filled apartments and turned the avenue into a thriving commercial center.[88] Another Brooklyn community, Sunset Park, was in the "throes of a long twilight" that began in the 1950s as the area was devastated by, among other things, a drastic cutback in jobs on its waterfront and in industry and the exodus of tens of thousands of white residents for leafier suburbs. Louis Winnick argues that immigrants in Sunset Park, as in other city neighborhoods "outside the yuppie strongholds of Manhattan and other favored areas of Brooklyn and Queens," have been the leading factor in neighborhood revitalization: "Owing to their high employment rates and multiple wage earners, the new foreigners have injected large doses of new purchasing power into the rehabilitation of an aging housing stock and the resurrection of inert retail streets. Their presence has been visible not only in the demand for housing but in the supply as well, displaying a willingness to undertake the disagreeable, if potentially profitable, tasks entailed in fixing up and managing decaying buildings."[89]

Outside of the five boroughs, immigrants have also been credited with helping a number of aging, industrial satellite cities in the region begin to recover from urban decline and the loss of middle- and lower-middle-class white families. And within the city, there is yet another pattern of neighborhood renaissance: as immigrant neighborhoods have filled up, and rents and house prices have risen, the most recent arrivals in some groups have begun to branch out to older native minority areas. Joel Millman, a journalist, writes of how West Indian home owners have begun to turn around Brooklyn's Brownsville, which by the 1970s had become one of the city's most desolate black ghettos, as they have moved there from nearby established West Indian neighborhoods in the search for housing.[90]

## The Road to Suburbia

It's a long way from Jacob Riis's exposé of tenement housing in *How the Other Half Lives* to crediting immigrants with rescuing New York City's sagging housing market. Riis and his cohorts would also have been surprised by another aspect of today's residential patterns—a different kind of suburbanization of immigration.

Immigrants in Riis's time, of course, ventured beyond the confines of New York City to places in the surrounding region. Indeed, in the search for work, Italians and eastern European Jews headed for many of the same areas in New Jersey, Westchester, and Long Island that attract newcomers today. At the time of the last great wave, industrial jobs had dispersed to a number of nearby satellite cities; construction projects in the region drew in low-skilled immigrant labor; and affluent residents of railroad suburbs in Westchester and Long Island required servants to work in their houses and gardens and to provide other services.

By 1910, some 132,000 foreign-born Italians and 96,000 Russian Jews lived in the twelve inner counties surrounding New York City—altogether, about a quarter of the size of New York City's Italian and Russian Jewish immigrant population. New Jersey's industrial cities drew the largest number. In 1910, when New York was the leading city of residence for foreign-born Italians in the country (340,770), Newark ranked fifth (20,500) and Jersey City, tenth (12,000). Newark, with some 22,000 foreign-born Russians, came in eighth in the nation for Russian Jews (New York City, with over 484,000, was first).[91] Italians became the most prevalent nationality in New Jersey's silk industry and also worked on gangs, digging sewers, excavating, or building railroads throughout the state. Many eastern European Jews left Manhattan's East Side to work in New Jersey's needle trades or become small shopkeepers. In New Jersey's northern cities, the newest arrivals succeeded the Irish and Germans in the least desirable neighborhoods. Italians, for example, took over the slums of Jersey City's "Horseshoe" from the Irish, whereas eastern European Jews moved into the tenements of Newark's Third Ward on the heels of their German predecessors. Of the new immigrants, it was said that "they settle in the congested districts of industrial centers and crowd together in tenements under unhealthy and unsanitary conditions."[92]

Although much smaller than Manhattan's Italian enclaves, Little Italys developed in several Westchester cities after the turn of the century, as Italians arrived to build roads and railways, pipelines and tracks, for inter- and intracity trolley systems and to work on huge construction projects like the Croton Dam.[93] Long Island's wealthy North Shore drew Italians, too, to labor on road, railway, and other construction projects and to develop and maintain the mansions there. By 1915, about 500 Italian immigrants and their children constituted one-sixth of Westbury's population; Glen Cove's 1,163 Italians represented over a tenth of that town's total.[94] In Westchester, eastern European Jews established themselves as artisans, junk collectors, factory workers, and shopkeepers in the developing cities, but their communities were small. In 1910, Yonkers was the only city with more than a thousand Russian-born Jews—about 3,000 (4 percent of the total population) supported a number of orthodox synagogues and kosher butchers.[95]

The dispersal patterns of today's immigrants around the New York region are not altogether different. Ronald Flores and Joseph Salvo's analysis of immigrant settlement patterns in the New York urban region shows that many new arrivals are moving to the same satellite cities that attracted immigrants in the past, although now they're more likely to work in service jobs than in industry.[96] Many of New Jersey's old industrial cities that attracted Jewish and Italian immigrants a century ago have fairly high proportions of recent arrivals. Some examples: in 1990, a third of Passaic's population, a fifth of Newark's, and a quarter of Jersey City's was foreign born. Some of the towns that attract immigrants are the same, too. On Long Island, the Orchard, a poor neighborhood on the margins of affluent Glen Cove that housed Italian gardeners and laborers at the turn of the last century, is now home to Salvadoran and other Latino immigrants who work as landscapers, construction workers, and pool-maintenance attendants.[97]

But the suburbs have undergone massive transformations since the last great wave, as have immigrant settlement patterns there.[98] The suburban population explosion after World War II changed the face of the suburbs forever. Nassau, which had about 84,000 people in 1910, was home to almost 1.3 million in 1990; Westchester County went from 283,000 to 875,000; Bergen County from 138,000 to 825,000. It is not surprising that immigrants have been increasingly drawn to the counties outside New York City—since all groups in the region have, regardless of their origins. Whereas in 1910, 33 percent of the foreign-born in the thirty-one-county New York urban region lived outside New York City, in 1990 it was up to 43 percent.[99]

Today it's more likely that suburbia is the first stop for immigrants rather than their eventual destination, after an initial stay in New York City. Indeed, moving right to the suburbs is a growing trend. In the 1970s, only about one in ten of the newly arrived immigrants in the New York urban region first settled outside New York City; ten years later it was one out of three.[100] Moreover, a number of immigrants today have the means to move into the kind of bedroom communities most Americans associate with middle-class suburbia—and some live right in the middle of extremely affluent communities, not on the fringes.[101]

Many suburbs have changed in the last few decades in ways that make them a realistic option for new arrivals looking for affordable housing and jobs. Older suburbs not far from New York City have gone through what Flores and Salvo call a "maturation process." Since the 1970s, many suburban communities have become home to increasing numbers of low-income, aged, and racial-minority households. On the whole, immigrants (and native minorities) have been moving into the less affluent and more rundown suburbs and satellite cities just outside New York City's borders but not far from the city's larger ethnic enclaves; meanwhile, native-born whites have been moving outward toward the region's periphery. There are, however, differences among groups. On average, Asians have settled in predominantly white suburbs that are more affluent and generally safer than those that other immigrant minorities enter. Hispanics have tended to move into another of the region's cities or to the older and poorer suburbs. West Indians end up in areas with sizable black populations.

Although a substantial number of immigrants in virtually every group live outside New York City, this trend is especially pronounced for certain groups. In 1990, over 60 percent of the post-1964 Cuban, Salvadoran, Portuguese, and Indian immigrants in the New York urban region lived outside New York City—as high as 95 percent in the case of Portuguese. In contrast, over three-quarters of the post-1964 Dominicans, Guyanese, Trinidadians, former Soviets, and Chinese in the region lived in New York City, no doubt attracted by the large ethnic enclaves that flourish there. In much the same way, Cubans and Portuguese have been drawn to large and dense ethnic communities in New Jersey. Asian Indians, who have no strong enclave in the five boroughs and who are often highly skilled and educated, have dispersed throughout the suburbs.

Immigrants have transformed many places in the metropolitan area. The old central cities in New Jersey not far from Manhattan—Jersey City, Passaic, Newark, Elizabeth, and Paterson—as well as older suburbs with a central-city character, like Union City and West New York, now have enormous numbers of immigrants. By 1990, the foreign-born accounted for 55 percent of the population in the heavily Cuban community of Union City and 60 percent in neighboring West New York. Many older New Jersey communities that are less dense in population and have a middle-class suburban feel are also popular immigrant destinations. Across the Hudson from Manhattan, Fort Lee, Palisades Park, and Englewood Cliffs, for example, each have populations that are a third or more foreign born. In Westchester, older suburbs and cities, like Port Chester, North Tarrytown village, and Mount Vernon, have a significant proportion of immigrant residents. And the list goes on—Cliffside Park and Perth Amboy in New

Jersey; Rye Town and Greenville in Westchester; and Spring Valley, Haver-straw, and Hillcrest in Rockland, all with populations that are at least a quarter foreign born.[102]

Edison, New Jersey, had only nine hundred Asian Indian residents in 1980; by 1990, that number had risen to six thousand, out of a population of eighty-nine thousand. "Twenty years ago, there was no alternative," said a leader of the Edison Indian community, referring to the special stores and services catering to Indians. "If you were an immigrant from India, you went to Queens. Now you can move to Jersey City or Middlesex County, where everything is available."[103] In Westchester, Port Chester's Hispanic population doubled in the 1980s to seventy-five hundred, or 30 percent of its residents, a mix of newcomers from such countries as Peru, Ecuador, Colombia, and Mexico.[104] Wealthy towns have attracted the most affluent immigrants—for example, Great Neck is home to many Iranians. Scarsdale, the Westchester suburb famous for its wealth and outstanding school system, was 7 percent Japanese and 3 percent Chinese in 1990.[105] At the other extreme, Salvadorans from peasant backgrounds have settled in low-income neighborhoods of Long Island's bedroom communities and established minority enclaves.[106]

### Polyethnic Neighborhoods

The ethnic ecology of today's immigrants differs from that of the past in still other ways. Although large and dense ethnic settlements continue to thrive, significant numbers of new arrivals do not live in them, even upon arrival. Indeed, many immigrant populations have no one neighborhood they can truly call their own and where they are the single dominant group. Understandably, this is true of groups that are small in number—but it's also the case for some larger groups that are highly dispersed. There's no one neighborhood that Filipinos dominate, for example. Much the same can be said of Asian Indians, who form communities of networks, not of space. New York's "Little India," consisting of a few blocks in Jackson Heights, Queens, is a concentration of businesses, not residences; it is a magnet for Indians from adjoining Queens neighborhoods as well as from the suburbs.[107]

Many of today's immigrant neighborhoods are an amalgam of newcomers from all parts of the world. Given the bewildering array of new groups—and dispersed settlement patterns in the region—this isn't surprising. The number 7 train that connects Times Square in Manhattan with Flushing in Queens has been dubbed the International Express as it weaves through polyethnic neighborhoods which have no parallel in previous waves of migration.[108] One observer writes: "Even at the time of its densest settlement, the Lower East Side . . . was a cross section of European nationalities plus a sliver from one Chinese region. The Flushing-Corona-Elmhurst-Jackson Heights cluster approximates an ethnic cross section of the planet."[109] Elmhurst is one of New York's most diverse immigrant areas, with large numbers of Chinese, Colombians, Koreans, Filipinos, Asian Indians, Dominicans, and Ecuadorians. Between 1991 and 1995, according to INS figures, the area constituting Elmhurst's zip code, 11373, received more people from more countries than any other zip code in the United States.[110] Although Flushing is sometimes referred to as a new Chinatown in the making, it is in fact home to a growing number of Central and South American as well as to Chinese, Indian, and Korean immigrants who join a native-born white population that remains substantial.[111] Astoria, known for its large Greek presence in the 1980s, welcomed large numbers of Asians and Latin Americans from different countries in the early 1990s—thereby becoming another ethnic stew.

By now, almost every part of New York City contains some immigrants, as does much of the region as well. Between 1990 and 1994 alone, even the yuppie stronghold of Manhattan's Upper East Side received eight thousand immigrants—a highly diverse group that included, in descending numerical order, Chinese, Irish, Filipinos, British, Japanese, French, Russians, Indians, Israelis, and Brazilians.[112] As Richard Alba and his colleagues document in their study of neighborhood change between 1970 and 1990, immigration has led to increasing racial and ethnic complexity in the New York City region. More and more neighborhoods contain multiple groups; fewer and fewer are ethnically or racially homogeneous. By 1990, only 8 percent of neighborhoods in the region were all white, down from 29 percent twenty years earlier. Nearly half of the region's neighborhoods could be classified as white, Hispanic, and Asian or as white, black, Asian, and Hispanic.[113]

Some better-off Asian and white immigrants have moved into the top-of-the-line residential mainstream immediately, and though they are a minority, their numbers are not unsubstantial. Because of their education and income (and because they're not black), they have been able to buy homes and rent apartments in neighborhoods without an immigrant cast, living side by side with well-to-do native whites. Israelis in high-status occupations, for example, live next to established Jewish New Yorkers in upscale areas of Manhattan and Riverdale. A small but significant number of Asians have moved into what used to be all-white areas in New York City, like the leafy and relatively affluent communities of Bayside, Little Neck, and Douglaston in northeastern Queens. A number of Asian professionals and entrepreneurs have been able to enter exclusive white neighborhoods in the suburbs, too, where they are the only nonwhites and a small minority (typically, 5 to 15 percent) of the population.[114]

In general, Asians have avoided the poorest areas in New York City and the region, and they are less segregated from whites than are blacks and Hispanics.[115] In the suburbs, according to an analysis of 1990 census data, their degree of segregation from non-Hispanic whites was a modest 33 percent (compared to 54 percent for Hispanics and 74 percent for blacks). Although some suburban communities had, by 1990, taken on a definite Asian flavor—for example, Asians were then a fifth of the population of Fort Lee, New Jersey—Asians outside of New York City were generally dispersed among many heavily white suburban communities where the Asian share of the population tended to be small.[116] In New York City, there are few predominantly white neighborhoods of any stripe without an Asian presence.[117] Asians are no longer the target of virulent racism. And because many Asian immigrants have started out in the middle rungs of the occupational ladder, they can afford to move directly into middle-class areas.

## Contemporary Housing

For some of today's immigrants, however, housing conditions are just as abysmal as they were a hundred years ago, perhaps even worse. There are reports of Mexican immigrants inhabiting tunnel-like spaces behind buildings in Washington Heights; of Korean workers "hotbedding" (that is, renting bed space by time) as they pay up to $175 a month for the privilege of sleeping in shifts; and of Chinese men being packed with ten or fifteen others into one-bedroom Chinatown apartments that have been subdivided into compartments smaller than many closets.[118] One journalist calls them the "all-but-homeless," squeezed by the withering stock of inexpensive apartments and mushrooming demand into "the kind of claustrophobic quarters that [Jacob] Riis sought to eliminate."[119]

Officials from various New York City agencies, according to a *New York Times* account, estimate that anywhere from ten thousand to fifty thousand immigrants live in cubicles illegally carved out of the basements of private homes and apartment houses, with little light or ventilation and inadequate means of escape.[120] In one East Flatbush building, the basement was sliced into six 5-by-8-foot cubbyholes by thin pieces of plywood, with a communal bathroom and kitchen area. Only two of the four burners worked on the stove; the shower produced only cold water; and the ceiling in the corridor consisted of exposed dripping pipes. Throughout the city, many immigrants "spend winters shivering without heat, their ovens on broil.... They bed down in illegal basements with nothing but plywood beneath their mattresses.... They confront frightening dilapidation—leaks that eat at their ceilings and rot their floors, rusted fire escapes and roller-coaster stairways.... And they endure vile infestation—rats gobble their garbage and nibble their slippers." A case in point on the Lower East Side: one Dominican family of five squeezed into an illegal $350-a-month room of only 120 square feet, with no sink and no toilet. At night, the mother said, "when the mice crawl over us in bed, it feels even more crowded."[121]

Substandard conditions are not confined to the city's boundaries. In the suburbs, too, many immigrants live in basements, attics, and garages that are sometimes partitioned into many tiny units. According to the anthropologist Sarah Mahler, for Salvadorans the high cost of housing on Long Island has meant that six or more adults and several children normally share an apartment or house. In one small house in Suffolk County, two men and a couple shared one bedroom; a couple and a small child lived in the second bedroom; several men slept in the living room; and a few tenants occupied the porch and garage. Roaches crawled all over the floor and walls in the house; the kitchen linoleum was nearly translucent from wear and the stove was covered with grease. Heat in the house was sporadic; the water was occasionally turned off because the landlord did not pay his bills; and the cesspool backed up repeatedly.[122] These "sliced and diced" illegal conversions, as journalists have called them, are often dangerous, without fire exits or adequate electrical wiring.[123] A fire caused by faulty wiring in an illegally converted house in Maspeth, Queens, which killed four Polish immigrant men (including the owner), dramatically highlighted the hazards posed by such dwellings.[124]

Appalling conditions like these are all the more upsetting given that living standards for the bulk of the population are so much better now than they were a century ago. In twenty-first-century America, people of all classes take steam heat, plumbing, and electrification for granted as necessities. When immigrants' housing conditions fall below even minimal standards of decency, it is, as critics rightly claim, a modern-day scandal.

Yet just as we can't ignore horrific cases of squalor, we also need to remember that only a minority of contemporary immigrants are consigned to woefully inadequate quarters. It's a complicated story—a mixture of crowded, often illegally converted, housing for many immigrants in combination with otherwise habitable conditions for the majority as well as an increase in home ownership.

An analysis of the 1996 New York City Housing and Vacancy survey, based on a sample of about eighteen thousand housing units, helps to get at some of the complexities.[125] On the down side, immigrants' low incomes and limited access to publicly subsidized apartments force them to devote a much larger percentage of their earnings to housing than do other New Yorkers. New York City has one of the tightest housing markets in the nation, and recent arrivals suffer the consequences. Almost half of all immigrant renters spent over 30 percent of their income for rent, compared to 42 percent of native-born renters. To cut housing costs, some 15 percent of immigrant households were crowded (defined as more than one person per room) and 5 percent severely crowded (more than one and a half persons per room). This was six times the rate for native-born white households in the city, and more than double the rate for native-born black households. In New York City, as in the suburbs, escalating rents, and the large outlays required for security deposits and broker's fees, make it impossible for many immigrants to rent entire houses or apartments on their own. Instead they rent rooms, and sometimes an entire floor, in apartments or houses that are leased or owned by compatriots. More often than not, these divisions and conversions violate building and occupancy ordinances.

Overall, however, the housing survey indicates that the large majority of immigrants, like most native-born New Yorkers, live in decent-quality housing. A relatively small minority, 17 percent of immigrant compared to 16 percent of native-born householders, reported living in poor-quality housing, defined as housing with three or more deficiencies such as heating or plumbing breakdowns, rat infestation, and water leakage from outside. Black and Hispanic immigrants, like their native-born counterparts, are the most disadvantaged in New York's housing market (see table 4). Immigrants from Europe, Russia, and Asia do not face the same difficult conditions as those from the Dominican Republic, Latin America, and the Caribbean. In fact, roughly the same proportion of Asian and European immigrant households are in seriously deficient housing as native white New Yorkers, whereas Dominican households face the most serious problems of all.

Ethnographic reports and informal observations also show that crowding and illegally subdivided units do not necessarily mean that living conditions are substandard. Middle-class Americans often recoil at the notion

Table 4   Deficient Housing in New York City Households, 1996

| Group | Percentage of Households |
| --- | --- |
| Foreign born (FB) | 17 |
| Native born (NB) | 16 |
| FB Dominican | 34 |
| Puerto Rican (mainland born) | 29 |
| NB, non-Hispanic black | 27 |
| Puerto Rican (island born) | 23 |
| FB Caribbean[1] and African | 22 |
| FB Mexican and Central and South American | 20 |
| FB Indian, Pakistani, and Bangladeshi | 10 |
| FB Chinese (China, Hong Kong, and Taiwan) | 10 |
| FB Korean, Filipino, and other Southeast Asian | 9 |
| NB, non-Hispanic white | 8 |
| FB Russian[2] | 7 |
| FB European | 7 |

Source: Schill, Friedman, and Rosenbaum 1998, based on the 1996 New York City Housing and Vacancy Survey of approximately eighteen thousand units.

Note: Deficient housing constitutes a dwelling with three or more serious problems, such as a heating or plumbing breakdown, rat infestation, or the lack of a bathroom or kitchen.

[1] Other than Dominican Republic and Puerto Rico.

[2] Includes Russia and successor states to Soviet Union.

of people living in basement apartments, and the idea of several families sharing a single-family house violates ideas about privacy and the sanctity of the nuclear family. Although many Jamaicans I met during my research in the 1980s lived in rooms or apartments in private houses that were not certified for this purpose, they had modern furnishings, appliances, and amenities like telephones and televisions. The rented rooms I visited in houses and apartments were well furnished and neatly kept.[126] Many illegally converted apartments make for decent quarters, for example, the basement apartment occupied by a Mexican immigrant and his three children in Jackson Heights; clean and well lighted, it had wall-to-wall carpeting throughout its four rooms and a full-size kitchen with a stove and large refrigerator.[127]

Or consider the rooming house owned by Dona Dahlia, a Brazilian immigrant. The house is a three-floor, semidetached brick structure in a neat, lower middle-class section of Queens. At any one time, about fifteen or sixteen newly arrived Brazilian immigrants are staying there, usually for a few weeks or, at most, a couple of months, at a cost of fifty dollars a week. Four to six men sleep in bunk beds jammed into the two bedrooms upstairs; they share a bathroom just off the landing. The women's quarters—a bedroom with two bunk beds and a small bathroom—is in the basement. Boarders can use the living room on the main floor, which is carpeted and furnished with two comfortable couches, a table, and a color television. Many of the lodgers cook for themselves in the kitchen. The refrigerator and cupboards are crammed with groceries carefully labeled with the names of individual residents. A piece of paper taped to the refrigerator lists telephone calls made to Brazil. Those who want privacy can use the telephone extension in Dona Dahlia's bedroom. Far from being a place of squalor, or merely a cheap place to live, anthropologist Maxine Margolis argues that Dona Dahlia's rooming house is also a school, counseling center, employment agency, and legal aid society that provides Brazilian immigrants with things they need to know and items they need to have during their first days in New York.[128]

Immigrant families that rent entire apartments or own their homes also often enjoy a range of modern amenities associated with a middle-class American lifestyle. One of the better-off Dominican workers Patricia Pessar interviewed lived in a spacious garden apartment, complete with guest room, living room, and den. Other Dominicans she met had also acquired modern kitchen appliances, color televisions, and automobiles in this country.[129] In my 1982 study of Jamaican immigrants, I found that of the forty people I interviewed, only one, a live-in domestic worker, did not have a telephone or television. As I asked questions to construct an amenity scale comparing housing in New York and Jamaica, most thought the question about whether they had an indoor flush toilet in New York was absurd. Of course they had one, they all said. Those who owned their homes, as well as some who lived in apartments, also had their own washing machine; nearly all owned a stereo; and many had an air conditioning unit. (Many owned a car as well.) My guess is that if I did the same survey today, most would now have other equipment that has become commonplace, like microwave ovens and videocassette recorders.

Tenement life of yore has, for a substantial minority of today's newcomers, given way to ownership of private homes. Housing opportunities are better today—and more immigrants have the financial resources to take advantage of them. Although New York City is still primarily a place of renters, home ownership is more common than at the turn of the century, when less than 15 percent of New Yorkers were home owners. In the early 1990s, the home ownership rate was 29 percent (nationally, the rate for central cities was 49 percent).[130] According to the 1996 New York City

Table 5   Household Income and Home Ownership in New York City, 1996

| Group | Median Household Income) ($) | Home Ownership (%) |
|---|---|---|
| Foreign born (FB) | 25,000 | 24 |
| Native born (NB) | 32,000 | 34 |
| NB, non-Hispanic white | 41,000 | 43 |
| FB European | 30,000 | 43 |
| FB Chinese | 38,510 | 41 |
| FB Korean, Filipino, and other Southeast Asian | 43,000 | 29 |
| FB Caribbean[1] and African | 30,000 | 27 |
| FB Indian, Pakistani, and Bangladeshi | 35,750 | 22 |
| NB, non-Hispanic black | 22,200 | 21 |
| FB Mexican and Central and South American | 30,000 | 19 |
| FB Russian[2] | 16,185 | 15 |
| Puerto Rican (mainland born) | 21,000 | 15 |
| Puerto Rican (island born) | 13,800 | 12 |
| FB Dominican | 14,844 | 6 |

*Source:* Schill, Friedman, and Rosenbaum 1998, based on the 1996 New York City Housing and Vacancy Survey of approximately eighteen thousand units.

[1] Other than Puerto Rico and Dominican Republic.

[2] Russia and successor states to Soviet Union.

Housing and Vacancy survey, a smaller proportion of immigrant (24 percent) than native-born (34 percent) householders own their own homes, although European and Chinese immigrants have about the same home ownership rates as native-born white New Yorkers (see table 5).[131] Unfortunately, the survey did not examine how long immigrants had lived in the United States. When they first come to this country, few immigrants have the assets to buy their own homes, but the rate increases substantially over time. Nationwide, immigrants who arrived in the 1970s and who were between the ages of twenty-five and thirty-four in 1980 achieved just 24 percent of the home ownership rates of native whites of the same age; by 1990, this same group had attained 76 percent of the native white rate.[132]

As one would expect, groups with relatively high household incomes tend to have the highest home ownership rates. European, Asian, and West Indian immigrants in New York City are more likely to own their own homes than Latin Americans and Russians (table 5). Once again, Dominicans fare the worst. This disparity is also revealed in a comparison of three Caribbean groups. At the time of the 1990 census, about a third of New York City's Jamaicans and Haitians were home owners, compared to only 8 percent of Dominicans. Jamaicans and Haitians had much higher household incomes than Dominicans, and this, Sherri Grasmuck and Ramón Grosfoguel argue, has to do with their better education and English skills, their early access to nonmanufacturing jobs, and their higher rates of female employment.[133] Because so many members of West Indian households work, they can pool family earnings in relatively low-paying jobs to finance the purchase of a home. West Indian rotating-credit associations are also a help in making the down payment possible. In these groups, commonly called "susus," each member makes a fixed weekly contribution, one member gets to keep the entire pool, and the recipient changes until everyone has had a turn. A number of banks now write mortgages in which susu proceeds are used as a financing source. Chase Manhattan Bank considers susu membership when allocating mortgages through its affordable mortgage program and accepts letters from susu bankers when evaluating loan applicants.[134]

Many neighborhoods in New York City are now filled with West Indian home owners, East Flatbush being a prime example. In the 1930s, young Jewish families eager to escape the tenements of Brownsville and the Lower East Side flocked to the small, newly built one- and two-family brick homes of East Flatbush, and in the 1950s a number of high-rise developments went up. In the late 1960s and 1970s, the neighborhood experienced a substantial white exodus, but because of the high rates of owner occupancy and the nature of the housing stock, the buildings did not suffer the kind of deterioration and destruction that followed the white abandonment of places like the South Bronx. Large numbers of small houses became available—and West Indian home buyers stepped in. Indeed, in 1988 one developer built seventy-two condominium units in East Flatbush, the first substantial construction in the area in three decades, specifically marketed toward West Indian households with incomes in the $35,000–$45,000 range.[135] In 1990, according to the census, 31 percent of foreign-born Jamaicans in East Flatbush owned their homes. The figure was even higher—37 percent—in the Williamsbridge-Wakefield section of the Bronx, an area on the northern edge of the borough with street after street of single-family brick houses.[136] As house prices have risen in established West Indian areas, immigrants have been branching out to less desirable neighborhoods, like Brownsville and Bedford-Stuyvesant, in the quest to purchase affordable homes.

Throughout New York City, increasing numbers of immigrants own homes in semisuburban communities such as Laurelton and Rosedale (home to West Indians) and Flushing (home to Asians) in Queens. The street on which I grew up in the 1950s in Fresh Meadows, Queens, was a mix of middle-class Jewish and Italian and Irish Americans who lived in single-family houses with carefully tended front lawns and backyards. By 1996, my parents were among the few "old-timers" in the neighborhood, which is increasingly made up of Chinese, Asian Indian, Korean, and Greek immigrants. Chinese-run real estate agencies flourish in the area, and many buyers depend on loans from the Chinese-owned banks that have mushroomed in Flushing in recent years and are more likely to give Chinese applicants the benefit of the doubt and to overlook some of the traditional indicators of poor credit ratings. In general, the support of Asian banks within the ethnic community as well as financial capital from abroad have made it possible for some Asian immigrants to enter the housing market as soon as they arrive, or not too long afterwards.[137]

Some immigrants, a small minority to be sure, are at the top of the housing hierarchy. As I've mentioned, established professionals and business people who arrive today often can afford, from the very start, to buy expensive homes in some of the region's—indeed, the nation's—most affluent suburban communities, such as those in Westchester County and Long Island and in yuppie neighborhoods in Manhattan and Brooklyn. According to a study of home ownership among immigrants in the state of New Jersey, Indians and Filipinos, the wealthiest of the recent arrivals, live in the newest housing—and the most expensive. In 1990, nearly half of New Jersey's Indian home owners and 40 percent of Filipino home owners had homes valued at two hundred thousand dollars or more.[138]

A hundred years ago, the vast majority of Italian and eastern European Jewish immigrants in New York City were crowded into airless tenements in densely packed ethnic neighborhoods in Manhattan and Brooklyn. Today, the picture is more complicated, because the latest immigrants come from so many countries and because a substantial minority have middle-class jobs and household incomes. Moreover, since the last great wave, the entire city and much of the region is more built up and heavily populated, and the general level of housing has improved dramatically. In the 1990s, the range of housing runs the gamut from basement cubicles in decaying Manhattan tenements to modern luxury homes in suburban Scarsdale. Although there are many distinctive immigrant neighborhoods, there are also multiethnic conglomerations of extraordinary diversity—and some communities where immigrants live in the midst of well-to-do native whites. Unlike their turn-of-the-century predecessors, most of today's arrivals do not live in New York City's worst slums—indeed, a significant proportion of the region's new arrivals do not live in New York City at all. There is a growing trend toward dispersal into the counties that border the city. All over the region, a modern version of ethnic succession has been occurring, as immigrants have replaced—and continue to replace—native-born whites who have left for greener pastures.

The differences stand out, yet there are also continuities with the past. In what seems like a timeless feature of immigrant settlement, many newcomers cluster in ethnic colonies, often sharing homes or apartment buildings with people from their home communities and, as they become a dominant presence, giving many neighborhoods a distinct ethnic flavor. Indeed, some of the latest arrivals have moved into the classic areas of immigrant settlement in Manhattan and Brooklyn as well as to satellite cities around the region. Whatever the neighborhood, low incomes—and recent entry into the housing market—also force many immigrant families today, as in the past, into crowded and sometimes substandard living quarters and to rent out space to their compatriots in order to make ends meet.

Past or present, clearly where one lives matters. At the most basic level, unsafe housing can cause or aggravate illness; crowded conditions can create or accentuate family tensions and stand in the way of children's success in school; and living in squalor can dampen immigrants' spirits and become a source of dissatisfaction with life in this country. When immigrant families spend half or more of their income on rent—which a great many now do—not much is left over to meet other necessary expenses, from subway fares and utility bills to food and clothing.

Outside the home, the neighborhood is a critical context in which immigrants learn about America and cope with their new lives; it influences a wide range of their activities and relationships. "Family neighbors" are at the core of many people's social networks.[139] New York City may seem like a cold and unfriendly place to those who do not know it, but immigrants, like other New Yorkers, frequently strike up friendships with residents of their apartment building or neighbors on their block, especially when they are of the same ethnic background and class. Novels and memoirs of tenement life in the past depict immigrants gossiping with neighbors in the same building, giving advice to each other's children, and helping out in times of emergency. "My mother went for an operation and the neighbor took the younger children," recalled one Jewish woman who grew up in a Lower East Side tenement. "Neighbors gathered in the halls, brought out their chairs, and chatted. If someone was bad off, they made a collection." This kind of sharing and support is found today as well.[140]

In general, ethnic communities provide immigrants with a range of social and moral resources. Much has been written about the way they cushion the impact of cultural change and protect against prejudice and initial economic difficulties. Personal contacts and friendship networks in ethnic neighborhoods are an important source of information about jobs both within and outside the community and a source of credit, labor, and clientele for entrepreneurial ventures.[141] Strength in numbers also translates into power at the ballot box and a critical mass to support other kinds of secular as well as religious organizations that help immigrants cope with their new environment. Ethnic neighborhoods play a role in keeping ethnic attachments alive because they make possible "a flourescence of ethnic cultural phenomena and institutions" and because they are a potential source of support for ethnic socialization. A family embedded within an ethnic community, write Richard Alba and his colleagues, "presumably finds that ethnic surroundings complement the ethnic socialization that goes on within the home."[142]

Ethnic clustering has a negative side, however, as native- and foreign-born black New Yorkers know too well. Confinement to black neighborhoods limits opportunities for decent schooling and access to other amenities of urban life.[143] Indeed, immigrants who can afford it often move out of the old neighborhoods in search of better public schools, higher-quality housing, and safer streets. Those who face fewer racial or ethnic barriers have a much wider choice. For example, many Koreans who initially settled in Flushing have relocated to middle- and upper-middle-class (largely white) neighborhoods in Queens and in the suburbs in the quest for high-quality schools.[144]

Looking ahead, many better-off Koreans, and other Asian and white European immigrants, are likely to continue to move into the residential mainstream, to communities where class rather than ethnicity is the common denominator. A countertrend is also a distinct possibility. Some areas where middle-class Asians have begun to settle may well contain seeds of new residential enclaves—as cultural preferences and the strength of ethnic- and kinship-based real estate markets lead more and more co-ethnics, over time, to join earlier pioneers.[145] In general, a number of immigrant groups (or substantial segments of immigrant groups) will probably remain highly segregated even as they become successful, creating more affluent versions of the ethnic ghetto. This is the pattern New York's Jews essentially followed from the 1920s through the 1950s. They continued to live apart from others as they climbed the social ladder, partly out of prejudice but partly, as historian Deborah Dash Moore observes, because, wanting to be "at home" in their neighborhood, they were happiest living among other Jews.[146] Even as late as the 1980s, roughly a quarter of the Italian

Americans in the greater New York region lived in ethnic neighborhoods, in the suburbs as well as in central-city enclaves.[147]

Whatever the future patterns of New York's ethnic geography, it's clear that the realities of immigrant settlement—during the last great influx as well as in the contemporary period—are more complex than the myths that have grown up about it. The struggles of poor immigrants to survive in a strange city have led to some inevitable similarities, but there are some unexpected and new twists to the neighborhood and housing story today as the newest immigrants chart their own course in a new New York.

# CHAPTER 3

# The Work They Do

O f all that we collectively remember of the immigration at the turn of the last century, nothing is more central than the image of hard, sweaty, unremitting work. The migrants, so popular legend goes, had nothing when they came—no skills, no stock in trade, no salable commodity except their extraordinary willingness to work from dawn to dark to get a start.

As we've seen, this is a distorted image, particularly when it comes to the Jews, who included huge numbers of skilled workers. Yet there are significant realities behind the legend. Both Jewish and Italian members of the last great wave of immigration had much in common when they looked for work: they were generally poor; they knew no English; and what formal education they possessed was not much use in finding jobs in late nineteenth- and early twentieth-century New York. For the overwhelming majority, there was no alternative but to toil long hours at backbreaking jobs.

The legend about the past colors how today's newcomers are perceived. Their extraordinary appetite for work—or their supposed laziness—is contrasted with images of migrants in the last wave. Their trials and triumphs, their initiative and drive, call up stories of past struggles. When politicians debate their contributions, the arguments are often cast in terms of those who came before.

And, admittedly, there are real similarities. Sweatshops haven't disappeared. Nor have ethnic businesses. New immigrants are frequently low-skilled and poor. Many end up in jobs that nobody else wants. Long hours at the bottom of the pay scale are still common. And grit and determination to get ahead are often what drive them as they strive to take advantage of better economic opportunities in America.

The differences, however, may outweigh the similarities—for three important reasons. First, because today's new immigrants arrive with much more occupational and educational variety. Second, because the city that receives them is a very different workplace than it was a hundred years ago. And third, because the racial and ethnic structure of the city has also changed in dramatic ways. Indeed, many issues that dominate scholarly accounts on the latest influx—for example, how immigrants have been able to get jobs in the face of New York's declining industrial base and whether they are hurting native minorities—reflect particular circumstances in the current period.

## The Immigrant Context

When today's immigrants look for work, a significant number have professional and technical skills, education, and even knowledge of the English language that would have been the envy of their predecessors a century ago. The range of human capital that contemporary arrivals bring with them is truly astounding.

In the last great wave, only a tiny number of Jewish and Italian immigrants came with professional skills.[1] As we saw in Chapter 1, less than 1 percent of the Italians and only 1.3 percent of the Jews arriving in America between 1899 and 1910 who reported an occupation were professionals. Enormous numbers came with no background in any kind of skilled work. Three out of four Italian immigrants had been common or farm laborers. Among Jews, the proportion of laborers and servants was about one in four.

Those who brought skills—67 percent of the Jews and 16 percent of the Italians with work experience—had practiced a trade or craft in the old country. Practically one-half of Jewish skilled workers had earned a living in the clothing trade. The remaining Jewish immigrant craftspeople knew town trades—carpentry, shoemaking, painting, and butchering—which they had practiced in the Russian Pale of Settlement. Another 5 percent of previously employed Jewish arrivals in the United States between 1899 and 1910 were merchants and dealers—occupations for which Jews had been well known in the Old World. Skilled Italians were shoemakers and masons, to name the two most common trades, as well as tailors, miners, and barbers.[2] In the early 1900s, Italian immigrants made up one-half to two-thirds of the barbers and hairdressers who arrived in the United States from all countries. One-half or more of all arriving masons were Italian, and in some years a third to a half of all stonecutters.[3]

Italian immigrants had an extraordinarily high rate of illiteracy. When new arrivals entered the United States, they were asked if they could read

and write. Among Italian immigrants over the age of fourteen arriving between 1899 and 1910, 47 percent answered no to both questions; among
southern Italians, the proportion was 54 percent, the highest of all European groups. When the first Italian-language daily was started in 1882, journalist Adolfo Rossi complained that it was extremely hard to find an Italian in New York who could "write his own tongue with accuracy."[4] Jewish
newspapers had an easier time. Literacy rates among Jewish immigrants
were much higher, although more than one in four, 26 percent, could not
read or write. The large proportion of females in the Jewish stream, who
were generally less well schooled than men, help explain these illiteracy
levels. Most Jewish men could at least read some Hebrew, given the near
universal enrollment of Jewish boys in the *cheder* (Jewish primary school).
Most were also literate in Yiddish, and some knew how to read Russian
as well.[5]

Neither Italians nor Jews arrived with much money. Of twenty-five
"races" of immigrants arriving in this country in 1900, southern Italians
were third from the lowest in terms of the amount of money they brought
—$8.84 per capita compared to $41.51 brought by Scots, the top group.[6] Ten
years later, 92 percent of arriving southern Italians and 87 percent of Jewish immigrants brought less than $50. This was at a time when the average
annual household income for New York's Italian immigrants was $519, and
for Russian Jews $520.[7]

For a substantial portion of today's immigrants, not much has changed.
A good many arrive with little more than the shirts on their backs. Many
have no funds to fall back on, and some, to pay to get here in the first place,
are heavily in debt. A significant number have little in the way of formal
education. According to an analysis of 1990 census data, almost a fifth of
New York City's foreign-born (ages sixteen to sixty-four) had less than a
ninth-grade education.[8] For some groups, the proportion was much higher.
Among post-1965 working-age immigrants, an astounding 43 percent of
Mexicans had less than a ninth-grade education. Dominicans (31 percent),
Salvadorans (29 percent), and Chinese (24 percent) were not far behind.
Altogether, more than half of New York City's Mexicans, Dominicans, Ital-
ians, and Salvadorans had not completed high school; this was also the
case for a third or more of the Chinese, Colombians, Cubans, Ecuadorians,
Greeks, Guyanese, Haitians, and Jamaicans (see table 6).

Many lack the skills or job training that would be of help in New York.
A few are from rural farm backgrounds. Six percent of immigrants entering the city in the early 1990s with a reported occupation had worked in
fishing, farming, and forestry—a small minority, it is true, yet the figure

Table 6    Education Completed by Post-1965 Immigrants Aged 16 to 64 in New York City, 1990 (Percentage Distribution)

| National Origin[1] | Less Than Grade 9 | Grades 9–12 | High School Graduate | Some College | College Graduate | Master's or More |
|---|---|---|---|---|---|---|
| Dominican Republic | 31.0 | 28.7 | 18.8 | 16.0 | 3.7 | 1.8 |
| China | 24.2 | 19.5 | 19.8 | 16.0 | 13.5 | 7.0 |
| Jamaica | 9.3 | 23.5 | 28.7 | 25.6 | 9.3 | 3.5 |
| Colombia | 16.3 | 23.7 | 29.5 | 21.7 | 6.4 | 2.4 |
| Ecuador | 20.6 | 24.8 | 26.3 | 21.5 | 5.1 | 1.8 |
| Haiti | 11.1 | 21.9 | 22.8 | 32.7 | 8.5 | 3.1 |
| Korea | 6.8 | 13.9 | 26.8 | 21.3 | 20.1 | 11.1 |
| Italy | 39.5 | 14.6 | 21.8 | 13.5 | 6.9 | 3.7 |
| India | 8.6 | 14.8 | 18.0 | 19.0 | 22.0 | 17.7 |
| Guyana | 9.6 | 25.3 | 31.3 | 25.4 | 6.5 | 1.9 |
| Mexico | 43.0 | 24.3 | 20.0 | 7.8 | 2.5 | 2.4 |
| Philippines | 2.0 | 5.0 | 7.9 | 21.9 | 50.7 | 12.6 |
| Trinidad | 8.1 | 21.3 | 33.4 | 27.3 | 7.6 | 2.5 |
| Former USSR | 5.5 | 13.3 | 26.5 | 21.9 | 18.1 | 14.7 |
| Poland | 10.8 | 17.0 | 26.3 | 22.0 | 11.5 | 12.4 |

*Source:* Cordero-Guzman and Grosfoguel 1998, based on U.S. Bureau of the Census, Public Use Microdata Sample, 1990.

[1] Top fifteen groups.

was 22 percent for the Chinese and 13 percent for Bangladeshis. Substantial numbers of new arrivals have backgrounds in other kinds of low-skilled jobs. About a quarter of men entering in the early 1990s with a reported occupation said they were operators or laborers; for Colombians, it was 75 percent, for Hondurans, 66 percent, and for Dominicans, 46 percent. Most have a language problem to contend with. A study of of the New York urban region's foreign-born between the ages of twenty-five and sixty-four, based on 1990 census data, found that the majority—52 percent—had a limited ability to speak, read, and write English. As one would expect, deficiency in English was worse among the least educated.[9]

This, however, is only part of the picture. Alongside the unlettered and unskilled are immigrant doctors, nurses, engineers, and Ph.Ds. In the early 1990s, more than a quarter of male and a third of female immigrants entering New York City who reported an occupation to the INS were professionals, executives, and managers—even higher proportions than among arrivals in the 1980s. Unlike the past, a significant chunk of the newcomers are highly educated. At the time of the 1990 census, 16 percent of New York City's working-age foreign-born residents (including island-born Puerto

Ricans) were college graduates—more than a third of the college graduates had a master's degree or more.[10] The best-educated groups are from Asia, Africa, Western Europe, and the Middle East. Most remarkable are Filipinos: nearly two-thirds of the post-1965 working-age adults in this group had college degrees.

Also unlike the past, many of today's newcomers arrive speaking fluent English. This is not surprising since a good number come from countries like Jamaica, Guyana, India, and the Philippines, where English is the official language or the language of educated discourse. In 1990, in the United States as a whole, almost a third of the immigrants who had arrived in the previous ten years told the census that they spoke English very well.[11]

Far from being penniless, moreover, some new arrivals, most notably among the Koreans, Chinese, and Indians, bring sizable amounts of financial capital. Given the limited data available, it is only possible to make guesses about how much money—and how many immigrants—we're talking about. In the 1980s and early 1990s, before the downturn in Korea's economy, some Koreans managed to bring tens of thousands of dollars in savings with them, accumulated by selling houses and emptying savings accounts at home.[12] In a predeparture survey of Korean immigrants conducted in Seoul in 1986, the average amount of money the respondents planned to take with them was $14,500.[13] Wealthy Hong Kong and Taiwanese businesspeople have also imported investment capital to New York.[14] On a more modest scale, successful professional and entrepreneurial immigrants from other countries often come with at least some funds to help them get a start.

Today's immigrants, therefore, can be divided roughly into two camps: those who arrive with college degrees and specialized skills, on the one hand, and those with little education and training, on the other. Taken as a whole, however, the newcomers come to New York with a good deal more human and financial capital than their turn-of-the-century predecessors, and this makes a huge difference in how they are faring as they enter the economy and the world of work.

## The Economic Context

"The new immigration," observed the influential Dillingham Commission *Report on Immigration* in 1911, "has been largely a movement of laboring men who have come . . . in response to the call for industrial workers."[15] Immigrants who arrived a hundred years ago found a city that was changing from a mercantile economy to a modern industrial center churning out low-level jobs. Today, New York's economy is also in the throes of change—but of a very different nature. Yesterday's thriving factory town has given way to a postindustrial economy that has shifted from goods to services and in which new jobs are more likely to require a college degree than brawn or muscle. Clearly, New York's economy has provided different kinds of job opportunities to immigrants in the two eras. There are other contrasts, too. In the past, ethnic succession or replacement played a role in providing jobs, but sheer economic expansion was far more important. Today, the reverse is true. A massive outflow of native New Yorkers from the city in the last few decades has been a significant factor in creating job openings for the newest arrivals, leading to direct, and indirect, succession by immigrants and a reordering of the hiring queue.

When Jews and Italians arrived a century ago, New York was a thriving city at the forefront of economic growth.[16] Although the port's share of foreign trade had begun to decline, the wharves and docks bustled as New York still handled almost half of the value of the nation's imports and exports. As the country's leading center of finance and business services, New York was becoming the headquarters for a growing number of major corporations. In 1892, according to a New York *Tribune* survey, New York City contained 1,265 millionaires, or 30 percent of the millionaires in the United States.

Low-wage factory work was expanding, too. Between 1880 and 1910, the number of industrial wage earners more than doubled, growing from 275,000 to over 554,000. By 1910, about four out of every ten employed New Yorkers worked in manufacturing. The biggest employers were publishing and printing and, above all, the clothing industry, which accounted for 40 percent of greater New York's industrial wage earners. The garment industry had grown by leaps and bounds as urbanization, the development of a national market, and rapid population growth spawned a market for ready-made women's wear, which was supplanting homemade clothes.[17] By the late nineteenth century, New York had become the fashion capital of America, leading all other American cities in the production of factory-made clothing. In 1910, the city was producing 70 percent of the nation's women's clothing and 40 percent of men's.[18]

As the economy flourished and the working population grew—in 1910 the employed workforce had reached 2.2 million, almost double the number for 1900—the city itself was literally bursting at the seams. New York was physically expanding in all directions, creating an ongoing need for construction projects. New houses, office buildings, tunnels, and bridges were being built, transit lines extended, and port facilities upgraded.[19]

Given this economic background, it's not hard to see how immigrants were able to find work. Ethnic succession was involved as large numbers of Jewish and Italian newcomers moved into bottom-level positions that had been the province of earlier Irish and German immigrants, many of whom had been able to obtain better jobs. For example, in 1910, although the Irish were still heavily concentrated in construction, they were mainly skilled workers.[20] Above all, New York's bustling and expanding economy generated new jobs and created a demand for the newest arrivals, whose labor power was itself an important engine of growth in, among other areas, the rapidly expanding clothing industry and the construction boom.

A hundred years later, New York is now a postindustrial city with an economy centered on processing information and facilitating high-level business transactions.[21] During the entire postwar period, manufacturing has been in steady decline. In 1950, 28 percent of employed New York City residents made a living in manufacturing; forty years later the figure had shrunk to 11 percent. During the same period, the number of manufacturing jobs declined from one million to 338,000. By 1996, the number had dwindled to 264,000. The garment industry has hemorrhaged, losing tens of thousands of jobs as work has shifted to southern states and overseas. The number of employees in the city's apparel and textile-manufacturing sectors fell from about 250,000 in the mid-1970s to about 83,000 in 1996.

The massive shift away from manufacturing has been accompanied by the ascent of the service sector. By 1990, four times as many New Yorkers worked in the combined services than on the factory floor. Put another way: in 1950, 20 percent of employed New Yorkers worked in services; in 1990, it was 47 percent.[22]

Long the nation's corporate and financial center, New York is, today, the world's financial capital. In 1998, the city led the world in securities trading—handling as many trades as London and Tokyo combined. New York City was home to twelve of the twenty largest international law firms and four of the five largest accounting firms in the world; and it had the nation's single largest concentration of international corporate headquarters. The widening of global trade has thrust major New York corporate service firms—in commercial and investment banking, securities, insurance, accounting, advertising, management consulting, and law—into the forefront of international commercial competition. The intensifying demand for information services has also worked to New York's advantage. The city is one of a handful of global information hubs. It is home to the nation's three major television broadcasting networks; six of ten large book publishers; leading newspapers, magazines, and print services; major on-line information providers; and the giants of communications and interactive multimedia.

The rise of corporate services and information processing—and the fall of manufacturing—have been accompanied by a shift from blue-collar workers to professionals, managers, secretaries, and service workers. In 1990, a quarter of employed New Yorkers held blue-collar jobs, down from 45 percent in 1950; over three-quarters were in white-collar jobs in 1990, up from 55 percent in 1950. By 1990, professional and managerial jobs employed as many New York City residents as all blue-collar categories combined.[23] Jobs that did not even exist a century ago, like computer programming, are flourishing. At the turn of the century, there was no such thing as a nursing home, and hospitals were often small institutions operating on minimal budgets. By the early 1990s, the health-care industry, although beginning to suffer job losses in the face of funding cuts in Medicare and Medicaid, was still one of New York City's largest employers, with over 70 public, voluntary, and private hospitals, about 160 nursing homes, and a sizable homecare sector. As of 1995, local government employment in the city was about 415,000, more than a sevenfold increase since 1900.[24]

The restructuring of the economy and the changing job mix have helped create a city that is increasingly "hollow in the middle." Although 1996 was a time of economic recovery, New York City's middle class was smaller than it was in 1977, at the end of a severe recession—and there were higher proportions in both the lower- and upper-income groups.[25] With a growing wage polarization between low-skilled workers and highly paid executives and professionals, New York State has the dubious distinction of having the largest income gaps nationally between the rich and the poor as well as between the rich and the middle class. From 1994 to 1996, the top 20 percent of families in New York State earned an average of $132,390 a year, not counting capital gains, while the bottom 20 percent averaged $6,787. The city's unemployment rate also remained relatively high in the 1990s—at 7.3 percent in August 1998, when the rate was 4.5 nationally.[26]

Overall, there has been no expansion in employment in New York City on the scale of that at the turn of the century, because job gains have been offset by job losses. Also, the growth in jobs has come in fits and starts. Employment contracted during hard times in the 1970s, then expanded in the recovery of the 1980s. In the downturn between 1989 and 1992 the city lost 281,000 jobs but, in another recovery, added about 100,000 jobs by 1996. In that year, city employment stood at 3.8 million—only about 213,000 more than in 1980.[27]

All these changes hardly sound propitious for newly arriving immigrants, yet New York's postindustrial economy has, in fact, provided plenty of opportunities for them. Although virtually every industry now has a higher ratio of high-level, white-collar jobs than only a few decades ago, there has been some growth at the bottom. As Saskia Sassen argues, the expansion of the advanced service sector has created not only highly skilled and highly paid jobs for stockbrokers, lawyers, and investment bankers but also low-skilled and low-wage jobs for messengers, janitors, and building cleaners. Also, there has been a demand for workers to support the affluent lifestyles of top-level professionals—for restaurant workers and apartment cleaners, for example.[28] A recent analysis of employment change in the city in the 1980s bears this out.[29] While job growth was most rapid in industries where the proportion of high-paying jobs and college-educated workers was increasing, some growth occurred at the lower end, too. For example, eating and drinking establishments, food stores, taxicabs, protective services, and repair services added about seventy thousand jobs. As more middle-class women with young children joined the labor force in the 1970s and 1980s, domestic child-care jobs also grew in number—though because so many undocumented immigrants are employed in this sector, relevant census data are particularly suspect.[30]

An important source of job openings for new immigrants, as Roger Waldinger argues, has been the erosion of the city's native white population base, a late twentieth-century phenomenon.[31] At the time of the last great immigration, more native-born whites were moving out of than into New York City, but the net outflow was relatively small, about 150,000 from 1900 to 1920.[32] Today, something different is going on. Indeed, the white exodus of the past few decades is unparalleled. In the 1970s, the non-Hispanic white population in the city fell by 1.3 million as a result of suburbanization, flight to the Sunbelt, and aging. Between 1980 and 1996, the non-Hispanic white population dropped by about another 900,000. Of importance here is that many of those who moved away from the city left jobs behind or retired, creating opportunities for immigrants in both direct and indirect ways. Altogether, native white employment in New York City declined by over 500,000 between 1970 and 1990.[33] In some cases—manufacturing and retailing, for example—immigrants stepped in to fill vacancies created by departing white workers. In other instances, the process was indirect. With the exit of many whites from the labor market, native-born New Yorkers seized the chance to move up the hiring queue into better-paying and more prestigious positions. In a ladder effect, this opened up positions at the bottom.

## Immigrants and Jobs

There's no such thing as an inevitable immigrant story when it comes to jobs. It may seem that immigrants always end up in the lousy jobs, toiling in sweatshops or running the corner grocery. Yet the employment picture, then as well as now, is more complicated. Which immigrants have been confined to the bottom of the heap? Why did Jews come to dominate the garment industry? Why did Italians build the subways? Why is the person changing your hospital bed West Indian and your greengrocer Korean? The way immigrants are incorporated into the labor market depends on the skills, abilities, and preferences they bring with them and the context they meet upon arrival. If, as sometimes happens, contemporary immigrants end up in the same kinds of jobs as their predecessors, this is because they resemble turn-of-the-century arrivals in important respects and because they find, though often for different reasons, similar opportunities and constraints in New York's economy.

### Italians and Jews Then

How did the Jewish and Italian immigrants who got off the boat a hundred years ago find work? And why did they become concentrated in particular industries? It's a tale, in part, of the ethnic niche, a perennial feature of the New York landscape—and especially important for those who arrive with modest skills and face labor-market discrimination in the search for work.

In general, immigrant occupational specialities take hold for a variety of reasons. They reflect a combination of the skills, cultural preferences, and human capital within the group as well as the opportunities available to the group within a given local economy. Sometimes, members of a group arrive with previous experience in fields for which a demand exists. English-language ability plays a role in steering some groups into jobs where interpersonal communication is important. By contrast, lack of transferable skills and of ability in English limits immigrants' scope. Sheer happenstance can be involved, too, as a few pioneers from a group go into a particular line of work and pave the way for others.

In the last great wave, garments were the great Jewish metier.[34] Russian Jews arrived at a propitious moment, when the garment trades were undergoing a rapid expansion as the demand for factory-made clothing surged. When Russian Jews started flocking to New York, the industry was already in the hands of Jews—albeit German Jews, who had immigrated in large numbers in the mid-nineteenth century. (Between 1846 and 1886 it is estimated that the German Jewish population of New York City grew from seven thousand to eighty-five thousand.) In 1870, German Jews owned virtually the entire New York clothing industry, both retail and wholesale.[35] Moreover, a high proportion of the Russian Jewish newcomers had had tailoring experience in the old country. Although most had worked with needle and thread, they quickly adapted to machine production. Those who had previously worked at other trades were also drawn to the garment shops, which were looking for workers. It took little time, and no very great skills, to learn how to run a sewing machine or press a garment. The shops were within walking distance of the familiar streets of the Lower East Side; in 1890, almost 80 percent of New York's garment industry was located below 14th Street.

By the turn of the century, Russian Jews had become the employers, having set up hundreds of small shops as contractors; for a preset price, contractors arranged to convert bundles of precut material obtained from manufacturers into ready-made clothing. Often, no more than fifty to one hundred dollars was needed to turn a tenement dwelling or rented loft into a workshop. The contractor purchased or rented sewing machines or, cheaper still, hired workers who furnished their own machines. Jewish workers often preferred to work in shops where the boss was a Jew, Yiddish was spoken, and the Sabbath and religious holidays were observed. "Separated by religious prescriptions, customs, and language from the surrounding city," Moses Rischin writes, "[Jewish immigrants] found a place in the clothing industry where the initial shock of contact with a bewildering world was tempered by a familiar milieu."[36] By 1897, about 60 percent of the New York Jewish labor force was employed in the apparel field and 75 percent of the workers in the industry were Jewish.[37]

Once Russian Jews established a presence in the industry, they were a conduit for additional friends and relatives. This is the second stage in the making of ethnic niches, described by contemporary social scientists to explain why particular groups come to dominate certain industries or occupations. An ethnic niche is simply a special place in the labor market in which members of an ethnic group are overrepresented. Ethnic niches, as Roger Waldinger puts it, become self-reproducing. Immigrants tend to flock to fields where settlers have established a solid foothold. Lacking information about the broader labor market and dependent on the support of their own kind, new arrivals typically learn about and get help finding jobs through personal networks in the immigrant community. Insiders tell their friends and relatives when job openings emerge. For their part, employers often prefer applicants who are recommended by existing employees and come to believe that members of a particular group are best suited to their job. As Suzanne Model points out, hiring applicants recommended by incumbents costs little; workers sponsored by fellow employees get along with their new co-workers and learn tasks more rapidly as a result; and such recruits are under pressure to perform well, since any shortcomings will reflect poorly on their sponsors.[38]

The great Italian beachhead into New York's economy was unskilled construction work. Lacking urban industrial skills, most Italians had nowhere to start but in the most menial occupations. Cheap, low-skilled labor was in demand in the booming building industry—and Italians fit the bill. Early on, in the 1880s, Italian *padroni*, or labor contractors, sent greenhorns to construction sites in response to orders from contractors for crews of men. As the padrone system became less important—by 1914 it had nearly disappeared—informal personal networks channeled Italian laborers into construction gangs as ditchdiggers, hod carriers, and mortar mixers and for other unskilled tasks.[39] Typically, they were recruited in the arduous and nonunionized sectors of the industry, such as road and subway construction. Italian immigrants joked that they were "born with a shovel in one hand and a pickax in the other."[40] In 1910, the construction sector employed 22 percent of Italian men in New York City, who constituted one in five construction workers.[41]

In 1890 New York's inspector of public works testified before Congress that Italians made up 90 percent of those involved in New York City's public works. More than four thousand Italians joined the crew that began excavation on the Lexington Avenue subway in 1900, a year in which one out of every four common laborers in New York was Italian. In 1904, Italians played a large role in building Manhattan's Grand Central Terminal; that same year some five thousand Italian workers helped build the Bronx aqueduct.[42]

Italians were also a significant presence on New York's docks, comprising at least a third of the labor force in the port by 1912, especially in coal hauling and unloading. The opening wedge for Italians, according to Thomas Kessner, was an 1887 strike by the Knights of Labor that temporarily crippled the shipping industry. Employers looking to break the Irish monopoly on the waterfront brought in lower-paid Italian laborers. One writer noted that bosses loved Italians because of their "eagerness . . . for the work, their willingness to submit to deductions from their wages, leaving a neat little commission to be divided between foreman, saloon keepers, and native bosses."[43] Once a sufficient number became longshoremen, an ethnic momentum was set in motion, as workers brought in relatives and Italian foremen gave preference to their fellow countrymen. With the enormous growth in the clothing industry, Italians moved into the "stronghold of the Jews," becoming second in numbers only to Jews in New York's garment workforce.[44] By some accounts, employers began hiring Italians because they were willing to work for lower wages than Jews and were less likely to join unions.[45] The mushrooming garment shops, located downtown near Italian neighborhoods, were looking for labor; no English was required; and most of the work they did, such as lining garments, sewing on buttons, trimming threads, and pulling bastings by hand, could be picked up quickly. "In some industries," Louise Odencrantz wrote, "the Italian's skill with a needle was a special asset . . . while in other cases, because of her ignorance of the language, and of how to get a job, she was forced to accept dirty, unskilled work."[46] In 1905, perhaps some 35 percent of the workers in the New York women's wear industry were Italian. By 1908, practically all the home finishers in the city's clothing industry were Italian women. They underbid Jewish women, working "for about two thirds of the price which other nationalities formerly received for the same work."[47] Also, Jewish women, whose husbands generally earned more than Italian men, gave up homework in favor of the more attractive alternative of taking in boarders.[48]

Italians who came with artisan skills — masons, barbers, and shoemakers — often were able to transfer their skills into jobs in New York. Barbering became an Italian occupation; only 7 percent of Italians were barbers in 1910, though they made up nearly two-thirds of the city's barbers. Shoemakers often took up shoe repair in New York or went to work in shoe factories; three-quarters of the factory shoe workers in New York City were Italian in 1919.[49]

For both Italians and Jews, the special needs and tastes of the ethnic market also gave rise to a host of jobs. Each community had a huge, residentially concentrated population speaking little or no English who wanted familiar foods and cultural products as well as other staples of daily life. Co-ethnics knew their customers' tastes and spoke their language; they sold goods at prices the new arrivals could afford and were more likely to offer credit than outsider merchants because they could rely on informal sanctions in the community to ensure being paid.

It may be an exaggeration to say, with Alan Kraut, that "no immigrant group to arrive in the United States had as many unique tastes or special dietary restrictions and taboos as the East European Jews," but they did provide a readily exploitable market for would-be entrepreneurs.[50] Russian Jews were well equipped to meet the demand. As Joel Perlmann argues, they knew about petty capitalist ventures, "about how to buy and sell, just as they knew how to use a needle and thread."[51] Quite a few arrived with a background in trade or as middlemen; Jewish artisans in Russia not only produced their goods but also usually sold them at market.[52] Whether or not they had been involved in selling in Europe, Jews dominated commerce in the Pale and were used to patronizing merchants who sold from carts and peddler's packs.[53]

It was not expensive to continue this Old World habit in New York. Pushcarts could be made, purchased, or rented for ten cents a day; pack peddlers carried their wares on their backs. The license fee for a pushcart cost a few dollars a year, an expense many probably avoided. The only substantial outlay was the daily cost of stock. At dawn peddlers would go to the fish or produce market on the docks, where they bought a small quantity of merchandise at wholesale prices. They would then push their carts uptown from the market, find their places along the curbs of the East Side, and wait for customers to tumble out of their apartments into the streets. All day and into the evening, Orchard Street, Hester Street, Grand Street, and Rivington Street were packed on both sides with continuous lines of pushcarts that extended from block to block. In 1890, a survey of three largely Jewish wards in lower Manhattan by the Baron de Hirsch Fund found that of 22,392 gainfully employed Jews, 24 percent were in trade, including 2,440 peddlers and pushcart vendors (46 percent of all those in trade). Altogether at this time, almost one quarter of the Jewish immigrant community on the Lower East Side was able to survive and prosper by catering to the remaining three quarters.[54] By 1910, 16 percent of Russian Jewish males in New York City were self-employed in trade, mostly as peddlers and store owners.[55]

These merchants sold in dribs and drabs, hoping to compensate with high volume. "The pushcart market had a kind of universal economics," Harry Roskolenko observed, "cheap. Everything in the cosmos was on a pushcart at some sort of price. . . . The pushcarts came small, came large, came bigger than large—and in double tiers."[56] Street merchants tended to specialize in a single type of commodity, perhaps books, eyeglasses, kitchen utensils, or clothing. This enabled them to get to know the market more thoroughly than a general merchant and to gain economies of scale denied to small shopkeepers.[57]

Food was probably the most popular merchandise among the pushcart peddlers and hucksters.[58] When Louis Borgenicht, a successful garment manufacturer, arrived in New York in 1889, herrings were his first venture: "Monday morning I took up my stand, flanked by two barrels of herring. . . .

My two barrels sold out quickly. . . . My hands stank from herring. My clothes stank from herring."[59] Herring was popular because it was cheap and could be eaten on the Sabbath, when fish was traditionally served. Then there were the traditional delicacies—bagels, blintzes, and knishes—as well as basic staples such as eggs, tea, coffee, and butter.

A peddler or pushcart vendor might make less than a skilled factory worker, but as Alan Kraut notes, he could run his business on his own terms and set his schedule according to his own priorities.[60] And there was the possibility of becoming the owner of a "real" store. In 1899, the Lower East Side's Eighth Assembly District had 140 groceries, 131 butcher shops, 36 bakeries, 14 butter and egg stores, 62 candy stores, 1 cheese store, 20 cigar stores, 3 cigarette shops, 10 delicatessens, 9 fish stores, 7 fruit stores, 16 milk stores, 2 matzoh stores, 14 tobacco shops, and 11 vegetable stores.[61] Hundreds of kosher butchers sprang up to provide meat slaughtered and prepared in the correct ritual way. Some expanded beyond the ethnic market: by 1900, 80 percent of the wholesale and 50 percent of the retail meat sold in the city was being handled by Jewish tradespeople.[62] The demand for seltzer, which was thought to be health enhancing, stimulated the growth of a large wholesale and retail seltzer enterprise dominated by Jewish bottlers, workers, and teamsters. In 1880, only two seltzer companies were in business in New York; by 1907, there were over a hundred, almost all on the Lower East Side.[63] In 1910, the Lower East Side had five hundred bakeries, a sevenfold increase since 1900. Besides the retail stores, coffeehouses, cake parlors, lunchrooms, and restaurants catered to the palates and observed the laws of the Russian Jewish community.

The Jewish community provided customers for other services, too. As eastern European immigrants branched out to east Harlem, Brownsville, and Williamsburg in the late 1890s and first decade of the twentieth century, immigrants found opportunities in the construction industry and in real estate. Barred by the unions from well-paid new construction, Jewish immigrants, some of whom had previous experience as carpenters or painters in the Old World, concentrated on alterations and the remodeling of old tenements.[64] Although their numbers were small, Jewish professionals, who had arrived as children and had been able to obtain advanced training in New York, found clients among their own kind. By the first decade of the twentieth century, a few hundred Russian Jewish doctors, dentists, pharmacists, and lawyers had hung up shingles on the Lower East Side.[65]

Like Jews, Italians found a ready market for their shops and wares among their compatriots. Nothing, Robert Foerster wrote, sold as well as food:

"Here a window displays voluminous round cheeses, or strings of sausages, or tinned eels; there are loaves of bread thirty inches from end to end, or great round loaves with holes in the center like gigantic doughnuts. Confetti or macaroni tempts in another window. . . . Capitalizing the timidity which the Italian often shows about trusting many people with his affairs, a versatile fellow will be at once a barber, banker, undertaker, wholesale and retail dealer, perhaps also a real estate and employment agent." [66] On Little Italy's Elizabeth Street, 16 percent of the 2,368 Italian males in 1905 made a living at petty trade; they dominated pushcart peddling and commerce in fruits and vegetables on this street. They also peddled fish, ran cafes, saloons, restaurants, and grocery stores, and dealt in coal, ice, and wood. [67]

Whatever their line of work, most Italian and Jewish immigrants had no choice but to put in long hours for low wages — and often under unsafe and uncomfortable conditions. The "pick and shovel" work so many Italians did was physically strenuous and dangerous; the pay was poor; and the seasonal nature of the building trades meant that laborers might go for weeks without work. Peddling, as Irving Howe observes, was "backbreaking and soul-destroying. There was only one reason to become a peddler: you had no skill and you wanted to stay out of the shops." [68]

Conditions in the garment sweatshops were notorious. The demands of New York's shirtwaist workers in the 1909 "uprising of 20,000" say it all: they were striking for a fifty-two-hour week, for limiting overtime to three evenings a week of no more than two hours, and for payment for supplies (thread, needles, and electricity). [69] "I went to work two weeks after landing in this country [in 1903]," wrote labor leader Clara Lemlich, recalling her first job in a small New York garment shop at the age of sixteen. "We worked from sunrise to sunset seven days a week. . . . Those who worked on machines had to carry the machines on their back both to and from work. . . . The shop we worked in had no central heating, no electric power. . . . The hissing of the machines, the yelling of the foreman, made life unbearable." [70] During the height of the season, the work might stretch to sixty-five or even seventy hours, with no overtime pay; in slack seasons, there was often no work at all. Larger factories were not much better. There were frequent speedups, and clocks might be slowed down during working hours. Accidents and shop fires were not uncommon. Workers had to pay for needles and the cost of electric power to run their machines and irons; they were fined if they broke needles, damaged garments, or were late to work. Until 1907, most workers had to provide their own sewing machines and pay a freight charge for transporting them from place to place. In 1914, more than 88 percent of the women employed in the city's shirt factories and 45 percent in the dress and shirtwaist industry earned less than the minimum subsistence wage for a single woman.[71] In 1890, the average annual wage for a New York City garment worker was $565, though a family of five required at least $850 to maintain itself; by 1910 clothing workers earned on average only $567, but by 1914 the minimum cost for a family of five had risen to $876.[72]

Working for co-ethnic employers may have had advantages, but it's important not to romanticize their relations with their workers, especially among Russian Jews, who invariably worked for other Russian Jews in the enclave economy.[73] On the positive side, old country ties between employers and employees in small garment shops contributed to the family tone and informality of workroom life.[74] The contractor typically worked alongside his employees—family members, *landslayt* (fellow townspeople), and neighbors—late into the night. It was not unusual for him to lend money to impoverished greenhorns in the shop, to help underwrite ship passage for workers' relatives, to offer advice and consolation, and, perhaps most important, to provide jobs for newly arrived family members. Ethnic bonds between employees and employers allowed ethnic businesses to function as a training ground for employees, who learned skills they could use to set up on their own or to move up in the job hierarchy.[75]

Yet co-ethnic employers were exploitative as well. The way to succeed in the garment industry was to undercut other contractors, a condition that not only drove many petty employers out of business after a few difficult seasons but also drove wage rates down. As Susan Glenn observes: "Conviviality and informality did not mask [cramped and unsanitary] conditions, nor did they mitigate the grueling pace of work in a sweatshop or the downward pressure on wages. As every immigrant who labored in this type of setting knew, 'to squeeze his own profit out the contractor must squeeze his workmen's wages down.' "[76] Italian men in construction work had their own problems with compatriots. In the 1880s and 1890s, many Italian men paid a padrone a fee for finding them work, and the most unscrupulous padroni lied in describing jobs, charged exorbitant fees, and even quickly discharged immigrant workers they had just hired and took on new ones, thereby collecting new fees.[77]

Russian Jews, who were more skilled to begin with, did much better than Italians in the labor market. (In 1905, nearly 60 percent of New York's Italian immigrant household heads had unskilled or semiskilled jobs, compared to about 20 percent of Russian Jewish immigrant household heads.)[78] Yet, in the pre–World War I era, both groups lagged behind native-born whites.

In an analysis of 1910 census data for metropolitan New York City, foreign-born Italian men's average occupational status was 71 percent that of native-born white men of native parents, and foreign-born Russian Jewish men's, 83 percent; Italian and Russian immigrant men trailed native-born Irishmen as well.[79] The 1910 census had no question about earnings, but the Dillingham Commission's national survey of male production workers in mining and manufacturing industries showed southern Italians at the low end, averaging only $9.61 a week compared to $12.71 for Russian Jews and $14.37 for native-born white employees.[80] As one would expect, those fresh off the boat had lower wages and occupational status than immigrants who had been here longer. Sociologist John Logan has calculated average values of occupational standing for different groups in New York City based on 1920 census data. Russians who had arrived in the preceding ten years had an occupational score of 28, compared to 45 for Russians who came before 1900 (native whites with U.S.-born parents had a score of 46); pre-1900 Italians had a score of 27, and those who came after 1910, a score of 21. Italian immigrants, whenever they arrived, lagged way behind the U.S.-born Irish and Germans, the two large earlier immigrant groups; Russian immigrants (with the exception of those arriving before 1900) also had lower average occupational standing than U.S.-born Irish and Germans.[81]

Turn-of-the-century immigrants provided the labor that helped fuel New York's industrial growth, but they did not move into a vacuum. Other groups were doing low-skilled work when they arrived, often in the same industries where the newcomers became concentrated. Although there was some competition between the newest arrivals and established residents at the bottom rungs of the occupational ladder, and a slowing of wage rates for the unskilled, this situation should not be exaggerated. Overall, it's a story of an expanding economy that allowed many earlier immigrants and natives to move into better positions, leaving the least desirable jobs for the newest arrivals. Native-born workers were also moving to greener pastures out west.[82] Although immigrants had a depressing effect on wages, New York was a high-wage city and, as economists Susan Carter and Richard Sutch note, had there been no immigrants, native-born workers probably would have moved there instead.[83]

Russian Jews displaced few already established workers because they worked mainly in the garment trades, which were expanding dramatically at the time, and in retailing, catering to their own community. As Roger Waldinger argues, the insularity of the Jewish ethnic economy, as in the case of clothing, kept head-to-head competition with non-Jews to a minimum; even in fields where both Jews and non-Jews were active, such as construction or real estate, connections to co-ethnic workers and clients helped Jews sidestep competitive obstacles.[84]

The impact of Italians is mixed. Although some were petty traders in their own neighborhoods, Italians were largely a proletarian population and, as such, they came into direct competition with established low-skilled workers, particularly the Irish, a huge group in the city that included large numbers of common laborers. Lower-paid Italians, according to Thomas Kessner, displaced the Irish from bottom-rung jobs on the docks and in unskilled street and construction work; in the first decade of the century, Italian tunnel workers in New York received from $1.75 to $3.00 daily, while Irish wages for the same work ranged from $3.00 to $5.00.[85] Italian barbers "scissored their way into a trade that had been controlled by Germans and Negroes."[86] Whereas the standard price in late nineteenth-century New York had been twenty-five cents for a haircut and fifteen cents for a shave, Italians commonly cut hair for fifteen cents and charged a dime or even a nickel for a shave.[87]

Yet Italians also met the demand for unskilled labor in expanding sectors of the economy and filled jobs that earlier immigrants left as better opportunities opened up. In construction, Italians worked mostly in the low-skilled, nonunionized sector, while the Irish predominated in more skilled, better-organized building trades. To defend themselves from competition from the newer immigrants, Irish-dominated unions in the building trades, such as plumbing and masonry, adopted nepotistic membership requirements that kept out the new arrivals. By 1910, 72 percent of the Irish in the construction industry were skilled workers, and significant numbers had moved up to become contractors.[88]

Although construction may have been booming, this was not the case on the docks, where many unskilled Irish were squeezed out of an over-crowded labor market by newcomers. Nevertheless, on the docks the Irish, Germans, and Scandinavians dominated the crews that loaded ships, leaving the less skilled tasks of unloading and coal handling to Italians. In racial terms (the subject of Chapter 6), many of the northwestern Europeans "referred to themselves as 'white men,' lumping the Italians, Poles, and Negroes as non-white."[89] Moreover, the expansion of certain industries, such as light manufacturing, allowed thousands of Irish American men to move into the lower rungs of management. Political connections and knowledge of English helped them rise to become foremen and superintendents. Political connections also helped the Irish to entrench themselves in city government jobs as policemen, firefighters, and rapid-transit workers.

And thousands of second and subsequent generations of Irish and German women found employment as teachers, nurses, and clerical workers[90]— positions (like city government jobs) often made possible by the huge increase in the city's population as a result of the Jewish and Italian immigration.

African Americans, however, benefited little from the immigrant influx, which resulted in their eviction from trades where they had previously been accepted and their confinement to the most menial, least attractive jobs—like janitors, elevator operators, and servants.[91] Yet, it must be remembered that in the pre–World War I years, when less than 2 percent of New York City's population was black, African Americans were a tiny proportion of the workforce. In fact, some argue that turn-of-the-century immigration helped postpone the great black migration from the rural South until war and immigration quotas removed much of the unskilled competition in northern labor markets.[92] Others say that oppressive forces, like the tenant farming system that locked southern blacks in a system of debt peonage, would have kept them bottled up in the South whether or not European immigrants had arrived.[93] All this is hypothetical. The fact is that at the beginning of the century, African Americans had not yet arrived en masse in New York. A hundred years later, they were a major presence in the city, and the question of whether their prospects in the job market were, once again, being hurt by the latest arrivals was of even more pressing concern.

## Immigrants Now

How are the newest New Yorkers finding a place in the city's economy? There are some strong continuities with the past, so that many of the occupational patterns found today—and the processes that underlie them—are simply modern-day variations on old themes. Yet, there are also some new twists, new puzzles, and new dilemmas that reflect the changing nature of New York's social and economic structure and the different backgrounds of the immigrants themselves.

One striking contrast has to do with the sizable number of newcomers from the middle and upper-middle classes in their home countries. Because of their backgrounds—and also because the city's occupational structure is more tilted toward white-collar and professional work than it was a hundred years ago—many of today's arrivals have been able to move, right from the start, into mid- and upper-level jobs in the mainstream economy. New York is home to Filipino and West Indian nurses, Chinese computer consultants, and Indian doctors and engineers. According to the 1990 census, a fifth of New York City's working-age foreign-born adults had managerial or professional jobs (see table 7). Turn back to the beginning of the century, and precious few Italians and Jews were professionals. In Kessner's analysis of 1905 census data, 2 percent of Italian immigrant household heads and 15 percent of Russian Jewish immigrant household heads in New York City held upper white-collar jobs, though nearly all were self-employed businessmen.[94]

Yet not all who now come equipped for high-level jobs in the mainstream economy are able to obtain them. Indeed, another marked difference from the past is that contemporary immigrants are much more likely to experience downward occupational mobility when they arrive. Not that this didn't happen before. A Hebrew teacher or religious scholar from Minsk might end up peddling goods or sewing garments in a sweatshop, though this kind of decline was unusual at the time. It is not today.

A lack of English, U.S. job experience, and network ties that connect them to the mainstream economy often prevent immigrants who held professional or highly regarded jobs in their home countries from getting work of comparable status here. Many cannot meet American licensing requirements to qualify for the positions they are trained for. Other highly skilled newcomers, who arrive without green cards, are forced to work in lower-level jobs in the informal economy. In my research, I met Jamaican accountants and policemen who drove cabs in New York, former secretaries in Guyana who became child-care workers, and Haitian nurses who were now nursing aides. Peter Kwong describes a Chinese teacher from Fouzhou province who had more than half a dozen jobs in his first year in New York, including short stints as a laborer for a Chinese building contractor and as a delivery boy for a Chinese restaurant.[95] A report on the Chinese community in Brooklyn's Sunset Park mentions, among many others, a drafting technician who became a dishwasher in New York, a linguistics professor turned housekeeper, and a physics engineer who found work as a shoe-store clerk.[96]

One of the main forces driving Koreans to set up small businesses is that they face limited opportunities for jobs congruent with their class background. (At the time of the 1990 census, more than a quarter of Korean men in the city were self-employed, far surpassing rates for other groups.)[97] Unlike his Jewish counterpart a hundred years ago, the owner of the corner Korean grocery store is likely to have gone to college and worked in a white-collar job before emigrating. The problem is that Korean professional certificates are not recognized here, and unfamiliarity with the English language and American culture makes it difficult for well-educated Koreans to obtain desirable jobs in the mainstream economy. Small business may be risky and grueling, but it is better than the alternative, which is a low-level service or factory job.

Granted, immigrants typically earn more money and enjoy better living standards in New York than they would in their homeland, even when they suffer a decline in occupational status. Some eventually manage to recover their former occupational position. Yet the decline in prestige can be a bitter experience, particularly in dealings with people outside their immediate circle who are unaware of their former status. Even among friends, it can be a sensitive subject. Indeed, according to one report, there are three topics that Korean immigrants are not supposed to ask one another about: past occupation, current occupation, and level of occupation.[98]

As is already clear, the ethnic niche is alive and well. Now, as before, distinct ethnic occupational specializations develop, as the newest arrivals steer their kin and compatriots into berths in the economy and as employers rely on ethnic recruitment to fill job openings. But the sheer diversity of today's immigrant population, in terms of national origins and educational and class backgrounds, has led to a far greater mix of occupational specialities than at the turn of the century. Given this diversity, it is not possible to discuss all the immigrant niches that have developed in recent years. A focus on the occupational concentrations among three of the larger groups, West Indians, Dominicans, and Chinese, shows that once immigrants begin to cluster in certain lines of work, the process of niche development proceeds in much the same way it did in the past. Sometimes, immigrants even concentrate in the same kinds of jobs as before. Yet if immigrants are still drawn to the needle trades, it's an industry that has been contracting, not expanding, as it was a hundred years ago. Meanwhile, the growth of other industries, like health care, has provided opportunities that were not available in 1900.

If you end up as a patient in a New York City hospital, the nursing aide who takes your temperature and makes your bed is likely to be a West Indian. In 1990, hospitals, nursing homes, and health services together provided employment to 22 percent of Caribbean New Yorkers, most of them women.[99] It was a measure of the dominant West Indian presence in the Manhattan nursing home I studied several years ago that the rotating credit associations that flourished among the service workers were called "susus," a term used throughout the New York West Indian community.[100]

West Indians benefited from the growth of the city's health-care industry in the 1970s and 1980s. Whereas southern blacks and Puerto Rican migrants dominated the menial hospital workforce in the 1950s and 1960s, their children were often loathe to follow their parents into low-level service work that, before unionization and contract gains, did not pay a living wage.[101] Besides, the better-educated were able to take advantage of growing opportunities in public-sector white-collar employment.[102] In the 1980s, white female college graduates, having achieved access to many other options, were no longer heading for professional nursing careers. This was at a time when New York's nursing shortage was so severe that hospitals were in a virtual bidding war for registered nurses.

The twin factors of supply and demand still don't explain why West Indian women in particular became so concentrated in health care. One factor is that hospitals had already adjusted to having a large African American nonprofessional workforce in the late 1940s and 1950s—a period when a small nucleus of West Indians had, in fact, begun to work in them as well.[103] If race wasn't a barrier to employment, command of English was a huge advantage in jobs requiring face-to-face contact with patients. When it came to hiring professional nurses, the West Indies, with its English-speaking, literate, and well-trained population, became a primary choice for filling vacancies. About one-third of the legal Jamaican immigrants classified as professionals between 1962 and 1973 were nurses; more recently, between 1990 and 1992, nurses were a quarter of the professional immigrants from the four major English-speaking Caribbean countries.[104] The Philippines, the other major supplier of nurses, also produces English-speaking nurses trained in an Americanized curriculum. New York hospitals in the 1980s actively recruited in Manila, where they advertised for nurses in the local newspapers;[105] in the early 1990s, a whopping 72 percent of all the female immigrants from the Philippines who entered New York City and reported an occupation were registered nurses.[106] By 1997, Filipinos made up some 10 percent of the city's nurses;[107] because they are an extraordinarily well-educated group, however, they have not, like West Indians, moved into lower-level service jobs in the health field.

Because of their English-language skills, West Indians were also able to take advantage of personal-service, clerical, and retail opportunities in the 1970s and 1980s. West Indian women are heavily represented in the finance, insurance, and real estate sector, often in clerical positions; many also work in domestic child care, another area where English fluency is a plus. Although some West Indian men work in hospitals and nursing homes, they are scattered in a variety of other fields as well, the most common jobs being security guards, truck drivers, construction workers, janitors, and carpenters.[108]

For the Dominicans and Chinese, lack of English is a major factor in their occupational specializations. Many have followed a familiar path to the garment shops. As in the past, the needle trades still depend on immigrants who lack the skills, capital, and English-speaking ability to easily move into other kinds of work. But there's a different dynamic currently, with the industry in decline, and immigrants, as a source of replacement labor, have become key to its very survival in the city.

When the newest immigrants began arriving in the late 1960s, the garment industry was short of labor. Many of the remaining European immigrant workers were aging and retiring. Minority workers were leaving the industry for better-paying jobs that opened up as the white-collar sector grew and discriminatory barriers fell. In the course of the "welfare explosion," allowances from public assistance began to approach, and in some cases surpass, earnings from low-wage manufacturing jobs.[109] The apparel industry itself was changing.[110] Many jobs disappeared altogether as standardized, stable production moved to the southern United States and, increasingly, abroad in search of cheap labor. Firms producing style-sensitive goods, however, had an advantage in manufacturing clothes locally so they could fill the racks in stores on time. Immigrants stepped into the breach. Those without English, without much education or readily transferable skills, and often without proper documents have been willing to accept the prevailing wage levels and working conditions in garment factories, where they quickly learn to operate a sewing machine and can get by in their own language. Indeed, immigrant entrepreneurs have been replacing aging Jewish and Italian factory owners, whose children have sought better opportunities elsewhere.

But why have particular groups clustered in the garment trades? In the case of Dominicans, it was partly a matter of timing: they started arriving in large numbers in the 1960s, when Puerto Ricans were leaving the industry; there were vacancies in factories not far from where they lived in Manhattan; and the industry had already adjusted to Puerto Rican workers, using bilingual supervisors and mediators between managers and employers.[111] At the same time, Dominicans were limited in their search for jobs by language problems and low educational levels. "I thought that I would get a job," said one Dominican immigrant, though "not any office job because I didn't know how to take care of any responsibility in an office. I thought that I would get what I am doing . . . a factory [job] . . . manual labor . . . no? . . . What else can you do?"[112]

Once Dominicans got a toehold in the industry, their compatriots followed—although, of late, the numbers have fallen off significantly. In 1990, in the New York urban region as a whole, manufacturing provided nearly three in ten jobs for Dominican immigrants, down from about 50 percent ten years earlier.[113] (Other Dominican concentrations are retail and wholesale groceries, auto repair, and services to buildings.) The latest Hispanic workers in the garment trades are Mexicans and Ecuadorians, who are concentrated in the city's 350 Korean garment shops.[114] Without an adequate supply of co-ethnics—Korean women have better opportunities in the Korean ethnic economy—Korean owners have turned elsewhere. Low-skilled, without English, and often without documentation, recent Mexican and Ecuadorian arrivals have been welcomed as an even more pliable labor force than longer-standing Dominicans.[115] Many Mexicans and Ecuadorians are informally funneled into the industry through sewing schools in midtown Manhattan, near the garment shops, and they frequently get jobs by canvasing door-to-door or learning about openings through friends and relatives; for their part, Korean owners are often comfortable with Spanish-speaking workers, since a number are "twice migrants," having lived in South America before moving to New York.[116]

It is the Chinese, however, who have become "the chief inheritors of New York's rag trade, tattered and torn as it may be."[117] In 1952, there were only three Chinese garment shops in the city; by the early 1990s the number had mushroomed to somewhere between four hundred and five hundred in Manhattan and about two hundred more in Brooklyn's Sunset Park. In the 1980s, Chinatown's garment factories alone employed as many as twenty thousand—mainly female—workers.[118] The Chinese of the pre-1965 era had already established an enclave economy in Chinatown, based on restaurants, hand laundries, and grocery stores; at the same time, a decline in manufacturing in areas near Chinatown left vacant many loft buildings in which the garment industry could develop. The new wave of immigration supplied a new group of entrepreneurs willing to invest in and manage the garment trade as well as a large pool of cheap female labor willing to work in it.[119] In addition, the capital needed to start a garment factory was minimal. Not unlike Jewish garment contractors of old, the average Chinese garment factory is really a small contracting shop in a loft or storefront, with little more than some thirty sewing machines, a steam press, and a few other pieces of equipment; there garments that have been designed and cut by large manufacturers are turned into finished products. Chinese women, hampered by their inability to speak English, their meager education, and their limited information about the larger employment market, flocked to the nearby garment shops, where they could learn, through informal on-the-job training, how to operate a sewing machine.

Restaurants are the other major Chinese ethnic niche. Together, restaurants and garments provide jobs for just over a third of the immigrant Chinese in New York; engineering services have become a niche for the better-educated.[120] Chinese restaurants are largely a male domain, staffed with an army of waiters, busboys, cooks, dishwashers, cashiers, and managers. Rigid work schedules, particularly evening shifts, make restaurant work difficult for women with young children; compared to garment work, restaurant jobs are more stable and remunerative, thereby allowing men to fill the role of principal family breadwinner.[121]

Like the garment business, the restaurant industry is part of a vibrant Chinese ethnic economy, where it's who you know, not what you know, that matters. Today's Chinese restaurants are an outgrowth of an earlier specialization. They originally developed in Chinatown to serve quick and inexpensive meals to male sojourners who did not have wives to cook for them. Chinatown restaurants also catered to the tourist trade, and even before the recent immigration, they had expanded outward to uptown areas, the outer boroughs, and the suburbs. Two sociologists write of how "eating Chinese" in restaurants has long been part of Jewish culture in New York City. By the 1950s, Cantonese Chinese restaurants had become a feature of New York Jewish neighborhoods, the menus sometimes explaining that won ton soup was "chicken soup with *kreplach.*"[122]

The advent of the new immigration reinvigorated the restaurant business. In addition to the expanding ethnic market, opportunities beckoned beyond. The influx of immigrants, as Roger Waldinger points out, "allowed Chinese restaurants to offer a relatively inexpensive meal just when American lifestyle changes led to a taste for more exotic foods and greater spending on meals made in restaurants, rather than at home."[123] By the early 1990s, Manhattan boasted some four hundred Chinese restaurants —and hundreds more in the rest of the city and the suburbs. According to one estimate, Chinatown's restaurants alone employed about fifteen thousand workers in the 1980s.[124] New York's Chinese restaurants vary in size and price from glitzy Chinatown establishments that serve elaborate banquets to fast-food take-outs in ghetto neighborhoods that compete with McDonald's and Burger King. Before 1975, Chinese restaurants in the United States were almost always Cantonese, but recent immigrants have brought myriad cuisines with them, including Szechuan, Hunan, Peking, and Shanghai. Some Chinese immigrants have even branched out beyond Chinese food; since 1991, dozens have opened taco stands.[125]

Finally, a few words on what is perhaps the most visible ethnic niche of all: Korean greengrocers. Koreans have turned the traditional produce store "into an art form" and reinvented the corner grocery, adding salad bars, deli counters, and bouquets of flowers.[126] By 1991, Koreans owned about eighteen hundred, or 60 percent, of the New York metropolitan area's produce stores and more than eleven hundred groceries.[127]

Koreans may seem to be repeating the Jewish success story in business, but the dynamics underlying the proliferation of Korean retail stores in the city are, on the whole, very different. I already mentioned their experience with blocked mobility. Unable to practice their professions in this country, Koreans opened up small businesses as the best way to make money. Family members, also with limited employment options, were often on hand to help out. The start-up costs to open a grocery or produce store were low, and some Koreans arrived with financial capital or had family members back home who could supply loans. Rotating credit associations, known as *kyes*, in which members contribute to a pool that is given out on a rotating basis, were another source of funds. And opportunities were there. Koreans arrived in New York at a time when Jewish and Italian retail shop owners were retiring or moving away and the older immigrants' children, who had entered the mainstream economy, were not interested in running the family store. Once the first wave of Koreans became entrenched in certain specialities, others followed; a dense web of trade associations, churches, and friendship and kinship ties in the Korean community has provided help with business information, loans, and staffing problems. Koreans have branched out as well into other retail lines, such as seafood stores, and have pioneered businesses, such as nail salons that are now ubiquitous in the city, by taking what were once more exclusive products or services and making them cheaper. In 1991, Koreans owned fifteen hundred dry cleaners, over seven hundred seafood stores, and some fifteen hundred nail salons in the New York metropolitan area.[128]

One thing that hasn't changed since the last great wave is the way immigrant communities themselves spawn job opportunities, although there is more variation today in the extent to which this occurs among various groups. As before, the immigrant market provides a base for a host of small businesses catering to special ethnic tastes and needs. In virtually every sizable immigrant neighborhood, local ethnic stores sell distinctive consumer goods; travel agents, lawyers, realtors, and accountants specialize in what Waldinger calls the "business of immigrant adjustment" as they help compatriots deal with problems caused by the strain of settlement.[129]

Manhattan's Chinatown is reminiscent of the old Jewish Lower East Side, with its hundreds of entrepreneurs tending their own stalls or shops. "Bushels of live crabs, crates of bok choy, and hordes of intense shoppers crowd the sidewalks . . . of the central business district of China-town. Shopkeepers hawk wares from every available nook: batteries and audiotapes, scarves, T-shirts, jewelry, and food of every description, from lobsters to doughnuts. . . . The pull of the ethnic market was so great as to make commercial rents higher than in other business areas, save the most prestigious downtown locations."[130] A host of restaurants, from tea-houses, coffeehouses, and fast-food take-outs to gourmet establishments, have sprung up to serve Chinatown's residents as well as immigrants who work in the neighborhood.[131]

One study estimated that in upper Manhattan's Washington Heights, or "Quisqueya Heights" (Quisqueya being the indigenous name of the Dominican Republic), there were between fifteen hundred and two thou-sand Dominican-owned enterprises; another found an average of twelve Dominican-owned businesses per block between 157th Street and 191st Street.[132] One finds restaurants specializing in *comida criolla* (Dominican cuisine); travel and money-transfer agencies; bodegas stocked with Domi-nican staples and brand-name products; pharmacies; and gypsy cab ser-vices.[133] In central Brooklyn, West Indian barbershops, beauty parlors, bakeries, record stores, and catering halls dot the landscape. Jamaican res-taurants serve curried goat; Guyanese bakeries sell coconut drops, pine-apple tarts, and currant rolls. "Dollar vans," so called because the standard fare is one dollar, cruise West Indian neighborhoods and directly (and ille-gally) compete with city buses, offering lower prices and more frequent service.[134]

A fascinating question is why West Indians have not managed to domi-nate all the retail businesses in their own neighborhoods, while other groups, like the Chinese and Koreans, have parlayed businesses catering to ethnic clientele into wider markets. In West Indian communities, Koreans own most of the fruit and vegetable markets, even those announcing that they specialize in West Indian products. In general, New York City's West Indians have remarkably low self-employment rates, under 4 percent for the three main groups, Jamaicans, Trinidadians, and Guyanese.[135]

Fluency in English is a major factor in that West Indians with skills and advanced education are better able than their Korean and Chinese counter-parts to find decent positions in the mainstream economy. West Indians' heavy concentration in large-scale bureaucratic organizations, such as hos-pitals and nursing homes, limits their exposure to the skills, information, and contacts needed to start their own businesses.[136] Nor do they bring with them an orientation to small-scale entrepreneurship. In their home societies, self-employment has traditionally been associated with marginal pursuits among the lower class, like peddling and backyard auto-repair shops; large-scale entrepreneurial activities have long been dominated by white, Middle Eastern, and Asian minorities; and education and the professions are seen as the routes to upward mobility. In New York, race is a barrier, too; racial segregation confines most West Indians to inner-city residential areas with weak local markets, and they run the risk of distrust and hostility in going outside their communities to find a white customer base or, as in construction, developing relationships with white networks that control access to larger private jobs.[137]

Working conditions for new immigrants also reflect their diversity. On the whole, immigrants who have reached the upper rungs of the occupational ladder—doctors, lawyers, and other professionals and successful businesspeople—enjoy working conditions not dramatically different from others of their station. Labor unions are now much stronger than they were in the last great wave, and office, service, and manufacturing workers covered by union contracts often earn fairly decent wages and receive a wide range of benefits. New York's hospital and nursing-home workers, for example, virtually all in unionized facilities, get health benefits, pension coverage, paid vacation, sick leave, and generous overtime pay; the least skilled among them, nursing aides and orderlies, start out at around thirteen dollars an hour.[138]

However, many immigrants work under dreadful conditions that are not much different from those of the past. Once again, the garment industry stands out. Many garment shops are crowded, unsafe, and poorly ventilated firetraps where new hands may work twelve-hour days for less than the minimum wage. Even in unionized Chinese sewing shops that provide health benefits, workers, paid by the piece, often average only two hundred dollars a week.[139] When they are paid off the books, garment workers, like others in the informal economy, are not covered by government-mandated provisions like workmen's compensation, unemployment insurance, and social security. As with earlier immigrants, co-ethnic employers are no guarantee of decent conditions. Owners of Chinese garment shops, for example, may dispense various favors and provide a family-like ambience for Chinese employees, but, in their own search for profits in a cutthroat industry, they are often exploitative nonetheless.[140]

Undocumented workers are particularly vulnerable in the labor market. Typically recent arrivals, they depend on employers who do not check their papers too carefully (if at all), a step that closes off opportunities in large firms and government bureaucracies in the regulated portion of the labor market. When immigrants without green cards do get jobs, they fear deportation if they exercise their legal rights to state protection. At street corners and other designated points throughout the New York area, undocumented Latino immigrants wait for vans or trucks to pick them up for unskilled and bottom-dollar jobs in construction, demolition, moving, and landscaping. Workers tell of employers who shortchange them or who promise three days of work but do not appear on the last day, payday.[141] In the West Indian community, it's usually the undocumented who are willing to take live-in domestic jobs, which isolate them from friends and relatives and often require that they be on call virtually twenty-four hours a day. In some cases, employers force them to share a room with children or pets, do not allow them access to certain public rooms except to clean them, and expect them to eat leftovers in the kitchen.[142] In general, according to a recent study, undocumented immigrants earn less than their legal counterparts; in New York State, in 1995, the average annual per capita income of the legal foreign-born was almost six thousand dollars more than that of undocumented immigrants.[143]

A final issue is how the latest immigrants stack up against the rest of New York City's residents. On the whole, they don't do as well in the labor market as native-born whites, which is what one would expect, given, among other things, that they are new to this country, often lack English proficiency, and generally have lower educational levels than native whites.

Of course, there is wide variation among groups (see table 7). At the low end, post-1965 Dominicans and Mexicans, hampered by low educational levels and lack of English, do particularly poorly. At the high end, Filipinos, with high levels of educational achievement, have a more impressive occupational profile than native whites. But Filipinos are unusual.[144] What emerges in general is a profile of immigrant disadvantage compared to native whites: a much smaller proportion of the foreign-born hold professional jobs than native whites, and a much larger proportion are in the services and operator and laborer categories. Immigrants also trail native whites in earnings,[145] although over time, as they gain experience and acquire skills needed here, that gap is likely to narrow for earlier entry immigrants.[146]

So far, the present scenario does not sound all that different from the past. But today there are two major population components that barely existed at the turn of the century: African Americans and Puerto Ricans. The product of a massive migration from the southern states and Puerto Rico that occurred after the last great immigrant wave, U.S.-born blacks and Hispanics were about a quarter of the city's working-age population in 1990.[147] What stands out is that on many measures, immigrants are doing

Table 7    Socioeconomic Characteristics of Immigrants Aged 16 to 64 in New York City, Compared with the Native Born, 1990

| National Origin/ Ethnicity | Less Than High School Diploma (%) | College Degree or More (%) | Professionals and Managers (%) | Operators and Laborers (%) | Average Earnings ($) | In Labor Force (%) | Unemployed (%) |
|---|---|---|---|---|---|---|---|
| Foreign born[1] | 40.4 | 16.3 | 19.6 | 18.8 | 14,593 | 70.3 | 9.7 |
| U.S. born | | | | | | | |
| non-Hispanic white | 12.5 | 39.0 | 41.2 | 6.6 | 27,382 | 76.7 | 5.2 |
| non-Hispanic black | 33.8 | 11.3 | 20.0 | 12.6 | 13,165 | 65.1 | 14.4 |
| Hispanic | 39.9 | 8.9 | 17.6 | 12.5 | 10,955 | 61.0 | 15.1 |
| Post-1965 Immigrants, by National Origin | | | | | | | |
| China | 43.7 | 20.5 | 17.7 | 25.7 | 12,653 | 73.7 | 5.9 |
| Colombia | 40.0 | 8.8 | 10.8 | 25.8 | 11,773 | 76.0 | 10.8 |
| Dominican Republic | 59.7 | 5.5 | 8.7 | 33.0 | 8,293 | 63.0 | 17.4 |
| Ecuador | 45.4 | 6.9 | 8.0 | 31.7 | 11,358 | 76.3 | 11.0 |
| Former USSR | 18.8 | 32.8 | 28.0 | 11.3 | 14,234 | 62.4 | 14.4 |
| Guyana | 34.9 | 8.4 | 16.1 | 16.2 | 14,018 | 75.2 | 8.2 |
| Haiti | 33.0 | 11.6 | 13.0 | 21.0 | 14,106 | 80.1 | 12.0 |
| India | 23.4 | 39.7 | 31.0 | 11.2 | 18,030 | 75.9 | 7.2 |
| Italy | 54.1 | 10.6 | 18.4 | 22.2 | 19,335 | 71.5 | 8.1 |
| Jamaica | 32.8 | 12.8 | 18.2 | 10.6 | 16,353 | 82.2 | 10.5 |
| Korea | 20.7 | 31.2 | 22.7 | 14.1 | 13,479 | 70.6 | 5.7 |
| Mexico | 67.3 | 4.9 | 5.1 | 31.7 | 8,731 | 77.6 | 8.5 |
| Philippines | 7.0 | 63.3 | 44.6 | 4.9 | 25,070 | 86.5 | 2.1 |
| Poland | 27.8 | 23.9 | 19.2 | 14.5 | 16,888 | 79.8 | 7.0 |
| Puerto Rico | 57.1 | 5.0 | 12.0 | 23.2 | 7,766 | 52.1 | 16.6 |
| Trinidad | 29.4 | 10.1 | 17.8 | 9.9 | 16,059 | 81.5 | 10.2 |

Source: U.S. Bureau of the Census, Public Use Microdata Sample, 1990. Data calculated by Hector Cordero-Guzman, New School for Social Research.

[1]All foreign born aged 16 to 64 in New York City, regardless of year of entry, including island-born Puerto Ricans.

better than native blacks and Hispanics, and this is especially pronounced among the most low-skilled and poorly educated.

As indicated in table 7, the foreign-born, as a whole, have higher earnings and higher rates of participation in the labor force and lower unemployment rates than native-born blacks and Hispanics. Among college graduates, however, the foreign-born have less of an advantage (see table 8). Indeed, among most non-English-speaking groups, post-1965 immigrants

Table 8    Socioeconomic Characteristics of Immigrants in New York City
Aged 16 to 64 by Educational Level, Compared with the Native Born, 1990

| National Origin/ Ethnicity | Less Than High School Diploma | | | College Degree or More | | |
|---|---|---|---|---|---|---|
| | In Labor Force (%) | Unem- ployed (%) | Average Earnings ($) | In Labor Force (%) | Unem- ployed (%) | Average Earnings ($) |
| Foreign born[1] | 59.8 | 12.8 | 8,852 | 85.7 | 5.2 | 29,129 |
| U.S. born | | | | | | |
| non-Hispanic white | 48.7 | 12.9 | 9,529 | 89.6 | 3.2 | 41,847 |
| non-Hispanic black | 45.1 | 27.1 | 5,989 | 89.6 | 4.0 | 27,881 |
| Hispanic | 40.9 | 27.1 | 4,418 | 88.5 | 5.2 | 25,799 |
| Post-1965 Immigrants, by National Origin | | | | | | |
| China | 70.4 | 6.1 | 7,752 | 83.6 | 4.3 | 24,959 |
| Colombia | 69.6 | 12.4 | 8,586 | 82.2 | 6.2 | 20,787 |
| Dominican Republic | 57.9 | 18.3 | 6,666 | 83.0 | 13.4 | 15,337 |
| Ecuador | 73.1 | 11.1 | 9,654 | 82.7 | 11.7 | 18,171 |
| Former USSR | 40.9 | 20.8 | 5,826 | 77.2 | 9.8 | 21,717 |
| Guyana | 63.4 | 11.7 | 9,176 | 87.1 | 5.2 | 25,075 |
| Haiti | 74.1 | 14.0 | 10,340 | 89.4 | 5.8 | 26,390 |
| India | 62.4 | 13.2 | 8,897 | 85.0 | 4.5 | 27,659 |
| Italy | 65.8 | 10.9 | 14,162 | 86.1 | 3.2 | 39,309 |
| Jamaica | 75.1 | 12.7 | 12,071 | 93.6 | 5.9 | 26,792 |
| Korea | 56.1 | 8.4 | 8,397 | 75.7 | 4.5 | 19,649 |
| Mexico | 75.6 | 8.4 | 7,853 | 78.6 | 9.7 | 13,036 |
| Philippines | 57.4 | 4.5 | 8,141 | 92.3 | 1.5 | 31,186 |
| Poland | 71.6 | 12.4 | 12,560 | 90.6 | 4.6 | 25,754 |
| Puerto Rico | 41.5 | 21.4 | 4,944 | 88.3 | 6.7 | 25,127 |
| Trinidad | 75.2 | 15.2 | 11,560 | 90.1 | 2.4 | 28,974 |

Source: U.S. Bureau of the Census, Public Use Microdata Sample, 1990. Data calculated by Hector Cordero-Guzman of the New School for Social Research.

[1] All foreign born aged 16 to 64 in New York City, regardless of year of entry, including island-born Puerto Ricans.

with a college degree have lower earnings than native minority college graduates. This is not the case for the low-skilled—and in 1990 more than a third of the immigrant and native minority working-age populations did not have a high school degree. Altogether, among those without high school diplomas, the foreign-born earn more than twice as much as native Hispanics and a third more than native blacks; their unemployment rates are half what they are for native minorities (see first four rows of table 8).[148] With the exception of Russians and island-born Puerto Ricans, who, as U.S.

citizens, are not immigrants, strictly speaking, the foreign-born advantage holds for all post-1965 groups.

Issues of race therefore become important in new ways. In the context of contemporary racial inequalities and concerns over joblessness in New York's ghetto neighborhoods, the question of why immigrants are faring better than, and whether they are displacing, native-born minorities at the lower ends of the occupational ladder has far-ranging implications.

There is little evidence that immigrants have directly displaced native blacks and Hispanics or have pushed them out of low-skilled jobs they once held. One analysis concludes that although foreign-born workers substantially increased their share of employment in African American job niches in New York City in the 1980s, much of the foreign-born gain—particularly for men—appeared to be at the expense of native-born white workers who retired or left the metropolitan area.[149] Large numbers of newcomers converge on industries such as retailing and manufacturing that had not been major employers of native blacks.[150] Indeed, many immigrants work in ethnic businesses in jobs created by immigrants for immigrants.

What, then, explains the disparity in earnings and unemployment rates between low-skilled immigrants and native-born minorities? Partly it's a matter of attitudes. Immigrants are more willing to tolerate harsh conditions, low pay, and dead-end jobs, because even rock-bottom wages look good compared to what they can earn back home. Also, many see their stay as temporary: they are here to save money with the intent of improving their status upon return. Native-born minorities, particularly those who have come of age in post-civil-rights America, have different expectations. To them, menial, minimum-wage jobs that offer no possibility for upward movement and require deference to better-off, often white, supervisors and customers are decidedly unattractive. They are less likely than immigrants to seek out these kinds of jobs in the first place, and when they do, they have less motivation to stay. According to a Chicago study, inner-city black men have a heightened sensitivity to exploitation, which fuels their anger and gives rise to a tendency to "just walk off the job"; although recent immigrants also feel exploited, this "somehow . . . comes with the territory."[151] For the native-born, public assistance (e.g., temporary aid for needy families, food stamps, Medicaid, and housing subsidies) often looks like a better choice than a lousy job. Indeed, it's interesting that, among those without a high school degree, Soviets, who as refugees are entitled to a wide range of federal and state benefits on arrival, have the highest unemployment rates of all post-1965 immigrants in New York City—though still not as high as the rates for native blacks and Hispanics.[152] (In addition, many New York Jewish agencies are on hand to help with the application process, and Soviet immigrants from one of the formerly communist republics have no compunction about requesting and accepting government aid.)

But the disparity in earnings and unemployment rates is not just a question of attitudes and expectations. There has been indirect displacement of low-skilled native minorities as well. For one thing, the immigrant influx has contributed to making low-level jobs more unattractive to native workers by lowering wage rates. The National Academy of Sciences report on the economic impact of immigration concluded that, in the United States as a whole, 44 percent of the decline in the real wages of high school dropouts from 1980 to 1995 resulted from immigration.[153] In New York City, one analysis found that an increasing share of recent immigrant workers in jobs between 1979 and 1989 had a strong negative effect on native-born blacks' earnings.[154]

A growing number of studies also reveal employers' preferences for hiring immigrants, whatever their race or ethnicity, over native blacks and Hispanics. In Brooklyn's Red Hook neighborhood, employers generally favored black immigrants over black natives and non–Puerto Rican Latinos over Puerto Ricans.[155] Likewise, Jewish, Korean, and black immigrant merchants prefer Caribbean and West African blacks over African Americans.[156] And, in central Harlem, where fast-food restaurants had, in the early 1990s, on average fourteen applicants for every minimum-wage job opening, immigrants were more likely to be hired than native-born African Americans, even when they had the same educational level and work experience.[157]

Employers often use ethnic markers to gauge productivity in a rough-and-ready way, and for low-skilled jobs in New York these days, they are picking among a variety of visibly identifiable and stigmatized groups.[158] They see immigrants as willing to work hard and long for low wages and to stay on the job.[159] It's not, as Philip Kasinitz and Jan Rosenberg note in their Red Hook study, that employers value immigrant cultures; many Red Hook employers indulged in crude ethnic stereotypes about their immigrant workers. "What is generally admired," they write, "are a few perceived attributes: punctuality, reliability, willingness to work hard and to be a pliable labor force."[160] If employers are positively inclined to hire immigrants, native blacks and Hispanics are often seen as a bad risk. For many employers there is a strong mental association between inner-city blacks and Puerto Ricans and a high rate of crime.[161] A common fear is that native minorities will be less productive, less reliable, and less tractable than immigrants—that they will be more likely to openly voice complaints, make claims on the firm, or contest managerial decisions.[162]

Finally, once immigrants become a dominant presence in particular firms, network hiring ends up perpetuating their advantage—and excluding native minorities. Most private-sector employers rely on referrals, typically from current workers, to recruit low-skilled employees. Network recruitment is efficient, saves time and money, and reduces the risk in acquiring unknown workers, because existing employees vouch for the newcomers and have an interest in the recruit working out. In this way, network hiring reinforces employers' belief that immigrants are a better bet than native minorities.[163] More than that, when immigrants recommend family, friends, and acquaintances, native minorities are out of the loop. They don't hear about openings, which are rarely advertised, and when they do, they often lack a sponsor on the job.[164] Moreover, once a particular ethnic group penetrates a workplace, employers are often reluctant to bring in native minorities for fear of interethnic conflict. And if the language on the shop floor is, say, Chinese or Spanish, native English speakers simply won't be able to communicate or fit in.[165]

There is no denying, therefore, that the immigrant influx has hurt low-skilled native minorities in the labor market. Indeed, had there been no massive immigration, employers might have made greater efforts to recruit native minorities—and, in the process, may have improved wage rates and working conditions as a way to attract them. Yet, bear in mind that there's a positive side to the balance sheet as well. Without the addition of immigrants to the city's population base, there would have been less need for workers to supply public services of all kinds. As Waldinger has pointed out, immigrants have provided "a fillip to employment growth [by adding to the local demand for goods and services]. Since immigrants receive the same public services as everyone else, from street cleaning to schooling, their presence has provided support for the African American employment base in the public sector." In this way, immigrants have especially benefited the more skilled segments of the native minority population, who have entered government employment in large numbers in the last thirty years.[166] And although native minorities no longer move into low-level manufacturing jobs, to the extent that manufacturing has ripple effects on the entire New York City economy, the immigrant presence has been a plus. Without the availability of a cheap, hard-working immigrant labor force, manufacturing would probably have suffered even greater losses;

more firms would have left the city or introduced labor-saving production techniques; and fewer new firms would have started up.

## Immigrants and Work: Continuity and Change

Work, work, and more work—the classic immigrant story seems to be repeating itself as a new group of arrivals enters New York. Immigrants come here to better themselves and their families, and if this means taking jobs that nobody else wants, they have generally been willing to do so. Italians once dug ditches and tunnels; now Mexicans wash dishes. Today, as in the past, the wages look good, at least at the start, compared to what they earned before migration; in any case, many immigrants now, like Italian "birds of passage" in the last great wave, see their stay as temporary and hope to accumulate enough to improve their lot back home (see Chapter 6).

This is not the only similarity between past and present. The underlying processes of niche development, which have been elaborated by sociologists to understand present-day ethnic concentrations, operated in both eras. Embedded in networks upon arrival, immigrants often rely on friends and kin to find jobs. Because network hiring benefits employers as well as immigrant job seekers, ethnic niches, once established, become self-reproducing so that today's garment workers are Chinese and, increasingly, Mexican and Ecuadorian, just as a hundred years ago they were Jewish and Italian. If the needle trades remain an immigrant speciality as the industry continues to rely on the cheap labor of low-skilled arrivals, so, too, many immigrants today, as in the past, set up shop to provide special goods and services to their compatriots.

Another continuity, unfortunately, is terrible working conditions that many immigrants must still endure. In general, immigrants continue to lag behind native whites in wages and occupational status, though how particular groups do now depends largely, as before, on the human capital they bring with them. A century ago, Russian Jews, arriving with more skills, did better than Italians; today, the more highly educated Asian groups outpace Latin Americans in the labor market. Moreover, all groups experience improvements over time, as immigrants acquire the skills and savvy needed to negotiate New York's job market.

Important as these similarities are, we are not simply witnessing a timeless immigrant saga. For one thing, New York City's economy has undergone radical changes. Jews and Italians arrived at a time of industrial expansion, filling a seemingly insatiable demand for labor as the city churned out jobs. In today's postindustrial economy, there's no similar kind of growth. In fact, what's often asked is how New York's economy has been able to absorb the more than two million immigrants of the past few decades when employment has not expanded much at all. Part of the answer has to do with a demographic change that is unique to the present era—namely, the enormous outflow of whites that has been a source of job openings in retailing, clothing manufacture, and other lines of work.[167]

New York's more complex, and more technologically advanced, economy has created a demand for immigrants to fill a much wider array of jobs than existed a century ago. Also, the immigrants themselves are different: there are more groups, more cultural styles, more ethnic job specialities. Most significant, today's arrivals range in background from illiterate peasants to engineers and computer specialists. Unlike previous groups, many of the latest newcomers have college degrees and speak fluent English; a small minority even bring substantial amounts of financial capital with them. Given such skills, it's no surprise that a much higher proportion of today's immigrants find employment easily in decent, often high-level jobs in the mainstream economy. Or that downward occupational mobility is more of a problem for immigrants now than in the past. And there's another basis of diversity among the current arrivals that was basically irrelevant for Jews and Italians a century ago: legal status. Although having a green card is hardly a recipe for success, without one an immigrant has more trouble getting a good job and making a living wage in the formal economy.

One final difference should be noted: New York now has a huge population of native-born blacks and Hispanics, so that it's especially significant that immigrants are outpacing them in the labor market. The pattern of immigrant advantage over native blacks is itself not new. At the beginning of the twentieth century, Jewish and Italian immigrants did slightly better occupationally than African Americans; the immigrant influx, moreover, crowded native blacks out of a number of skilled trades.[168] Yet blacks at that time were but a tiny proportion of the city's population, and Hispanics even smaller. Today, this is not the case, and the question of whether immigrants are hurting native racial minorities is more pressing—as well as more complex now that the majority of immigrants are themselves black and Hispanic. Low-skilled, poorly educated native-born blacks and Hispanics have borne the brunt of the negative impact of immigration, as new arrivals are willing to accept lousy conditions and wages for low-level work, build up networks that connect them to jobs, and are often preferred by employers. So far, better-educated native minorities, as Roger Waldinger observes, have been sheltered from immigrant competition by their concentration in public-sector jobs. Yet this will surely change; immigration will soon mean that "there will be more claimants for a piece of the public sector pie."[169] And another development also lies ahead. In the future, the native minorities competing with immigrants for jobs will include the children of many of today's newcomers, thereby adding yet a further complication to an increasingly complex picture.

# CHAPTER 4

# Immigrant Women and Work

*I*t is impossible to talk about immigrant women today and one hundred years ago without considering the enormous changes that have taken place in the lives of American women.

Women now vote—a right they gained only in 1920—and hold political office. More go to college, and beyond: by 1979, women students outnumbered men in the nation's colleges; some ten years later they earned over half of the bachelor's and master's degrees awarded and a third of the doctoral degrees.[1] Women executives and high-level professionals are no longer the rarity they once were. In 1910, only 1 percent of lawyers and 6 percent of physicians in the nation were women. By 1995, the figures had risen to 25 percent for lawyers and 22 percent for physicians.[2] Divorce is easier and more acceptable, and women on their own have access to social welfare benefits to a degree unknown earlier in the century.

Perhaps most dramatic, there has been a virtual revolution in women's involvement in the labor force. More women in the United States are now working for wages for more of their lives. Whereas in 1900 only 20 percent of women in the nation were in the paid labor force, by 1995 the figure had reached nearly 60 percent.

There is also a difference in who works. At the turn of the twentieth century, the vast majority of women workers were young and single. It was generally assumed that work outside the home was temporary for a young girl; when she married, she would move back into the domestic domain. Indeed, there was a social stigma attached to the working wife, who was often considered beyond the pale of middle-class respectability.[3]

Today, working daughters have given way to working mothers.[4] Women now enter the labor force later—and they stay. Whether they work for economic need, to maintain or raise their family's living standards, or for personal satisfaction, the fact is that by 1990 almost three quarters of married women with children under eighteen worked in the paid labor force, many doing so full-time and year-round.[5]

How these broad changes in women's participation in the American labor force have affected the experiences of immigrant women today as compared to the past is the focus of this chapter. Wage work, as we shall see, has empowered immigrant wives and mothers in late twentieth-century New York in ways that were not possible for Jewish and Italian married women of an earlier era. Comparing a time when few married immigrant women worked for wages to a period when most do brings into sharper focus the relationship between migrant women's work and their overall status—and helps us understand the conditions that lead women to experience gains as well as losses when they come to the United States.

An important issue in both periods is how women's status changed in the process of moving to New York. A common popular perception about the past is that migration was liberating for European women who left traditional cultures, with their old-fashioned and repressive customs, for a freer America. To some degree, this view captures the experiences of young unmarried Jewish and Italian women in the past, but it most certainly misrepresents the situation of adult migrant women at the time, who were more constrained in many ways after the move to New York.

In the contemporary period, in contrast, migrant women of all ages in New York have tended to experience improvements in their status as women, although it is too strong to say that migration has emancipated them. Lately, feminist scholars have emphasized that migration's impact on women should not be conceptualized in stark either/or terms. Migration often leads to losses—as well as gains—for women, and traditional patriarchal codes and practices may continue to have an impact.[6] In the spirit of the new feminist scholarship, this analysis makes clear that even when migration improves women's access to economic resources, as it often does today, they are not fully liberated.

Gender inequalities are still very much with us, and women—immigrants as well as the native-born—continue to experience special burdens and disabilities as members of the "second sex." The Chinese say that women hold up half the sky, but many immigrant women in New York appear to be holding up more than their half. Indeed, immigrant mothers' continued responsibilities for child-care and domestic tasks add new complications for them when they are more likely to work outside, as well as inside, the home.

## Jewish and Italian Women in the Great Migration

From the beginning, in the move itself, Jewish and Italian women typically followed men—husbands, fiancés, and fathers—who led the way. Women were a minority, too. The Italian migration was, more than anything else, a movement of single men coming to make money and go home. In most years of the peak migration between 1880 and 1910, about 80 percent of Italian immigrants to the United States were male.[7] The Jewish movement was mainly a family affair, but even then men predominated: between 1899 and 1910 women made up 43 percent of the migration stream to the United States.[8]

A common pattern among male Italians at the turn of the century was to make the trip between America and Italy several times, either on their own or in the company of male kin or fellow villagers. Some returned to Italy for good. Many, however, settled in New York permanently once they had saved enough money and then sent for family members. Most Jewish men came to stay, but they, too, usually made the journey first, later sending for working-age children and then arranging for wives and younger family members to follow. Occasionally, Jewish daughters came first, becoming "emissaries of family survival" in America. According to Susan Glenn, once a network of relatives was established in New York, many Jewish families were willing, and found it practicable, to send one or more children, including working-age daughters, in advance.[9]

Although women usually had husbands and fathers to greet them, the voyage to the New World was nonetheless daunting. In his autobiography, Leonard Covello recalls that his mother had never been more than a few miles outside her Italian village when, in 1896, she made the long trip with her young children, first to Naples and then on the choppy seas for twenty days to New York. In the two-day wait at Ellis Island, before Leonard's father came to meet them, his mother "hardly closed her eyes for fear of losing us in the confusion."[10] About the same time, in 1891, eleven-year-old Rose Cohen and her unmarried aunt left Russia for New York. They were joining her father, who had migrated a few years earlier, gotten a foothold in New York, and sent prepaid steamship tickets to his family. Rose and her aunt's trip involved being smuggled across the border (for lack of proper local passports), a week-long wait in Hamburg in a dismal building owned by the steamship company, and an ocean crossing, in steerage, marked by days of terrible seasickness. About a year after Rose arrived, the rest of the family, including her mother, joined Rose and her father in New York.[11]

## Immigrant Daughters

No sooner had Rose Cohen settled in New York than she, like so many other Jewish girls, went to work in a garment sweatshop, recalling that her "fingers often stiffened with pain" as she "rolled and basted the [coat] edges."[12] Jewish daughters, as Susan Glenn notes, were expected to go out and earn a living as a matter of course. It was as inevitable, said one worker, "as eating and breathing and finally dying. It was just part of the scheme of things."[13] Stereotypes about the freedom that America offered European migrant women are based on the experiences of immigrant daughters, although even in their case, there is a risk of exaggerating the extent to which they were empowered by the move to New York in this period. Although work outside the home often expanded young Italian and Jewish daughters' horizons, factory jobs were debilitating, poorly paid, and sometimes downright dangerous and did not lead to much economic independence.

In 1910, more than three-quarters of unmarried Jewish immigrant daughters over sixteen worked for wages, the vast majority in the needle trades; even younger girls, those only fourteen and fifteen years of age, often worked outside the home.[14] Italian girls were more likely to stay home helping with household chores or to engage in industrial homework, but large numbers also went to work in factories. By one count, in 1905 in New York City 62 percent of single Italian-born women between the ages of sixteen and twenty-one were wage earners, typically in the garment industry but also in paper-box, candy, jewelry, and tobacco factories. For Italian girls from rural backgrounds, factory work in New York often represented the first experience with wage labor.[15] Although some Jewish daughters in eastern Europe had worked in small factories or, more commonly, done industrial homework, their economic role expanded in New York, where, in the context of increased industrial opportunities, many more went out to work.[16] Among the American-born or -raised, there was even some movement out of the factory into the office during this period; by 1905 one out of four Russian daughters in New York City was in white-collar employment, as a school teacher, clerk, salesperson, or shopkeeper, whereas the proportion among Italian daughters, 9 percent, was still very small.[17]

Immigrant daughters' earnings were crucial to the family budget. A 1911 Bureau of Labor study of wages, hours, and economic conditions of women and children in the men's clothing industry showed that Jewish working daughters brought in nearly 40 percent of their family's yearly earnings, slightly more than Italian daughters in the same situation.[18] Their wages, nonetheless, were extremely low. In 1910, when a New York State Factory Investigating Commission estimated that a single woman living alone needed to earn ten dollars weekly to maintain a minimal standard of living, Italian and Jewish daughters typically earned between six and nine dollars a week. In addition, they worked in industries that experienced slack periods; for several weeks or months a year they might earn nothing at all.[19]

Young women's expanded wage-earning role in New York did not translate into economic independence or control. Italian and Jewish daughters understood their wages to be part of the family fund. They customarily handed over all their earnings, many giving their unopened pay envelopes to their mothers in return for small allowances to cover weekly expenses. "I gave my pay envelope to my mother," said Amalia Morandi, an Italian garment worker. "I wouldn't dare open it up. I'd give it to my mother because I knew that she worked hard for us and I thought this was her compensation."[20] A 1916 report, based on a survey of seven hundred single (mostly Jewish) women in New York shirtwaist factories, noted that the majority gave their "untouched and unopened" pay envelopes to their parents. The same was true for young Italian women, though some evidence suggests that Jewish daughters were allowed to retain a greater proportion of their earnings for personal use than their southern Italian sisters.[21]

Boys were less pressured to contribute all their earnings and typically received larger allowances than their sisters.[22] Theresa Albino gave all her earnings to her mother, while her eighteen-year-old brother contributed three or four dollars a week. "But you know how it is with a boy," she explained; "he wants things for himself." Mothers also expected daughters to help them with housework or tend to younger siblings, an expectation not placed on sons, who had more freedom to roam the streets, play sports, and seek adventures with their friends.[23]

There was a double standard educationally, too. Jewish daughters often went to work to support their brothers' pursuit of education. My own grandmother, who came from Russia as a child, remained bitter that she had to go to work as a secretary, without even finishing high school, while the family savings financed her brothers' education at private universities. Census reports for the beginning of the century show Russian Jewish boys more likely to go to high school and college than girls; moreover, in high school, boys predominated in the academically elite programs.[24] Although Italian families were less sure of the value of an American education in general, here too boys, as one immigrant recalled, "had always more privileges than girls. . . . When girls at thirteen or fourteen wasted good time in school, it simply made us regret our coming to America."[25] An analysis of census data leads Miriam Cohen to conclude that if Italian families in New York invested in advanced schooling for their children at all, they were more likely to invest in the boys' than the girls'. [26] It wasn't hard in this period to get around the various regulations designed to keep children in school. Before 1903 in New York, only four years of schooling were required before a child could legally go to work, and working papers were relatively easy to obtain. Even when stricter compulsory education laws were enacted, requiring children to attend school until the age of fourteen, little effort was made to enforce the law, and children routinely obtained false working papers.

Conditions in the factories and sweatshops that employed Jewish and Italian daughters were grim. "Fourteen hours a day you sit on a chair, often without a back, felling coats"—this is how one union organizer described working conditions to Rose Cohen and other garment sweatshop workers at a union meeting in the 1890s. "Fourteen hours you sit close to the other feller hand [a worker who stitched the inside flaps of seams so that they would lie flat] feeling the heat of her body against yours, her breath on your face. Fourteen hours with your back bent, your eyes close to your work you sit stitching in a dull room often by gas light."[27]

Even after 1910, when shorter, nine- to ten-hour workdays became the rule, many Italian and Jewish women factory workers extended their hours by overtime or taking work home. There was no alternative, they felt, to doing the additional work. They feared losing their jobs if they did not agree to the added work, and they were spurred on to sacrifice by economic pressures at home and the need for extra earnings. Seventeen-year-old Louisa Trentino was able to increase her weekly earnings of six dollars by fifty cents if she worked until 8:30 three nights a week. Her wages were the mainstay of the family: her father was employed irregularly as a hod carrier, and her mother and the young children earned a few dollars making flowers at home every week.[28]

In addition to the long hours and low wages, the various fines and charges for supplies cut into earnings. An Italian corset operator who made about $5.50 a week at piecework had to pay thirty cents a spool for thread and might use one or two spools a week.[29] In garment shops, girls had to rent their chairs and pay twenty-five cents to store their hats in a locker. Being five minutes late often cost an hour's pay, and fines were levied for mistakes on garments. A young Italian girl who trimmed the threads off of neckwear at four dollars a week had to pay for the collar if she made a cut that could not be mended.[30] In other cases, there were charges for breaking a machine: one girl who earned about seven dollars a week at making padding for coats by machine had to pay $1.50 when she broke part of it.[31]

In the factories, working conditions were notoriously unsafe: doors were often locked when work began; fire escapes were inaccessible; stairways were dark and dangerous; and machines and workers were crowded together. The disastrous fire at the Triangle Shirtwaist Company in 1911, which resulted in the death of 146 workers, exposed the terrible overcrowding and dangerous conditions that plagued even the most modern garment factories.

There were some bright spots, however. Work outside the home brought opportunities to make new friends and to speak freely with peers without the presence of elders. Within female factory work groups, immigrant daughters broadened their cultural and social worlds. Susan Glenn writes of young Jewish workers cultivating new tastes in dress and adornment in garment factories and learning about American mores and modern conceptions of romance. Likewise, Italian daughters discussed current boyfriends and the latest romantic novels and magazines with friends on the job.[32]

In fact, the move to New York gave immigrant daughters greater freedom over marriage choice. Old World patterns of arranged marriages began to give way in the context of new ideas and norms in America. In eastern European Jewish communities, matchmakers, or *shadkhens*, typically arranged marriages between a bride and groom, who were wed sight unseen. In New York, some dispensed with the services of matchmakers altogether as young people chose their own mates, often meeting—free of chaperones—at the array of public venues available in America, such as dance halls, amusement parks, lecture halls, and evening schools.[33] When matchmakers were used, they assumed a different role, introducing prospective mates who might reject the match.[34] Italian girls, too, had greater freedom to decide on prospective husbands than in Italy. As among Jews, parental influence remained strong. But no matter how much parents tried to restrict their daughters' social life, many young Italian women met and socialized with single men in the streets and parks, in walks around the block, and on trips to the beach and the movies.[35]

As one historian suggests, young Jewish women's ability to earn their own living allowed them more control over whom they married and the power to resist the services of marriage brokers.[36] As time went on, Jewish daughters also gained more control over their earnings. They still felt obliged to contribute most of their wages to the family fund, yet it became accepted to keep back at least a portion for their own use. By the 1920s, many Jewish parents had begun to believe that their daughters were entitled to some of the money they had earned for clothing and entertainment. Rather than have their daughters hand over all their wages and receive back an allowance, parents now accepted that daughters could decide how much money they required for expenses and then give their mothers the rest. "I just told my mother, 'This is what I need,' " recalled one woman. "And when I had to buy clothing, I went out and bought it." Young Italian women, generally living in poorer families than their Russian Jewish counterparts, were forced to accept for much longer—by one account, into the 1930s and 1940s—the expectation that they turn over their entire paychecks.[37]

### Immigrant Mothers

When newly arrived Rose Cohen asked her father whether everybody in America goes to work early, comes home late, and goes to sleep, day after endless day, he replied, "No, you will get married."[38] His comment reflects the realities for most American women at the time. Married white women were a rarity in the American workplace, with fewer than 5 percent of them working for pay in 1890 and 1900.[39] For the vast majority of Jewish and Italian immigrant women, marriage, typically at around the age of twenty to twenty-two, spelled the end of factory work.[40] In the 1930s and 1940s, some eventually returned to the paid workforce when their children were grown. But immigrant women who came to New York as married adults often never worked outside the home.

In one view, immigrant women's "retirement" to the domestic arena was a blessing.[41] By taking in boarders and doing piecework at home, they contributed much-needed money to the family income while also rearing children and performing time-consuming domestic duties. Cleaning, cooking, and doing the laundry were labor-intensive chores for poor immigrant women who could not afford mechanical conveniences or hired help. The weekly laundry, for example, involved the laborious process of soaking, scrubbing, wringing, rinsing, drying, and ironing clothes. Although women did a tremendous amount of daily housework, they defined their own rhythms. Unlike the factory, where bosses were in control, women exercised real authority and set the pace in their own households. In *Call It Sleep*, Henry Roth's autobiographical novel of his Lower East Side childhood, Aunt Bertha looks forward to marriage: "Ten hours a day in a smothering shop. Ten hours, afraid to pee too often because the foreman might think I was shirking. . . . I don't want to wear my buttocks to the bone sitting in a shop and weave paper flowers and rag flowers all my life."[42]

In the home, immigrant wives nurtured and disciplined children. They also managed the family budget: husbands and sons usually gave them the larger part of their wages each week, and, as we have seen, most daughters handed over their entire paycheck. The role of housewife and mother, moreover, if done well, carried with it respectability and the approval of family and neighbors.

Yet it is important not to glorify immigrant wives' housebound existence. It had a downside as well. Although it may be too strong to say, along with one historian, that immigration disempowered women who came as wives and mothers and intensified their subordination, clearly there were aspects of life in the New World that represented a change for the worse.[43] For many Jewish and Italian women, the journey to New York imposed new constraints, and they were forced to lead more sheltered lives than they had in the Old World.

Jewish women came from a culture that offered them contradictory messages. On the one hand, patriarchy ran deep. Women were excluded from seats of power in the community and from positions in the religious sphere. The most respected people in the social order, religious scholars, were almost without exception men. Boys were encouraged to study rabbinic learning and the texts of the Hebrew Bible, and no sacrifice was too great to send a boy to *yeshiva,* or advanced religious school. "In Russia," said Ida Richter, an immigrant from a small town near Minsk, "a woman was nothing. . . . When my father used to pray in the morning with his prayer shawl, I used to hear him say in Hebrew, 'Thank God, I'm not a woman.' A girl wasn't much."[44]

At the same time, women had a central role in economic life. The ideal Jewish man was a full-time scholar who withdrew from the mundane world while his wife labored to support him. Most men did not have the talent, education, or resources to live up to this ideal, but religious scholars, as the cultural elite, set the tone for the society as a whole. It was no shame for men to lack interest in business and no embarrassment for women to earn a living for her family.[45] "The hard-working scholar's wife acted as a legitimating symbol of the female breadwinner for the masses of east European Jews," Susan Glenn observes. "If the scholar's wife worked, then why not the merchant's, the trader's, the watchmaker's, or the tailor's? And that was the pattern." Women's work, throughout the world of eastern European Jews, was considered necessary and respectable. Says Glenn: "The frequency of married women's work was high enough and had sufficient cultural support to make it something of a norm."[46]

Large numbers of Jewish wives worked in business or trade, sometimes helping in a store formally run by their husbands or keeping a store or stall on their own where they sold food, staples, or household wares. Some women were peddlers who stood in the marketplace or went from house to house selling rolls and bagels and other food they had prepared at home.[47] Others bought small lots of manufactured goods in cities to trade with peasants in the market. Jewish wives, in these circumstances, became tough bargainers. They developed a knowledge of the marketplace and a certain worldliness about the society outside their own communities. In the market, women had a better command of local languages spoken by the peasants—Russian, Hungarian, and Polish—than did the more learned men, and many developed a reputation for being outspoken and aggressive.[48]

The Jewish community itself provided some jobs for women, for example, as attendants at the *mikvah* (ritual bath) or as bakers of matzos at Passover. By the end of the nineteenth century, with the development of factory production in Russia and the movement of many Jews to cities, increasing numbers of young unmarried Jewish women were drawn to artisans' shops and small factories, where they made matches, cigarettes, and other goods. The sewing machine created new opportunities for doing outwork, and thousands of married and single homeworkers made dresses or did other kinds of needlework for contractors, who then distributed the garments to stores. As a last resort, some unmarried girls went into domestic service. When they married, Jewish women rarely took factory jobs or paid work that demanded long hours away from home. Instead, many were involved in various kinds of home-based artisanal or outwork production.

The move to New York altered notions of a married woman's proper role. In Russia, one immigrant woman explained, often "the women made a living for the man." In New York, she added, it was widely acknowledged that "a man of character never let his wife work."[49] The husband was expected to be the main support of his family. A character in Abraham Cahan's novel *The Rise of David Levinsky* tells Levinsky that before he came to America his wife "had a nice little business. She sold feed for horses and rejoiced in the thought that she was married to a man of learning." In this country, however, "instead of supporting him while he read Talmud, as she used to do at home, she persisted in sending him out to peddle. 'America is not Russia,' she said. 'A man must make a living here.' "[50]

Formerly respected for their abilities as breadwinners, married women increasingly stressed their domestic over their economic role. The practical problems of child-care and domestic responsibilities in New York made it hard to work outside the home. Because grandparents seldom migrated, they were not around to help out; older daughters were in school or at work themselves. Household tasks were more demanding in the context of new standards of cleanliness and new acquisitions. Moreover, in the American cultural environment, female labor was seen as a necessary evil to be tolerated only if a family was in difficult economic circumstances or, for single women, as a brief interval between adolescence and marriage. Wives' income-producing activities took place, by and large, in the home and often remained hidden and unacknowledged as "work."[51]

Hardly any Jewish wives worked for wages. In 1880, census materials show only 2 percent of immigrant Russian Jewish households in New York City reporting wives who worked for wages; in 1905, the figure fell to 1 percent.[52] A United States Immigration Commission survey of households in seven cities (including New York) a few years later revealed an average of only 8 percent of Russian Jewish wives in paid employment.[53]

In the early years of the immigration, in the 1880s and 1890s, many Jewish women did piecework at home in the needle trades. After this, the increasing shift of garment production to factories, legislation on tenement manufacture, and competition with lower-paid Italian women who came into the clothing industry sharply cut the participation of Jewish women in the homework market.[54] Taking care of boarders, virtually indistinguishable from other domestic duties, became a more attractive alternative— and the main way Jewish wives contributed to the family income.

According to the Immigration Commission's 1911 study, as many as 56 percent of New York Russian Jewish families had boarders living with them.[55] Rose L. observed that Jewish women did not work outside the home once they were married. "Boarders you had," she recalled; "you worked for them, you cooked for them, you cleaned for them."[56] In Judith Weissman's Lower East Side tenement apartment, two men who worked in the same factory as her father boarded with her family. The two boarders shared a bedroom, while she slept on the couch with her brother—until her father thought she was too old for this. Her brother then moved into the kitchen, where his bed consisted of two chairs placed close together. Even when the family moved to a better apartment, they had three boarders who, in addition to rent, paid thirty-five cents a month for a big dinner every day.[57]

Many immigrant wives helped their husbands in mom-and-pop stores, and some ran the shops on their own. "Minding" the store was considered an extension of a woman's proper role as her husband's helpmate. Often the family lived above or in the back of the store so that wives could run back and forth between the shop counter and the kitchen. "If you had to help out in the store," one immigrant woman said, "you were still at home." Even if the store or stall was physically apart from the family apartment or if wares were peddled on the street, such enterprises had more legitimacy for a Jewish married woman than wage work, because they gave her more independence and greater flexibility regarding child rearing and domestic tasks.[58]

The result of Jewish mothers' work patterns in New York was their "heightened centrality" in the home, where the overwhelming majority did all their work, both paid and unpaid. In his memoirs of his Brownsville childhood, Alfred Kazin recalls how the kitchen, where his mother cooked and sewed, was her life. "All my memories of that kitchen are dominated by the nearness of my mother sitting all day long at her sewing machine. . . . Year by year, as I began to take in her fantastic capacity for labor and her anxious zeal, I realized it was ourselves she kept stitched together."[59]

By and large, married women's lives were more circumscribed in New York. Jewish immigrant mothers did, of course, socialize with friends and neighbors and go out to shop. As the family member most responsible for decisions about household purchases, the Jewish housewife presided over the acquisition of consumption items. Jewish women are said to have excelled in the American custom of bargain hunting as they scoured the Lower East Side in search of goods at low prices.[60] But whereas in eastern Europe, Jewish wives were often the worldly ones, in America their housebound existence made it more difficult to learn the new language and customs.[61] Their husbands picked up English in the workplace, and their daughters learned American ways in factory work groups. Many mothers, however, remained fluent only in Yiddish and felt uncomfortable in new situations outside the Jewish community.[62] They had to depend on their children to teach them American customs or, as a few managed to do, attend night school to learn English.[63]

Jewish wives from small towns and villages, used to doing chores like laundry in the company of other women, now faced the more lonely and difficult task of washing clothing by themselves inside cramped tenement apartments.[64] According to Elizabeth Ewen, housework was generally more demanding in America. In small European towns and villages, women went to the nearest stream or lake once a month to wash clothes; now the laundry was a weekly task. Another example: mattresses in eastern Europe were generally made of straw, and in cold weather feather bedding was common. In America, beds came with mattresses that required sheets and blankets, all of which needed to be washed and aired on a regular basis.[65]

Immigrant wives' income-earning activities rarely represented the major contribution to the family economy. Industrial homework or taking in boarders was not as lucrative as work outside the home, and wives were seen as helping out their husbands in family businesses. From being charged with providing a major portion of the family livelihood in eastern Europe, married women in America were now outearned by their working daughters in the industrial labor force, who emerged as the main female breadwinners in the Jewish family.[66]

Italian immigrant wives also became more housebound in New York, and their wage-earning daughters also earned more than they did. Although they took an active role in the family economy in both Italy and New York, the nature of this participation inevitably changed in significant ways in the New World.

In the rural Sicilian and southern Italian villages immigrants left behind, married women supervised household chores, organized the making of clothes and food preparation, and managed the family budget. Often, they tended animals and tilled the garden, producing food for family consumption and for sale at the local market. Artisans' wives also helped out in the shop. Although it was a mark of poverty for women to work in the fields, wives in poorer families often had no choice but to help as day laborers during harvest periods, picking fruits and nuts, husking almonds, and threshing wheat.[67]

Peasant women's day-to-day work took them out of the house and brought them into contact with people of varying status. Although artisans' wives worked inside the privacy of their homes, the small, dimly lit houses of peasant women made poor workplaces. Whenever the weather allowed, they did their household chores outside, alongside neighbors in the street or courtyard. The Sicilian *cortile*, or shared courtyard outside a group of houses, was, according to one writer, a kind of shared living room.[68] Sicilian peasant wives met as they hauled water from the fountain or distant springs and sat together at open streams laundering clothes. It was not unusual for them to help better-off families with heavier household chores in return for food or money or to sell eggs or other produce to more prosperous neighbors.[69]

When they moved to New York, most Italian wives did not go out to work for wages, although the percentages were higher than for their Jewish counterparts. The 1905 census recorded only 6 percent of immigrant Italian households in New York City with wives employed outside the home, mainly in tailoring shops and textile factories.[70] These figures are probably too low. A 1913 study of Italian women in lower Manhattan found that in more than half (279) of the 515 families where the mother was living at home, she contributed to the family income. As many as a third of the income-earning mothers did factory work, largely in men's and women's clothing and in the flower and feather industries. More than a third did industrial homework; about a fifth kept lodgers and boarders.[71] More Italian than Jewish married women worked in shops outside the home or in formal employment, because their husbands generally earned less.[72] As Kathie Friedman-Kasaba puts it, Italian women's continued participation in "the lowest-paid and most exploitative segments of clothing production owed largely to the low-paid and highly irregular employment available to the Italian immigrant men of their households."[73]

Once they had children, most Italian women earned money by working at home. Although many Italian wives supplemented their husbands' income by taking in boarders, it was a less frequent practice than among Jews.[74] Homework was common. By the first decade of the century, most industrial homeworkers in New York City were Italian. Wherever home garment finishers exist in large numbers, one investigator wrote, "we may be sure that they are Italians. . . . Among the Italians may be found whole blocks that are practically colonies of home finishers."[75] The typical Italian homeworker was in her mid-thirties, and most were between the ages of twenty-one and forty-five.[76] Working in the kitchen or a bedroom, Italian women finished garments or made artificial flowers while raising their children and caring for the house. Children in the family had to pitch in, too. Accounts of homework in the artificial-flower industry describe Italian children of three and four helping make violets by picking apart petals and dipping stems into paste.[77] Older children relieved their mother of the need to walk the few blocks to carry bundles of clothing and boxes of flowers back and forth from the contractor to their homes.

In one Italian family of ten, the father earned $7.00 a week selling lunches in a saloon; the oldest daughter made $6.50 in a box factory; and the sixteen-year-old son brought in $3.00 as a wagon boy. Four children were at school, and two babies were at home. Every member of the family except the father and two babies helped make flowers. The mother worked irregularly during the day, the school children after school hours, and the working daughter and son in the evening. They made three-petaled violets at $.07 cents a gross, earning a total weekly wage of $3.00. They lived in three rooms for which they paid $12.50 a month.[78] The pressure to increase earnings, and the demands of housework, meant that homeworkers often worked late into the night. More than one-third of a group of Italian artificial flower makers reported that they had worked after 10 P.M. the week before, two-thirds of the late-night group having worked past 3:00 A.M. at least once during the week.[79]

Homework paid distinctly less than factory jobs. One study of artificial flower makers in New York found that the average weekly wage for factory workers was $6.72; for home workers it was $4.92, and this represented combined earnings for an average group of more than three workers.[80] Women were well aware that factory jobs paid better, but the demands of caring for young children and household duties, as well as the widely accepted notion that women should leave the workplace after marriage, usually kept them at home. One Italian homeworker with four children under the age of four had worked in a candy factory before she married. "That's better than making flowers," she said, "but we can't go to work after we're married."[81]

Like Jewish immigrant wives, Italian women working at home were more insulated from American ways and language than other family members. One Italian minister of the time wrote of hearing Italian women say "I have been down to America today" to describe going a few blocks outside the Italian enclave.[82] Whereas Andrea Bocci's father frequented a Prince Street saloon every night, her mother never went out: "If one of her friends would be sick, she would go and help them out, but otherwise she would stay at home."[83] Italian, like Jewish, wives visited with neighbors in the halls and stairways, on front stoops, and in their apartments, but they led a more "inside"—more isolated—life than in Italy.

Most household chores, as well as industrial homework, were done within the four walls of their tenement apartments. By 1911, according to the Immigration Commission's report, women in Little Italy did not have to leave their tenement buildings to get water, although a considerable number shared a sink with people in other apartments.[84] Whereas washing in Italy was a social function, in New York it was a task for the individual woman.[85] Laundry was done in the apartment in big tubs filled with water boiled on the kitchen stove. The kitchen was also the place for cooking meals and for doing industrial homework. Women went out to do some of their shopping, but they also often sent children to make purchases for meals as well as to pick up materials from contractors. The move from Sicily to Elizabeth Street, Donna Gabaccia concludes, "limited immigrant women's opportunities to interact with others," and these limitations were a source of dissatisfaction with their new environment.[86]

Even as modern plumbing freed women from some of the more rigorous chores they had known in southern Italy, new standards of living and new household acquisitions complicated housework. "We had no blinds, no curtains and the floors were all made of stone," said one Sicilian woman. "You have no idea how simple life is over there. Here one must wash two or three times a week; over there once a month."[87] New York ovens could not produce a satisfactory Sicilian bread; those who did not buy bread in New York now had to mix the dough and take it to a nearby baker.[88] Certainly, life in America for Italian wives and mothers, like their Jewish counterparts, meant hard work from dawn to dusk, but it was mainly work in the home—and, by and large, unpaid. This is something that would change in radical ways for the immigrant women who came in the next great wave.

## Contemporary Patterns

Today's immigrant women have advantages unknown a century ago. They arrive with different educational and occupational backgrounds than their Jewish and Italian predecessors. More important, the world they live in gives women opportunities and benefits unheard of then.

The very composition of today's immigrant streams gives women a numerical edge. Women immigrants now outnumber men in virtually all of the major groups coming to New York (see table 9). In large part, this is because U.S. immigration law favors the admission of spouses and children as a way to reunite families and has made it easier for certain kinds of workers, like nurses, to get immigrant visas.[89] In the early 1990s, there were ninety-two male immigrants for every hundred females entering New York City, down from ninety-eight males per hundred females in the 1980s. The balance in favor of women is especially striking among Filipino immigrants: in the 1980s, there were sixty-seven males per hundred females in this group; in the early 1990s it was sixty-three per hundred. The Filipino migration stream includes a relatively large proportion of spouses of American citizens. Also, many Filipino women have gained entry on the basis of their occupations in the health-care field.[90]

It is not just that women, rather than men, predominate today. More women come on their own rather than follow in the footsteps of men. The structure of U.S. immigration law, changing gender roles, and economic opportunities for women are all responsible for this trend. Immigrant women's concentration in specific high-demand occupations—like private household work and nursing—has enabled many to play a more

Table 9   Number of Males per 100 Females among Legal Immigrants
Arriving in New York City, 1990–94

| Country of Birth | Males per 100 Females | Country of Birth | Males per 100 Females |
|---|---|---|---|
| Poland | 95 | Trinidad and Tobago | 81 |
| China | 94 | Haiti | 80 |
| Dominican Republic | 93 | India | 80 |
| Former USSR | 90 | Korea | 78 |
| Guyana | 89 | Colombia | 72 |
| Ecuador | 88 | Philippines | 63 |
| Jamaica | 88 | All Immigrants | 92 |

Source: Lobo, Salvo and Virgin 1996: 20, fig. 2.6, based on Annual Immigrant Tape
Files, 1990–1994, U.S. Immigration and Naturalization Service.

pivotal role as pioneer immigrants, establishing beachheads for further immigration.[91]

   In the early years of the new immigration, women's ability to obtain
labor certification enabled many to lead the way. Susan Buchanan describes
how Haitian families in the 1970s often picked a female member to pioneer
the migration process, because women could qualify for labor certification
as domestic workers more easily than men. Getting a tourist visa, it was
felt, was also easier for women; they were seen by immigration officials as
less likely than men to overstay their tourist visas, since they would presumably want to return to their children in Haiti. Once in the United States,
women were a better bet at legalizing their status. They could get domestic
work, which offered the possibility of achieving permanent resident status
through an American sponsor.[92]

   When I studied the Jamaican village of Coco Hill in the late 1960s, many
women had left their families to take jobs in New York as private household
workers.[93] Mrs. Riley, for example, a middle-aged higgler (market woman),
lived on a hill behind the house where I stayed. Soon after I left Jamaica, I
learned that she had moved to New York as a live-in domestic worker. Like
Mrs. Riley, once Jamaican women established themselves in New York,
they frequently sent money and plane tickets for children and sometimes
husbands as well. A few Jamaican women I spoke with in New York in the
1980s told me they had been reluctant to emigrate but were pushed to pave
the way for men. They came first because they, rather than their husbands,
could get an immigrant visa.

   Today, immigrant women are, as a group, more highly educated than at
the turn of the century and include more individuals with professional and

middle-class backgrounds. Compared to rural Italy and the Russian Pale a hundred years ago, the countries from which contemporary immigrants come now offer women greater opportunities for advanced education and professional training. Some groups have an especially high proportion of college-educated women—for example, Koreans, Taiwanese, Indians, and Russian Jews.[94]

Data from the Immigration and Naturalization Service (INS), although limited, show that between 1982 and 1989 a fifth of the working-age immigrant women intending to live in New York City who reported an occupation were in professional, technical, administrative, managerial positions; in the early 1990s, the share in these categories went up to 36 percent.[95] In line with the worldwide growth of clerical occupations over this century, about one in every six immigrant women coming to New York City in the 1980s and 1990s reported an administrative-support occupation such as secretary, typist, or office clerk.[96]

Once in New York, the majority of contemporary immigrant women go out to work. Adult immigrant women are now the main female contributors to the family income, while their teenage daughters are generally in school. This is a pattern found throughout American society. With the expansion of high schools—and colleges—over the course of the century and the rise in the age at which children leave school, women (and men) start working later than they used to.[97] Today's immigrant daughters are often eighteen or older when they enter the labor market full-time, compared to fourteen or fifteen a century ago. Marriage no longer spells a retreat from paid employment outside the home. Industrial homework, while not entirely a thing of the past, is much rarer than in the era of Italian and Jewish immigrants.[98] Now it is socially accepted, even expected, throughout American society that wives and mothers will go out to work.

Figures from the 1990 census show how active immigrant women are in New York City's labor market (see table 10). Overall, 60 percent of New York City's working-age immigrant women were in the labor force. (This compares to 66 percent of New York City's working-age women generally.) At one end, Filipino women, who often came specifically to work in health-care jobs, stand out as having the highest labor-force participation rate at over 85 percent. West Indian women are not far behind, with rates in the range of 70–80 percent. Dominicans come out near the bottom, with 52 percent in the work force. In trying to explain the different rates among Caribbean immigrants, Sherri Grasmuck and Ramón Grosfoguel argue that Dominican women's lower levels of education and limited English language skills have made it more difficult for them to find

Table 10    Labor-Force Participation for Female Immigrants Aged 16 to 65 in
New York City, 1990

| Country of Birth | Female Participation in Labor Force (%) | Country of Birth | Female Participation in Labor Force (%) |
|---|---|---|---|
| Philippines | 87.0 | Ecuador | 61.6 |
| Jamaica | 79.5 | India | 59.9 |
| Trinidad | 77.5 | Korea | 59.8 |
| Haiti | 76.3 | Dominican Republic | 51.9 |
| Guyana | 70.7 | Former USSR | 51.9 |
| Colombia | 66.3 | Italy | 50.1 |
| China | 65.6 | | |
| Poland | 63.9 | Total of all foreign born[1] | 60.2 |

*Source:* Kasinitz and Vickerman 1995, based on U.S. Bureau of the Census, Public Use
Microdata Sample, 1990.

[1] Includes island-born Puerto Ricans.

jobs—especially jobs that pay enough to cover the costs of child care. Because Jamaican women arrive with English and, on average, higher educational levels, they have better employment prospects. They are also more disposed to go out to work, because they come from a society with a strong tradition of female employment: almost 70 percent of women in Jamaica were in the work force in 1990, compared to only 15 percent in the Dominican Republic.[99]

As among men, there is enormous variety in the kinds of jobs occupied by female immigrants in New York City; a good many have professional and managerial positions, while others end up in low-level service and factory work. Census data for 1990 on immigrant women in the labor force who arrived in the 1980s show this variation. Twenty-seven percent of women from Asia, 13 percent from the Caribbean, and 10 percent from Central and South America were classified as professionals and managers; at the same time, 21 percent of Asians, 14 percent from the Caribbean, and 23 percent from South and Central America were operators.[100]

That many immigrant women are able to obtain professional and managerial jobs is not surprising given the human capital they bring with them. Unfortunately, as among men, many who held professional or white-collar jobs in their home society experience downward mobility when they arrive in New York. Without American-recognized training, English proficiency, or green cards, highly qualified migrant women are often consigned, at least temporarily, to relatively low-level positions when they arrive. Many West Indian private household workers I interviewed in my research, for example, had been teachers and clerical workers back home; some, who used to employ domestics themselves, experienced what Maxine Margolis has called the transition from "mistress to servant." [101] A number of Haitian and Hispanic aides in the nursing home I studied were full-fledged nurses before they emigrated, but their qualifications were not recognized here, and language problems stood in the way of passing the requisite licensing exams to practice nursing in New York.

In a time-worn pattern, women in each immigrant group gravitate in large numbers to particular occupations. Thus, as we saw in the last chapter, one finds large concentrations of West Indian women in the health-care field as well as the ubiquitous West Indian nanny; many Dominican and Chinese, and recently Mexican and Ecuadorian, women work in garment factories. The Chinese are garment workers par excellence. Over half of immigrant Chinese women who work in New York City are in the needle trades, virtually all as sewing machine operators. The entire Chinese garment industry, Min Zhou writes, has been turned into a female occupation. More than 80 percent of Chinese immigrant workers in Chinatown's garment industry are women, most married and with children.[102]

## Outside Work: Blessing or Burden?

For most immigrant women today, work outside the home is both a blessing and a burden. It gives wives and mothers the ability to obtain a kind of independence and power that was beyond the reach of their Jewish and Italian sisters a century ago and beyond their own reach before migration. Less happily, wage work is a source of additional pressures, constraints, and burdens.

That wage work has, in many ways, improved the position of substantial numbers of migrant women in New York is not just the perception of the women themselves. From the outside looking in, it is clear that migrant women often gain greater independence, personal autonomy, and influence as a result of earning a regular wage for the first time, earning a higher wage than in the sending society, or making a larger contribution to the family economy than previously. How much improvement women experience depends to a large degree on their role in production and their social status in the home country as well as on their economic role in New York. What is important is that, for the majority of migrant women, the move to New York and their involvement in work here lead to gains in some domains of their lives, particularly the household.

In cases where women did not earn an income or earned only a small

supplementary income prior to migration, the gains that come with regular wage work in New York are especially striking. The much cited case
of Dominican women fits this pattern. Now that so many Dominican immigrant women work for wages—often for the first time—and contribute a larger share of the family income, they have more authority in the
household and greater self-esteem. They use their wages, observes Patricia
Pessar, "to assert their right to greater autonomy and equality within the
household."[103]

In New York, Dominican women begin to expect to be copartners in
"heading" the household, a clear change from more patriarchal arrangements in the Dominican Republic. "We are both heads," said one woman,
echoing the sentiments of many other Dominican women in New York. "If
both the husband and wife are earning salaries then they should equally
rule the household. In the Dominican Republic it is always the husband
who gives the orders in the household. But here when the two are working, the woman feels herself the equal of the man in ruling the home."[104]
In a telling comment, a Dominican migrant visiting her home village told
her cousin about New York: "Wait till you get there. You'll have your own
paycheck, and I tell you, he [your husband] won't be pushing you around
there the way he is here."[105]

The organization of the household budget is in fact more equal in New
York. In the Dominican Republic, men generally controlled the household budget even when wives and daughters put in income on a regular or
semiregular basis. Commonly, men doled out an allowance to their wives,
who were responsible for managing the funds to cover basic household
expenses. The men had the last word when it came to decisions about long-
term and costly outlays. When women contributed income, it was used
for "luxuries" rather than for staples, reinforcing the notion that the man
was the breadwinner. In New York, Pessar found that husbands, wives,
and working children usually pool their income; they each put a specific
amount of their wages or profits into a common fund for shared household expenses such as food, rent, and utilities. Some also pool the rest of
their paychecks; in other cases, household members keep the remainder
of their incomes for personal expenses and savings. With this kind of arrangement, women's contributions are no longer seen as supplementary
and men's as essential. As men become more involved in developing strategies for stretching the food budget, they also begin to appreciate more fully
the skills women bring to these tasks. How critical women's wage work is
to these new arrangements is brought out by what happens when women
significantly reduce their contributions to the household budget, either

in New York or when they return to the Dominican Republic. The man usually asserts his dominance once again by allocating a household allowance to his wife and reducing her authority over budgetary decisions.

No wonder Dominican women are eager to postpone or avoid returning to their homeland, where social pressures and an unfavorable job market would probably mean their retirement from work and a loss of new-found gains. One strategy to prolong their families' stay in the United States is to maximize expenditures on expensive durable goods like appliances, furniture, and automobiles; these purchases not only make life more comfortable in New York but also reduce the amount of savings available for a return to the Dominican Republic.[106]

Of course, many immigrant women, including some Dominicans, had regular salaries before emigration. Even these women often feel a new kind of independence in New York, because jobs in this country pay more than most women could ever earn at home and increase their contribution to the family economy. Many Jamaican women I interviewed, for example, had white-collar jobs as secretaries, clerks, or teachers before they emigrated. Still, they said they had more financial control and more say in family affairs in New York, where their incomes are so much larger. "We were brought up to think we have to depend on a man, do this for a man, listen to a man," said a New York secretary. "But here you can be on your own, more independent." Many told me that in Jamaica women usually have to depend on their husbands, whereas in New York they can "work their own money." Also, for those with training, there is a wider range of good jobs available. And there are better opportunities for additional training and education than in Jamaica, something that holds true for those from other Latin American and Caribbean countries as well.

The sense of empowerment that comes from earning a wage—or a higher wage—and having greater control over what one earns comes out in studies of many different groups. Paid work for Chinese garment workers, according to one report, not only contributes to their families' economic well-being but also has "created a sense of confidence and self-fulfillment which they may never have experienced in traditional Chinese society. 'My husband dares not look down on me,' one woman said; 'he knows he can't provide for the family by himself.' " Or as another put it: "I do not have to ask my husband for money, I make my own." For many Salvadoran women, the ability to earn wages and decide how they should be used is something new. As one woman explained: "Here [in the U.S.] women work just like the men. I like it a lot because managing my own money I feel independent. I don't have to ask my husband for money but in El Salvador, yes, I would have to. Over there women live dependent on their husbands. You have to walk behind him." Or listen to a Trinidadian woman of East Indian descent: "Now that I have a job I am independent. I stand up here as a man." [107]

The female-first migration pattern involving adult married women that is common in some groups reinforces the effects of wage earning on women's independence. Many women who have lived and worked in New York without their husbands become more assertive; one Dominican woman noted that she had changed "after so many years of being on my own, being my own boss." [108] One study suggests that Asian men who move to the United States as their wives' dependents often have to subordinate their careers, at least initially, to those of their wives, since the women have already established themselves in this country. [109]

Work outside the home in New York brings about another change that women appreciate. Many men now help out more *inside* the home than before they moved to New York. Of course, this is not inevitable. Cultural values in different groups as well as the availability of female relatives to lend a hand influence the kind of household help men provide. A study of the division of labor in Taiwanese immigrant households found that, as in Taiwan, men who held working-class jobs or owned small businesses did little around the house. [110] Korean men, staunch supporters of patriarchal family values and norms, generally still expect their wives to serve them and resist performing household chores like cooking, dishwashing, and doing the laundry. Such resistance is more effective when the wife's mother or mother-in-law lives in the household, a not infrequent occurrence in Korean immigrant families. Yet much to their consternation, Korean men in New York with working wives often find themselves helping out with household work more than they did in Korea—and wives often make more demands on them to increase their share of the work. [111]

Research on a number of Latin American and Caribbean groups shows that when wives are involved in productive work outside the home, the organization of labor within it changes. [112] We are not talking about a drastic change in the household division of labor or the emergence of truly egalitarian arrangements. Indeed, Latin American and Caribbean women strongly identify as wives and mothers and like being in charge of the domestic domain. What they want—and what they often get—is more help from men. Mainly, men oblige because they have little choice. Evidence also suggests that women's, and men's, conceptions of what men should do in the household begin to shift in the immigrant context.

West Indian men are definitely more helpful in the household than they were in the Caribbean. There men hardly ever did housework, even when their wives had cash-earning activities. Work back home did not always take women out of the house for long periods. In the West Indies, neighbors and kin, especially mothers and sisters, frequently helped with minding the children. Those with salaried jobs employed domestics and nannies to cook, clean, and watch their children.

Although West Indian women in New York still do most of the cooking, cleaning, shopping, and washing, men often help out with this "women's work." However much they resent pitching in, men recognize that there is no alternative when their wives work and their children (particularly daughters) are not old enough to lend a hand. "If she's working, we both chip in," remarked one Trinidadian man.[113] Working women simply cannot shoulder all of the domestic responsibilities expected of them, and they do not have relatives available to help. Even if kin live nearby, they are usually busy with work and their own household chores. Wives' wages are a necessary addition to the family income, and West Indians cannot afford to hire household help, which is much more expensive here. "In order to have a family life here," said a middle-class Trinidadian woman, "[my husband] realizes he has to participate not only in the housework but in the child-rearing too. It's no longer the type of thing where he comes home and the maid is there, having prepared the dinner. . . . Here if you're going to have a household, he has to participate. He has to pick up the children, or take them to the babysitter, or come home and begin the dinner."[114] Several Jamaican men I met in New York—exceptions to be sure—even served as the main family cooks.

West Indian couples with young children often arrange their shifts so that the husband can look after the children while the wife works. I interviewed a number of Jamaican men in New York who worked night shifts and stayed at home with the children during the day. "In Jamaica, oh please," a Jamaican nurse told me, "that was slavery. Bring the man his dinner and his slippers, do the laundry, you're kidding. Not anymore." In New York, her husband does the laundry, makes the children's breakfast, and, in the past, got up at night to feed and change the babies.

More than behavior changes. As men become accustomed to doing more around the house, their notions of what tasks are appropriate—or expected—often also shift. Research shows that Dominican and Jamaican men and women believe that when both partners have jobs, and daughters are too young to help, husbands should pitch in with such tasks as shopping, dishwashing, and child care. Women tend to view their husband's help as a moral victory;[115] men accept their new duties, however reluctantly.

Although the exigencies of immigrant life—women working outside the

home, a lack of available relatives to assist, and an inability to hire help—
are mainly responsible for men's greater participation in household tasks,
American cultural beliefs and values have an influence, too.[116] Many of the
Dominicans whom Patricia Pessar and Sherri Grasmuck spoke to claimed
that they self-consciously patterned their more egalitarian relations on
what they believed to be the dominant American model. They saw this
change as both modern and a sign of progress. One Dominican man and
his wife said that soon after they were both working, they realized that "if
both worked outside the house, both should work inside as well. Now that
we are in the United States, we should adopt Americans' ways."[117] Whatever men think, immigrant women may feel they can make more demands
on their husbands in this country, where the dominant norms and values
back up their claims for men to help out.

In addition to the independence, power, and autonomy that wages
bring, there are the intrinsic satisfactions from work itself. Women in professional and managerial positions gain prestige from their positions and
often have authority over others on the job. Certainly, this was true of the
immigrant nurses in the nursing home I studied. The registered nurses
were proud of their professional achievements, received deference from
nursing aides below them, and exercised enormous authority in their units.

Many women in lower-level work also get a sense of satisfaction from
doing their job well and from the new skills they have learned in New York.
Dominican garment workers take pride in meeting the rigorous demands
of the workplace, and many immigrant women who do "caregiving work"
in private homes or institutions get enormous pleasure from giving good
care and from feeling needed and becoming close to their charges.[118] "I like
to help people," said a Jamaican woman who cared for a frail elderly couple
on a live-in basis. "People don't realize how hard it is to work in the home
and deal with sick people. Have to please them, make them comfortable,
keep them happy. I like to work and I love my job. I may not be an R.N. but
I help people."[119] Deep attachments often develop between West Indian
babysitters and the children they look after, and I found that many immigrant nursing home aides were close to elderly patients whose needs they
saw to day after day.[120]

An important aspect of work is the sociability involved. In factories,
hospitals, and offices, women make friends and build up a storehouse of experiences that enrich their lives and conversations. Indeed, when women
are out of work, they often complain of boredom and isolation. Mrs. Chow,
a Chinese garment worker, said that when she was laid off, "I had too much
housework to do and I felt even busier than when I worked. Sometimes I

get frustrated if I am confined at home and don't see my co-workers."[121] Dominican women say that when they are laid off they feel isolated at home; they miss not only the income but also socializing with workmates and the bustle of the streets and subways.[122] Typically, informal work cultures develop on the job that make work more interesting and liven up the day. Workers often chat and joke while they work and socialize at lunch and on breaks. Sometimes, they celebrate weddings or birthdays during free time or take up collections for sick co-workers. In the nursing home I studied, workers had formed a number of savings groups among themselves, with regular weekly contributions. Nursing aides also routinely lent each other a hand in difficult chores. In general, friendships formed on the job may extend outside the bounds of the workplace as women visit and phone each other, attend parties, and go on shopping jaunts with co-workers.[123]

Just as most immigrant women are in the labor force, they expect their adult daughters to follow suit. They have career aspirations for their daughters, whom they hope will move into higher-status and better-paying jobs than their own. Compared to a century ago, today's immigrant parents are less likely—indeed, are unlikely—to ask daughters to sacrifice their education for the sake of brothers, although an educational double standard may still prevail in some groups in terms of educational expectations and the way family resources are allocated for private schools or college. Some Indian parents, for example, retain the belief that a woman with too much education will have difficulty getting married. There are cases where parents insist that sons attend four-year colleges while daughters are channeled into two-year institutions.[124] In other groups, however, education may be considered more important for women than for men—or at least as important.[125] Korean parents in New York now consider girls' educations as important as boys', a major change from Korea, where boys were given preference. Indeed, Korean immigrant mothers' emphasis on equal educational opportunity for boys and girls, Pyong Gap Min argues, is partly a reaction to the unequal treatment they received in Korea and their awareness that women face fewer social barriers and have more career opportunities in this country.[126]

Although the focus here is on the benefits that immigrant women reap from working outside the home, the move to New York has improved their status as women in other ways that are particular to the current period.

In the wake of liberalized legislation, divorce is often easier and more acceptable in New York than it was in the home country. Despite the increasing prevalence of divorce in Taiwan, Chen explains, it is still very embarrassing for a divorced woman there to face family and friends. In New York, Taiwanese divorced women can take care of themselves; "no one will question your past, and you can restart life here." [127] Divorce, of course, is a risky business for immigrant women, since without the husband's financial contributions their standard of living is in jeopardy and making ends meet becomes more of a struggle. Female-headed households typically have lower incomes and higher poverty rates than those with two working partners.

Still, better wage-earning opportunities in this country and the availability of social welfare benefits have meant that women can often manage on their own more easily than back home. And certainly more easily than they could have a century ago, before government welfare programs were vastly expanded. [128] (Although 1996 federal welfare legislation curtailed access to these programs for most noncitizens, some benefits have since been restored.) Some immigrant women are more willing to make demands on their husbands than they would have done in the old country—and insist on more egalitarian relations—because they know that government economic supports are on hand if the union breaks up. Also, they are spurred on by American norms that emphasize the husband as a marriage partner who helps out around the house and makes decisions in concert with his wife. Moreover, they may be less willing to tolerate severe abuse from their spouses in New York than they would have been before migration, because they know that the American legal and social service systems will support them. [129]

Women from some countries see the chance *not* to work as a gain. According to Fran Markowitz, many émigré women from the former Soviet Union are freed from the triple role of worker, wife, and mother in New York because they are eligible, as refugees, for government assistance—another benefit not available a hundred years ago—or because their husbands earn enough for them to stay at home. While some Soviet émigré women feel depressed and useless because they no longer need to work full-time, others are glad to be able to take time off to care for young children. Couples who would never have dreamed of having more than one child in the Soviet Union may now have two or three. [130]

Or consider the case of Dominican women on their own with young children. In the Dominican Republic, the lack of a system of public assistance increased the pressure on women without a man in the household to enter the labor force; in New York, Dominican women with young children and no spouse in residence have often preferred to seek public assistance than take the low-paying jobs available, since they could then care for their children (rather than spend a significant part of their wages on child care) and perhaps advance their own education and obtain future marketable skills.[131]

For many immigrant women, housework and other domestic chores are easier in New York now that they can afford modern appliances like washing machines, vacuum cleaners, and microwave ovens, which were luxuries in their home countries. In the case of the Russian Jewish émigrés studied by Fran Markowitz in the 1980s, cooking, cleaning, and shopping, among other tasks, were less time-consuming than they were in Russia, where keeping a family fed often meant standing on lines for hours each day just to purchase basic foodstuffs, bribing grocery-store workers, and keeping abreast of news about special black-market shipments.[132]

Modern-day New York also offers many immigrant women greater scope outside the home than was possible before. They may be able to engage in certain activities that were unacceptable or at least unusual for women in their home countries, thereby contributing to their sense that living abroad offers a new kind of freedom. Maxine Margolis describes a scene she observed in a Queens nightclub one Friday night, where a group of five Brazilian women in their forties and fifties sat at the bar drinking, smoking, and talking among themselves. Occasionally, the women were asked to dance by male patrons of the establishment. "What was so memorable about the scene is that it could not have occurred in these women's native land. In Brazil, it would be unthinkable for 'respectable' middle-aged women from the middle strata of society to go to a bar or a nightclub 'alone,' meaning without appropriate escorts."[133] Several Jamaican women I met spoke of the new opportunities to expand their cultural horizons in New York through the theater, concerts, and films—and of the opportunity to pursue their interests and lead their lives without the eyes, and censure, of the local community so closely upon them.[134] Dominican women, too, say they feel liberated in their ability to travel widely on their way to and from work or to other activities without people gossiping that "they spend too much time away from their homes . . . [and] think[ing] the woman is up to no good."[135] And while women may have negotiated with bureaucratic institutions on behalf of the household in the home country, this mediating work takes on new dimensions here. Dealing with public institutions like welfare agencies, schools, and the health-care system often expands the scope of women's activities and broadens their networks and skills.[136]

If wage work enables many immigrant women to expand their influence and independence, these gains often come at a price. Indeed, wage work in New York brings burdens as well as benefits to immigrant women and may create new sets of demands and pressures for them both on the job and at home. Moreover, despite changes in women's status in New York, premigration gender-role patterns and ideologies do not simply fade away; they continue to affect the lives of migrant women, often in ways that constrain and limit them. Cultural ideals about gender and spousal relations held at the point of origin, observes Pierrette Hondagneu-Sotelo in another context, influence the outcome of the changing balance of economic resources in New York.[137]

Wage work, as immigrant women commonly explain, is not an option but a necessity for their family's welfare. As one Korean woman put it: "Without me helping out economically, it is absolutely impossible to survive in New York City."[138] Wage work typically brings a host of difficulties for women. On the job, women's wages are still generally lower than men's. In addition, women are limited in their choice of work owing to gender divisions in the labor market—often confined to menial, low-prestige, and poorly paid jobs that can be described as industrialized homework. Working in the ethnic economy does not help most women either. Recent studies of Chinese, Dominican, and Colombian women in New York who work in businesses owned by co-ethnics show that they earn low wages and have minimal benefits and few opportunities for advancement.[139] Indeed, Greta Gilbertson argues that some of the success of immigrant small-business owners and workers in the ethnic enclave is due to the marginal position of immigrant women. The many Korean women who work in family businesses are, essentially, unpaid family workers without an independent source of income. Although many are working outside the home for the first time, they are typically thought of as "helpers" to their husbands; the husband not only legally owns the enterprise but also usually controls the money, hires and fires employees, and represents the business in Korean business associations.[140]

For many immigrant women, working conditions are extremely difficult. Among the worst are those endured by garment workers, who often have to keep up a furious pace in cramped conditions in noisy lofts. Despite federal and state laws, some sweatshops are physically dangerous, located in windowless buildings with sealed fire exits and broken sprinkler systems. Often paid by the piece, many women do not even make the minimum wage and are forced to work overtime at straight-time wages if they want to keep their jobs.[141]

Domestic workers often have to deal with humiliating or demeaning treatment from employers as well as long hours, low pay, and lack of benefits.[142] For those who clean houses, there are the dangers that come with using noxious and often toxic substances as well as the sheer physical strenuousness of the job. House cleaners, like many Salvadoran women on Long Island, have to piece together a number of daily cleaning jobs so they can keep busy all week. Some immigrant women with full-time jobs have more than one position to make ends meet. I know many West Indian women, for example, who care for an elderly person on the weekend to supplement what they earn from a five-day child-care job. Others supplement their income through informal economic activities like selling homemade food or beauty products in various cosmetic lines.

Added to this, of course, are the demands of child care and the burdens of household work. Going outside to earn means that child rearing is more complicated than at the turn of the century, when married women typically worked at home. Only very affluent immigrants can afford to hire maids or housekeepers, and female relatives, if present in New York, are often busy at work themselves. Occasionally, women can juggle shifts with their husbands so that one parent is always around, and sometimes an elderly mother or mother-in-law is on hand to help out.[143] Many working women pay to leave their children with babysitters or, less often, in day-care centers.[144] Child-care constraints are clearly a factor limiting women to low-paid jobs with flexible schedules. One reason Chinese women gravitate to garment shops is the flexible hours, a benefit provided by Chinese contractors in part to compensate for the miserable wages. In Chinatown, workers can take time off during the day to drop off and pick up their children at school, buy groceries, or nurse their babies. They are even allowed to bring their babies to the workshop, and school-aged children are allowed into the garment shop after school. For Mrs. Chow, who had a four-year-old daughter and an eighteen-month-old son, the flexible schedule in her factory made it possible for her to manage a job. She could take time off during the day to go to the babysitter's house to see her baby. When the children were sick, she could take a day or two off or take the garment work home.[145] Not all women are so lucky, however. Child-care responsibilities may prevent women from working full-time—or, in some cases, at all. Some women leave their young children with relatives in the home country so as to manage work more easily, a common pattern among West Indian live-in household workers.[146]

Immigrant women of all social classes have the major responsibilities for household chores as well as child rearing, so that a grueling day at work is often preceded or followed by hours of cooking, cleaning, and washing. "I'm always working" is how Mrs. Darius, a Haitian nursing home aide with eight children, put it. Although her husband, a mechanic, does not help much around the house ("Some men are like that"), Mrs. Darius gets assistance from her mother, who lives with her. Still, there is a lot to do. "I have to work 24 hours. When I go home, I take a nap, then get up again; sometimes I get up at two in the morning, iron for the children, and go back to sleep."

Korean working wives, according to Pyong Gap Min, suffer from overwork and stress owing to the heavy demands on their time. After doing their work outside the home, they put in, on average, an additional twenty-five hours a week on housework, compared to seven hours contributed by their husbands. Altogether, working wives spend seventy-six hours a week on the job and doing housework—twelve more hours than men do. Although professional husbands help out more around the house than other Korean men, their wives still do the lion's share.[147] Kim Ai- Kyung, the wife of a physician, has run a boutique in New Jersey for more than thirteen years. She explained that she has not visited her family in Korea for many years because she cannot leave her husband and children alone: "The older boy is in medical school, and the younger one is working at a bank in New York City. But, when they come home, they still don't even open the refrigerator to get their own food or drink. I always serve them. And my husband—he does not know anything about the house. He doesn't even know how to make . . . instant noodle soup. If I went to Korea, he would starve to death."[148]

Or take the case of Antonia Duarte, a Dominican mother of three who put in a seventeen-hour day. At 5:00 A.M., she was up making breakfast and lunch for the family. She woke her three children at 6:00, got them dressed, fed, and ready for school and then took them to the house of a friend, who cared for the four-year-old and oversaw the older children's departure to and return from school. By 7:15, Antonia was on the subway heading for the lamp factory, where she worked from 8:00 A.M. to 4:30 P.M. five days a week. She collected her children a little after 5:00 and began preparing the evening meal when she got home. She didn't ask her two oldest children to help—the oldest is a twelve-year-old girl—because "I'd rather they begin their homework right away, before they get too tired." Her husband demanded a traditional meal of rice, beans, plantains, and meat, which could take as long as two hours to prepare. She and the children ate together at 7:00, but her husband often did not get back from socializing with his friends until later. He expected Antonia to reheat the food and serve it upon his arrival. By the time she finished her child-care and other domestic responsibilities, it was 11:30 or 12:00. Like other Dominican women, she explained that if she did not manage the children and household with a high level of competence, her husband would threaten to prohibit her from working.[149]

Women in groups where strong traditional patriarchal codes continue to exert an influence may experience other difficulties. In some better-off Dominican families, wives are pressured by husbands to stay out of the work force altogether as a way to symbolize their household's respectability and elevated economic status.[150] It is still a point of pride for a Latin American man to say that his wife doesn't work; part of making it into the middle class is seeing to it that the women in the household remain at home.[151] In many groups, working women who are now the family's main wage earners may feel a special need to tread carefully in relations with their husbands so as to preserve the appearance of male dominance.[152] Indeed, one study shows professional Korean women making conscious attempts to keep their traditional lower status and to raise the position of their husbands by reducing their incomes. A nurse explained: "My basic salary exceeds his. If I do overtime, my income will be too much—compared to his—and so, when overtime work falls on me, I just try so hard to find other nurses to cover my overtime assignments. . . . By reducing my income, I think, my husband can keep his ego and male superiority."[153]

Finally, there is the fact that women's increased financial authority and independence can lead to greater discord with their spouses. Conflicts often develop when men resent, and try to resist, women's new demands on them; in some cases, the stresses ultimately lead to marital breakups. Special problems may develop when men are unemployed or unsuccessful at work and become dependent on women's wage-earning abilities—yet still insist on maintaining the perquisites of male privilege in the household.[154] In extreme cases, the reversal of gender roles can lead to serious physical abuse for women at the hands of their spouses.[155] Indeed, in some instances, increased isolation from relatives in the immigrant situation creates conditions for greater abuse by husbands, who are freer of the informal controls that operated in their home communities.[156]

## Immigrant Women in Two Eras

Today's immigrant women, it is clear, are not simply a copy of earlier arrivals in modern dress. They come with what sociologists call different human capital—many with more education and more training than immigrant women of a century ago. Moreover, since the last great wave, there have been enormous changes in the status and role of women in American society.

Contemporary immigrant women benefit from, among other changes, the expansion of educational and employment opportunities for women, from liberalized legislation concerning divorce and gender discrimination, and from social welfare programs that have made it easier for them to manage on their own. Gone are the days when women had to boil pots of water for laundry on the kitchen stove or depend on coal for cooking and heating their apartments. The widespread availability of modern labor-saving devices has made housework less taxing than it used to be. The growing number of female officeholders, professionals, and high-level managers also makes a difference, if only because the notion filters down to all immigrant women that they—or their daughters—can aspire to such roles. Indeed, immigrant women now populate the professions to an extent that would have seemed unimaginable a century ago.

Women's involvement in the world of work is critical to understanding why moving to New York has been liberating in many ways for so many contemporary immigrants—and why, at least for immigrant mothers and wives, it was more limiting in the past. Jewish and Italian women came to New York at a time when there was a social stigma attached to the wife who worked for wages outside the home; the mother's wage was considered a "final defense against destitution," to be undertaken only on account of severe economic or family emergency.[157] Often, Jewish and Italian immigrant wives found themselves more cloistered in their homes than in the Old World. The work they did to earn money—taking in boarders and industrial homework—did not lead to reallocating household tasks among other household members. Because virtually all their income-producing activities were done in the home, these activities ended up preserving and intensifying the gender division of housework and child care.[158] The main female wage earners in the family, immigrant daughters, handed over their pay to their mothers, who, as managers of daily financial affairs, used it for running the household.

Now that female wage earners are typically wives and mothers, they have more leverage in the household than working younger daughters once had. Indeed, adult women's employment has transformed their family relationships more so than in the earlier generation. Because an immigrant working mother today is often absent from the home for forty or forty-five hours a week, or sometimes longer, someone must fill her place—or at least help out. Often, it is her husband. Women's labor force participation, in other words, frequently increases husbands' participation in household work and leads to changes in the balance of power in immigrant families. Daughters in modern-day families, growing up in an era when female labor-force participation is increasing and the working mother is common-place, may go even further in redefining their family roles as they enter the labor force for an extended period of their lives.[159]

As the main female wage earners in the family, today's immigrant mothers contribute a larger share of the household income than they did early in the century. Their regular access to wages—and to higher wages—in the United States often gives them greater autonomy and power than they had before migration. Working outside the home also broadens their social horizons and enhances their sense of independence. "A woman needs to work," said one Cuban sales worker. "She feels better and more in con-trol of herself. She doesn't have to ask her husband for money. It seems to me that if a woman has a job, she is given more respect by her husband and her children."[160] Many contemporary immigrant women would heartily agree. For a good number, the opportunities to work—and to earn more money—represent a major gain that has come with the move to New York.

If immigrant wives and mothers have come a long way in the past hun-dred years, it is clear that they are not fully emancipated. Not only do they suffer from gender inequalities that are a feature of American society gener-ally, but important vestiges of premigration gender ideologies and role pat-terns may place additional constraints on them. Wage labor, as one schol-arly observer puts it, both oppresses and liberates immigrant women.[161] Many work in low-status, dead-end positions that pay less than men's jobs. Immigrant working wives in all social classes experience a heavy double burden, since the household division of labor remains far from equal. If husbands help out with domestic burdens, they may do so only grudgingly, if at all, and it is women, more than men, who make work choices to ac-commodate and reflect family and child-care needs. While many, perhaps most, immigrant women feel that the benefits of wage work outweigh the drawbacks, others would, if they could afford it, prefer to remain at home. As a Korean woman who worked as a manicurist in a nail salon fifty-four hours a week said: "If my husband makes enough money for the family, why should I take this burden?"[162]

A comparison of women in the two eras should not, in short, blind us to the barriers and difficulties immigrant women still face. Improvements in women's status go hand in hand with the persistence of male privilege. At the same time, the comparison is a powerful reminder, once more, that the New York we have lost, to paraphrase Peter Laslett, was hardly a utopia for immigrant women and that working outside the home, for all its problems, has brought significant benefits to women who arrive today.[163]

# CHAPTER 5

# The Sting of Prejudice

*A*n important and conspicuous difference between then and now is that immigrants today are, in significant numbers, people of color, whereas those at the turn of the century were, in the main, phenotypically white. There are also vast differences in the New York that immigrants find when they arrive. In 1900, blacks made up a little under 2 percent of the city's population, and an even smaller proportion were Asian or Hispanic. Immigrants now enter a city that was on the receiving end of an enormous internal migration. A massive flow of African Americans from the South between World War I and the 1960s and a huge migration of Puerto Ricans after World War II transformed New York's racial dynamics. By 1960, the city was more than one-fifth black and Hispanic. In 1998, the figure was up to 57 percent, and of that group about four out of ten were still of native stock.[1]

Not only have the realities of New York's racial composition changed, but the very idea of race is different, too. Today, New Yorkers of eastern and southern European ancestry are considered fully and unquestionably white. They didn't look that way, however, to commentators at the turn of the century. There was considerable prejudice against Jews and Italians, and, to a surprising degree, it was expressed in racial terms.

Racial differences may seem permanent and immutable—as if they are inevitable and "natural"—but, in fact, race is a changeable perception. Indeed, the awesome power of race is related to its ability to pass as a feature of the natural landscape.[2] Races are not fixed biological categories, and dividing human populations into "races," as physical anthropologists have shown, has no basis in genetics.[3] Regardless of its dubious roots in biology, however, race "is real because, to paraphrase W. I. Thomas, people act as though it is real and thus it has become real in its consequences."[4] Race, in other words, is a social and cultural construction, and what is important is how physical characteristics or traits are interpreted within particular social contexts and are used to define categories of people as inferior or superior.[5] At the turn of the century, Jews and Italians were seen as belonging to different races—and one of the current groups, Asians, is undergoing a contemporary metamorphosis.

Another window on current racial perceptions involves the way West Indians and Hispanics are seen. The experiences of West Indians, as blacks of African descent, are testimony to the durability of the black-white divide in American society. As for Hispanics, although they share strong cultural and linguistic similarities, and often come from the same sending countries, racially they are extremely diverse. The way they are seen sheds light on their self-perceptions and the way the culture as a whole views racial and, just as important, class distinctions.

Last, the whole question of racial prejudice is complicated by enormous changes in the nature of public discourse on racial issues. What was acceptable and commonplace in 1900 would be considered unthinkable today. In fact, it is arguable that the only totally prohibited form of public discourse in America is overt language that deals with racial and ethnic stereotypes.

## When Jews and Italians Were Inferior Races

It seems obvious that Jews and Italians are white, but to many Americans, this was not clear at the time of the last great immigration wave. Then, the white population was seen as divided into many sharply distinguishable races. Jews and Italians were thought of as racially distinct in physiognomy, mental abilities, and character. A common belief was that they belonged to inferior "mongrel" races that were polluting the country's Anglo-Saxon or Nordic stock.

Contemporary historians have coined phrases like "in-between peoples," "probationary whites," and "not-yet-white ethnics" to describe Jews' and Italians' ambiguous racial status.[6] On the one hand, southern and eastern European immigrants were typically placed above African and Asian Americans. Indeed, the courts consistently allowed Jews and Italians to be naturalized as "white" citizens and almost as consistently turned down non-European applicants as "nonwhite." On the other hand, eastern and southern European immigrants were seen as below other "white" people.[7] In the essay "How Did Jews Become White Folks?" Karen Sacks asks why so many prominent Americans early in the twentieth century did not think her ancestors were truly white.[8] Earlier generations of Americans, as Matthew Jacobson observes, saw "Celtic, Hebrew, Anglo-Saxon or Mediterranean physiognomies whereas today we see only subtly varying shades of a mostly undifferentiated whiteness."[9]

Far from being on the fringe, full-blown theories about the racial inferiority of eastern Europeans and southern Italians were well within the mainstream of the scientific community at the turn of the century. Openly propounded by respected scholars, such views were also propagated and given the stamp of approval by public intellectuals and opinion leaders and the press.

*The Passing of the Great Race,* the most influential of the books proclaiming a scientific racism—it "inspired a bevy of popular writers and influenced a number of scholarly ones"—appeared in 1916 but achieved peak popularity in the early 1920s.[10] Written by Madison Grant, a patrician New Yorker who was founder and later chairman of the New York Zoological Society, it had an introduction by Henry Fairfield Osborn, a prominent biologist and president of the American Museum of Natural History. The book set forth the notion that America had originally been settled by descendants of a genetically pure and biologically superior "Nordic" race with "fair skin, blond hair, straight nose, and splendid fighting and moral qualities." Grant warned that American stock would be mongrelized by inferior Europeans such as the Alpines from central Europe, Mediterraneans and, worst of all, Jews. People of inferior breeding, he believed, were overrunning the country, intermarrying and diminishing the quality of American blood. The "dark Mediterranean subspecies" are "long skulled like the Nordic race, but the absolute size of the skull is less. The eyes and hair are very dark or black, and the skin more or less swarthy. The stature is stunted in comparison to that of the Nordic race and the musculature and bony framework weak." Of Polish Jews, Grant wrote, their "dwarf stature, peculiar mentality, and ruthless concentration on self-interest are being engrafted on the stock of the nation." Inevitably, the mixing of two races "gives us a race reverting to the more ancient, generalized and lower type." Thus, "the cross between any of the three European races and a Jew is a Jew."[11] America, he feared, was being swept toward a "racial abyss." "If the Melting Pot is allowed to boil without control . . . the type of native American of Colonial descent will become as extinct as the Athenian of the age of Pericles, and the Viking of the days of Rollo."[12]

Edward A. Ross, one of the most race conscious of American social scientists, was also troubled that newcomers, with their inborn deficiencies, would dilute America's sturdier Anglo-Saxon stock. He condemned Jews for their inborn love of money, and southern Italians for their volatility, instability, and unreliability. Steerage passengers from Naples "show a distressing frequency of low foreheads, open mouths, weak chins, poor features, skew faces, small or knobby crania, and backless heads. Such people lack the power to take rational care of themselves." Ross spoke of the "dusk of Saracenic or Berber ancestors" showing in the cheeks of Italian immigrant children. "One sees no reason," he wrote, "why the Italian dusk should not in time quench what of the Celto-Teutonic flush lingers in the cheek of the native American."[13]

According to Ross, the massive influx of new immigrants would, if unchecked, lead to a falling off of good looks: "It is unthinkable that so many persons with crooked faces, coarse mouths, bad noses, heavy jaws, and low foreheads can mingle their heredity with ours without making personal beauty yet more rare among us than it actually is." With more Italians coming to the United States, intelligence would suffer: "So far as the American people consents to incorporate with itself great numbers of wavering, excitable, impulsive persons who cannot organize themselves, it must in the end resign itself to lower efficiency, to less democracy, or to both." With more Jews, the moral standards of the nation were in danger since lower-class eastern European Jews are "moral cripples, their souls warped and dwarfed by iron circumstance. . . . Life amid a bigoted and hostile population has left them aloof and thick-skinned. A tribal spirit intensified by social isolation prompts them to rush to the rescue of the caught rascal of their own race . . . and many of them have developed a monstrous and repulsive love of gain."[14]

Articles in the press and popular magazines echoed racial views of this kind. Influential publications like the *New York Times* and the *Saturday Evening Post* ran editorials sympathetic to Madison Grant's theories. In a series of widely read articles for the *Saturday Evening Post* in 1920–21, Kenneth Roberts cast his findings on immigration into the framework of the Nordic theory, concluding that a continuing deluge of Alpine, Mediterranean, and Semitic immigrants would inevitably produce "a hybrid race of people as worthless and futile as the good-for-nothing mongrels of Central America and Southeastern Europe."[15] Articles with titles like "Are the Jews an Inferior Race?" (1912) and "Will the Jews Ever Lose Their Racial Identity?" (1911) appeared in the most frequently read periodicals. A story in the *New York Times* (1893) referred to the "hatchet-faced, pimply, sallow-cheeked, rat-eyed young men of the Russian Jewish colony."[16] The "marks of their race," said *Harper's* of Lower East Side Jews, "appear in the formation of the jaw and mouth and in the general facial aspect."[17] Jewish racial features, the *New York Sun* (1893) argued, made them unassimilable: "Other races of men lose their identity by migration and by intermarrying with different peoples, with the result that their peculiar characteristics and physiognomies are lost in the mess. The Jewish face and character remain the same as they were in the days of PHARAOH. Everybody can distinguish the Jewish features in the most ancient carvings and representations, for they are the same as those seen at this day. Usually a Jew is recognizable as such by sight. In whatever country he is, his race is always conspicuous. . . . After a few generations other immigrants to this country lose their race identity and become Americans only. Generally the Jews retain theirs, undiminished, so that it is observable by all men." [18]

Even the social reformer Jacob Riis unabashedly used racial stereotypes in his classic exposé *How the Other Half Lives*. The Italian, wrote Riis, "is a born gambler. His soul is in the game from the moment the cards are on the table, and very frequently his knife is in it too before the game is ended. . . . With all his conspicuous faults, the swarthy Italian immigrant has his redeeming traits. He is as honest as he is hot-headed. . . . The Italian is gay, lighthearted and, if his fur is not stroked the wrong way, inoffensive as a child." As for the Jews: "Thrift is the watchword of Jewtown . . . at once its strength and its fatal weakness, its cardinal virtue and its foul disgrace. . . . Life itself is of little value compared with even the leanest bank account. In no other spot does life wear so intensely bald and materialistic an aspect as in Ludlow Street." [19]

Many politicians of the Progressive Era tailored their thinking about the racial desirability of the new European immigrants to appeal to the "foreign" vote—for example, in the election of 1912, Woodrow Wilson repudiated the contemptuous phrases he had written about southern and eastern European immigrants in his history text a decade earlier. [20] But it was not unusual for political figures to speak, in the racial symbolism of the day, of the dangerous possibility that the "inferior European races" would alter the essential character of the United States. In 1921 no less a figure than Calvin Coolidge wrote that "there are racial considerations too grave to be brushed aside. . . . The Nordics propagate themselves successfully. With other races, the outcome shows deterioration on both sides. Quality of mind and body suggests that observance of ethnic law is as great a necessity to a nation as immigrant law." [21]

The racial attack on southern and eastern European immigrants was, as John Higham notes, a powerful ideological weapon of the movement to reduce immigration, helping to mobilize public sentiment in favor of restriction. [22] Genetic arguments about inferior races gave those wanting to cut immigration from southern and eastern Europe a scientific sanction; restriction against the new immigration seemed like a biological imperative.[23] Ultimately, the restrictionists won, and 1924 legislation—reducing the number of European immigrants allowed yearly to 2 percent of the foreign-born of each nationality in the United States according to the 1890 census—marked the end of the massive influx of southern and eastern Europeans.[24]

If the notion that Jews and Italians were inferior races was commonplace in public discourse at the beginning of the twentieth century, in everyday life there was a racial vocabulary to describe—and abuse—them. As James Barrett and David Roediger note, the words themselves were important: "They were not only the means by which native born and elite people marked new immigrants as inferiors, but also the means by which immigrant workers came to locate themselves and those about them in the nation's racial hierarchy."[25]

The racialization of Italians was especially pronounced, and the language of color was sometimes involved. Italians were often described as swarthy, and a common epithet for them, guinea, had long referred to African slaves, particularly those from the continent's northwest coast and their descendants.[26] "You don't call an Italian a white man?" a member of a congressional committee asked a West Coast construction boss. "No sir," he answered, "an Italian is a dago."[27] In all sections of the country, John Higham concludes, "native-born and northern European laborers called themselves 'white men' to distinguish themselves from southern Europeans whom they worked beside."[28] As late as the 1930s, a second generation Italian in New Haven told a researcher that "our skin gives us away. . . . It's dark and oily." Another described a conversation with his employer, who called Italians names. When asked why he felt this way about all Italians, the employer said: "I don't mean you, Henry. You're white."[29]

Eastern Europeans were also racialized in the popular mind, according to Barrett and Roediger: "While racist jokes mocked the black servant who thought her child, fathered by a Chinese man, would be a Jew, racist folklore held that Jews, inside-out, were 'niggers.' "[30] Jews were thought to have visible physical characteristics that marked them off and made them "look Jewish."[31] To refute the racial stereotypes, Dr. Maurice Fishberg, a professor of medicine at New York University and Bellevue Medical College and Russian Jewish immigrant himself, actually classified the noses of 2,836 Jewish men in New York City, finding "that only 14 percent had the aquiline or hooked nose commonly labeled as a 'Jewish' nose."[32] In 1923, New York University was plastered with signs that told Jews to drop out so the school could be a "white man's college."[33] As late as the 1930s, an American history textbook asked whether it would be possible to absorb "the millions of olive-skinned Italians and swarthy black-haired Slavs and dark-eyed Hebrews into the body of the American people."[34]

Not only was it acceptable to speak about the inferiority of Jews and Italians in newspapers, magazines, and public forums, but discrimination against them was open and, by and large, legal. Elite summer resorts made no bones about shutting out Jews. In the 1880s, many in upstate New York set up placards: "No Jews or Dogs Admitted Here." Although a 1913 New York State law forbade places of public accommodation from advertising their unwillingness to admit anyone because of race, creed, or color—with violations punished as misdemeanors—in states without such laws, resort owners still flaunted such slogans as "Altitude 1869 feet. Too high for Jews."[35] Where the law applied, more subtle means were employed. When resorts and private clubs announced that they served "restricted clientele," it was understood that Jews were not allowed.

"Restrictive covenants," clauses in real estate titles that limited the sale or transfer of property to members of certain groups, kept Jews out of some of New York City's most desirable suburban neighborhoods. Toward the end of the 1920s, apartment-house owners in Jackson Heights, Queens, advertised that their buildings were "restricted" and prohibited Catholics, Jews, and dogs. A legal battle over the exclusions ensued, but the court upheld the rights of the property owners to choose their own tenants. It was not until a 1948 Supreme Court case outlawed restrictive covenants that such agreements became unenforceable in the courts of law.[36]

There were various forms of open discrimination in employment, too. At the end of the nineteenth century, for example, pay rates for common laboring jobs often varied by racial group. In 1895, a public notice recruiting laborers to build the Croton Reservoir listed the daily wage schedule of three groups: common labor, white, $1.30 to $1.50; common labor, colored, $1.25 to $1.40; common labor, Italian, $1.15 to $1.25.[37] For Jews, the bars were felt higher up the job scale. In 1917, the United States Army inserted ads in the *New York World* blatantly stating its need for "Christian" carpenters, although after objections from the president of the American Jewish Committee, a directive was issued forbidding such bigotry. After World War I, as more Jews sought white-collar jobs with private firms, newspaper advertisements indicating a preference for Christians proliferated.[38]

Also in the post–World War I years, many colleges, universities, and medical schools adopted quota systems that set limits on Jewish admission. Although in 1922 President Lowell of Harvard University openly recommended limiting the number of Jewish students, the allotments there, as elsewhere, were covert, and institutions developed discreet ways to achieve their objectives. The application for Sarah Lawrence College, for example, asked, "Has your daughter been brought up with strict Sunday observance?" Columbia College wanted to know the student applicant's "religious affiliation," whether his parents had ever been known by another name, the parents' place of birth, the mother's full maiden name, and the father's occupation. Harvard came up with the idea of enforcing a geographical distribution, assuming that one would find few Jews outside of the major cities of the east and midwest. It was not until 1946 that New York's City Council passed a resolution threatening the tax-exempt status of nonsectarian colleges and universities that used racial or religious criteria in selecting students; in 1948, New York State (soon followed by New Jersey and Massachusetts) forbade discrimination on grounds of religion and race in higher education.[39]

## Race and the Newest New Yorkers

Today, immigrants of European ancestry, whether from Ireland or Poland, England or Russia, Italy or Israel, are fully and unquestionably white. Europeans, of course, are a minority of the current newcomers. Most of the latest immigrants are "nonwhite" or "people of color," but what this means in the New York of today is staggeringly complex.

The white-black cleavage remains central in New York, as it did for much of the twentieth century, ever since the massive migration of African Americans from the South and the fading of Euro-American racial distinctions.[40] This dichotomy has a special resonance and significance given the history of American slavery, the government policies of legal segregation in the South, and the fierce prejudice and institutionalized discrimination throughout the country. Whereas white denotes European antecedents, black stands for Africa. No matter how light their skin tones, Americans with known African ancestry continue to be delineated as black. Although legally in retreat, the peculiarly American "one drop rule" that defined as black a person with as little as a single drop of black blood has had an enduring legacy.

As people of African descent, West Indians are clearly on the black side of the racial divide. Where Hispanics and Asians fit in is much more complicated. Hispanics are generally thought of as nonwhite, although they include people of extraordinary racial diversity, ranging from dark-skinned Dominicans to white-skinned Latin Americans who claim a strong European heritage. Asians may well be the present-day in-between peoples. Neither black nor white, they appear to be moving closer to whites in the racial hierarchy. In general, "nonwhite" immigrants who are *not* defined as black have had the most success in being recognized for their nationality, rather than their color, and in benefiting from the "whitening" effects of class.

### Being Black: West Indian New Yorkers

For West Indians, being black is the master status that pervades and penetrates their lives. The term West Indian refers here to people of African descent from the English-speaking Caribbean, although what I say about race also pertains to immigrants from Haiti, who are also considered black. I do not include the growing number of Trinidadian and Guyanese immigrants of East Indian descent, whose ancestors were brought to the Caribbean as indentured laborers to replace slaves after emancipation. East Indians, as they are called in the Caribbean, are a separate, and fascinating, case, since they typically attempt to establish an Asian identity in New York as a way to avoid being labeled black.

West Indians of African descent cannot avoid this designation. In New York, they often find themselves lumped with American blacks—virtually invisible to most white New Yorkers in a sea of anonymous black faces.[41] Two especially dramatic racial incidents illustrate this invisibility: the Howard Beach murder in 1986 and the Crown Heights riots in 1991. The focus in the mainstream media was on the fact that the victims were black, and most New Yorkers never knew, or cared, that they were West Indian.

Given the realities of American race relations, this focus is not surprising—but that is precisely the point. Indeed, in the Howard Beach incident, Michael Griffith, a Trinidadian immigrant, was attacked because he was black. He was killed—struck by a car—after being chased on the highway by a group of white teenagers. The victim who sparked the riots in the Crown Heights section of Brooklyn was a seven-year-old Guyanese boy named Gavin Cato, who was killed when a car driven by a Hasidic Jew jumped a curb (his sister was also seriously injured) . Rumors spread that a Hasidic ambulance service had ignored the children while rushing to the slightly injured driver. Several hours later, a band of black youths fatally stabbed a Jewish rabbinical student, Yankel Rosenbaum, which precipitated several nights of rioting, mostly by young African American and Caribbean black males.[42] The protests and publicity surrounding the incidents, which defined them in black-white terms and largely ignored the ethnic identity of the victims, brought home to West Indians, in a powerful way, that in New York, regardless of the differences they see between themselves and black Americans, others often see them only as blacks.[43]

This is not always the case, of course. In another violent incident that dominated the local news in 1997, the media described the man who was brutally attacked by police officers inside the station house of a Brooklyn precinct as a Haitian immigrant. But even when other New Yorkers recognize Caribbean immigrants as West Indian, as foreign, or, as many whites say, "from the islands," West Indians are seen as an ethnic group within the larger black population. Their racial status, in other words, is always salient. Being viewed as black, and being identified with black Americans, has enormous consequences for their lives. Certainly it is true, as many studies show, that American whites have become much more racially tolerant and less likely to voice racist sentiments to pollsters and in public since the civil rights revolution of the 1950s and 1960s.[44] Today, most white Americans would like to convey an image of themselves as unprejudiced and compassionate.[45] Yet racial stereotypes, prejudice, and discrimination against blacks have had a tenacious hold—and persist in a variety of forms.

At one extreme, racially motivated violent attacks, though the exception, clearly still happen. Some other examples: in 1990, a West Indian family who bought a house in Canarsie, Brooklyn, saw their property torched before they could move in; in 1992, a fourteen-year-old West Indian boy and his sister were attacked on the way to school in the Bronx by four young white men who squirted them with white paint and yelled racial epithets; and in 1995, a West Indian Episcopalian priest and his family who were the first blacks to move into an all-white section of Midwood, Brooklyn, had their car set on fire.[46] Less dramatic, but also painful, West Indians tell of racial slurs, insults, and slights and of their sense that whites do not want to socialize or associate with them. When Andrew Hacker writes that "every black American knows . . . how it feels to have an unfavorable—and unfair—identity imposed on you every waking day," I would add that, as blacks, West Indians in New York know it too.[47]

According to Joe Feagin, no matter how affluent or influential blacks may be, in public places they cannot escape the stigma of being black.[48] A West Indian social worker recalled how once, when he was the only black person on an airplane, he was also the only passenger whom the hostess neglected to offer a magazine.[49] Well-dressed black professionals often find that taxis are unwilling to stop for them in Manhattan. West Indian teenagers describe being followed in stores because they are suspected of shoplifting and having whites recoil from them in fear on the street, in the subway, and in parks.[50] "Because when you go to the stores . . . people follow you around, you go on the bus and people hold their pocketbooks," one fourteen-year-old West Indian girl explained. "They don't discriminate against you because you're West Indian. They are discriminating against you because you are black."[51] Young black men, whom many whites see as potentially dangerous, have an especially hard time. It is not unusual for whites to cross the street or clutch their handbags when they see a young black man approach—and they do not stop to wonder whether the man is West Indian or American. Regardless of their socioeconomic status, Feagin claims, most black males, by the time they are in their twenties, have been stopped by the police because "blackness" is considered a sign of possible criminality by police officers.[52]

If social distance marks relations between most blacks and whites in New York, residential segregation by race also has been remarkably persistent. Sociologists have developed a statistical measure of residential segregation, called the index of dissimilarity, that gives the percentage of people in a group who would have to move in order to achieve an even or completely integrated pattern; 100 represents total segregation between two groups, and 0 minimum segregation. This measure shows that West Indians are extremely segregated from whites—as segregated as American blacks. Using 1990 census data, Kyle Crowder calculated that the index of dissimilarity between West Indians and non-Hispanic whites in the New York metropolitan area was 82, almost the same as for African Americans (81).[53]

Like other newcomers, many West Indians congregate in distinct West Indian neighborhoods because that is where they want to be. As I described in Chapter 2, West Indians generally move into areas with fairly decent housing, and have high rates of home ownership. But race—and racial isolation—put severe constraints in their way. Real estate agents, for example, often steer them to black neighborhoods or withhold information on housing availability elsewhere, and West Indians themselves often prefer communities where there can avoid racism and rejection. "Some neighborhoods," observed one West Indian New Yorker, "are not yet ready for black people. And I don't want to be a hero."[54] Those who have braved open hostility and branched out from West Indian areas in Brooklyn and Queens to adjacent white communities find that their new neighborhoods become increasingly black. So, for example, Canarsie-Flatlands, a lower-middle-class white ethnic enclave in the 1980s, had a population that was 65 percent black by 1996.[55] Antiblack prejudice tends to fuel a process of racial turnover, as whites begin to leave and no new whites move in; at the same time, the growing number of black families in the neighborhood makes it seem more welcoming to West Indians looking for homes. The result is a pattern of segregation in which West Indian residential enclaves are located in largely black areas of the city and the suburbs. Indeed, West Indians are not very segregated from African Americans—in 1990, the index of dissimilarity between the two groups in the New York metropolitan area was 43, a fairly moderate rate.[56] If figures for all black New Yorkers are anything to go by, and the evidence shows that they are, higher class standing does little to buy West Indians a racially integrated environment.[57]

This continuing American apartheid, to use Douglas Massey and Nancy Denton's phrase, has far-reaching implications.[58] West Indians' lack of access to white neighborhoods—and the inevitable racial turnover that takes place when middle-class "pioneers" move into white communities—confines the majority to areas with inferior schools, high crime rates, and poor government services and limits their informal contacts with white Americans. Outside of work (and sometimes at work as well), most West Indians find themselves moving in all-black social worlds. This is fortified, it should be noted, by patterns of marriage, which are another indication of continuing racial prejudice and the distinctive social distance separating whites and blacks in America. Again, we have to rely on figures for the entire black population, but they are no doubt similar for West Indians as well. Although 98 percent of married whites in the United States in 1990 had a white spouse, when they married outside of their group, they were several times more likely to marry members of groups other than blacks. Put another way, among married couples, more than one out of four (nearly 30 percent) Asians and Hispanics had white spouses, compared to only one in eighteen (5 percent) blacks.[59] Among native-born married people twenty-five to thirty-four years old in 1990, 70 percent of Asian women and 39 percent of Hispanic women, but only 2 percent of black women, had white husbands; 5 percent of black men had white wives compared to 33 percent of Hispanic men and 40 percent of Asian men.[60]

The sting of racial prejudice in New York is especially painful, because West Indians come from societies with different racial hierarchies and conceptions of race. There is no denying that the long history of West Indian plantation slavery and colonial social arrangements have left, in their wake, the assumption that African ancestry is inferior; dark skin, moreover, continues to be correlated with poverty.[61] But blackness does not have the same stigma that it does in the United States—and blackness is not, in itself, a barrier to social acceptance or upward mobility. In most West Indian societies, people of African ancestry are the overwhelming majority (the exceptions are Trinidad and Guyana, with their enormous East Indian populations), and there are hardly any whites or Europeans. Black and colored West Indians in influential and important jobs are hardly token representatives of their race. That they occupy high-status roles is normal and unremarkable. Indeed, since the end of World War II, black and colored West Indians have dominated public affairs and routinely fill prestigious and professional positions.[62]

The very notion of who is considered black differs in the West Indies. Whereas in the United States, the category black includes those who range from very dark skinned to very light skinned, in the West Indies blackness is a matter of ancestry, skin color, hair type, facial features, and socioeconomic status. As Milton Vickerman observes, those defined as black in the United States belong to different groups in Jamaica, where there is a keen consciousness of shade—the lighter, the better.[63] In Jamaica, blacks are generally thought of as impoverished individuals with African ancestry, dark skin, and Negroid facial features and hair type. People who combine features from several types (African plus European, Asian, or Middle Eastern) are traditionally considered brown or colored. Moreover, money still "whitens"; as individuals improve their income, education, lifestyle, and financial status, they seem progressively whiter. What matters, above all, is having education, wealth, manners, and well-placed associates, not race.

Obviously, this changes in New York, where West Indians are considered black and are victims of racial discrimination, whatever their achievements or shade. It is not surprising that a number of Jamaicans I met in the course of my research told me that they never knew what it meant to be black until they came to America. This new racial awareness—or, as Sutton and Makiesky put it, the "heightened consciousness of themselves as a black minority enclosed within a sometimes menacing, sometimes friendly, world of more powerful whites"[64]—gives West Indians a sense of common cause with African Americans on issues and in political struggles where black and white interests are seen to be in conflict.

At the same time, however, West Indians often try to distance themselves from—and avoid the stigma associated with—African Americans. They do this by emphasizing cultural, linguistic, and behavioral features that, in their view, make them different from, indeed superior to, African Americans. In other words, race unites West Indians and African Americans; ethnicity divides them.[65]

West Indians come to New York to improve their lives, and although there are, as the late journalist Orde Coombs noted, "no guarantees that identification with the white ruling class assures upward mobility, it is certain, they feel, that affiliation with the black underclass does not."[66] West Indians see themselves as "harder workers, more ambitious, and greater achievers" than African Americans. Many Jamaicans told me that they are more likely to buy homes than American blacks and that they place more value on education and discipline. Another common theme was that they are less hostile to whites than American blacks—they "don't have chips on [their] shoulders"—and have more dignity and greater self-assurance in dealing with whites.[67] Many Jamaicans I interviewed felt that when whites found out that they were Jamaican, and not African American, they viewed and treated them more favorably. "Once you say something," one man explained, "and they recognize you're not from this country, they treat you a little different." To what extent this is actually the case is hard to say. What is clear, however, is that many West Indians believe it to be true—and the belief itself further bolsters their sense of ethnic pride and distinctiveness, and their feeling of superiority to African Americans.

## Hispanic Newcomers

The racial status of New York's Hispanic immigrants is a much more complicated matter: it shows enormous ambiguity, inconsistency, and flux. Although scholars debate whether it is justifiable to call Hispanics a race, in popular discourse they are often thought of this way. To most Americans, Hispanics are not white, though they are not imagined as black either. Hispanics are commonly thought of as brown or of mixed race, even though, in fact, they display remarkable racial diversity. As one journalist notes, there are black Hispanics from the Dominican Republic, Argentines who are almost entirely European white, and Mexicans who would be counted by census takers as American Indians if they had been born north of the Rio Grande.[68]

The term Hispanic is a recent creation in the United States, coined only a few decades ago by census takers as a statistical term of convenience to deal with counting the Latin American population. Some scholars argue that the label is no more than a statistical fiction that bears little relation to reality. Latin American immigrants prefer to be known by their group of national origin not as Hispanics or Latinos, and although they share linguistic and cultural roots, they do not comprise a single, coherent community.[69] Yet what started out as a statistical label of convenience has gradually been transformed by public use into a real social entity from the perspective of American society.[70] Indeed, a recent book, entitled *His-*

*panic Nation,* examines how a combination of state policies, the Spanish-language media, and political movements is turning the statistical fiction "Hispanic" into a social reality in American society.[71]

What do most New Yorkers think of when they hear the term Hispanic? Is it just an ethnic category, a synonym for people whose origins are in Latin America and the Spanish-speaking Caribbean and who are seen as having a distinctive cultural heritage or background? The census treats Hispanics this way, since it asks people who say they have Hispanic origins to indicate their race as well (the choice in 1990 including White, Black, American Indian, Asian or Pacific Islander, and Other). Thus, the census category "non-Hispanic whites" was invented. But read nearly any New York newspaper or hear people talk on the street and it becomes clear that Hispanic stands for something more than ethnicity. There has been a gradual racialization of Hispanics — a belief that physical characteristics, particularly skin color, are involved. Indeed, by treating Hispanics as a group equivalent to blacks in antidiscrimination and affirmative-action policies, the federal government has contributed to raising Hispanic to the status of a racial category.[72]

Increasingly, in political and street-level discourse, New Yorkers think in terms of a four-race framework of white, black, Hispanic, and Asian. (American Indians, the fifth race, are not often mentioned as such in New York City.) "When people in the contemporary United States talk about racial politics, racial discrimination, or racial violence," observes Roger Sanjek "it is this white-black-Hispanic-Asian (plus American Indian in some localities) framework that they speak within."[73]

In New York, politicians and political pundits as well as the media routinely refer to blacks, Hispanics, and Asians as minorities in opposition to whites. It is not unusual for New York police to describe a perpetrator or victim as Hispanic, based only on his or her appearance. This generally means someone who is "too dark to be white, too light to be black, and who has no easily identifiable Asian traits."[74] A comment by a Salvadoran immigrant on Long Island indicates an awareness of this kind of racial stereotyping: "The police hassle Hispanics everywhere," he explained; "as soon as they see the *face of a Hispanic* [italics mine] inside a car they immediately turn on their lights and stop his car to ask him for his papers."[75] The presumption that Hispanic immigrants are nonwhite also comes out in casual conversations when New Yorkers describe Hispanics who are phenotypically white. "She's Colombian, but she's white," I have heard people say. New Yorkers feel no need to mention the skin color of European immigrants, who are assumed to be white as a matter of course.

The label Hispanic carries a stigma in New York, often conjuring up images of people who are brown- or tan-skinned, foreign in speech and manner, and unable or unwilling to adapt to U.S. laws, culture, and norms of hygiene.[76] A Cuban-born stock broker, whose only contact with clients was on the phone, described how he changed his surname (Gonzalez) so that when he solicited new clients they would "listen to me and trust me more than they would with a Hispanic name." (In fact, he was phenotypically white and had no accent, having moved to the United States as a small child; he had not told his mother, in Florida, about the name change, fearing that "she would be crushed.")[77] New Yorkers are generally not sensitive to the differences among immigrants from the Dominican Republic, Cuba, Ecuador, Colombia, Mexico, and Honduras. And they often lump the most recent Spanish-speaking arrivals with Puerto Ricans, who are still New York's single largest Hispanic group, have extraordinarily high rates of poverty, and are imagined, by many New Yorkers, as an underclass mired in crime and drugs. Indeed, for much of the post–World War II era, before the recent immigration wave, the all-encompassing minority category in New York City was "blacks and Puerto Ricans." No wonder that Spanish-speaking immigrants from the Caribbean and Latin America often make efforts to distinguish themselves by nationality from blacks and Puerto Ricans, the city's most stigmatized minorities. Robert Smith, for example, tells of how Mexican immigrants define themselves as neither black nor Puerto Rican, emphasizing their strong community institutions, tightly knit families, and solid work ethic.[78]

The case of New York's Brazilian immigrants is especially interesting, since even though most are phenotypically white (and speak Portuguese), they are often labeled Hispanic. They strongly object to this designation, which, they believe, results in discrimination. Doubtless they wish to escape the color connotations of the Hispanic label. Also, class is involved. Most Brazilian New Yorkers are from the middle strata of Brazilian society and are well educated; they consider it an insult to be confused with the rest of the city's Latino population, who typically come from poorer backgrounds and have less education. Brazilians believe that they receive better treatment from white Americans when they make clear that they are not Hispanic, something they try to do by emphasizing their linguistic and cultural distinctiveness.[79]

And this leads to yet a further complication. If Hispanics are increasingly thought of as a race in popular discourse, in their day-to-day lives they also often identify, and are seen by others, in terms of the black-white dichotomy. On one end are white Hispanic immigrants of European an-

cestry who, if self-identification is anything to go by, are a substantial number. In the 1990 census, a quarter of New York City's Dominicans and
over half of the Colombians and Cubans described themselves as white.[80]
Like New York's white Brazilians, white Hispanic immigrants often cannot escape the stigma associated with the Hispanic label. The remark by
one Puerto Rican New Yorker, recorded in Oscar Lewis's La Vida, would
doubtless strike a familiar chord with many new arrivals. "I'm so white,"
the respondent said, "that they've even taken me for a Jew, but when they
see my Spanish name, they back right off."[81] Ramón Grosfoguel and his
colleague argue that "no matter how 'blonde or blue eyed' a person may
be, and no matter how successfully he can 'pass' as white, the moment
that person self-identifies as Puerto Rican, he enters the labyrinth of racial
Otherness."[82]

Yet there are obvious advantages to being white. A recent study found
that Dominicans who are perceived as white have much lower poverty
levels than, and enjoy advantages in the labor market over, their darker-
skinned compatriots. "When I got my job in the laundry," said one extremely fair-skinned Dominican, "the owners said that even though I spoke
Spanish, they would hire me because they didn't want any Blacks working for them."[83] An analysis of residential segregation patterns based on
1980 census data found that white Hispanics from the Caribbean region in
the New York metropolitan area were less segregated from non-Hispanic
whites than Hispanics who described themselves as "other race" with some
Spanish identification or as "black."[84] Presumably, many of the Hispanics
who marry non-Hispanic whites—nationwide, in 1990, nearly half of the
white men who intermarried wed Hispanics—are white or very light-
skinned.[85]

As one might expect, the reality of the American color line creates special problems for dark-skinned or black Hispanics. (This has a significant
impact on the Dominican population. In 1990, a quarter of the Dominicans
in New York City, compared to 13 percent of the Cubans and 3 percent of
Colombians, described themselves on the census as black.)[86] In the study
of Caribbean Hispanic residence patterns, Hispanics who described themselves as black (as opposed to white or "Spanish race") in the 1980 census
were the most segregated from non-Hispanic whites and the least segregated from the wider black population. Apart from residence, there are
the day-to-day humiliations. A dark-skinned young New York–born man
of Dominican descent explained, "When I was jumped by whites, I was
not called a spic but I was called a nigger."[87] Or consider the experience of
another dark-skinned Dominican who tells of waiting in a corporate office

for a job interview: "A woman wandered out into the room I was sitting in, looked at me, looked around, and returned to her office. A few minutes later she did the same thing again. After the third time, she finally asked, 'Are you Luis Rodriguez?' I replied 'Yes,' as the woman tried to explain her way out of the blunder she had just made. 'I was looking for someone who looked different, I mean Hispanic, I mean . . .' "[88]

Dominicans with African features or dark skin find it especially unsettling to be confused with African Americans, since they come from a society where the category black is reserved for the highly disdained Haitians and where to be partly white (the case for most Dominicans ) is to be nonblack. In the Dominican Republic, Dominicans of mixed phenotype tend to discount their African heritage and say they are "indios," seeing themselves as descendants of the Spanish and indigenous populations.[89] Dark-skinned immigrants from other Latin American countries experience a similar clash of racial orders in New York. Although each country in Latin America has evolved its own racial context because of its unique history, race is generally thought of as a continuum from black to white, with a large number of terms to describe those in-between. People can be more or less white, black, or Amerindian. A *trigueño*, or "wheat-colored" person, for example, is generally lighter skinned than a *moreno*. Moreover, income and education can have a lightening effect so that "a person who is called *negro* or *prieto* when he is poor and uneducated will almost always be described by some more flattering term, such as *trigueño*, if he rises in status."[90]

Where does this leave the many—indeed, probably most—Hispanic immigrants in New York, whose skin color and other physical features do not qualify them as white but who tend not to be considered black either? In many ways, very much in the middle. These are the people New Yorkers usually have in mind when they use or hear the term Hispanic. And they are the people likely to describe themselves as "other" when the census asks about race—a selection made, in 1990, by half the Dominicans, a quarter of the Cubans, and 43 percent of the Colombians in New York City.[91]

On occasion, "not white, not black" Hispanic immigrants may find that they are taken for "light-skinned blacks."[92] But on the whole, they have avoided the presumptions of inferiority associated with Africa and slavery and have been able to put a visible distance between themselves and black Americans. Hispanics who checked off the "other race" category in the 1980 census and gave some Spanish identification were highly segregated from non-Hispanic blacks. Although their residential patterns indicate that they are accepted on the basis of common ethnicity by white Hispanics, they appear not to be accepted as neighbors by non-Hispanic whites, from whom they remain highly segregated.[93]

Class distinctions add further complexity to the way Hispanic immigrants are seen. Whereas West Indians find that race remains a barrier whatever their class status, for white or light-skinned Hispanics, income, education, and occupation enhance and solidify the advantages they already enjoy. White or very light-skinned Hispanic New Yorkers who enter the upper reaches of the middle class and become fluent English speakers are able to move fairly easily in a white social world. It is worth noting that the light-skinned Puerto Rican who complained that New Yorkers backed off when they heard his Spanish name was from a poor slum family.

By the same token, lower-class status reinforces and intensifies racial prejudice against mixed race and black Hispanic immigrants. The case of Salvadorans on Long Island is instructive in this regard. The mayor of a town where many Salvadorans live and work put it bluntly: "People don't want to live with people with brown skin." Another consideration is that most Salvadorans come from poor peasant backgrounds and hold menial jobs in the town. Out of necessity, they live in overcrowded quarters, and many have to walk or bicycle to work, school, and social events because they cannot afford cars. When white old-timers see Salvadoran laborers— boot-clad, unshaven, and dusty—treading down Main Street as they return from work, it heightens animosity toward Hispanic immigrants, who are seen as eroding the quality of suburban life. Interestingly, white old-timers do not express antipathy toward better-educated and middle-class Korean or Chinese immigrants who live in their communities.[94]

### Asians: The Elasticity of Race

Asians in America have long been seen as a separate racial category, but perceptions of them have changed remarkably in recent decades. Once looked down upon as the "yellow peril," East Asians are now frequently touted as the "model minority." Several popular articles have depicted high-achieving Asian American students as "proto-whites," and a number of scholarly accounts suggest that Asians may eventually blend into the white category through intermarriage and personal achievement. Such crystal-ball gazing is of course highly speculative, especially given the continued racial distinctions between whites and Asians. But the fact that such possibilities are under popular and academic scrutiny brings out the enormous transformations in the way Asians are seen.

In the past, Asians were subject to blatant exclusion and discrimination on racial grounds. Until the recent immigration, Asian in New York meant Chinese. Not black, and not white, they were often portrayed as "slanty-eyed" and belonging to the "yellow race." One reason that Chinese immigrants huddled together in Chinatown was fear of racism in the world outside.

Racial prejudice against Asians was enshrined in restrictive immigration and naturalization laws. The Chinese Exclusion Act of 1882 singled out the Chinese as the first and only group to be excluded from the United States on the basis of race, ethnicity, or nationality, and by 1917 Congress had banned the immigration of most other Asians as well. For much of the country's history, Asian immigrants were denied the right to become citizens. After Congress passed a statute in 1870 expanding naturalization to include persons of African descent, legal measures were taken to deny this right to Asian immigrants. The 1882 Chinese Exclusion Act specifically defined Chinese as "aliens ineligible to citizenship"; over the next few decades the rule was extended, through a series of decisions in state and federal courts, to all other immigrants from east and south Asia. The judgment of a 1921 Federal District court stated that Congress required someone to be white for naturalization because "color [is] . . . evidence of a type of civilization which it characterizes. The yellow or bronze racial color is the hallmark of Oriental despotisms."[95] It was not until 1943 that Chinese immigrants gained the right to become citizens and that the discriminatory immigration laws affecting Asians began to be relaxed. Only in 1952, with the passage of the McCarran-Walter Act, was naturalization eligibility extended to all Asians.[96]

On the West Coast, where anti-Asian sentiments were particularly virulent, several states adopted laws prohibiting intermarriage between Asians and whites. A 1913 California law, targeted at Japanese farmers, barred Asian immigrants from owning land. When a California court held, in 1885, that the public schools had to admit Chinese children, the state legislature passed a bill allowing school districts to set up separate schools for "Mongolians."[97] Most devastating of all, during World War II more than one hundred thousand Japanese Americans who lived on the Pacific Coast were forcibly evacuated and moved to internment camps.

Today, over fifty years later, it is hard to imagine that Asians, as "aliens ineligible for citizenship," used to be cast, as Yen Le Espiritu puts it, as "almost blacks but not blacks." Now, the model minority stereotype renders them "almost whites but not whites."[98] New York's Asians rank just below whites in the city's racial hierarchy—and they generally meet with greater acceptance from middle-class white New Yorkers than other racial minorities. Even the modern-day nativist Peter Brimelow, author of *Alien Nation,* who sees the latest arrivals as swamping white America, admits to a certain "sentimentality" about Asian immigrants whom, he writes, are often viewed as "the most 'Anglo Saxon' of the current wave."[99]

As compared to blacks and Hispanics, Asians are the least residentially segregated from non-Hispanic whites in the New York metropolitan area. Especially striking is the growing number of affluent suburban communities, like Scarsdale, where small numbers of Asians live in the midst of large white majorities.[100] Susan Slyomovics reports that white middle-class New Yorkers in the Bronx neighborhood she studied accepted the Muslim mosques of South Asians but rejected African American Muslim places of worship.[101] Nationwide, there is a high rate of intermarriage between the children of Asian immigrants and non-Hispanic whites. Moreover, a growing number of affluent white families in New York have adopted Asian children. Since the early 1990s, so many orphan Chinese girls have been adopted by upper-middle-class white professionals that, by 1997, about eighteen hundred families belonged to the Greater New York chapter of Families with Children from China; by one account, there were at least one thousand adopted Chinese orphan girls under the age of five in the New York area.[102]

For their part, most Asian immigrants see themselves as superior to blacks and Hispanics—and wish to avoid being lumped with these groups at the bottom of the racial-ethnic hierarchy. A black journalist reports how an Asian colleague described the sorts of people who got off at different subway stops. At one stop, the Asian colleague said, all the "minorities" got off, meaning the blacks and Hispanics. "He did not consider himself a minority, despite the fact that blacks and Latinos vastly outnumber Asians in the city. In his mind, as in many others, blacks and Latinos are the true minorities here."[103] At Columbia University, the president of the Korean Students Association explained why his group refused to participate in an umbrella body known as the United Students of Color Council: "My skin color is closer to a Jewish shade."[104] In fact, in terms of skin color, Koreans, like the Japanese and Chinese, "tend to register rather mildly on screens of 'white' American color sensitivity."[105] Indian immigrants, whose darker skin color puts them at risk of being confused with African Americans, emphasize their ethnic identity and distinctive history, customs, and culture as a way to avoid such mistakes. First-generation Indian immigrants, according to Johanna Lessinger, "do not acknowledge they are anything other than white—they think of themselves as white."[106]

What accounts for the greater acceptance, and changed perceptions, of

Asians today? Partly it is the class composition of the recent Asian immigration and the successes of their children. A large number of the new arrivals from Korea, the Philippines, Taiwan, Hong Kong, Japan, and India come with college degrees, ready to compete for middle-class careers, able to afford homes in middle-class areas, and intent that their children advance through education. Many of their children have done extraordinarily well. National figures show that native-born Asians are substantially more likely to complete college than whites and other groups.[107] In New York City, Asian students are overrepresented at the top of the academic ladder. They now make up about half of the student body at Stuyvesant High School, the city's most selective public high school. So many Koreans attend Horace Mann School—one of New York's most competitive private high schools, known for its outstanding college admission record—that a special Korean parents' group has been organized (see Chapter 6).

Views of Asian immigrants' home countries have changed—and this is another factor behind the new racial perceptions. In the past, Americans saw Asia as a backward region. Now, Japan is a modern advanced nation and a world economic power; Singapore, Taiwan, South Korea, and Hong Kong emerged, in the postwar period, as important modern economies; and China is a major player in world politics. Although many Americans have resented Japan's economic successes and Japanese takeovers of American firms, the Japanese, and by extension other east Asians, are no longer viewed as inferior. Indeed, in the early 1990s, Japan and other Asian economies were often held up as models for American companies.

Asians may now seem almost white to some New Yorkers, but they are still seen as racially distinct—and they still confront racial prejudice and discrimination.[108] There are reports of racial insults and slurs—Korean immigrants, for example, being faced with "go back to China" or "no chinks allowed."[109] One Filipino American college student recalls being rejected by her white boyfriend's parents in high school because she wasn't white ("They didn't even know that I was Filipino. They thought I was Chinese"); such an experience would strike a responsive chord among many other Asian Americans as well.[110]

Although Asians often live in communities with substantial numbers of whites, they have sometimes met with resistance, especially when they move into lower-middle-class white areas. In the late 1980s in Brooklyn's Bensonhurst neighborhood, anti-Asian flyers were distributed to mailboxes urging residents to boycott Korean and Chinese businesses as well as real estate agents who sold property to Asians.[111] A few years later, in 1995, in Bellerose, Queens, real estate agents were reported to be trying to drum up business by calling and writing white residents with what seemed to be tips that more Indian and Pakistani immigrants were moving into the community.[112]

Although they are less likely to be subjects of racial attacks than blacks and Hispanics, Asians are occasionally victimized this way as well. Consider two incidents in the late 1980s and early 1990s: three Korean men were assaulted in Woodside, Queens, by two white men who began yelling racial slurs and physically attacked one of the Koreans, breaking his leg; and a gang of forty white youths jumped five Asian American teenagers in a predominantly white neighborhood of Bayside, Queens. In 1987, troubling attacks took place in a New Jersey town where large numbers of Indians had moved. Groups of young white and Hispanic hoodlums, who called themselves dotbusters, pushed, shoved, and insulted Indian housewives who walked down the street wearing saris and *bindi* (the cosmetic dot on the forehead of Hindu women). Dotbusters beat up Indian students at a nearby technical college, and eventually two young Indian men were set upon and brutally beaten; one suffered permanent brain damage, and the other was fatally injured.[113]

Asian immigrants, especially Koreans, confront the additional issue of racial hostility from African Americans and Afro-Caribbeans. Many Korean stores in Brooklyn and Manhattan have been targets of racial threats and verbal attacks by blacks; several Korean-owned stores in black neighborhoods have been destroyed by arsonists; and between 1981 and 1991, five long-term black boycotts of Korean stores took place in New York City. This hostility has a familiar ring, much like that experienced by Jewish shopkeepers and landlords in black neighborhoods in the not too distant past.

Korean merchants, like their Jewish counterparts before them, are convenient scapegoats for black residents' economic frustrations because of their classic role as middleman minorities, acting as intermediaries between large numbers of low-income African American customers and predominantly white-owned suppliers and manufacturers. There are inherent tensions in commercial transactions in this context. African American and Afro-Caribbean customers complain that Korean proprietors are rude, overcharge or shortchange them, treat them like potential thieves, and resort to force in dealing with shoplifters. Koreans counter that they have to worry about shoplifting and that customers often pay less than they owe or damage merchandise. Added to these complaints are the preexisting prejudices that each group brings to their interactions. Korean shop owners tend to be biased against blacks, viewing them as less intelligent, less honest, and more criminally oriented than whites. In fact, according to one survey, Korean merchants are more prejudiced against black customers than black customers are against Korean merchants. For the sake of their business interests, Korean shopowners try to hide their prejudiced attitudes; black customers have little to lose by displaying their hostilities.[114]

## Public Discourse about Race

Along with enormous changes in perceptions of race, the very rhetoric of race has also undergone a striking transformation since the last great immigration wave. A hundred years ago, politicians, public intellectuals, and the press had little hesitation about expressing blatantly racist views, including those about the newest immigrants. It is hard to imagine a contemporary national figure of the prominence of then Vice President Calvin Coolidge writing, as he did in *Good Housekeeping* in 1921, that "America must be kept American. Biological laws show . . . that Nordics deteriorate when mixed with other races."[115] Or of a New York City congressman claiming, in the manner of the late-nineteenth-century Tammany candidate Tim Campbell, that "the local issue is the dago Rinaldo. He's from Italy, I am from Ireland. Are you in favor of Italy or Ireland?"[116]

Today, a different etiquette about race prevails in public discourse. The civil rights revolution ushered in a series of laws and court decisions banning discrimination and setting up new agencies and systems to enforce the law. The result has been a whole new climate and understanding about what is acceptable to say about race in public. Racial, religious, and ethnic slurs are now condemned when uttered by public officials and candidates and by those in private institutions with a visible responsibility to the public. By the 1970s and 1980s, Lawrence Fuchs writes, candidates for high office and public officials could not disparage, or even tolerate the disparagement of, any ethnic or religious group without suffering severe and widespread public condemnation.[117] In reaction, conservative critics complain about what they call the liberal culture of political correctness that makes it impossible to "tell it like it is." Peter Brimelow goes so far as to say that Americans are unwilling to own up to the negative social consequences of immigration because of the fear of being accused of racism.[118]

Now that racism is less acceptable in public, the movement to restrict immigration has a different tone than it did earlier in the century, when important officials and public leaders wrote and spoke about southern and eastern European races polluting the nation's superior Nordic stock. Today, most public appeals for restriction shy away from blatantly racist arguments. Even Peter Brimelow—who writes about the impending breakdown of American society if immigration continues and the white core declines —presents himself as courageous for being willing to buck what he sees as the current trend of avoiding discussion of anything that smacks of racism.[119] Objections to the current scale of immigration are couched primarily in terms of concerns over the number of illegal immigrants, or the drain on public budgets, or the competition for jobs between immigrants and native-born Americans, or the dangers of overpopulation.[120]

In the new atmosphere of public tolerance, there are more subtle ways of casting aspersion on racial and ethnic groups. Instead of egregious epithets or slurs, "code words" are now used to refer to negative characteristics of minorities. One journalist speaks of the "slur-cum-apology," in which politicians profit from public prejudices by playing to them, then absolving themselves.[121] And although it is now taboo for public figures to make moral judgments of different races, when these differences are put in terms of "scientific" evidence, they acquire an aura of respectability. A notable example is the much publicized book *The Bell Curve*, which claims that differences in intelligence between blacks and whites have an important hereditary component.[122]

For all the changed rhetoric, race continues to be the basis for profound inequalities and prejudices. New York remains a highly segregated city in which blacks and Hispanics are more likely than whites—or Asians—to live in areas of concentrated poverty, with inferior schools, inadequate city services, and high crime rates.[123] Crimes motivated by bigotry have not disappeared, despite the creation of bias-investigation teams to prevent them. Police brutality against minorities is a serious problem. In 1996, almost 80 percent of police-misconduct complaints to New York City's Civilian Complaint Review Board were made by blacks, Hispanics, and Asians; in the same year, an Amnesty International report found a pattern of ill treatment of suspects, deaths in custody, and unjustified shootings by officers, with most abuses in black, Hispanic, and Asian neighborhoods.[124] Many whites are unwilling to support government programs aimed at assisting racial minorities; affirmative action has lost political support in the nation and is under attack in the courts. Thus, while contemporary immigrants benefit from entering a society that has witnessed remarkable progress since the civil rights revolution, racial divisions continue to matter in significant ways.

The racial difference between today's nonwhite immigrants and their white European predecessors seems like a basic—and obvious—fact. Yet much is not obvious about racial matters then and now. At the turn of the century, Jews and Italians were not recognized as fully white, and negative views of them were often expressed in racial terms. At a time when nearly all New Yorkers were of European descent, Jews and Italians were seen as racially distinct from and inferior to those of Anglo-Saxon stock. Today, although immigrants from Latin America, Asia, and the Caribbean are often referred to as nonwhite or people of color, these blanket terms oversimplify the nature and impact of race among them.

One of the benefits of a historical comparison is that it highlights the elasticity and changeability of racial perceptions. Today, New York's racial order is in a state of flux as the white share of the population continues to shrink and the proportion of Hispanics and Asians grows. In the context of contemporary New York, the term racial minority, as currently used, is in fact a misnomer now that whites are actually a numerical minority—some refer to New York as a majority minority city. In 1998, according to census estimates, only 35 percent of New Yorkers were white; Asians had reached 8 percent of the citywide total; blacks, 26 percent; and Hispanics, 31 percent.[125] In light of these changes, as Reynolds Farley observes, "the way we think about race, the meaning of the term, and the way we define and measure racial categories are all topics of debate as the old black-white dichotomy proves inadequate for the many-hued nation we are becoming."[126]

And the many-hued New York. A new racial hierarchy is evolving in the city in which Hispanics, in many contexts, are seen as a separate race and Asians have become the "whitest" of the nonwhite groups. This enormous change in perceptions of Asians has led to speculation that, with more intermarriage and intermingling, the category "white" may eventually be expanded to include Asians as well as lighter-skinned Hispanics, although a more pessimistic view holds that persistent discrimination will prevent Asians from ever being accepted as belonging to white America.[127]

Another new dynamic is that New York has a huge population of African Americans and Puerto Ricans, the groups many New Yorkers still have in mind when they use the term minority. This has enormous implications for black and Hispanic immigrants. On the positive side, blacks and Hispanics have the potential of joining together politically to further common aims and agendas—a potential that is realized on many occasions. Less happily, black and Hispanic immigrants often face the same kind of discrimination and prejudice as native minorities. One reason many of today's immigrants stress their ethnic identity is to set themselves apart from African Americans and Puerto Ricans. This is the case for West Indians, many Latino newcomers, and even some dark-skinned Indians who run the risk of being confused with African Americans.

Despite the striking changes, the social construction of race in black-white terms has had a grim tenacity. As blacks of African descent, West Indians suffer extraordinary disabilities, and black Hispanic immigrants confront more severe discrimination than their lighter-skinned compatriots. A key issue for many of today's darker-skinned immigrants is not whether they will become white—which is currently out of the question—but whether they will gain recognition on the basis of their ethnicity or national heritage rather than be identified in terms of skin color.

The most intractable racial boundary in the United States remains that separating those deemed black from so-called whites. Consequently, although Asians and lighter-skinned Hispanics may well be the current "in-between peoples," the fate of black immigrants and their children is more problematic. Certainly, new racial conceptions are likely to evolve that erode the black-white dichotomy. It is also possible, however, that the crucial line will remain between blacks and all others, as black immigrants and their children remain on the black side of the racial divide and experience persistent discrimination well into the future.

# CHAPTER 6

# Transnational Ties

The conception of citizenship itself is rapidly changing and we may have to recognize a sort of world or international citizenship as more logical than the present peripatetic kind, which makes a man an American while here, and an Italian while in Italy. International conferences are not so rare nowadays. Health, the apprehension or exclusion of criminals, financial standards, postage, telegraphs and shipping are today to a great extent, regulated by international action. . . . The old barriers are everywhere breaking down. We may even bring ourselves to the point of recognizing foreign "colonies" in our midst, on our own soil, as entitled to partake in the parliamentary life of their mother country. — Gino Speranza

S ound familiar? This reflection on the globalizing world and the possibility of electoral representation for Italians abroad describes issues that immigration scholars are debating and discussing today. The words were written, however, in 1906 by the secretary of the Society for the Protection of Italian Immigrants.[1] They are a powerful reminder that processes that scholars now call transnational have a long history. Contemporary immigrant New Yorkers are not the first newcomers to live transnational lives. Although immigrants' transnational connections and communities today reflect many new dynamics, there are also significant continuities with the past.

The term transnationalism, as developed in the work of Linda Basch and her colleagues, refers to processes by which immigrants "forge and sustain multi-stranded social relations that link together their societies of origin and settlement. . . . An essential element . . . is the multiplicity of involvements that transmigrants sustain in both home and host societies." It's not just a question of political ties that span borders of the kind that Gino Speranza had in mind. In a transnational perspective, contemporary immigrants are seen as maintaining familial, economic, cultural, and political ties across international borders, in effect making the home and host society a single arena of social action.[2] Migrants may be living in New York, but, at the same time, they maintain strong involvements in their societies of origin, which, tellingly, they continue to call home.

In much of what is written on the subject, transnationalism is treated as if it were a new invention; a common assumption is that earlier European immigration cannot be described in transnational terms that apply today. Perhaps, as Nina Glick Schiller notes, the excitement over the "first flurry of discovery of the transnational aspects of contemporary migration" led to a "tendency to declare . . . transnational migration . . . a completely new phenomenon."[3] A few years earlier, she and her colleagues argued that transnationalism was a new type of migrant experience—that a new conceptualization, indeed a new term, transmigrant, was needed to understand the immigrants of today.[4] Recently, Alejandro Portes has argued that present-day transnational communities—dense networks across political borders created by immigrants in their quest for economic advancement and social recognition—possess a distinctive character that justifies coining a new concept to refer to them.[5]

Of course, there have been hints in the literature that modern-day transnationalism is not altogether new—suggestions, for example, that it differs in "range and depth" or "density and significance" from patterns in earlier eras.[6] A recent essay by Glick Schiller marks an important step forward by beginning to systematically compare current transnational migration to the United States with past patterns.[7] Following this lead, Luis Guarnizo analyzes differences in the meanings, implications, and effects of transnational political practices among contemporary and turn-of-the-century immigrants.[8] Historians, too, have been jumping on the transnationalism bandwagon, pointing out that they've been writing about transnational practices and processes all along—they just haven't used the term.[9]

In this chapter I take a closer look at what's really new about transnationalism through an analysis of New York's immigrants in two eras. What emerges is that many transnational patterns often said to be new have been around for a long time—and some of the sources of transnationalism seen as unique today also operated in the past. At the same time, there is no denying that much is distinctive about transnationalism today, not only because earlier patterns have been intensified or become more common but also because new processes and dynamics are involved.

## Continuities between Past and Present

Like contemporary immigrants, Russian Jews and Italians in turn-of-the-century New York established and sustained familial, economic, political, and cultural links to their home societies at the same time as they developed ties and connections in their new land. They did so for many of the same reasons that have been advanced to explain transnationalism today. There were relatives left behind and ties of sentiment to home communities and countries. Many immigrants came to America with the notion that they would eventually return. If, as one anthropologist notes, labor-exporting nations now acknowledge that "members of their diaspora communities are resources that should not and need not be lost to the home country," this was also true of the Italian government in the past.[10] Moreover, lack of economic security and full acceptance in America also plagued the earlier immigrants and may have fostered their continued involvement in and allegiance to their home societies. Of the two groups, Italians best fit the ideal transmigrant described in the contemporary literature; many led the kind of dual lives said to characterize transmigrants today.

Russian Jews and Italian immigrants in New York's past, like their modern-day counterparts, continued to be engaged with those they left behind. What social scientists now call "transnational households," with members scattered across borders, were not uncommon a century ago. Most Italian men—from 1870 to 1910 nearly 80 percent of Italian immigrants to the United States were men—left behind wives, children, and parents; Jewish men, too, were often pioneers who later sent money to pay for the passage of other family members. Those who came to New York sent letters to relatives and friends in the Old World—and significant amounts of money. Jake, the young Jewish immigrant in Abraham Cahan's story *Yekl*, was following a common pattern when he regularly sent money to his wife in Russia. Whenever he got a letter from his wife, Jake would hold onto his reply "until he had spare United States money enough to convert to ten rubles, and then he would betake himself to the draft office and have the amount, together with the well-crumpled epistle, forwarded to Poveodye." The New York Post Office sent 12.3 million individual money orders to foreign lands in 1900–1906, half the dollar amount going to Italy, Hungary, and Slavic countries.[11] Gino Speranza claimed that "it was quite probable that 'Little Italy' in New York contributes more to the tax roll of Italy than some of the poorer provinces in Sicily or Calabria."[12]

There were organized kinds of aid, too. Between 1914 and 1924, New

York's Jewish *landsmanshaftn,* or home town associations, sent millions of dollars to their war-ravaged home communities. The societies' traditional activities—concerts, balls, banquets, regular meetings, and Sabbath services—all became occasions for raising money. Special mass meetings were held as well. In one week in December 1914 more than twenty rallies took place in New York, raising between seventy-five and fifteen hundred dollars each for the war victims of various towns. After the war, many Jewish immigrant associations sent delegates who actually delivered the money. A writer in one Yiddish daily wrote: "The 'delegate' has become, so to speak, an institution in the Jewish community. There is not a single *landsmanshaft* here in America . . . which has not sent, is not sending, or will not send a delegate with money and letters to the *landslayt* on the other side of the ocean."[13]

Putting away money in New York to buy land or houses in the home country is another long-term habit among immigrants who intend to return. In the last great wave, Italian immigrants were most likely to invest in projects back home. "He who crosses the ocean can buy a house," was a popular refrain celebrating one goal of emigration.[14] An inspector for the port of New York quizzed fifteen entering Italians who had previously been to the United States. "When I asked them what they did with the money they carried over, I think about two-thirds told me they had bought a little place in Italy, a little house and a plot of ground; that they had paid a certain sum; that there was a mortgage on it; that they were returning to this country for the purpose of making enough money to pay that mortgage off." It was not unusual for Italians in New York to send funds home with instructions about land purchases. An Italian told of his five years of back-breaking construction work in New York. Each day, he recalled, "I dreamed of the land I would one day buy with my savings. Land anywhere else has no value to me."[15]

Many did more than just dream of going back—they actually returned. Nationwide, return migration rates are actually lower now than they were in the past. In the first two decades of the century, for every one hundred immigrants entering the United States, thirty-six left; between 1971 and 1990, the number had fallen to twenty-three.[16] Return migration, as Glick Schiller observes, should be viewed as part of a broader pattern of transnational connection. Those who have come to America with the notion of going back truly have their "feet in two societies." Organizing a return, Glick Schiller argues, necessitates the maintenance of home ties and entails a continuing commitment to the norms, values, and aspirations of the home society.[17]

Russian Jews in turn-of-the-century New York were unusual for their time in the degree to which they were permanent settlers. Having fled political repression and virulent anti-Semitism, the vast majority came to the New World to stay. Even so there was more return migration than is generally assumed. Between 1880 and 1900, perhaps as many as 15 to 20 percent who came to the United States returned to Europe.[18]

Many Russian Jewish migrants planned to return only temporarily in order to visit their home towns, although "not a few turned out to be one-way visits." Some had aged relatives whom they longed to see; others sought brides, young Jewish women being in short supply in America; still others went home merely to show off, to demonstrate that they had somehow made good; and in a few cases immigrants returned home to study. Some Russian Jews went back, savings in hand, to found businesses. Sarna tells us that a few "enterprising immigrants employed their knowledge of English and Russian to engage in commerce. In 1903, according to Alexander Hume Ford, there was 'a Russian American Hebrew in each of the large Manchurian cities securing in Russia the cream of the contracts for American material used in Manchuria.'" Russian statistics indicate that 12,313 more U.S. citizens entered Russian territory from 1881 to 1914 than left. According to American government investigators, "Plenty of Jews living in Russia held United States passports, the most famous being Cantor Pinchas Minkowsky of Odessa, formerly of New York."[19]

After 1900, however, events in Russia led immigrants in New York to abandon the notion of return. With revolutionary upheaval and the increasing intensity of pogroms, the rate of return migration among Russian Jews fell off to about 5 percent.[20] In the post-1900 period there were also few repeat crossers. Of the Jews who entered the United States between 1899 and 1910, only 2 percent had been in the country before, the lowest rate of any immigrant group in the United States in this period.[21]

Many more Italians arrived with the expectation of returning home. They were the quintessential transnational New Yorkers of their time, as much commuters as many contemporary immigrants. Many were "birds of passage" who went back to their villages seasonally or after a few years in America. Italians called the United States "the workshop"; many arrived in March, April, and May and returned in October, November, and December, when layoffs were most numerous.[22] For many Italian men, navigating freely between their villages and America became a way of life.[23] They flitted "back and forth," writes Mark Wyman, "always trying to get enough for that additional plot, to pay off previous purchases, or to remove the load of debt from their backs." By the end of the nineteenth century, steamships were bigger, faster, and safer than before; tickets for the sixteen- or seventeen-day passage in steerage from Naples to New York cost fifteen dollars in 1880 and twenty-five in 1907 and could be paid for in installments.[24] Prefiguring terms used today, one early twentieth-century observer of Italian migration wrote of how improved methods of transportation were leading to the "annihilation of time and space."[25] Overall, between the 1880s and World War I, of every ten Italians who left for the United States, five returned. Many of these returnees—*ritornati,* as the Italians called them—remigrated to the United States. According to reports of the United States Immigration Commission, about 15 percent of Italian immigrants between 1899 and 1910 had been in the United States before.[26]

If economic insecurity, both at home and abroad, now leads many migrants to hedge their bets by participating in two economies, it was also a factor motivating Italians to travel back and forth across the Atlantic. The work Italian men found in New York's docks and construction sites was physically strenuous and often dangerous: the pay was low and the hours long; and the seasonal nature of the building trades meant that laborers had many weeks without any work. During economic downturns, work was scarcer, and, not surprisingly, Italian rates of return went up during the financial depression of 1894 and the panic years of 1904 and 1907.[27] Many Jews in the late nineteenth century, according to Jonathan Sarna, returned to Russia because they could not find decent work in America—owing to "the boom-bust cycle, the miserable working conditions, the loneliness, the insecurity."[28] Fannie Shapiro remembers crying when her father returned from a three-month stay in America, since she had wanted to join him. (She later emigrated on her own in 1906.) In Russia, she explained, her father "put people to work . . . [because] he was the boss," but in New York "they put him in a coal cellar."[29]

Lack of acceptance in America then, as now, probably contributed to a desire to return. Certainly, it fostered a continued identification with the home country or, in the case of Jews, a sense of belonging to a large diaspora population. Because most current immigrants are people of color, it is argued that modern-day racism is an important underpinning of transnationalism; nonwhite immigrants, denied full acceptance in America, maintain and build ties to their communities of origin to have a place they can call home.[30] Unfortunately, as recounted in Chapter 5, rejection of immigrants on the grounds of race has a long history, and, in the days before "white ethnics," Jews and Italians were thought to be racially distinct from—and inferior to—people with origins in northern and western Europe.

Whether because they felt marginalized and insecure in America or maintained ethnic allegiances for other reasons, Italians and Jews then, like many immigrants today, avidly followed news of and remained actively involved in home-country politics. As Matthew Jacobson puts it in his study of the "diasporic imagination" of Irish, Polish, and Jewish immigrants, the homelands did not lose their centrality in "migrants' ideological geographies." Life in the diaspora, he writes, remained in many ways oriented to the politics of the old center. Although the immigrant press was a force for Americanization, equally striking, says Jacobson, "is the tenacity with which many of these journals positioned their readers within the envisaged 'nation' and its worldwide diaspora. . . . In its front-page devotion to Old World news, in its focus upon the ethnic enclave as the locus of U.S. news, in its regular features on the groups' history and literature, in its ethnocentric frame on American affairs, the immigrant journal located the reader in an ideological universe whose very center was Poland, Ireland, or Zion."[31] Continued connections to the homeland influenced immigrants' political orientations and involvements in other ways. According to Michael Topp, the ideas, activities, and strategies of Italian American radicals in the years just before and just after World War I were shaped, at least in part, by communications with unionists and other activists in Italy, their reactions to events in Italy, and their physical movement back and forth between countries.[32]

New York immigrants have also long been tapped by home-country politicians and political parties as a source of financial support. Today, Caribbean politicians regularly come to New York to campaign and raise money; earlier in the century, Irish nationalist politicians made similar pilgrimages to the city. Irish immigrants, who arrived in large numbers in the mid-1800s, were deeply involved in the Irish nationalist cause in the early decades of the twentieth century. In 1918, the Friends of Irish Freedom sponsored a rally in Madison Square Garden attended by fifteen thousand people, and street orators for Irish freedom spoke "every night of the week" in Irish neighborhoods around the city. In 1920, Eamon de Valera traveled to New York seeking support for Sinn Fein and an independent Irish Republic, raising $10 million for his cause.[33]

Moreover, home governments were involved with their citizens abroad. The enormous exodus to America and return wave brought a reaction from the Italian government, which, like many states that send immigrants today, was concerned about the treatment of its dispersed populations—and also saw them as a global resource.[34] The Italian government gave subsidies to a number of organizations in America that offered social services to Italian immigrants and set up an emigration office on Ellis Island to provide the newly arrived with information on employment opportunities in the United States. The current of remigration, an Italian senator said in 1910, "represents an economic force of the first order for us. It will be an enormous benefit for us if we can increase this flow of force in and out of our country." In 1901, the Italian government passed a law empowering the Banco di Napoli to open branches or deputize intermediaries overseas to receive emigrant savings that could be used for Italian development. Beyond wanting to ensure the flow of remittances and savings homeward, Italy tried to retain the loyalty of emigrants overseas as part of its own nation-building project. A 1913 law addressed the citizenship issue: returnees who had taken foreign citizenship could regain Italian citizenship simply by living two years in Italy; their children were considered Italian citizens even if born elsewhere.[35] Although it never came to pass, there was even discussion of allowing the colonies abroad to have political representation in Italy.

## What's New

Clearly, transnationalism was alive and well a hundred years ago. But if there are continuities with the past, there is also much that is new. Technological changes have made it possible for immigrants to maintain more frequent and closer contact with their home societies and, in a real sense, have changed the very nature of transnational connections. Today's global economy encourages international business operations; the large number of professional and prosperous immigrants in contemporary America are well positioned to operate in a transnational field. Dual nationality provisions by home governments have, in conjunction with other changes in the political context, added new dimensions to transnational political involvements. Moreover, greater tolerance for ethnic pluralism and multiculturalism in late twentieth-century America, and changed perspectives of immigration scholars themselves, have put transnational connections in a new, more positive light.

Transformations in the technologies of transportation and communication have increased the density, multiplicity, and importance of transnational interconnections and made it possible for the first time for immigrants to operate more or less simultaneously in a variety of places.[36] A century ago, the trip back to Italy took about two weeks, and more than a month elapsed between sending a letter home and receiving a reply. Today, immigrants can hop on a plane or make a phone call to check out how things are going at home.[37] As Patricia Pessar observes with regard to New York Dominicans: "It merely requires a walk to the corner newsstand, a flick of the radio or television dial to a Spanish-language station, or the placement of an overseas call" to learn about news in the Dominican Republic.[38]

In the jet age, inexpensive air fares mean that immigrants, especially from nearby places in the Caribbean and Central America, can fly home for emergencies, like funerals, or celebrations, like weddings; go back to visit their friends and relatives; and sometimes move back and forth, in the manner of commuters, between New York and their home community. Round-trip fares to the Dominican Republic in 1998 ran as low as $330. Among the immigrant workers I studied several years ago in a New York nursing home, some routinely spent their annual vacation in their home community in the Caribbean; others visited every few years.[39] A study of New York's Asian Indians notes that despite the distance and cost, they usually take their families back to visit India every year or two.[40] Inexpensive air travel means that relatives from home also often come to New York to visit. In the warmer months, Lessinger reports, when relatives from India make return visits to the United States, "a family's young men are often assigned to what is laughingly called 'airport duty,' going repeatedly to greet the flights of arriving grandparents, aunts and uncles, cousins and family friends."[41] Thanks to modern communications and air travel, a group of Mexicans in New York involved in raising money to improve their home community's water supply was able to conduct meetings with the *municipio* via conference call and to fly back to the community for the weekend to confer with contractors and authorities when they learned the new tubing had been delivered.[42]

Now that telephones reach into the far corners of most sending societies, immigrants can hear about news and people from home right away and participate immediately in family discussions on major decisions. Rates have become cheap—in 1998 a three-minute call to the Dominican Republic cost as little as $1.71, and to India $3.66; phone parlors, ubiquitous in New York, and prepaid phone calls are even cheaper.[43] Cristina Szanton Blanc describes how a Filipino couple in New York maintained a key role in child-rearing decisions although several of their children remained in Manila. On the phone, they could give advice and orders and respond to day-to-day problems. When their only daughter in Manila had an unfortunate romance, they dispatched a friend visiting the Philippines to investigate the situation. Adela, the mother of the family, had herself been back to the Philippines three times in six years.[44] Asian Indian New Yorkers typically phone relatives in India weekly or biweekly, and Johanna Lessinger reports that one rich young woman called her mother in Delhi every day.[45] Most Brazilians whom Maxine Margolis interviewed in New York City ran up phone bills of between $85 and $150 a month, and a few admitted that they typically spent $200 a month or more. She offers an illustration of how readily Brazilians call home: "When I was in a home furnishing store in Manhattan and asked the Brazilian owner, a long time resident of New York City, how to say 'wine rack' in Portuguese, he was disturbed when he could not recall the phrase. As quickly as one might consult a dictionary, he dialed Brazil to ask a friend."[46]

Faxes and videotapes also allow immigrants to keep in close touch with those they left behind. Some Brazilians in New York, Margolis tells us, regularly record or videotape sixty- to ninety-minute messages for family and friends back home. Like other immigrant New Yorkers, they can participate vicariously, through videotape, in important family events.[47] Johanna Lessinger recounts how Indians in Queens gather to watch full-length videos of weddings of widely scattered relatives, able to admire the dress and jewelry of the bride and calculate the value of pictured wedding gifts.[48] The better-off and better-educated may use e-mail as well. Said an Irish journalist in New York: "My grandfather, who came here in the late 1800s . . . he was an immigrant. . . . We don't have the finality of the old days. I can send E-mail. I can phone. I can be in Bantry in twelve hours."[49] Immigrant cable-television channels, moreover, allow an immediate, and up-close view, of homeland news for many groups; Koreans in Queens can watch the news from Seoul on the twenty-four-hour Korean channel, while Russian émigrés can turn to WMNB-TV for live performances from a Moscow concert hall.[50]

Modern forms of transportation and communications, in combination with new international forms of economic activity in the new global marketplace, have meant that more immigrants today are involved in economic endeavors that span national borders. Certainly, it is much easier today than a hundred years ago for immigrants to manage businesses thousands of miles away, given, among other things, modern telecommunications, information technologies, and instantaneous money transfers. Alejandro Portes and Luis Guarnizo describe how Dominican entrepreneurs in New York reap rewards by using their time in New York to build a base of property, bank accounts, and business contacts and then travel back and forth to take advantage of economic opportunities in both countries.[51] A few years after a Dominican man Patricia Pessar knew bought a garment factory in New York, he expanded his operations by purchasing (with his father and brother) a garment factory in the Dominican Republic's export processing zone. He and his wife and children continue to live in New York, where he has become a U.S. citizen, though he has also built a large house in the Dominican Republic.[52]

Many Asian Indian New Yorkers, encouraged by the Indian government's attempt to capture immigrant capital for development, invest in profit-making ventures in India, including buying urban real estate and constructing factories, for-profit hospitals, and medical centers. Often, relatives in India provide on-the-spot help in managing the business there. After receiving a graduate degree in engineering in the United States, Dr. S. Vadivelu founded a factory in New Jersey that makes electrolytic capacitors. He later opened two factories in his home state of Andhra Pradesh, where he manufactures ceramic capacitors for sale to Indian electronics manufacturers. His father and brothers manage both plants on a daily basis; Dr. Vadivelu travels back and forth several times a year to check on the factories.[53]

The Indian example points to something else that's new about transnationalism today. Compared to the past, a much higher proportion of newcomers today come with advanced education, professional skills, and sometimes substantial amounts of financial capital that facilitate transnational connections—and allow some immigrants to participate, in the manner of modern-day cosmopolitans, in high-level institutions and enterprises here and in their home society. The affluence of Indian New Yorkers, Lessinger argues, makes them one of the most consistently transnational immigrants in behavior and outlook. Indeed, *within* the Asian Indian community, it is the wealthiest and most successful professionals and business people who maintain the closest links with India and for whom "extensive transnationalism is a way of life." They are the ones who invest in India, make numerous phone calls, and fly home frequently, where they mix business with pleasure; such individuals have "a certain influence and standing wherever they go."[54] The Chinese "astronauts" who shuttle back and forth by air between Taiwan or Hong Kong and America are typically well-educated and well-off professionals, executives, and entrepreneurs who move easily in financial, scientific, and business worlds around the globe.[55] Pyong Gap Min describes international commuter marriages involving high-level Korean professionals and business executives who have returned to Korea for better jobs while their wives and children remain in New York for educational opportunities. The couples talk on the phone several times a week; the husbands fly to New York two to five times a year while the wives visit Korea once or twice a year.[56]

When it comes to transnational political involvements, here, too, technological advances play a role. The newest New Yorkers can hop on a plane to vote in national elections in their home countries, as thousands did in a recent Dominican presidential election. (With new Dominican electoral reforms, due to go into effect in 2002, such trips will be unnecessary, since it will be possible to vote in Dominican elections from polling places in New York.) Politicians from home, in turn, can make quick trips to New York to campaign and raise funds. Candidates for U.S. electoral positions have been known to return to their country of origin for the same reason. Guillermo Linares, for example, during his 1991 campaign for New York's City Council, briefly visited the Dominican Republic, where rallies held in support of his candidacy generated campaign funds and afforded opportunities for photos that were featured in New York newspapers.[57]

Apart from technological advances, there are other new aspects to transnational political practices today. Russian Jews brought with them a notion of belonging to a broader Jewish diaspora community, but they had no interest in being part of the oppressive Russian state they left behind. Italians, coming from a country in the midst of nation-state consolidation, did not arrive with a modern "national identity." Except for a tiny group of political exiles, migrants did not care much about building an Italian state that "would welcome them back, protect them from the need to migrate further, or represent the character and glories of the Italian people."[58] Among other groups in the past, such as the Irish, migration became part of their continuing struggle for national liberation. What's different today is that immigrants are arriving from sovereign countries, with established nationalist ideologies and institutions, and are a potential basis of support for government projects, policies, and leaders in the homeland. As a new way of building support among migrants abroad, former president Jean-Bertrand Aristide of Haiti popularized the notion of overseas Haitians as the Tenth Department in a country that is divided into nine administrative departments and set up a Ministry of Haitians Living Abroad within the Haitian cabinet.[59]

Moreover, today, when the United States plays such a dominant role in the global political system and development strategies depend heavily on U.S. political and economic support, a number of sending states view their migrant populations as potential lobbies. It has been argued that one reason some nations are encouraging their nationals to become United States citizens is their desire to nurture a group of advocates to serve the home country's interests in the American political arena.[60]

Of enormous importance are the dual-nationality provisions that now cover a growing number of New York's immigrants. Early in the century, a new citizen forfeited U.S. citizenship by voting in foreign elections or holding political office in another country. Today, the United States tolerates (though does not formally recognize or encourage) dual nationality—and many countries sending immigrants here have been rushing to allow it. As of December 1996, seven of the ten largest immigrant groups in New York City had the right to be dual nationals.[61] Legislation passed in Mexico in 1998 allows Mexicans, one of the fastest-growing immigrant groups in the city, to hold Mexican nationality as well as U.S. citizenship although, as of this writing, dual nationals cannot vote in Mexican national elections or hold high office there.[62]

The details of dual-nationality policies vary from country to country. In Trinidad and Tobago, for example, dual nationals can vote only if they have lived there for a year prior to elections, whereas Colombian nationals can vote at the Colombian Consulate or polling sites in Queens and run for office in their homeland even after they become U.S. citizens. In 1994 the Dominican Republic recognized the right to dual nationality; three years later, as part of an electoral reform package, the government adopted a proposal to give naturalized American citizens of Dominican descent the right to vote in Dominican elections and run for office while living in New York. When implemented, the reforms will make the Dominican community in New York the second largest concentration of voters in any Dominican election, exceeded only by Santo Domingo.[63] Currently, there are proposals in the Dominican Congress to create seats to represent Dominican emigrants.

A powerful economic incentive is involved in the recognition of dual nationality by various sending countries. In the Dominican Republic, for example, immigrant remittances rank as the most important source of foreign exchange, and there, as elsewhere, the government wants to ensure the flow of money and business investment homeward.[64] The record-breaking naturalization rates in the United States, in large part a response to recent U.S. legislation depriving noncitizens of various public social benefits, may have increased concern about losing the allegiance—and dollars—of emigrants.[65] On his first visit to New York City as president of the Dominican Republic, Lionel Fernandez Reyna (who grew up in New York City, where he attended elementary and high school on the Upper West Side) publicly urged Dominicans to feel free to pursue dual citizenship. "If you, young mother, or you, elderly gentleman, or you, young student, feel the need to adopt the nationality of the United States in order to confront the vicissitudes of that society stemming from the end of the welfare era, do not feel tormented by this," he said in a speech televised on New York's Channel 41. "Do it with a peaceful conscience, for you will continue being Dominicans, and we will welcome you as such when you set foot on the soil of our republic."[66] Political calculations come into play, too. The extension of dual nationality or citizenship provisions may be a way of trying to secure the role of overseas nationals as "advocates of *la patria's* interests in the United States, the new global hegemon."[67] And though the migrant community's economic clout is an important reason why, as in the Dominican case, migrant lobbying efforts for dual citizenship were successful, political developments and conflicts in the home country are also involved.[68]

Although some scholars and public figures worry about the trend toward dual nationality—it makes citizenship akin to bigamy, says journalist Georgie Anne Geyer, in *Americans No More: The Death of American Citizenship*—by and large transnational connections are viewed in a more favorable light today than they were in the past.[69] Early in the century, return migration inflamed popular opinion. "Immigrants were expected to stay once they arrived," writes historian Walter Nugent. "To leave again implied that the migrant came only for money; was too crass to appreciate America as a noble experiment in democracy; and spurned American good will and helping hands."[70] Another historian notes: "After 1907, there was tremendous hostility . . . toward temporary or return migrants. . . . The inference frequently drawn was that [they] considered the United States good enough to plunder but not to adopt. The result was a high degree of antipathy."[71] Indeed, Randolph Bourne's classic essay "Transnational America," published in 1916, responded to rising anti-immigrant sentiment, arguing that the nation should "accept . . . free and mobile passage of the immigrant between America and his native land. . . . To stigmatize the alien who works in America for a few years and returns to his own land, only perhaps to seek American fortune again, is to think in narrow nationalistic terms."[72]

At the time, a common concern was that the new arrivals were not making serious efforts to become citizens and real Americans. Public schools, settlement houses, and progressive reformers put pressure on immigrants to abandon their old-fashioned customs and languages. A popular guide on becoming American advised immigrant Jews to "forget your past, your customs, and your ideals." The Americanization movement's "melting pot" pageants, inspired by Israel Zangwill's play, depicted strangely attired foreigners stepping into a huge pot and emerging as immaculate, well-dressed, accent-free "American-looking" Americans.[73] Expressions of ethnicity were suffocated in New York City's schools, where, in the words of Superintendent Maxwell, the goal was "to train the immigrant child . . . to become a good American citizen."[74] Much of the scholarship concerning the earlier immigration emphasized the way immigrants were assimilating and becoming American; ties to the home society were often interpreted as "evidence for, or against, Americanization" and, in many accounts, were seen as impeding the assimilation process.[75]

Today, when there's an official commitment to cultural pluralism and cultural diversity, transnational ties are more visible and acceptable—and sometimes even celebrated in public settings. Anti-immigrant sentiment is still with us, and immigrant loyalties are still often questioned, but rates of return are not, as in the past, a key part of immigration debates. In an era of significant international money flow and huge U.S. corporate operations abroad, there is also less concern that immigrants are looting America by sending remittances home. Indeed, as Luis Guarnizo observes, U.S. corporations unintentionally reinforce and encourage transnationalism by developing marketing incentives to promote migrants' monetary transfers, long-distance communications, and frequent visits to their countries of origin.[76] Increasingly today, the message is that there is nothing un-American about expressing one's ethnicity. In New York, officials and social service agencies actively promote festivals and events to foster ethnic pride and glorify the city's multiethnic character. Practically every ethnic group has its own festival or parade, the largest being the West Indian American Day parade on Brooklyn's Eastern Parkway, which attracts between one and two million people every Labor Day. Exhibits in local museums and libraries highlight the cultural background of different immigrant groups; special school events feature the foods, music, and costumes of various homelands; and school curricula include material on diverse ethnic heritages. In the quest for votes, established New York politicians of all stripes recognize the value of visits to immigrant homelands. As part of her mayoral campaign, for example, Democratic candidate Ruth Messinger traveled to the Dominican Republic and Haiti for four days of official meetings, news conferences, and honorary dinners, which led to coverage in newspapers and radio and television stations reaching Dominicans and Haitians in New York.[77] This kind of campaigning across borders, Luis Guarnizo argues, lends legitimacy, status, and a sense of empowerment to groups like Dominicans, who maintain intense transnational relations.[78]

Scholars are now more interested in transnational ties and see them in a more positive light than in the past. In emerging transnational perspectives, the maintenance of multiple identities and loyalties is viewed as a normal feature of immigrant life; ties to the home society complement—rather than detract from—commitments in this country. At the same time, as immigrants buy property, build houses, start businesses, make marriages, and influence political developments in their home societies, they are also shown to be deeply involved in building lives in New York, where they buy homes, work on block associations and community boards, join unions, run school boards, and set up businesses.[79] Generally, the literature stresses the way transnational relationships and connections benefit immigrants, enhancing the possibility of survival in places full of uncertainty. In an era when globalization is a major subject of scholarly study, it is perhaps not surprising that immigrants are seen as actors who operate in a transnational framework or that commentators in the media are following suit. "Today," writes journalist Roger Rosenblatt, "when every major business enterprise is international, when money is international, when instant international experiences are pictured on T.V., more people think of themselves as world citizens. Why should not immigrants do likewise?"[80]

Obviously, there is much that is new about transnationalism. Modern technology, the new global economy and culture, and new laws and political arrangements have all combined to produce transnational connections that differ in fundamental ways from those maintained by immigrants a century ago. Once ignored or reviled, transnational ties are now a favorite topic at conferences and are sometimes even celebrated in today's multicultural age. Yet the novelty of contemporary conditions should not be exaggerated. Immigrants who move from one country to another seldom cut off ties and allegiances to those left behind, and turn-of-the-century immigrant New Yorkers were no exception. It may have been harder to maintain contacts across the ocean than it is today, but many immigrants in the last great wave maintained extensive, and intensive, transnational ties and operated in what social scientists now call a transnational social field.

A comparison of transnationalism then and now raises some additional issues. If many academic observers who studied earlier immigrants were guilty of overlooking transnational ties in the quest to document assimilation, there is now a risk of overemphasizing the centrality of transnationalism and minimizing the extent to which contemporary immigrants "become American" and undergo changes in behavior and outlook in response to circumstances in this country. Indeed, as David Hollinger notes, today's immigrants "are more prepared for a measure of assimilation by the worldwide influence of American popular culture; most are more culturally attuned to the United States before they arrive here than were their counterparts a century ago."[81] Moreover, as a recent study of Mexican and Central American migrants points out, transnationalism tends to put too much stress on ephemeral migration circuits and understates the permanency of migrant settlement.[82] Although many, perhaps most, immigrants come with the idea of improving their lot and returning home, as they extend their stay and as more family members join them, they become increasingly involved with life and people in this country. Ties to the homeland seldom disappear, but they often become fewer and thinner over time.

Perhaps because studies using a transnational approach are in their infancy, we still know little about how pervasive and extensive various transnational ties actually are for different groups. The new immigration, like the old, to quote Hollinger again, is very mixed. "It displays a variety of degrees of engagement with the United States and with prior homelands, and it yields some strong assimilationist impulses alongside vivid expressions of diasporic consciousness."[83] In the past, Italians were more transnational in behavior and outlook than Russian Jews. This was mainly because Jews came to stay, whereas large numbers of Italians were labor migrants, who aimed to—and often did—go back home after a spell of work in New York.

Today, as well, some groups are likely to maintain more intense, regular, and dense transnational connections than others, but we don't know which ones—or why. It is much more than a question of having significant numbers who go back and forth in low-level jobs like the Italian sojourners of old. Peggy Levitt suggests several factors that help explain why the groups she is studying in Boston differ in type, intensity, and durability of transnational ties. She lists geography, including the home country's distance from the United States and the extent of residential clustering here; institutional completeness or the degree to which the group creates institutions enabling migrants to satisfy most of their needs within their own ethnic community, particularly transnational institutions such as churches that extend across borders; and the role of the state, both the home government's role in reinforcing and encouraging migrants' ties with people back home and the American government's history of political and economic involvement in the homeland. She also mentions socioeconomic factors, including high levels of social parity between migrants and those in the home community that make it easier for members to stay attached to one another and to sanction those who do not.[84] Additional factors are also likely to be important: the nature of social organization and cultural patterns in the home community that may encourage the maintenance of transnational connections as well as the particularities of homeland political movements, leaders, and organizations that may lead them to actively recruit support abroad.

There is also variation *within* groups in the frequency, depth, and range of transnational ties. Just as well-off Asian Indian immigrants have more resources to maintain transnational connections than their poorer counterparts, so, too, this may be true in other immigrant groups. Legal status is likely to affect the types and extent of transnational connections maintained; undocumented immigrants cannot easily go back and forth, to give one obvious example. Whether migrants came on their own or with their families also must be considered. There are also bound to be differences in the nature and impact of transnational ties between men and women and between the old, young, and middle-aged. And as I've noted, transnational connections may well lose force with the length of stay in America, as suggested by research showing that remittances tend to taper off over time.

Finally, there are the consequences of transnational connections for migrants' lives here. If scholars of turn-of-the-century immigration once tended to blame home-country ties for a host of problems, from poor English skills to lack of interest in naturalizing, today's transnational perspectives often have a celebratory tone. Transnational ties are seen as helping migrants cope with discrimination and prejudice in this country and providing access to a wide range of resources, including business and investment opportunities, political and organizational leadership positions, and assistance with child care. In an insecure world, they allow migrants to keep their options open. As Glick Schiller and her colleagues write: "By stretching, reconfiguring, and activating . . . networks across national boundaries, families are able to maximize the utilization of labor and resources and survive within situations of economic uncertainty and subordination."[85] Even involvement in home country–based organizations is often said to strengthen migrants' ability to mobilize a base of support for political issues and elections in New York.[86]

But it is important to bear in mind that modern-day transnationalism has costs as well. Financial obligations to relatives left behind may be a drain on resources needed for projects in New York.[87] The family separation involved in transnationalism often brings great personal strain. Transnational mothers worry about the children left behind in the home country —about the care they're receiving, whether they'll get in trouble in adolescence, and whether they will transfer their allegiance and affection to the "other mother."[88] In the realm of politics, involvement in political and organizational affairs of the home country may draw energies and interests away from political engagement and activism on behalf of the immigrant community here; this is what one study suggests happens among Latin American men in Queens. Having experienced a loss of occupational status in New York, many of the men want to return to Latin America, and, as a result, they tend to form, participate in, and lead ethnic organizations that focus on the country of origin. These ethnic organizations raise money for charitable concerns in the home country, not the United States. It's unlikely, Jones-Correa predicts, such ethnic institutions will, in the short run, be an instrument for redirecting immigrants' focus to political and social issues in the United States.[89]

That scholars are debating the contradictory pressures of transnational ties is a sign of their importance for today's immigrants—and perhaps for their children as well. What is clear is that for the first generation, transnational practices are very much part of the modern scene. It is also clear, to return to the comparison, that they are not just a late twentieth-century phenomenon. Transnationalism has been with us for a long time, although in its modern guise it appears to be more far-reaching and more intense—and may also turn out to be more durable and long-lasting.

# CHAPTER 7

# Going to School

"*E*astern European Jews showed almost from the beginning of their arrival in this country a passion for education that was unique in American history." So wrote Nathan Glazer and Daniel Moynihan in *Beyond the Melting Pot* (1963), their study of the major ethnic groups then predominating in New York City.[1] Sentimental notions about the Jews' love affair with education and their zeal for the life of the mind have become part of our picture of the "world of our fathers." Jews are remembered as a "people of the book" who embraced learning on their climb up the social ladder.

Partly because so many of the writers, scholars, and popular image makers who shape our views of the last great wave are themselves Jewish, the Jewish experience looms large in the collective memory. The Jews are commonly viewed as the archetypal success story, pictured as making a miraculous rise through education. As for the schools, they are often recalled in popular opinion as places that took poor and ill-prepared immigrant children and turned them into an educated and Americanized middle class—what Colin Greer has called the great school legend.[2] There's nostalgia for a time when the schools aimed to transform immigrants into 100 percent Americans—when immigrants had to learn one language, English, and one national American culture.

These memories of the past matter today because they set up expectations about what immigrants can and should achieve in the schools. If my grandparents and great-grandparents could succeed in New York City's schools a hundred years ago without special programs to help them adjust, say many descendants of the earlier wave, why can't today's immigrants and their children do well when they get so much more assistance?

But, in fact, did immigrants in the last great wave succeed in the schools? And how is the current crop of newcomers doing? In assessing what actually happened then—and what's happening now—this chapter shows that popular myths give a distorted, rose-colored view of immigrant children's educational accomplishments in the past. Nor are the newest arrivals doing as badly as many imagine. Despite a dramatically different context and significant problems in the schools, many of today's immigrant children are doing remarkably well.

As for the role of the schools in turning immigrant children into Americans, did the schools really do a better job in the past than now, when the very term Americanization is under fire? And what difference does it make that today, as Nathan Glazer claims, "we are all multiculturalists now"?[3] A fascinating new twist is added by contemporary scholars who argue that it is risky for immigrant children to become too American and that those who hold onto their traditional culture often do better in school.

This leads to the final topic of the chapter: the role of immigrants' culture in explaining why some immigrant groups have produced so many high achievers in the schools while others have lagged behind. Insights from historical research on the relative success of Jews, compared to Italians, makes clear that it is not just culture but immigrants' social class that makes a difference. Today, another factor—race—must also be considered.

## Jewish Educational Achievements: Myths and Realities

Inspirational tales about the eastern European Jews' rise through education and their success in New York's schools in the so-called immigrant golden age do not stand up against the hard realities of the time. In the years before World War I, the period of concern here, most eastern European Jews did not make the leap from poverty into the middle class through education. Those who made substantial moves up the occupational ladder in this period generally did so through businesses in the garment, fur, shoe, and retail trades and in real estate. It was only in later decades, in the 1920s, 1930s, and beyond, that large numbers of eastern European Jewish children used secondary and higher education as a means of advancement.

For most Russian Jewish children, school was a short-term affair. Until 1916 or later, most left school with at best an eighth-grade education. During the 1890s, enrollment figures for District 1 on the Jewish Lower East Side declined sharply after grade 5B, indicating that many children left school when they reached twelve, the age at which one could get working papers. When, after 1903, the age limit was raised to fourteen, the most precipitous drop in enrollments took place at that age.[4] In fact, a study done for the Metropolitan Life Insurance Company reported that 37 percent of the working papers issued in New York City in 1914–15 went to Jewish children. In 1908, when the United States Immigration Commission conducted a study of New York's schools, over eighteen thousand Russian Jewish students were in the first grade, but only about five thousand were in the eighth.[5]

Few Russian Jewish children went to high school, and even fewer graduated. In 1908, only about 3,000 of the 109,000 Russian Jewish pupils in New York City were attending high school. A study that followed New York City school children who entered high school in 1906 found that 70 percent of the Russian Jews had dropped out four years later, and only 16 percent had graduated.[6] In 1908, 1,586 Russian Jewish students were in the first year of high school in New York City, but only 293 in the fourth. Altogether, well below 5 percent of the Russian Jewish children in the city graduated from high school.[7]

Going to college was even rarer—to the overwhelming majority of the newest Jewish immigrants, more a matter of mythology than experience. Indeed, in the first decade of the twentieth century less than 1 percent of Russian Jewish young people of college age ever reached the first year of college.[8]

The City College of New York (CCNY) may have already become a largely Jewish school—in 1908, three quarters of its all-male students were listed as Jews, mostly of eastern European background—but Jewish undergraduates at CCNY and other New York colleges were a select few. Only a tiny number made it to graduation. Moreover, according to Selma Berrol's account, the Jews who graduated from City College were mainly from German families who had come earlier in the nineteenth century. According to her analysis of City College's alumni registers, for four decades German Jewish names outnumbered all others; in 1883 less than 1 percent of the graduates had Russian or Polish names, and in 1923, only 11 percent.[9] At all-female Hunter College, the other tuition-free college in New York at the time, eastern European Jewish daughters had become the majority of the graduating Jewish population by 1910. Still, in the college as a whole, this group of women was a minority of the graduating class for a number of years after the First World War—going from less than 1 percent of the graduates in 1889 to 8 percent in 1906 to 24 percent ten years later.[10]

The numbers we're talking about are very small. City College's entire graduating class in 1913 had only 209 students; if eastern European Jews represented less than 11 percent of the graduates, then there were fewer than twenty-three men in the class. The 25 percent of Hunter College graduates who were eastern European Jews in 1916 included only fifty-eight women. This was at a time when the Jewish population of New York was almost a million![11] It was not until the 1930s that there were big graduating classes at City College that contained large numbers of Jews of Russian and Polish origin.[12]

Why is it that so few Russian Jewish children made it to high school and college? For one thing, there weren't many high schools in the city at the turn of the century, and a diploma wasn't necessary for the jobs employing most New Yorkers. This was a period when few employers required their employees to be high school graduates and when job opportunities were abundant for young people with little schooling. In fact, white-collar jobs were available even for the eighth-grade graduate. Before 1900, and into the first decade of this century, only a small fraction of any group graduated from high school, which was generally viewed as an institution for the bright child whose parents were willing and able to forgo his or her labor. An even smaller proportion of the population reached college. A business career did not require four years of college, nor did teaching and the law; indeed it wasn't until the late 1890s that a high school diploma was required for teacher certification in New York. Morris Hillquit, the distinguished Jewish socialist leader, recalled how he took up the study of law after dropping out of high school in the late 1880s. "Having passed the requisite 'Regents' examination,' I enrolled in the New York University Law School and was admitted to the bar in the spring of 1893."[13]

Before 1898, Manhattan and the Bronx had no public high schools for full-time study except for the preparatory divisions of the City College of New York (for young men) and Hunter College (for young women), both highly selective programs that provided a single year of "daunting post eighth-grade education."[14] Four evening high schools existed in Manhattan and the Bronx at the time, but in practice few enrolled in them (in 1895 enrollments totaled 6,973), far fewer attended (the average was 2,571), and only a handful earned diplomas (162).[15] Even immigrants who were motivated to attend the evening high schools found it hard after a long day's work to study or go to classes, which often left no time for dinner and involved considerable travel.[16] By 1911, the number of public high schools in the city had grown to nineteen, with an enrollment of fifty-four thousand students (a fourfold increase from 1899), but the high school student body was still only about a quarter of the size of the four preceding elementary school grades.[17]

There were even fewer places in New York's colleges.[18] When eastern European Jewish immigrants began to arrive in New York in large numbers in the 1880s and 1890s, City College (founded in 1847) was still mainly a place for the sons of prosperous families (often merchants), and its classical curriculum was meant to give cultural polish to men of independent means who went on to become ministers, doctors, or simply cultivated gentlemen.[19] At the turn of the century, however, CCNY modernized its curriculum; and starting in 1903, Regents scholarships, which provided enough to cover carfare and lunches, were available to students who scored well on examinations in academic subjects. But there were few seats available at the two tuition-free colleges: City College, with around half of New York's Jewish college students, had only 676 men enrolled in 1908; Hunter had only 703 women.

Extended schooling was a luxury beyond the means of most newly arrived immigrant families, who needed their children's contributions to the family income. Even those who managed it rarely saw all their children go to high school. In 1912, when Bella Cohen Spewack tried to persuade the parents of her thirteen-year-old friend Celia to let her go to high school, Celia's mother responded in a way that was not unusual for the time: "But you don't understand. . . . Every little money that comes into the household counts. Celia must go working. We know it's hard, but what can we do? There are three more [children] that must go through public school, no? Three more need shoes and shirts and dresses and food. There isn't enough. My husband makes but very little. He is no more a young one. Wouldn't we let Celia go if we could? Of course! Don't talk foolish!"[20] Two days later Celia entered a factory. In his memoirs, Morris Hillquit, who would later become a lawyer, wrote of dropping out of high school in the late 1880s because his parents were "frightfully poor. My elder brother and the older of my sisters were working. I felt uncomfortable in the role of the drone of the family and determined to go to work."[21] He ended up teaching evening school for three years, earning three dollars a night, before resuming his studies.

Finally, there's the fact that New York's elementary schools did a poor job of educating Russian Jewish immigrants' children, so that many were not prepared or motivated to continue their education beyond the elementary level.[22] The schools were severely overcrowded, a result of the enormous influx of immigrants and the inability of new school construction to keep up with demand. From enrollments of less than 250,000 in 1881, the public school population nearly doubled by 1898; by 1914, it had grown to 793,000 students. The Lower East Side, Brownsville, and Williamsburg—all Jewish areas—were among the most overcrowded districts in the city.

Given the shortage of seats, many Russian Jewish children were unable to start school at the usual age of seven and had to wait until they were eight or older. In 1894, almost a thousand children were turned away from three Lower East Side elementary schools for lack of room. A near riot took place in 1897, when five hundred Jewish children were turned away from P.S. 75 on the Lower East Side because the school already had two thousand pupils in a building meant for fifteen hundred. Bear in mind that the schools on the Lower East Side, as in other Jewish neighborhoods, were heavily Jewish owing to the residential concentration of the Jews and the local character of the public schools. In 1905, 95 percent of the sixty-four thousand pupils in a school district below Houston Street were Jewish; ten of the district's thirty-eight schools were 99 percent Jewish.

When children were admitted, their classes on the Lower East Side, according to Lillian Wald, a social worker, frequently had "as many as sixty pupils in a single room and often three children on a seat."[23] In Brownsville, the most congested school district in the city in 1910, there were three classes with as many as eighty-two students. One student later recalled having to sit in the same seat with another girl and put her arm around her seatmate's waist "so that I shouldn't fall off on the other side."[24] Educators of the time joked that teachers should have prior experience in a sardine factory before being hired to work in the New York schools.[25] On the Lower East Side, conditions were so crowded that an army hospital ship was converted into a school, and between 1905 and 1910, ten thousand children received instruction on board at its mooring at the foot of Corlear's Hook. Moreover, lack of seats consigned many to going to school only part-time; this way, the same room could be used for two classes in one day. In two Brownsville school districts in 1910, all children up to the fourth grade were on half-day sessions.[26]

Compounding the overcrowding was the fact that many immigrant children did not know English. Until the introduction of "C" or "steamer" classes in 1904, non-English-speaking children were placed in the lowest grade regardless of their age. The C classes were designed to give students, through a total immersion approach, enough English quickly so they could enter normal classes, but they were woefully inadequate. No matter how children did in the C classes—many spent only six weeks in them—they had to transfer into a regular class after five or six months. Moreover, owing to lack of funds, problems of overcrowding, and the inertia and opposition of teachers and principals, there were very few of these classes, only enough for some fifteen hundred students throughout the city in 1906 and seventeen hundred in 1908. Although nearly every school on the Lower East Side had at least one C class, many schools in Williamsburg and Brownsville had none at all.[27]

Given language difficulties and the late age at which many Jewish children started school, it is not surprising that many were older than the usual
for their grade level. Teachers were the ones to decide whether a child
should be promoted or not; children who could not do the required work
were simply left back to repeat the grade, often with the very same teacher
who had denied them promotion the previous term. In 1908, 35 percent of
the Russian Jewish elementary school pupils in New York City were overage for their grade. When Julia Richman was district superintendent on
the Jewish Lower East Side, she wrote of the armies of "holdovers" who
repeated the class they had taken previously. In 1908, according to the U.S.
Immigration Commission reports, over a thousand Russian Jewish twelve-
year-olds had not made it beyond the third grade.

The teaching methods didn't help either. Mechanical drill and rote
learning were the order of the day into the first decade of the twentieth
century. A survey in the 1890s described a recitation in which the children
bobbed up and down so rapidly in giving answers that "the class represented the appearance rather of traveling pump handle rather than of a
large number of human beings." Answers were screamed rapidly and the
children were not permitted time to think.[28]

If schooling for most eastern European Jewish students in turn-of-the-
century New York was nasty, brutish, and short, how did they stack up
compared to other groups? By any standard, they did much better than
Italians, the city's other greenhorns at the time. Undoubtedly, this favorable comparison is one reason Jewish academic achievements have stood
out and received so much attention. Compared to New York City's native
whites (the term studies then used for native-born whites with a native-
born white parent or parents), the picture is mixed.

At the elementary school level, Russian Jewish students' progress was
fairly similar to that of native white New Yorkers—though it was much
more impressive than Italians'. (Virtually all Russian Jewish schoolchil-
dren attended public schools, as did about 90 percent of Italians.)[29] A number of studies sought to measure rates of retardation for different ethnic
groups, the unfortunate phrase then used to describe being older than the
normal age for a grade level. In a 1908 study by the Immigration Commission, 41 percent of native white ten- to twelve-year-olds were two or more
years overage for their grade, compared to 46 percent of Russian Jewish
children and 69 percent of southern Italian children. Another survey of
students in fifteen New York City schools found Russian Jewish children
only a little more overage than the German and native-born youngsters
tested and much less retarded than Italians.[30] A few years later, according

to a study made in 1911 for the superintendent of schools, the greatest number of nonpromotions in the city were in Little Italy.[31] A similar pattern emerges in another measure of school progress: in 1908, about the same proportion of Russian Jewish seventh graders (71 percent) continued to eighth grade as native whites (75 percent), while fewer southern Italians stayed (60 percent).

According to records of the Board of Attendance, truancy was higher in Italian East Harlem and Little Italy than elsewhere in the city. Italian parents were more likely than Russian Jews to keep their children out of school to help with housework or to earn money. "My mother told me to stay at home" and "My parents cannot afford to send me to school every day" were standard comments from Italian pupils explaining their absence.[32] Although the superintendent of schools praised Jews for obeying the compulsory education laws, he wrestled with the problem of truant Italians, suggesting the appointment of several Italian-speaking truant officers to deal with Italian parents who were keeping their children home.[33]

A greater proportion of Italian students dropped out altogether before the legal working-paper age, as compared to Russian Jews, who were more likely to complete the minimum grades required.[34] According to the U.S. Immigration Commission, in 1908 Italians had a larger number of child laborers aged six to fifteen who were not in school than any other ethnic group in the city.[35] Lax enforcement of the law meant that it was possible to get working papers before the legal age or to go to work without them. False papers certifying a child's age were available in immigrant neighborhoods, and physical examinations by the Health Department, if given at all, were cursory. Manufacturers had little fear if they hired adolescents without proper papers, since few factory inspectors were around to enforce regulations. The city's magistrates usually refused to fine parents for allowing their children to stay out of school, even if they had not obtained certification. School officials themselves were known to certify students they knew to be underage as a way to be rid of "unruly and uneducable" pupils.[36]

Higher up the educational hierarchy, Russian Jews surpassed southern Italians but did not do as well as native whites. In 1908, the Immigration Commission's study found that a third of New York's native-white sixth graders made it to high school, compared to 16 percent of Russian Jews and 6 percent of southern Italians. Students who stayed until eighth grade had a better chance of going to high school, but the same pattern prevailed: over half of the native white eighth graders started high school, compared to 31 percent and 22 percent of Russian Jewish and southern Italian eighth graders, respectively. Once they reached high school, the dropout rates for all groups were astoundingly high, but Russian Jews (18 percent) had about the same chance of reaching the senior year as native whites (20 percent) and a better chance than southern Italians (11 percent). A study that tracked a sample of students who entered New York City high schools in 1906 found that Russian Jewish students (16 percent) had higher graduation rates than native whites and indeed than all other ethnic groups; Italians came out at the bottom, with none in the sample graduating after four years.[37]

At the college level, Jews stood out with an extraordinarily high proportion of New York's undergraduates, no doubt another reason for their reputation for educational success. In 1908, when they were a third of New York's public school population, they formed close to a quarter of the students in the eight colleges in the city surveyed by the Immigration Commission.[38] Although they were still a small minority at places like Barnard and Columbia, they were by far the dominant group at City College and made up more than a quarter of the student body at Hunter College. Precious few Italians attended college at the time. In the Immigration Commission survey, they accounted for less than 1 percent of New York's college population, though they made up 10 percent of the public school student body. With seventeen Italians (compared to 146 Jews), Columbia had the largest contingent of Italians of any college in the city; Adelphi and Barnard had no Italians.[39]

If Jews had a high rate of college attendance for the time, native whites in this period did even better—and continued to dominate higher education. Although children with native white fathers were a distinct minority—27 percent—of the public school student body, they made up about half of New York City's college population.[40]

## How Are Contemporary Immigrants Doing?

To hear many native New Yorkers tell it, the city's school system has never been as bad as it is today. The schools are dangerous, dirty, and decaying; the students perform poorly, many graduating from high school without being able to read or write English. The growing number of immigrants, it seems to many, is just another part of the problem. Indeed, New York City school personnel often attribute the low academic performance of students in many districts to the influx of large numbers of inadequately prepared immigrant students.[41] Because the new immigrants are, by and large, nonwhite, many New Yorkers lump them with native-born minorities who dominate the city's schools today—three out of four New York City public school students are black or Hispanic—and assume that immigrants share the same educational problems and difficulties commonly associated with poor native-born black and Hispanic youth.[42] Such pessimistic views are as misleading as myths about the educational giants of the immigrant past. Whereas some immigrant children are having trouble in the schools, many others are making remarkable progress.

How does this compare with the educational achievements of immigrants and their children at the turn of the century? It's difficult to say, because the context in which education is a path to mobility is so radically different today. To compare the present proportion of immigrant children graduating from high school or college with past figures is to ignore the different meaning of a high school and college education in the two periods. On the one hand, the latest immigrants benefit from new programs and educational opportunities; on the other, formal education—and a more extended education—is now more important in getting a job as a consequence of educational upgrading and transformations in the nature of work. It's necessary, therefore, to first get a sense of the context in which the latest arrivals go to school and advance through the educational system before looking at their actual accomplishments.

Since the beginning of the century, educational requirements have, in essence, been racheted up several rungs. At the time of the last great wave, high schools were just starting to become mass institutions. Now, getting a high school diploma is the norm, achieved by more than 70 percent of New York City's adult population.[43] Whereas one hundred years ago an eighth-grade education would do for most manual jobs, now a high school diploma is a must for many low-skilled positions. Indeed, in 1990, the four leading occupations for the nation's male high school graduates (aged sixteen to thirty-four) were truck drivers, carpenters, auto mechanics, and janitors and cleaners; and for women, secretaries, cashiers, waitresses, and nursing aides.[44] High school graduates not only have a better chance of getting a job than high school dropouts but also earn more money.

College is no longer an institution for a tiny elite.[45] Indeed, by 1990, a quarter of New Yorkers twenty-five and older had completed a college education.[46] Today, college graduates find themselves competing for positions that immigrants with a high school diploma could have obtained a century ago. Graduating from college—and beyond—has become essential for the growing number of professional, technical, and managerial positions.

Whatever the actual utility of a college degree for many jobs, the fact is that in a competitive job market, employers often regard it as a marker of a worker's desirability.

There is a significant earnings premium for a college diploma. In 1990, according to one analysis, men with a college degree in New York City had earnings that were 118 percent higher than those with just a high school diploma; women college graduates' earnings were 164 percent higher than those of high school graduates.[47] The economic returns to advanced education have increased in recent years. The average annual earnings (adjusted for inflation) of high school dropouts declined in New York City during the 1980s; they slightly increased for high school graduates and went up substantially for college graduates.[48]

Although immigrants need more education today to get ahead, this is balanced by the fact that the educational system now offers a much broader range of programs and opportunities than were available in the past. Probably the most significant change since the beginning of the century has been the enormous expansion, and wider availability, of higher education. For New York's recent arrivals, college mainly means one of the institutions of the City University of New York (CUNY), now a gargantuan system unrecognizable from the days when Hunter and City were the only municipal colleges and had enrollments in the hundreds. In 1995, CUNY had more than 213,000 students enrolled in ten senior colleges, six community colleges, a technical college, a graduate school, a law school, a medical school, and an affiliated school of medicine. Free tuition disappeared in 1976—twenty years later, tuition was thirty-two hundred dollars a year at four-year colleges and twenty-five hundred dollars at community colleges—although many students receive state and federal grants that cover much of the cost.

At the turn of the last century, the entrance requirements to City College were minimal, and once there, many students had trouble with the rigorous examination standards.[49] For the last three decades, CUNY's graduation standards have also been considerably higher than admissions criteria, but there has been more help for those having difficulty—although CUNY is now toughening the admissions process and has adopted a plan to eliminate remedial classes at the four-year senior colleges. Under the open-admissions policy introduced in 1970, high school graduates with an 80 average or a rank in the top half of their class—which after 1976 was raised to the top third—were guaranteed a place in one of the senior colleges; everyone else was offered a seat in a community college. The four-year colleges offered an array of remedial programs as well as classes in

English as a Second Language to help students with basic skills.[50] A new system is designed to change this. In 1995, the senior colleges were allowed to set their own admissions standards. Even more radical, beginning in 2000, according to the new plan, students unable to pass proficiency tests in English and math will be barred from the four-year colleges.[51] The community colleges, however, will still admit students needing remediation, and special immersion programs will also offer remedial classes; if students later pass the proficiency tests, they can enter the bachelor's degree programs at the four-year colleges. Hostos Community College, whose student body is about 80 percent Hispanic (many from the Dominican Republic and Central America), has even offered many classes in Spanish.

Outside the city itself, the State University of New York (SUNY) now has a network of over sixty senior and community colleges, several of which are in the New York area (including the one where I teach in Westchester County, which attracts a number of immigrants from New York City and the suburbs). The state's Educational Opportunity Program has made it possible for students from economically disadvantaged households to be admitted to SUNY colleges with grades that otherwise would be too low; at campuses like my own, the program comes with grants toward tuition, money for textbooks, and personal counseling.[52]

In public as well as private colleges, many black and Hispanic immigrants from the Caribbean and Latin America have benefited from affirmative-action programs originally designed to help black Americans. Under affirmative action, special consideration is given to underrepresented minorities in the admissions process. Although most low-income blacks (and other minorities) have been left untouched by affirmative action, a small percentage who are attractive to good colleges are wooed and financed. The result is that, despite steep tuition costs, some high-achieving black and Hispanic immigrants and their children have gained admission to, and been offered scholarships by, private colleges and universities in the New York metropolitan area and elsewhere. A special program (Prep for Prep) to recruit minority students to New York City's expensive elite private schools has also been a channel for upward educational mobility for a small number of immigrant students.

At the elementary and high school levels, various programs have been designed to help students learn English: bilingual programs in which students receive instruction in their native language (until they learn enough English to switch to regular classes) and English as a Second Language (ESL) programs, where children are pulled out of regular classes for several hours a week for intensive instruction in English. For all the problems associated with such classes—which I'll discuss below—most would agree that they represent an improvement from the days when immigrants who spoke no English were put in the first grade whatever their age and when quick-fix steamer classes, the only other possibility, were available to but a fraction of children who needed them. Those who look with nostalgia to the good old days when immigrants learned English "the hard way," without any special help, overlook problems in the past as well as benefits of the new approaches. Rather than simply dropping newcomers into classes where they cannot read the texts and do not understand what is going on—and where they fall further and further behind as they struggle to figure out the rudiments of English—bilingual programs and ESL classes aim to ease the transition process to American schools and help many students learn English. This is especially critical today, when schooling lasts much longer than it did earlier in the century and is more essential in getting jobs, and when many immigrants arrive ready to go to high school. Indeed, even critics of bilingual instruction generally support efforts to provide English as a Second Language classes.

Several new schools in the city have been specifically designed for recent immigrant children with limited English proficiency. As of 1996, seven such schools at the high school level served over two thousand students, and several more were being planned, to include the elementary and middle school levels. Some of these schools take students through to graduation; others are intended to be transitional so that after a year or a year and a half, students move to regular schools.[53] At the Newcomers School: An Academy for New Americans, the daily schedule consists of one or two hours of English instruction; classes in math, social studies, and biology, however, are in one of the several native languages. The school is also geared to helping students make the social and emotional adjustment to the United States. The first classes at the beginning of the school year are "survival courses" that teach students how to use a pay phone, take the subway, and ask directions to the rest room.[54] As the principal of another New York newcomer high school put it, "These students need to know how the city works, how to get around, and how to deal with regular Americans. The school can't prepare them for everything but it can give them a start."[55]

In listing the new educational opportunities, I don't want to give the impression that New York has experienced nothing but improvements since the turn of the century. Far from it. The city's public schools—and here I'm speaking of schools below the college level—are still not doing a very good job of educating the new arrivals. In part, it's because they face many of the same problems that confronted schools in immigrant districts in the past.

One problem is overcrowding. The surge of immigrants moving into the city has led to major increases in public school enrollment, which is now over the million mark and rising; between 1990 and 1996, enrollment grew by an average of nineteen thousand students annually.[56] (According to one estimate, by 1995–96 immigrants represented nearly a third of the student population of New York City's public schools.)[57] With so many new students and a limited budget, the public schools are squeezed for space. Once again, the most overcrowded schools are often in immigrant neighborhoods, Corona being a case in point. In 1998, a Corona elementary school of twenty-seven hundred children had burst its seams. Although the cafeteria was no longer doing double duty as a classroom, some children were assigned to ten portable metal shacks and a mini-building in the school yard and to a school annex five blocks away.[58] Class size has been increasing, although, partly owing to teachers' union contracts, the figures are much lower than at the turn of the century. A study of several hundred elementary schools in the early 1990s found the average size of third-grade classes to be about twenty-six students, and twenty-nine students for the sixth grade.[59] Classes of over thirty-five or forty are not uncommon; in one Brooklyn high school, an ethnographer tells of forty-two to forty-six students registered for classes that have seats for only thirty.[60] In 1996, students at more than a third of the city's high schools were attending split sessions, implemented as a way to cope with overcrowding.[61]

Given chronic underfunding and recent budget cuts, many of the schools that immigrants attend are in a state of disrepair, with leaking roofs, antiquated heating systems, and broken windows. There are shortages of textbooks, supplies, and equipment, as well as of qualified teachers. Inequities in the financing of public education—average spending in New York City per pupil is well below the statewide average—hamper the schools' ability to serve students.[62]

Many, perhaps most, immigrant children attend schools where student skill levels are low, dropout rates high, and attendance rates poor. In 1995, only about half of the city's students in grades three to eight scored at or above grade level on math and reading tests.[63] Overage students that worried turn-of-the-century educators are still a problem. According to a recent Board of Education study, 36 percent of the students who entered the ninth grade in the fall of 1992 were over the expected age for their grade. Many of them were simply held back; others were recent immigrants who were overage when they started school in New York.[64] In one Lower East Side high school with a high proportion of new arrivals, the principal reported in the late 1980s that one fourth of new freshmen were seventeen years old—the traditional age for that grade being fourteen.[65]

Not surprisingly, a high proportion of overage students drop out before graduation. But then, so do many others. High school attendance may now be nearly universal, but large numbers do not graduate. Sixteen percent of the students in the city's public schools who started ninth grade in 1992 dropped out before graduation; only 48 percent graduated after four years. Less than a quarter of the graduates in 1996 received a Regents-endorsed diploma signifying that they had passed the statewide Regents exams in a number of basic academic subjects. At the beginning of the century, when high schools were institutions for a minority of the better and more motivated students, violence and crime were not issues. Today they are a definite problem, with occasional shootings and stabbing incidents taking place on school grounds or nearby and muggings, robberies, and violent fights all too frequent occurrences.

As in the past, immigrant students enter the public schools with a host of special needs and problems. Many have to overcome poor educational preparation in their home country or, at the very least, unfamiliarity with many subjects taught here and with the teaching methods (and discipline) used. At the same time as they are starting school, they are adjusting to new norms and customs in America and, if they have been separated from parents who migrated here earlier, new family arrangements as well. And there is language. As one would expect, students who don't speak English well have higher dropout rates and lower scores on standardized tests than those who do; in 1997–98, about 156,000 students in the city's public schools were labeled as limited English proficient (LEP) because they scored below a certain percentile on tests measuring English competency.[66] Whereas a hundred years ago, New York schools mainly had to cope with Yiddish- and Italian-speaking children, today they confront a bewildering array of languages; a count by the Board of Education indicates that more than a hundred languages are spoken by students from over two hundred countries. In one of the most diverse schools in the city, located in Flushing, the children came from over sixty countries and, among them, spoke more than four dozen languages.[67]

The new language programs, though a help, are plagued with problems. There are not enough bilingual or ESL classes or qualified teachers to meet the enormous need.[68] Teachers who speak languages other than Spanish are in especially short supply. (The public schools also offer bilingual programs to significant numbers of children in Chinese, Haitian-Creole, Russian, and Korean.)[69] If teachers know the language in question, they do not always have preparation in teaching methods or the ability to teach math, science, and social studies, especially in junior high and high school. ESL teachers often labor under the burden of teaching English to classes that can contain students from as many as ten different language groups.

There are intense debates about the relative merits of bilingual as opposed to ESL programs, as well as criticisms of the assessment tests that decide which children should enter them. Some parents are concerned that their children are languishing in bilingual programs, where they are stigmatized, lack access to services available to students in the academic mainstream, do not spend enough time learning English, and too often fail to test out after three years. A Board of Education study added further ammunition against bilingual education when it showed that students made more rapid progress learning English in ESL classes than in bilingual programs.[70] For their part, West Indian parents complain that the language needs of their children, who often speak a Caribbean Creole rather than standard English, are ignored and that many are inappropriately placed in special education classes.[71]

Despite all these problems, many immigrant students are doing remarkably well. Indeed, a number of recent studies in New York and in the nation show them doing as well as or better than the native-born in significant ways.

First consider immigrants as a whole. Although the data available on immigrant students in New York are woefully inadequate—the only data the Board of Education collects on immigrants refer to "recent immigrant students" who have entered a U.S. school system for the first time in the past three years—they show immigrants comparing favorably with other students in several ways. Students who were recent immigrants to the school system in middle school graduate from high school on time by a slightly greater percentage than their native-born peers. They also have lower dropout rates.[72] And although recent immigrants' median test scores in math, reading, and English are somewhat lower than those of other students, they *improved* their scores between 1989–90 and 1990–91 more than the rest of the student body.[73]

Immigrants make up a high—and growing—proportion at the City University of New York. In 1992, 41 percent of CUNY's freshman class was foreign born—at a time when about 40 percent of the students graduating from New York's public high schools went to CUNY. Predictions are that by the year 2000, a full half of CUNY's freshmen will be born outside the

United States or in Puerto Rico. In 1992, seven CUNY colleges had reached this proportion, and at City College and Hostos Community College immigrant (or Puerto Rican- born) students made up more than 60 percent of the freshman class.[74]

Two studies based on large representative national samples show immigrants often outperforming their native-born peers. Using data from a national sample of eighth graders, Grace Kao and Marta Tienda conclude that children of immigrants—both those born abroad and those born in the United States—earned higher grades and math scores than children of native-born parents, even after the effects of race, ethnicity, and parental socioeconomic status were held constant.[75] Another national study of more than twenty-one thousand tenth and twelfth graders interviewed in 1980 and then followed over a six-year period made two types of comparisons: between immigrants and native-born students in the aggregate as well as between immigrants and the native-born in four different ethnic-racial groups (Asian, white, black, and Hispanic). Whichever way they were compared, immigrants were more likely to follow an academic track in high school than their native-born counterparts; once graduated, immigrants were also more likely to enroll in postsecondary education, to attend college, and to stay continuously through four years of college.[76]

What about differences among immigrant groups? Every group, of course, has both its high achievers and its academic failures, students who end up at Harvard or Yale and students who drop out of high school. Yet, taken as a whole, some groups are conspicuously more successful than others. Like the Jews of an earlier era, today's educational exemplars are Asian groups; white European immigrants are also doing comparatively well.[77]

Consider the evidence from studies by the New York City Board of Education. On reading and math tests given to students in grades three through twelve, recent immigrants from Korea, the former Soviet Union, and India did better than other students; newly arrived students from the Dominican Republic, Haiti, and Mexico did much worse.[78] An evaluation of bilingual programs found that elementary school students who spoke Korean, Chinese, or Russian tested out of both bilingual and ESL classes far more quickly than did Haitian Creole- and Spanish-speaking students.[79] And, finally, considering the foreign- and native-born together, Asians in the class of 1996 had much higher on-time high school graduation rates—and much lower dropout rates—than blacks and Hispanics; Asians' on-time graduation rates were not quite as high as those of whites, but because a greater proportion of Asians were still enrolled, they had lower dropout rates than whites.[80]

Asians (native as well as foreign born) are overrepresented in the city's elite public high schools that select students on the basis of notoriously difficult entrance exams. In 1995, an astounding half of the students at the most selective high school of all, Stuyvesant, were Asian; at the Bronx High School of Science, 40 percent were Asian, and at Brooklyn Technical High School, 33 percent.[81] This is at a time when Asians were 10 percent of the city's high school population. Asians are also overrepresented in CUNY's four-year colleges as well as at New York University and Columbia. Outside of New York, they have become a significant presence on many Ivy League and other elite college campuses. By the early 1990s, Yale and Harvard had entering classes that were 13 percent and 15 percent Asian, respectively. At Stanford the figure was close to 20 percent, while at MIT it was close to a quarter. Of the high school seniors who took the Scholastic Aptitude Test in 1990, Asians had an average score that was five points higher than that of whites; at higher family incomes, the difference was even more pronounced.[82]

In the national study of tenth and twelfth graders who were followed for six years, Asian immigrants and natives generally did best on every measure of preparation for and participation in higher education, followed by whites and then blacks and Hispanics. The differences were large. Eighty-four percent of Asian immigrant high school graduates went on to college, compared to much lower rates for black immigrants (59 percent), Hispanic immigrants (65 percent), and white natives (62 percent) and immigrants (67 percent).[83]

The big question is why Asians stand out in this way, a topic I take up later in the chapter when I consider the role of immigrant culture in educational achievements. For the moment, I want to look at another set of myths about immigrants and education: the role of the schools in turning immigrants into good American citizens.

## Going to America, Going to School

When Hyman Kaplan, the "irrepressible" fictional student at the American Night Preparatory School for Adults ("English—Americanization—Civics —Preparation for Naturalization"), spoke to the student assembly on three national heroes, "Judge Vashington, Abram Lincohen, an' Jake Popper," he was ahead of his time.[84] In the days of Hyman Kaplan, and in the decades before, men like Jake Popper, a hardworking Jewish shopkeeper in whose store "even poor pipple mitout money always gat somting to eat," were not even mentioned in the classroom. Then, George Washington and Abraham Lincoln were the two most prominent American heroes, and Harriet Tubman—who, by one account, has now achieved iconic status[85]—would have been as unfamiliar to students as Jake Popper.

Although many New Yorkers look back to the confident Americanizing role of the schools with nostalgia, they forget that it came at a price. Fears that present approaches will fail to make the latest newcomers "Americans" are also overblown. Going to school, as the title of one book suggests, is still to go to America—though, of course, to a very different, post–civil rights America than in the past. Moreover, while conservative critics lament that immigrants may not be assimilating fast enough, a growing body of research shows that becoming American can be bad for immigrants' educational progress.

## Americanization the Old Way

The public schools that Jewish and Italian immigrants attended a century ago intended to "make Americans out of immigrant greenhorns" and did not seek to encourage or reinforce cultural differences.[86] The schools were rigid in their approach, had no place for the culture, history, or language of the immigrants, and generally saw Italian and Jewish practices as inferior. "It didn't matter," Nathan Glazer writes, "that one came from a home in which one had coffee and a roll for breakfast; one should have orange juice and milk."[87]

School leaders saw their great task as weaning immigrants away from their ethnic heritage and transforming them into loyal and proper Americans. This was the case even before Americanization programs became more strident, harsh, and oppressive at the time of World War I. "The majority of the people who now come to us have little akin to our language; they have little akin to our mode of thought; they have little akin to our customs; they have little akin to our traditions," City Superintendent Maxwell told a public conference. "It is a great business of the department of education in this city . . . to train the immigrant child . . . to become a good American citizen."[88] According to District Superintendent Julia Richman, immigrants "must be made to realize that in forsaking the land of their birth, they were also forsaking the customs and the traditions of that land; and they must be made to realize an obligation, in adopting a new country, to adopt the language and customs of that country."[89]

Above all there was the need to teach the newcomers English. Whereas public grade schools in several midwestern cities with large German populations offered bilingual German and English programs in the late nineteenth century, New York's educational authorities, as Irving Howe observes, rejected bilingualism out of hand and never saw it as a serious option.[90] Yiddish and Italian were taboo in the classroom, including the special steamer language classes. In her Lower East Side school district, Julia Richman even forbade children to speak Yiddish among themselves during recess or in the halls and bathrooms. She assigned teachers to patrol lunchrooms, restrooms, and school yards and told them to give demerits when the hated "jargon" was heard; she encouraged teachers to wash out with soap the mouths of those who relapsed.[91] The teachers themselves had to speak English without a trace of an accent. The oral portion of the licensing examination held by the New York City Board of Examiners was looked upon with dread; Jewish applicants were penalized if their speech had traces of a Yiddish accent; examiners looked upon their "t's and d's and sibilant s's as unacceptable."[92]

All things that were Jewish or Yiddish—and Italian—were outside the school. School leaders may not have consciously aimed to denigrate the parents' culture, but ignoring it had this effect.[93] In the East Harlem school he attended before World War I, Leonard Covello could not "recall one mention of Italy or the Italian language or what famous Italians had done in the world, with the possible exception of Columbus, who was pretty popular in America. We soon got the idea that 'Italian' meant something inferior, and a barrier was erected between children of Italian origin and their parents. This was the accepted learning process of Americanization. We were becoming American by learning how to be ashamed of our parents."[94]

History and civics lessons emphasized American holidays and the country's English roots. As in Hyman Kaplan's night school, national heroes like George Washington, Abraham Lincoln, and Benjamin Franklin were extolled as models to follow. There were no Jewish figures in the texts for reading, writing, literature, social studies, or history. History texts portrayed immigrants as a problem; they gave no information about how immigrants lived, what they did, or where they came from, much less why they came.[95] It was not until 1922 that Italian was put on an equal footing with French and Latin in the high school language curriculum and not until 1930 that Hebrew was offered anywhere, and even then only on an experimental basis at two Brooklyn high schools.[96]

Educators of the day saw Old World cultures as inappropriate to life in the New World and the schools as a place for what David Tyack calls compensatory socialization.[97] Health care and hygiene were high on the agenda. Jewish immigrants recalled hygiene checks when they were children: teachers probed their hair for lice with pencils, and they remembered having to carry a clean white handkerchief, the "preeminent symbol of cultural transformation and imposition." One teacher came to school with stacks of clean handkerchiefs and would call students up to the front of the room to blow their noses.[98] Sometimes it seemed that the main object of school was to be clean. In addition to the dreaded public weekly search for head lice, there were daily lectures on "nail brushes, shoe polish, pins, buttons, and other means to grace." Since many immigrant parents lived in tenements where water had to be fetched from six floors below, the amount of bathing and washing demanded by teachers was a struggle.[99]

Teaching foreign girls housekeeping methods was said to improve nutrition in immigrant households; physical education was to provide a healthy outlet for boys and girls who lived in cramped tenement apartments.[100] School nurses treated minor ailments in school and, if the medical condition was serious, visited the child's home and told the parents where to go for treatment. In June 1906, one Lower East Side principal even arranged to have doctors come to the school to remove the swollen adenoids of a number of youngsters—a condition then thought to cause feeblemindedness because of excessive breathing through the mouth. The result was rumors of children bleeding heavily, their throats slashed by knife-wielding physicians, and riots in the streets as parents stormed the public schools protesting the "murder" of their children. School officials and Progressive reformers saw the public schools as the best place to ensure that immigrant children had healthy bodies and sound minds and to defend against dangerous germs bred among the foreign-born; to immigrant parents, the provision of medical care to public school children often seemed an unwelcome intrusion.[101]

## Becoming American in School Today

Although the term Americanization has long been out of favor,[102] New York's schools continue to play a role in turning immigrant students into Americans. A key mission of the schools is still to teach newcomers English, which is regarded as essential to making it in this country. Remnants of older ideological versions of education for citizenship, as David Tyack observes, continue to appear.[103] The symbolism of the flag remains important in some schools, as illustrated by the comment of an elementary school principal in a heavily immigrant Queens neighborhood. He described his school as so overcrowded that students only have "enough [space] to bump elbows when they stand behind their desks to pledge allegiance to the flag." [104] New figures have been added to the pantheon of heroes, but Abraham Lincoln and George Washington remain among them. History lessons still pay attention to the Constitution and the structure of American government.

New York schools that are most sensitive to immigrants' special needs and adjustment problems try to introduce students, in a variety of ways, to customs and values in this society. One of the goals of special newcomer schools—to "teach the rudiments of American manners, grooming, workplace deportment, and citizenship" [105]—does not sound much different from the aims of educators a hundred years ago. At a conference on immigrant education, the director of a recently opened newcomer school for middle schoolers discussed programs that taught students about American culture, including lessons on Halloween and an international dinner (parents made the food) held at the school right before Thanksgiving.[106]

One difference today is that newcomers are less likely than those in the past to enter school at "some point near American cultural ground zero." With the global diffusion of American consumption patterns, lifestyles, and popular culture, many immigrant children have already been Americanized to some degree before they even set foot in New York. Moreover, a substantial number, who come from countries where English is the main or official language, arrive speaking and understanding English well or fairly well.[107]

What is also different is that when they get to school, they learn about a strikingly different America in which there is an increasing acceptance of pluralism as a central American value.[108] Now, the schools no longer tell immigrants they have to wipe out their old culture to become American. American customs are often taught in the student's own language and in a way that deliberately avoids condescension. Indeed, expressions of ethnicity are encouraged and celebrated in the name of a multicultural America, where all races, both sexes, and different lifestyles are deserving of respect and of protection against discrimination. When Nathan Glazer declares that we are all multiculturalists now, it is clear that there has been a massive change. Whether one likes it or not, the fact is that, as he observes, "those few who want to return American education to a period in which the various subcultures were ignored, and in which America was presented as the peak and end-product of civilization, cannot expect to make any progress in the schools." [109]

Students are told to be proud of their ethnic heritage; they are asked to tell classmates about the customs and traditions of their native lands; and they learn about the histories of countries around the world as part of the standard curriculum. An official manual advises new teachers in New York City on the ways to create a "multicultural classroom" in which students and teachers are sensitive to "myriad aspects of difference." Teachers are encouraged to learn about and appreciate students' family traditions, customs, beliefs, and foods and to display pictures, artwork, maps, charts, and flags representing the homelands of students and their families. An activity sheet for an elementary class includes selections—to be read to the whole class by the teacher—describing naming customs and ceremonies in African, Chinese, Puerto Rican, and Jewish cultures. For junior high and high schoolers, there is Project Roots, a five-week unit that encourages students to explore their personal and family histories through thinking about, examining, and gathering memorabilia from the past.[110]

Textbooks have been revamped to include the contributions of minorities and women to American history, and there are new heroes and heroines from various national and racial backgrounds. The social studies curriculum in New York City for grades seven and eight offers a multicultural perspective on United States and New York State history, with lessons on, among other things, ethnic and racial intolerance in the 1920s, the causes of African American migration from the South to northern cities after World War I, and U.S. policies toward Latin America and the Caribbean.[111] The history taught at all levels goes beyond America and Europe to embrace the wider global arena—including countries from which many recent immigrant groups come.

Outside the classroom, special ceremonies, festivals, and events in schools celebrate students' ethnic heritage. In the Queens schools studied by Roger Sanjek, what he calls "ceremonies of incorporation" featured ethnic foods, music, and costumes and used languages in addition to English during their programs. At one school, "International Day" began with a parade through the surrounding neighborhood by the entire school, with all of the students wearing ethnic costumes. Each class then performed ethnic dances for an audience of parents; later, ethnic foods, prepared by parents, were available in each classroom.[112] Sometimes a particular ethnic group gets its own special day. In one multiethnic Queens school, for example, the principal gave a party to celebrate the Dominican Republic's day of independence. About twenty parents brought in Dominican food, told stories about their homeland, and sang the Dominican national anthem.[113] Since the early 1990s, Korean festivals have been held annually in several Queens public schools under the sponsorship of Korean parents' associations.[114]

And, of course, the teaching of English has undergone a sea change. Bilingual and English as a Second Language programs, a by-product of civil rights laws of the 1960s, are a far cry from the days when schools prohibited any language other than English from being used in the classroom or school yard.[115] Although these programs, as I have noted, are not without problems, fears that they are producing a new generation of immigrant students who do not know English are exaggerated. Evidence from a variety of large-scale studies shows the impressive rapidity with which immigrant children acquire English fluency. In 1990, almost half of the young people in the country under eighteen years of age who had immigrated in the past ten years could already speak English very well, as could fully three-fourths of those who arrived before 1980. Children of immigrants also demonstrate an unambiguous preference for English in everyday communication.[116] Richard Alba even suggests that immigrant children are acquiring English more rapidly now than in the past because there is less possibility for immigrants to isolate themselves and their children from the Anglophone culture of the majority, "which bombards them even in their home countries." Also, the emergence of English as a worldwide lingua franca and the general currency and prestige of cultural products produced in English have intensified the pressures to convert to English.[117]

### Americanization as a Problem: A New View

Whether learning the English language or American values, turn-of-the-century educators and commentators were adamant that immigrant students had to Americanize to get ahead. Today, current research has a different message. A growing concern is that becoming American has high costs for immigrant youth and, under certain circumstances, can lead to academic failure.

Partly it's a matter of acquiring the habits and attitudes of teenagers in the American mainstream. This means spending more time hanging out with friends, more time partying and dating, and more time with peers who value socializing over academics, according to a large national study of American high school students. The author of this study puts it strongly: "Because part of what it means to be an American teenager in contemporary society is adopting a cavalier attitude toward school, the process of Americanization leads toward more and more educational indifference."[118]

Research on immigrant students in Miami and San Diego shows that although their English improves the longer they stay in the United States, they also spend more time watching television and less time doing homework—and, not surprisingly, their grades suffer as a result.[119] A Jamaican-born male student at a Brooklyn high school describes the negative process of Americanization that newcomers (including himself) experience in this country: "If a child comes from another country that normally is always into their books and then they discover all this free will, you know, all this talking to different people, hanging out with girls and drinking and smoking and having fun and going to parties, once you have all that stuff coming into play, one time or another, you're going to be doing less and less school work and you're going to turn more and more Americanized."[120]

Immigrant youngsters who adopt the adversarial academic orientation of disaffected native minority youth face even greater problems. This is a risk for many recent immigrants in New York, who not only go to school in inner-city ghetto neighborhoods but also share a bond of race or ethnicity with their native-born classmates. Becoming American for the children of many new arrivals means adopting the peer culture of significant numbers of their native black and Hispanic ghetto schoolmates—what has been called segmented assimilation.[121] This peer culture has its roots in the structure of opportunities and constraints facing native minority teenagers, including racial inequality and the grim realities of poverty and crime in their neighborhoods as well as overcrowded, unsafe, poorly equipped, and often "out of control" schools with low academic standards.

Whatever its origins, the peer culture has serious negative consequences. While offering young people a way to cope with their situation, it also has the effect of devaluing educational achievement and encouraging behavior that impedes academic success. Students, native and immigrant alike, feel pressured to conform by adopting an oppositional stance. To strive to do well in school—to get good grades and "to be in good" with the teachers—is to "act white" and be disloyal to the group.[122] In the Brooklyn high school he studied, Mateu-Gelabert found a "street ethos" among a good many students that led to disruptive and dangerous behavior in the school. To maintain respect, students developed a tough demeanor and, for fear of being branded cowardly, were ready to fight anyone who challenged them. Loyalty to friends was a code of honor, requiring that they come to their friends' aid, often through physical confrontation.[123]

One way immigrant parents counteract these negative influences is to remove their children from inner-city neighborhood schools altogether.

They can send them to private or parochial schools that foster learning and studying among students, native and immigrant alike, and provide an environment more conducive to doing well.[124] Or they can move to middle-class areas where the schools are of higher quality academically. The catch is that these options require substantial economic resources that are beyond the reach of most new arrivals.

Among immigrant students who have no choice but to attend substandard inner-city schools, those who manage to *resist* the onslaughts of Americanization—and remain immersed in their ethnic cultures and communities—have an advantage. Obviously, this does not mean a total rejection of American culture. To get ahead, students need to acquire skills in English and the dominant American culture. Rather, the theory is that selective Americanization or acculturation is beneficial. Tight kinship and dense ethnic networks, Alejandro Portes argues, enable parents to monitor and encourage their children's performance and protect them from "negative outside messages" and the "downward leveling norms of the inner city."[125] To the extent that immigrant children are enmeshed in tightly knit ethnic communities—and attend ethnic churches, participate in ethnic festivals, and visit ethnic shops—parents continue to exert social control over and monitor their children's behavior and social relationships. They can also draw on the support of ethnic-community friends and neighbors to back them up and help supervise the younger generation's behavior. Mary Waters found that West Indian parents who were heavily involved in ethnic churches and voluntary associations seemed to have more ability to provide guidance and positive social contacts for their children.[126] Gender roles and expectations also play a role (see Chapter 8). Immigrant parents are typically more effective in keeping daughters away from the temptations of American youth culture and the ethos of the street because they subject the young women to greater controls and keep them more tied to the home than sons.[127]

Whether immigrant children who remain committed to "traditional" cultural values and rooted in ethnic networks when they are in school will remain so later in life is an open question. If they do well in school and move into middle-class occupations in the wider economy, they may well end up assimilating into the majority or minority middle class so that "taking refuge in the ethnic community" is really just one stage on the road to assimilation into the mainstream. Even so, the notion that ethnic communities and cultures are a resource for immigrant children while they are still in school represents a new way of thinking about immigrant mobility—and definitely a change from the days when newcomers were told that they had to become American and shed their immigrant culture to get ahead.

## Educational Achievement: Culture, Social Class, and Race

Just how important are immigrants' cultures in accounting for their educational achievements? On the face of it, they would seem to be of overriding significance today, when immigrants come to New York with a strong work ethic and high expectations for their children's success. But then why are some immigrant groups, most notably Asians, outperforming others in the educational arena? Are there particular cultural traits that Asians bring with them that give them an advantage in the way Jewish culture was said to have done in the past? Cultural background helps to explain group differences in educational success both then and now, but, I would argue, it interacts with—and ultimately is probably of less importance than—social-class factors and, in the present context, race.

First, let's look at the role of culture. One reason eastern European Jews did so much better academically than Italians in the old days was that they placed a high value on education. Jews came from a culture where religious scholars were the most honored individuals in the community; families proudly supported the learned men who spent their days reading the Talmud and disputing its meaning. In stark contrast, southern Italians' cultural heritage made them less oriented to book learning and less sensitive to the economic advantages of schooling.[128] By some accounts, southern Italians were antagonistic to schools and intellectuals in their home country. At the least, they were skeptical about the value of education. In peasant communities back home, formal schooling was viewed as largely irrelevant to their lives. There was "no obvious need for more than a trifling amount of formal education"; the practical skills needed for survival could be taught at home or through apprenticeship. Knowledge beyond the everyday requirements was a luxury for the "better classes." Time spent in school simply took children away from work.[129] That Italian cultural heritage mattered comes out in Joel Perlmann's detailed study of Providence, Rhode Island: Italian children from middle-class homes left school earlier than Russian Jewish children from working-class homes and earlier than other children from working-class homes as well. Families had to make choices about resources and needs, he suggests, and these were determined partly by cultural factors.[130]

This generalization still holds true, although in today's changed context no immigrant group has the kind of negative, indeed some might say oppositional, attitudes to education that characterized southern Italians at the turn of the century. In contemporary New York, most immigrant parents, in all groups, arrive with positive attitudes toward education and high educational expectations for their children. Indeed, national studies reveal that immigrant parents, as a whole, have higher educational aspirations for their children and more positive attitudes toward schooling than native-born parents.[131]

As one might expect in light of their children's achievements, Asian immigrants have been found to have especially high aspirations for their children—much higher, nationwide, than other immigrant and native-born groups.[132] It is hard to say how much these aspirations, and Asian students' academic successes, are due to the cultural values and resources they bring to America as opposed to social-class advantages. But cultural background doubtless plays a role. This is supported by a number of national studies that show Asian students outperforming all other racial/ethnic groups, even after taking into account such factors as family income, household composition, and parental education.[133]

Much has been made of Korean and Chinese immigrant parents' strong belief in and zeal for their children's education. "Our main concern," said one Korean man, "Education—Number One quality. Most people, that's all they think about."[134] In Korea, one of the worst things a person can say about another, according to Pyong Gap Min, is "You are uneducated."[135] In Chinatown, when parents greet their children, often the first things they say are "Did you behave in school today?" "Have you got your grades yet?" "How good are they?"[136] Chinese and Korean parents put intense pressure on their children to excel and often make enormous personal sacrifices to ensure that they get a good education. An extreme example is a Korean woman who believed that by fasting she would help her children get into a selective New York City high school: "For my son's admission into Bronx High School of Science, I fasted for two years and prayed. At that time, I worked [in the family gas station business] like an insane woman for sixteen hours each day. But I never ate anything until twelve noon. For lunch, I drank a cup of water and had a bowl of soup for dinner. After my son got into Bronx Science, I again fasted for a whole year for my daughter's admission to the same school. Both of them graduated from Bronx Science and went to good colleges."[137] While Chinese immigrant parents value thrift and denounce consumption of name-brand clothes and other "too American" luxuries, they do not hesitate to spend money on books, after-school programs, Chinese lessons, private tutors, music lessons, and other educationally oriented activities.[138]

Hard work and discipline, not innate intelligence, are the keys to educational success in the eyes of Chinese immigrant parents. If their children study long hours, parents believe, they can get As—and they push their children to "work at least twice as hard as their American counterparts."[139] Confucian teaching, it is said, not only puts a high value on education but also emphasizes discipline, family unity, and obedience to authority, all of which contribute to academic success. Children who do poorly in school bring shame to Chinese families; those who do well bring honor.[140]

The traditional respect for scholars and teachers in Chinese culture also contributes to positive student-teacher interactions. Chinese children typically try to please teachers, who are looked upon as authority figures second only to parents. In turn, teachers and administrators are favorably disposed to well-behaved Chinese pupils and often expect them to perform well.[141] In a time-worn pattern, high teacher expectations help bring about high student performance. Indeed, Jewish pupils at the turn of the century, with their positive attitude to schooling, were said to be the "delight of their teachers"; Italian children were "more or less difficult to discipline and irresponsible." Many Jewish students strove to live up to their teachers' high expectations, whereas Italian children had to struggle against negative stereotypes.[142]

In contemporary New York, the cultural background of Koreans and Chinese operates in another way, in that they have imported after-school institutions that prepare their children for exams for the city's specialized high schools and, later on, elite universities. Called *hagwon* in Korean and *buxiban* in Chinese, these private academies are a tradition in Asia, where competition to get into the top universities is fierce. In Chinatown, where tutor services and test preparation programs are readily available, "school after school," according to Min Zhou, has become an accepted norm.[143] In 1995, the Korean-language yellow pages listed about three dozen cram schools in the New York area; in Flushing alone, there were about twenty Korean-run private institutions specializing in English and mathematics. According to one survey, a fifth of Korean junior and senior high school students in New York City were taking lessons after school, either in a private institution or with a private tutor.[144] The C.C.B. Prep School in Woodside, Queens, boasted that in 1994, 95 percent of its junior high students were admitted to Stuyvesant, Bronx Science, or Brooklyn Tech. About 50 percent of the pupils were Korean, 40 percent Chinese, and 10 percent Caucasian. Tuition was $595 for eight weeks of Saturday instruction, $695 for eight weeks of Tuesday and Thursday.[145]

This leads to the crucial matter of social class. In the past, a major factor explaining eastern European Jews' greater educational achievements was their occupational head start.[146] Compared to southern Italians, Jews were more urban and arrived with higher levels of vocational skills, which gave them a leg up in entering New York's economy. Because the Jewish immigrant population was, from the start, better off economically than the Italian, Jewish parents could afford to keep their children in school more regularly and for longer. The poorer, less skilled southern Italians were more in need of their children's labor to help in the family. Indeed, Miriam Cohen has argued that because more Jewish mothers could afford to remain out of the paid workforce, fewer daughters had to leave school to assist in either homework tasks or child care.[147]

Although eastern European Jews who came to New York were not, as a group, highly educated, the fact that they were more literate than Italians was also a help. Only about a quarter of the Jewish immigrants over the age of fourteen entering the United States between 1899 and 1910—compared to more than half of the southern Italians—told immigration officials they could not read or write. If Jewish children were more likely to have literate parents, they, too, often arrived with a reading and writing knowledge of one language, making it easier to learn to read and write English than it was for southern Italian immigrant children, who generally arrived with no such skills.[148]

Today, educational background plays a much larger role in explaining why the children of Asian immigrants are doing so well. At the time of the 1990 census, a full third of adult Asian immigrants in New York City who had arrived in the previous ten years—and about half of the Indians and Taiwanese and almost 70 percent of Filipinos—were college graduates. So were a third of Soviet immigrants, another group known for its academic success. By comparison, only 8 percent of Caribbean adult immigrants— 6 percent of Dominicans and 11 percent of Jamaicans—were college graduates and the figure for Central and South Americans was 11 percent.[149]

Although they often experience downward occupational mobility in New York, the fact is that highly educated parents, as many studies show, have higher educational expectations for their children and provide family environments more conducive to educational attainment.[150] If their children started school in the home country, they typically attended excellent—and rigorous—institutions. (Here, by the way, it's worth noting that certain sending countries have a reputation for particularly good schools,

Korea being one of them. Students in Korean schools, for example, significantly outscore American students in math and science as early as the fourth grade.)[151] Well-educated parents, moreover, are usually more sophisticated about the way the educational system works here and have an easier time, and more confidence in, navigating its complexities—and steering their children into the good schools—than those with less education.

Read a journalistic account of a high-achieving Asian immigrant and more often than not the parents turn out to be from a middle-class or elite background in the home country. One example: two individuals profiled in a *New York* magazine cover story on Koreans were children of grocery store owners. The mother of the assistant district attorney had been a music teacher in Korea; the mother of the Brown University student had been trained as a violinist at Seoul University, and the father had studied literature at another Korean university.[152] The Korean woman who fasted to get her children into Bronx Science had graduated from college in Korea, where she worked as an elementary school teacher; her husband, also a college graduate, had been a translator. In 1987, of the nine Chinese finalists in the Westinghouse Science Talent Search, six had parents who were research scientists, physicians, or college professors.[153]

In large part because so many come from professional and middle-class backgrounds, Asian New Yorkers are also doing fairly well economically, which has implications for their children's achievements. (At $47,997, their average household income in 1990 was a little higher than the citywide average, $47,145.)[154] A century ago, economic resources were important because they allowed immigrants to keep their children in school; now they make it possible (or easier) to send children to better schools. Korean and Chinese after-school academies don't come cheap. Neither do private institutions or parochial schools that are an alternative to the inferior public schools in many immigrant neighborhoods. Moreover, those with better family incomes can afford to move to areas within the city (and suburbs) with better schools, a common strategy among Asian immigrants. "First comes Flushing, then Bayside, then Long Island," said one successful Korean entrepreneur, describing the trek of successful Koreans to communities with the best high schools.[155] By 1995, nearly two out of five of the students in northeast Queens School District 26, the best in the city, were Asian, mostly Korean and Chinese.[156] Wherever the school, a decent family income means that supplying books and other school equipment is less of a struggle; students also have more time to study if they don't have to take part-time jobs to help out with expenses.

Bear in mind that not all Asians are academic highfliers; some are experiencing serious difficulties in school. The Chinese in New York stand out in this regard mainly because they have such a high proportion of poorly educated arrivals in their ranks, with the census reporting that a quarter of post-1965 working-age Chinese immigrants had less than a ninth-grade education.[157] The growing number of children from rural Chinese peasant families in New York, often barely literate in their own language, have a much harder time in the schools than children of Taiwanese or Hong Kong professionals. They are more likely to become discouraged, lose interest in school, and become involved in youth gangs than the children of highly educated parents from middle-class backgrounds.

Finally, there is the role of race. At the turn of the century, race was irrelevant in explaining why Jews did better academically than Italians. Both groups were at the bottom of the city's ethnic pecking order, considered to be inferior white races. Today, the way Asian—as opposed to black or Hispanic—immigrants fit into the racial hierarchy makes a difference in the opportunities they can provide their children. Because they are not black, Asian (and white) immigrants have greater freedom in where they can live and, in turn, send their children to school. Moreover, their children are less likely than black or Hispanic immigrants to feel an allegiance with native minorities and be drawn into an oppositional peer culture.

A comparison of the educational achievements of Korean and West Indian children brings out these points. Although they did not bring a tradition of cram schools and "exam hell" with them, West Indians, like Koreans, arrive with cultural orientations associated with educational achievement: a belief that education is the key to success and a drive for their children to do well. Education has long been valued as a major avenue to occupational mobility in West Indian societies where it is, in itself, an important basis of prestige. In the West Indies, those with a good education can get jobs that support a desired lifestyle; they also have cultural characteristics such as speech patterns (they speak "proper" or standard English) and manners that command respect. When I studied a Jamaican village in the late 1960s, a constant topic of conversation was the need to work hard to finance children's education, and many parents made extraordinary sacrifices, including selling land, to do so. "We have to deprive ourself to help our children so they can get qualification to help them out," explained one woman, who spent long hours buying and selling produce at market to get the money for books and uniforms for her daughter, who attended secondary school on a partial scholarship.[158]

Yet, despite West Indian parents' intense desire for their children to succeed in school—and their emphasis on discipline and respect for teachers and authorities—West Indian students in New York have not done as well as Koreans. Of course, there are many success stories. On its education page, the *Carib News* regularly features West Indian students in New York who have graduated at the top of their class, been admitted to prestigious colleges, and received awards in their high schools or at various branches of CUNY. Yet, compared to Koreans, far fewer West Indians attend the city's selective high schools or the nation's elite universities. Although West Indians at CUNY senior colleges often feel that getting there has been a major accomplishment, Koreans at the same places are likely to think of themselves as failures who have not made the Ivy League.[159]

Social-class factors definitely play a role, though what seems to matter is not so much income—according to the 1990 census, West Indian New Yorkers' average household income ($42,939) was actually slightly higher than Koreans' ($41,600)[160]—but that a far smaller proportion of West Indian parents are themselves highly educated. A quarter of the Korean adults in New York City who arrived in the 1980s had college degrees, compared to only 11 percent of Jamaicans, 7 percent of Guyanese, and 8 percent of Trinidadians.[161] Indeed, among West Indians themselves, students who excel in local New York City schools typically come from middle-class backgrounds or had some of their schooling at the top selective schools back home. Better-educated and better-off parents are also more likely to send their children to parochial schools or citywide magnet schools or to move to neighborhoods where the schools are of higher quality and there is greater exposure to a middle-class minority culture of mobility.[162]

Whatever their class, however, the realities of race in late twentieth-century New York create problems for West Indians that Koreans do not experience. Koreans have been able to move into heavily white neighborhoods with good schools fairly easily. Because they are black, West Indians are more likely to live in racially segregated areas, and even when they move to integrated communities, white flight tends to turn the neighborhoods all—or nearly all—black. The result of segregated residential patterns is that the majority of West Indians send their children to all-black or predominantly black neighborhood high schools, where the dropout rates are high, violence and the availability of weapons are a problem, and there are few experienced or dedicated teachers. Mary Waters describes an all-black Brooklyn high school where she did field research among second-generation West Indians: "The number of weapons entering the school was enough to color all interactions between teachers and students, the academic standards of the vast majority of the classes were not enough to prepare a student for a competitive college, the problems of teenage pregnancy, drug and alcohol use were widespread, and the odds of a freshman graduating four years later were less than 50–50."[163] Often the staff in this school were either inexperienced, first-time teachers or burnt-out individuals who had no other options. Many had little control over their classrooms; some had given up altogether, like one teacher who typically taught for ten minutes and then stopped, or another who gave out answers to tests beforehand. Some troubled students got away with spending day after day hanging out in the hallways or right outside the school. For those who attended classes regularly, the fear of violence affected their ability to learn. Many students gave harrowing accounts of being afraid to walk through the hallways because of the danger of inadvertently bothering someone with a weapon.[164]

On top of this, West Indian students—as blacks—experience pressure in the local schools to be black American, which often means adopting an oppositional identity that sees doing well academically as "acting white." In any case, West Indian students' own experiences with racial discrimination and their perceptions of blocked social mobility lead many to reject their parents' immigrant dream and to be receptive to the peer culture of the neighborhood and school that emphasizes racial solidarity and opposition to school rules and authorities. All too often, this adversarial stance toward school is a recipe for academic failure.[165]

An examination of schooling then and now highlights, once again, the dangers of judging today's immigrants by a set of myths rather than actual facts. New York's Jewish immigrants may have valued education, but before World War I most of their children did not receive much of it. At a time when educational requirements were minimal, educational opportunities limited, and most Jews still mired in poverty, only a small minority of Jewish children graduated from high school and hardly any from college. Early in the century, the academic failures of Italians, whose even poorer parents had little belief that education would help their children advance, were cause for concern. As late as the 1930s, teachers were often open in their contempt of the "bunch of little garlic-eating greasers" they had to "try to pound learning into" in Little Italy. "What a bunch of animals they are, one and all!" teachers often thought. "If one could only get transferred! They are so dirty!"[166]

If immigrant children at the turn of the century were less successful academically than many recall, today's newcomers are doing better in school than is commonly believed. There are of course many dropouts and failures —a more serious problem today, when a decent job requires more education. But a substantial number are making it. A combination of new opportunities and programs and the entry of large numbers of immigrant children with highly educated parents and previous experience in fine schools in their home country have translated into academic success for many newcomers. Indeed, now that education is a key to mobility in the United States as well in immigrants' home societies, virtually all immigrants arrive with a positive attitude toward education and high aspirations for their children.

Although conservative critics worry that the advent of multicultural and bilingual education will prevent the latest newcomers from becoming real Americans, the fact is that immigrant children are still subject to strong Americanizing influences in the schools from teachers as well as fellow students. Indeed, academic researchers today are worried that immigrants are becoming too much like their American peers as they spend less time studying and doing homework and more time watching television and hanging out with their friends. Immigrants who attend schools in poor ghetto neighborhoods run the risk of adopting the oppositional outlook or disruptive ethos of the in-crowd or dominant group, something that is more likely when there exists a shared bond of race or ethnicity. The message is that immigrant children should stay involved with their ethnic community and ethnic culture as a way to get ahead. An ideal pattern, according to Alejandro Portes and Rubén Rumbaut, is selective acculturation, where strong bonds with the ethnic community combine with learning English and American ways.[167]

Clearly, we need more studies to refine and clarify the complex relationship between social-class factors, ethnic networks, and cultural values in immigrant educational achievement. I have tried to explain different rates of success among groups, but obviously it is also critical to understand why, within each immigrant population, some do better than others. Because immigrants are so often compared with native-born Hispanic and black youth in inner-city neighborhoods, we must also remember that native-born minority youth are not a unified group either—and not all have developed an oppositional outlook or an ethos that encourages disruptive school behavior. In late twentieth-century America, when racial inequalities represent the most profound divisions in our cities, we should guard against valorizing the experiences of immigrants who are somehow able, through their own culture and social networks, to resist the assaults of downward assimilation. It is all too easy, using this kind of framework, to blame American-born minorities for their position and a short step to arguing that if only they adopted immigrant cultural and social patterns, they, too, would be successful. In our enthusiasm for aspects of immigrants' cultures and communities that help them get ahead, we should not forget the advantages that come from having better-off and better-educated parents —and the need to keep in the forefront the role of racial discrimination, economic inequalities, and inferior and underfunded inner-city schools that make it difficult for many immigrant children to get a good education and that perpetuate the kind of oppositional or adversarial stances that emerge among many native and immigrant children alike.

# CHAPTER 8

# Looking Backward—and Forward

W hat, then, in a broad sense, can be learned from this comparison of New York's two great waves of immigration? That our view of the past is shaped by our perceptions of the present. That the remembered past is not the same thing as what actually transpired. That what seems novel isn't always new. That there is nothing inevitable about the immigrant story.

The past also illuminates the future. The paths that immigrants' children will take in tomorrow's New York are made clearer if we look back at what happened to the descendants of the last great migration. A basic question is whether an understanding of the trajectories followed by the second generation in the past offers any hints or guides about what is to come. This means looking at yet another slice in time—the period between the 1920s and the 1960s—when the children of Jewish and Italian immigrants became adults, workers, and parents. It also means making some projections about the years ahead. The focus in this final chapter is on three issues that have already been discussed at some length for immigrants themselves: changing perceptions of race; prospects for occupational mobility; and transnational connections.

## Will the Descendants of Today's Immigrants Become "White"?

If the historical literature on race teaches us anything, it is that racial categories are highly changeable. The notion that dark skin color will impede the progress of the current second generation rests on the assumption that today's racial views will continue to be dominant. This may not be the case. After all, there has been a radical change in the meaning of race in the past hundred years. A century ago, the difference between a "swarthy" Italian

224

and a "white" German was every bit as visible as the difference today between an "Asian American" and a "European American." It is a measure of how dramatic the transformation has been that most Americans have forgotten that Italians and Jews were ever seen as separate races and an inferior kind of European. How did Jews and Italians become unquestionably accepted as white? Will any of the new groups repeat this pattern? Or will entirely new racial categories and divisions emerge in the wake of the recent immigration so that the very category white will become a twentieth-century relic?

The whole notion of becoming white is a complicated one. So mired are we in current racial categories and views that it is hard to get away from them in discussions of race. Race today is basically a color word, but it was not that way in turn-of-the-century New York, when virtually the entire population was of European ancestry. Jews and Italians were thought to be of a different race than people with origins in northern and western Europe. They looked different to most New Yorkers, and they were believed to have distinct biological features and innate character traits. The courts recognized them as white, and they were seen as superior to blacks and Asian groups, yet they were not the equals of northern and western Europeans. They were, as Matthew Jacobson puts it, "both white and racially distinct from other whites."[1] One of the remarkable changes of the twentieth century is that southern and eastern Europeans are no longer thought of as separate races in the popular mind. They have been gathered, along with other Americans of European origins, under the one umbrella of "whiteness." It is in this sense that historians speak of Jews and Italians as becoming "full-fledged whites" or "unquestionably" and "fully" white.

It was not a foregone conclusion, however, that Jews and Italians would become fully "white." Historical processes have a way of seeming inevitable after they've happened, but, given a different set of circumstances, there could have been a different outcome. For example, an alternative, middle grouping—neither white nor black but some distinctive stigmatized "other"—could have emerged.[2] Why didn't this happen? A full history of the way Jews and Italians, each in their own way, came to be thought of as members of a unified white race remains to be written, yet it is possible to sketch out the underlying factors involved.

One was the end of the massive influx of eastern and southern Europeans, in the wake of restrictive legislation in the 1920s. The dramatic decrease in the flow of new arrivals reduced the fears of old-stock Americans about the deluge of "racial inferiors"; it also facilitated assimilation by depriving Italians and Jews of constant, large-scale reinforcements.[3] Indeed, by the time World War II ended, most of New York's Jews and Italians were American born. The Nazi genocide made anti-Semitism less respectable, and in the scientific world, theories of nurture and culture eclipsed theories of nature and biology. A spate of books in the 1930s and 1940s, from Ashley Montagu's *Race: Man's Most Dangerous Myth* to Franz Boas's *Race and Democratic Society,* challenged the view, championed by earlier advocates of eugenics and scientific racism, that race determined character, customs, and behavior; new views that argued for the primary role of environment and culture became dominant in intellectual circles.[4] Whereas formerly the literature of race discussed "capacities," "traits," "characters," and "deficiencies," the rising literature on race relations now spoke in a language of "equality," "justice," "discrimination," and "prejudice."[5]

Entirely independent developments among African Americans had the indirect effect of helping to consolidate the whiteness of Jews and Italians. The massive migration of African Americans from the rural South to New York from World War I on altered New York City's racial composition, adding large numbers of people who were below Jews and Italians in the racial hierarchy. Indeed, Jews and Italians themselves made efforts to distance themselves from African Americans: they did this by stressing their whiteness. As blacks poured into Harlem in the 1920s, Jews left, in part, as Eric Goldstein argues, to establish their position as whites. In the years following the Depression, Jewish women asserted a distinctiveness from black women by hiring African American domestic workers to clean their homes.[6] The civil rights movement, paradoxically, contributed to the emergence of a new racial order that benefited eastern and southern Europeans. By putting black-white issues on center stage in the national agenda, the struggle for African American civil rights reduced the salience of racial distinctions among European groups, thereby allowing Jews and Italians to "vanish into whiteness."[7]

The economic successes of Jews and Italians, and their increased intermingling with other European groups, also helped to erode the once salient racial differences among New Yorkers of European origin. With postwar prosperity, as well as generous GI housing and educational benefits, the children, and later grandchildren, of turn-of-the-century Jewish and Italian arrivals did well. As the groups climbed the socioeconomic ladder and mixed residentially with people of northern and western European descent, Richard Alba and Victor Nee note, "their perceived distinctiveness from the majority faded. . . . Intermarriage both marked the shift and accelerated it."[8]

Obviously, climbing the socioeconomic ladder and adopting the dominant society's ways were not enough to achieve unqualified whiteness. Other immigrant groups in this same period—Asians, for example—who also became economically successful and assimilated to American ways did not become white. Jews and Italians were in-between peoples to begin with —recognized in some contexts as white, albeit an inferior kind of white— and did not experience the same kind of systematic, legal, and official discrimination that faced black and Asian immigrants.

American courts consistently allowed southern and eastern Europeans (unlike Asians) to be naturalized as white citizens. That the law declared them white—and fit for naturalizable citizenship—was a powerful symbolic argument in their favor. The ability to naturalize also gave them added numbers at the ballot box with which to exert political influence. Indeed, politicians often tailored their thinking about the racial desirability of new European immigrants in the context of campaigns in which the foreign vote counted.[9]

Italians and Jews may have ranked lower than northern and western Europeans but, in the racial continuum of the time, they were a step above Asians who, in turn, were relatively more desirable than blacks.[10] African Americans, it is well to recall, had only just been released from slavery when the last great immigration wave began—and not until the civil rights revolution of the 1960s would the structures of segregation in the American South begin to be dismantled. The racial notions underlying the response of whites toward blacks, as Stanley Lieberson has written, were both deeper and more pervasive than toward European immigrants, wherever they came from. Despite notions about the inherent inferiority of Jews and Italians, it was believed they could become more acceptable by abandoning their strange cultures and becoming more "American." "There was a much less powerful concept of 'place' or 'station' obstructing the . . . [European] groups," Lieberson writes. "The emphasis called for blacks to remain in their station whereas for [European] immigrants it was on their ability to leave their old-world traits and become as much as possible like the older white settlers."[11]

The fact is, too, that Jews and Italians physically resembled members of the older European groups. It was often possible for children of Jewish and Italian immigrants to blend into the majority population (to "pass") if they shed their distinctive dialects, dress, and other cultural features; this was not an option for Chinese or West Indian immigrant children of the period, who were more visibly distinct.[12] In his study of second-generation Italians in New Haven in the 1930s, Irvin Child described a young man who passed as non-Italian. "I don't hear it [derogatory epithets]," the young man explained, "except from people I know because the others don't guess that I'm Italian."[13] In my own family history, my mother tells me that when she applied for a job on Wall Street in the 1940s, friends advised her not to reveal her Jewish identity (she didn't), and quite a few Jews tried to hide their Jewishness by changing their surnames. Among movie stars, Betty Joan Perske became Lauren Bacall, and Issur Danielovitch was transformed into Kirk Douglas. But the ability to hide one's identity was impossible for the vast majority of African Americans, whose skin color made them more visible. Whatever name she used, Lena Horne was black. The emphasis on skin color had different results for European immigrants and African Americans who intermarried. An Italian or Jewish woman who intermarried and took the surname of her husband would be less identifiable as Italian or Jewish; a black woman who married a white man, by contrast, would still be labeled black. Similarly, when Jewish and Italian women married husbands of "old European stock," their children bore their fathers' surnames; if a black woman had a child with a white man, the child was socially defined as black.[14]

If the transformation of Italians and Jews into members of an all-encompassing white community had a lot to do with their starting-off points, their economic achievements, and their attempts to distance themselves from African Americans, will these factors play a role in the future? Of course, some of today's immigrants, like Russians, Poles, and other Europeans, are already unquestionably white. But what about those who are now labeled nonwhite? Will the immigrant groups currently thought of as in-between come to be seen as white? Or is it misleading to pose the question this way? Just as there was no all-encompassing white community a hundred years ago, so, too, the very category white may become outmoded in the future as new ways of thinking about racial and ethnic differences, and new racial divisions, emerge. Whereas in the past, Jews and Italians were transformed from races into white ethnics without undergoing any physical change, today, when the language of color is so prominent in racial discourse, intermarriage and the blurring of physical differences among mixed-race offspring are often predicted to be the key agents of racial change.

Already, the centrality of the black-white divide, which dominated New York race relations for much of the twentieth century, is being challenged and changed by the growing numbers of Asians and Hispanics who do not fit clearly into either category. Indeed, given the high Hispanic birthrates, and the prospect of continued Asian and Hispanic immigration, the proportion of Asian and Hispanic New Yorkers will surely rise. (By 1998, it will be recalled, census estimates put Hispanics at 31 percent of New York City's population, Asians at 8 percent.) High rates of intermarriage—and the growing number of multiracial offspring—are also an indication that we are moving toward a new kind of racial order. According to Zhenchao Qian's analysis of 1990 census data, nearly two-thirds of young U.S.-born Asians marry non-Asians, the great majority of them whites; and nearly 40 percent of their Latino counterparts marry non-Latinos, again the majority of them white.[15] Racially mixed ancestry is nothing new in American history, but the mixed-race issue hits with fresh force today because of the much greater acceptance of racial intermarriage, which was illegal in some states as late as 1967.[16]

One scenario for the future suggests that there will be a shift in the way people are assigned to the category white. The lighter of the multiracials will join whites of European ancestry and light-skinned Hispanics to constitute an expanded white group. The white category, in other words, will be widened to include some new strands, perhaps even successful Asians as well.

In another scenario, the very category white will cease to be salient, and the current white-nonwhite division will give way to a new black-nonblack dichotomy. In this scenario, a white-Asian-Hispanic melting pot will be offset by a minority consisting of those with African ancestry—African Americans, black Caribbean and African immigrants, and Hispanics of visible African ancestry. A number of sociologists have speculated that the black category itself could expand, as the most unsuccessful portions of some immigrant groups (presumably darker in skin color) assimilate into the existing black population.[17] Whiteness, in this forecast, would be much less meaningful than it is today; indeed a new term might emerge, as Joel Perlmann and Roger Waldinger note, "to replace white—a term that can include Asians and Hispanics easily enough and that essentially means 'native born, and not black.'"[18] The black category, however, would not lose its significance.

A shift to a black-nonblack—or as Michael Lind puts it, a black-beige—racial order is a troubling forecast, for it sees the boundary dividing blacks from other Americans as intractable, and blacks as being consigned, once again, to racial exclusion.[19] It is based, unfortunately, on some hard realities. Although black-white intermarriages rose from a reported 65,000 in 1970 to 328,000 in 1995, the intermarriage rate is still dramatically lower than for Hispanics and Asians.[20] Just as the salience of the "Negro question" helped Jews and Italians fuse with Anglo-Americans into a unified white race, so today's immigrants often make efforts to distance themselves from

African Americans as a way to gain acceptance and assert claims to equality with whites. Moreover, as I discussed in Chapter 5, Asians and most Hispanics started out in the 1980s and 1990s in an in-between status, neither black nor white. As such, they could easily become part of a new nonblack or beige majority.

Some may say that the physical characteristics distinguishing Asians and many Hispanics will make it impossible for them to blend into one racial category alongside whites. In Shawn Wong's novel *American Knees*, the thoroughly Americanized, third-generation Chinese American hero, Raymond Ding, can never forget that he is Chinese because others classify him as Chinese or Asian when they see his color and physical features. "Don't you know in America skin color is your identity?" he says. "This is a racist country. You can't be invisible."[21] Yet race, as I have shown, is in the eyes of the beholder—conditioned by cultural understandings of difference. The Chinese are no longer stigmatized the way they were earlier in the century, and if a black-nonblack racial order does emerge, the Chinese and other Asians would become, if not invisible, then less visible as part of a new racial majority. Presumably, whiteness would then no longer be the metonym for power and inclusion the way it is now.

If the nonblack-black scenario is a worrisome prospect for blacks, a more optimistic forecast sees black-white relations evolving in a different way. In this scenario, increasing intermarriage and intermingling will reduce the salience of current racial and ethnic boundaries, including the black-white divide. "In a society characterized by increasing rates of movement, mixing, and intermarriage, and by growing numbers of persons who assert their multiplicity," write Stephen Cornell and Douglas Hartmann, "boundaries become less obvious, less potent, and far more difficult to maintain."[22]

The argument is that rates of intermarriage between blacks and whites, though low, are rising, and many children of these marriages are demanding social recognition of their mixed ancestry. A hundred years from now, Stanley Crouch predicts, "Americans . . . will find themselves surrounded in every direction by people who are part Asian, part African, part European, part Indian. . . . The sweep of body types, combinations of facial features, hair textures, eye colors, and what are now unexpected skin tones will be far more common."[23] If many Asians and Hispanics are brought into the racial majority, this expansion could "dissolve the transparency of racial distinctions and thus impact upon the distinctions that set African Americans racially apart."[24] In the aftermath of the civil rights revolution, there has been a remarkable growth in the black middle class as well as an expansion of black college enrollment. With increased mixing at work, on campus, and in other social settings, prejudices may begin to lessen. This is especially likely in the upper-middle classes, where class may end up trumping race as common school ties, elite occupational status, and various social connections and interests begin to blur ethnic and racial boundaries.

Just which scenario will triumph is hard to say, and it may be that something altogether different will come to pass, involving an amalgam of some of the forecasts outlined above. The process of change is likely to be gradual, though it is bound to involve struggles and divisions, as some groups attempt to alter or widen existing racial categories while others resist. It seems a safe bet, however, that the racial order will look very different in thirty or forty years from the way it does now and that the changes will have enormous implications for the children of today's immigrants as well as for the immigrants of tomorrow.

## Will Today's Second Generation Move Up the Occupational Ladder?

When it comes to issues of mobility, the rags-to-riches story is a basic part of the American dream. European immigrants, the story goes, sweated and struggled when they got here, but their children were able to "make it" in America. If "we" did well, say many New Yorkers whose parents and grandparents came a century ago, why can't "they?" In fact, the ascent up the socioeconomic ladder was more difficult for yesterday's second generation than many of their descendants remember. Like the whitening process, it was not inevitable. It was the outcome of specific historical forces, rather than the simple passage of generations.[25] Today, the big question is how different social and economic conditions, particularly the emerging "hourglass economy" and the need for increased levels of education to qualify for decent jobs, will affect the ability of the second generation to get ahead.

"My son the doctor" may have been a cherished phrase of Jewish immigrant parents, but "my grandson the doctor" is more accurate. The children of Jewish immigrants, like their Italian counterparts, generally did better occupationally than their parents, but the great leap into the professions waited another generation or two. Second-generation Italian and Jewish New Yorkers made relatively modest moves up the occupational ladder; some, we should recall, did not move up at all. Census data for 1950

Table 11    Occupations of Employed Second-Generation Italians and Jews, New York–Northeastern New Jersey Standard Metropolitan Area, 1950

| | Men | | Women | |
|---|---|---|---|---|
| Occupation | Italian (%) | Jewish (%) | Italian (%) | Jewish (%) |
| Professional and technical workers | 6 | 19 | 5 | 16 |
| Managers and proprietors | 10 | 27 | 2 | 8 |
| Clerical and sales workers | 17 | 28 | 40 | 63 |
| Craftspeople | 22 | 10 | 2 | 1 |
| Operatives | 29 | 12 | 44 | 8 |
| Private household workers | — | — | — | — |
| Service workers | 6 | 3 | 4 | 3 |
| Laborers | 9 | 1 | — | — |
| Not reported | 1 | 1 | 1 | 1 |
| Total employed (in thousands) | 370 | 217 | 177 | 81 |

*Source:* Glazer and Moynihan 1970: 322–23, tables 6, 7, based on U.S. Census of Population, 1950.

and 1960 show that, in the aggregate, second-generation Jewish and Italian New Yorkers outpaced the first in occupational standing,[26] though a fair number of Jewish and Italian offspring must have ended up in jobs that were similar in status to those held by their parents.

What kind of work did Italian and Jewish second-generation New Yorkers do? In 1950, some thirty years after the massive influx from southern and eastern Europe ended, the majority were clerks, skilled workers, and small business owners (see table 11). Only a small proportion of second-generation Jews—and an even smaller proportion of second-generation Italians—were then in the professions. Blue-collar work continued to be the mainstay in the Italian second generation among males and females alike; Jews were more likely to be found in clerical and sales jobs and as managers and proprietors. Given the greater success of Jews in the immigrant generation, it is not surprising that their children held onto this lead. Cultural attitudes aside, Jews, more than Italians, were able to provide children with access to capital, to entrepreneurial skills, and to opportunities—including white-collar positions—in the ethnic economy. Moreover, Jewish immigrant parents were more likely than Italians to have the material resources to absorb the direct and indirect costs of added years of schooling.

Mobility paths were gendered.[27] For boys, education was less crucial in getting ahead. Many more manufacturing jobs were available for Italian American sons than daughters, and after the Depression men could earn relatively good wages in blue-collar jobs, particularly if they were skilled laborers and worked in strongly unionized industries. The oppositional culture that flourished among Italian American working-class boys did not spell economic disaster. Richard Gambino recalls how the values of his childhood street-corner group in Brooklyn's Red Hook of the 1940s and 1950s were cynical and hostile to school and teachers: "The values of these street corner groups took precedence over the demands of the public school, and the things we valued did not include high achievement in school. In fact any child who achieved high grades was suspect, a fact that tormented me in my earliest years in school because I did well in studies without much effort. . . . The values that dominated boys' groups in my childhood . . . were loyalty to the group, a close-mouthed and distrustful attitude toward all outside the group (except blood family), a cynicism about our school and teachers . . . and concern with our physical powers expressed in athletics . . . and fighting."[28] Despite not doing well in school, Gambino's friends managed to enter the unionized blue-collar labor force through the help of relatives and neighborhood friends and to earn enough to support a stable and secure middle-class lifestyle. Even among Jews, some American-born sons went into skilled blue-collar work, and many of the white-collar jobs they held were as small-scale entrepreneurs, an occupation that did not require much education.[29]

For girls, the job opportunities that beckoned required more education. The growth in New York's white-collar sector generated a demand for more educated workers. By 1940, a high school diploma was a standard requirement for most secretarial or bookkeeping jobs, and clerical workers and salespeople at least needed to know how to read and write English readily and be competent at simple arithmetic.[30] As a high school education became a practical necessity for young women, more of them sought it out. In 1950, a larger proportion of native-born Italian women born between 1926 and 1936 had high school diplomas than native-born Italian men, a reversal of earlier gender patterns; the same thing was happening among New York's Jews, although when it came to higher education, more men than women completed college among both second-generation Jews and Italians. In the Jewish community, as Miriam Cohen observes, it was common for women to help out in the family business as bookkeepers or secretaries and to marry businessmen who were wealthier but less well educated than themselves.[31]

Bear in mind that it was not until the 1950s that Jews really began a mass program of college education; for Italians it would not be until a decade or two later.[32] Before then, to be sure, Jews had flocked to New York City's public colleges; during the Depression years, Brooklyn, City, and Hunter were around 80 to 85 percent Jewish. The 1920s and 1930s were also the decades when teaching became known in New York as the Jewish profession. (And, I should note, a predominantly female Jewish profession.) In the 1920s, New York's expanding school system needed teachers, and rising salaries promised teachers a chance of middle-class status. By 1940, Jews made up more than half of those joining a teaching staff of nearly forty thousand in New York City's public schools.[33] Still, before World War II, a high school diploma was the best that most second-generation Jews achieved—and among second-generation Italians, even this was unusual. In 1950, only about a third of native-born Italian New Yorkers who grew up in the 1920s and 1930s had graduated from high school, compared to about two-thirds of their Jewish counterparts.[34]

Before World War II, moreover, discrimination in employment severely limited the options of those who managed to get a high school or college degree. As Jews moved up the educational ladder, barriers were erected to block their ascent. During the Depression years, New York City's largest employers—including public utilities, banks, insurance companies, and home offices of major corporations—rarely hired Jews. Non-Jewish law firms seldom took on Jewish attorneys; medical and dental offices did not welcome Jewish graduates.[35] Jewish professionals—accountants, lawyers, doctors, and dentists—fell back on a pattern of self-employment, setting up their own practices and catering largely to a Jewish clientele. In the process, they provided employment for a host of Jewish secretaries, bookkeepers, and clerks, as did the large number of businesses in the Jewish ethnic economy. In the 1930s, moreover, Jews were a growing presence in the civil service after Mayor LaGuardia implemented a merit system for hiring and promotion.[36]

Although most second-generation Jewish and Italian New Yorkers came of age and entered the workforce in the 1920s, 1930s, and 1940s, the spectacular expansion of the economy in the 1950s and 1960s improved and consolidated their progress. The second-generation cohort born in the 1920s and 1930s benefited even more from postwar economic prosperity. The decline in discriminatory barriers after World War II opened up doors in education and employment. And government assistance, in the form of low-interest home loans and educational benefits for World War II veterans, enabled many GIs to go to college and establish a middle-class life in suburbia. The third generation, born in the prosperous postwar years, was therefore well situated to catapult even further ahead, through education, into the upper reaches of the economy. By 1990, management and the professions engaged almost 40 percent of New Yorkers of Italian ancestry—and for Jews it was well over 50 percent.[37]

Will today's second generation do as well as their predecessors? In academic circles, the predictions are gloomy. The fear that a significant number of the children of today's immigrants will not only fail to move ahead but will actually fall behind the status of their parents—what Herbert Gans calls "second generation decline"—dominates current thinking on the new second generation.[38]

The main problem, according to the literature, is the changing structure of the economy, which has reduced the supply of relatively high-paid, low-skilled jobs. More and more, in the emerging hourglass economy, it's a question of getting a good job at the top or a bad job at the bottom. Well-paid blue-collar jobs are scarcer than in the past, and the declining viability of small business makes it harder to move up through expanding the businesses of the immigrant generation. Increasingly, the premium is on an extended education to get ahead. Whereas a high school degree was all it took to move into decent white-collar work in the past—and not even this was required for well-paid blue-collar jobs—immigrants' children today have to acquire a level of skills in one generation that many European immigrants took several generations to attain. A college diploma is required for highly skilled positions in professional services and information processing that offer high wages, good working conditions, career stability, and promotional possibilities. Those who do not do well in school will find their prospects limited to "immigrant jobs"—poorly paid, low-skilled service positions that involve long hours, unpleasant working conditions, and offer few chances for upward mobility.

Members of the second generation whose parents themselves did not escape poverty could end up in a bad way. Confined to poor inner-city schools, living in neighborhoods beset by drugs and violence, and exposed to an adversarial street and school culture, many immigrant children are at risk for academic failure. Gans also predicts they are at risk for downward mobility:

> If the young people are offered immigrant jobs, there are some good reasons why they might turn them down. They come to the world of work with American standards, and may not even be familiar with the old-country conditions . . . by which immigrants . . . judged the urban job market. Nor do they have the long-range goals that persuaded their parents to work long hours at low wages; they know they

cannot be deported and are here to stay in America, and most likely they are not obliged to send money to relatives left in the old country. From their perspective, immigrant jobs are demeaning; moreover, illegal jobs and scams may pay more and look better socially—especially when peer pressure is also present.[39]

If mass immigration continues—which it is likely to do for many years to come—employers will have their pick of new arrivals for low-end jobs, making it tougher for the second generation to get work at all and having a depressing effect on wages and working conditions in bottom-level positions.

Preliminary findings from an ongoing study of second-generation immigrants in the New York area suggest that "unambiguously black groups" —West Indians, Haitians, and many Dominicans—will have the most trouble. The main reason is that they have less access to educational opportunities than other groups, partly because of the racially segregated housing market. If racial segregation limits them to dangerous neighborhoods and inferior schools, few college degrees will be forthcoming.[40] If they develop oppositional attitudes and behavior, which, as we saw in Chapter 7, many are likely to do, this will have more dire consequences than it did for the second generation in the past. In the service-sector jobs that predominate today, conformity to middle-class norms in interpersonal relations is far more important than in the traditional blue-collar work available to Italian working-class boys in the past. A "tough guy" and antiauthoritarian stance may not have been a problem in the work culture of the factory floor, but in many service jobs today, it is. Second-generation black immigrant youth, Mollenkopf and his colleagues speculate, will be reluctant to take jobs that require deferential behavior to white employers; employers, for their part, may be reluctant to employ second-generation youth who have come to culturally resemble African American youth.[41] The end result: second-generation decline.

Is the hypothesis of a second-generation decline too pessimistic? I think so. The second generation without much education may not like the jobs they can get, but unemployment and the pathologies that go with poverty —crime, drug use, and alcoholism—are not the only, or even the most likely, result. Whatever they think of the low-level jobs available, they may end up taking them anyway, especially when they leave adolescence, marry and settle down, and have children to support. For many in the second generation, it will be a matter not of decline but of staying at the same socioeconomic level as their parents. The son of a Jamaican security guard, for example, may become a bus driver, and a Dominican factory worker's daughter a nursing aide. Even if the second generation reject their parents' values and standards, the fact that they have grown up in immigrant communities with dense job networks will probably give them access to bottom-rung positions—and perhaps even slightly better jobs that require little formal education, for example, as supervisors or skilled workers.[42]

Gender also needs to be considered, particularly since women stay in the labor force so much longer today. Although many second-generation men from poor working-class families will be stalled or headed downward, their sisters are in a better position to make modest gains. One reason is that girls in immigrant families are, on the whole, doing better in school than boys. Paradoxically, gender inequalities that tie girls to the home and reward female compliance and passivity end up helping them succeed academically. Being responsible for domestic chores and helping to look after younger siblings take time away from studies, yet these activities keep young girls away from the temptations of the street. Boys have fewer family responsibilities and are often encouraged to be independent, which is often counterproductive for school work. Parents are often stricter with their daughters than their sons, feeling a need to protect the girls from early sexual activity and pregnancy. Also, teachers in overcrowded inner-city schools may reward traditional feminine traits such as cooperativeness, compliance, and passivity.[43]

When they go on the job market, second-generation women may not only have better educational qualifications than their brothers, but they may also be preferred for, and find it less difficult to work in, service jobs that demand deference and good people skills. With a modest amount of schooling—a high school degree, perhaps some technical training, or a few years of college—second-generation women can qualify for lower-level white-collar jobs, for example, as receptionists, secretaries or health technicians. Openings may be available in these kinds of occupations through ethnic succession if, as Roger Waldinger and Joel Perlmann predict, native white women leave them as their own job profile is upgraded.[44]

And, remember, a good many of today's second generation—men and women alike—are poised to make dramatic improvements through obtaining college degrees and advanced professional qualifications. It may be going overboard to say, with Waldinger and Perlmann, that "there is little question that many, possibly even most immigrant children are heading upward,"[45] yet as they point out—and as the previous chapter indicated—a good number of the current second generation are making remarkable educational progress. A substantial proportion of today's immigrant parents are from middle-class backgrounds and are college-educated themselves. Although they often suffered status declines in this country, their children are well positioned to use education in upward mobility. Asian Americans, in particular, are already well represented in the nation's leading universities; their advance into New York City's elite magnet schools and into higher education is phenomenal. The more open society of the late twentieth century also offers advantages that were not available to immigrants in the past. Affirmative-action programs and more generous scholarships have helped speed the entry of the second generation into elite educational institutions. Whereas the Jews met open discrimination and quotas when they tried to climb the occupational ladder, in post–civil rights America it has been more difficult for dominant groups to engage in these kinds of closure strategies.[46]

Because the current second generation is just starting to enter the labor force in significant numbers, the literature on their economic prospects is still in the speculative stage. By necessity, second-generation research has focused on children and adolescents and often includes what Rubén Rumbaut calls the 1.5 generation, who were born abroad and came here before the age of twelve.[47] The results of an ongoing, large-scale study of second-generation young adults (aged eighteen to thirty-two) in the New York area will give us a picture of their early work careers,[48] but it will be a while before we can gather large enough samples of older second-generation adults to fully assess how they fare in the workforce. In the meantime, unforeseen changes in the economy could further stall or impede the progress of the second generation—or, alternatively, give them an unexpected boost. After all, few would have predicted back in 1910 that an economic boom some forty years later would help the descendants of Jewish and Italian immigrants get ahead. There is no such thing as an inevitable climb up the social ladder for the children of immigrants of any era, and the future of the present second generation clearly depends to a great degree on economic circumstances in the coming years.

## Is Transnationalism a One-Generation Phenomenon?

Finally, there is the fate of transnationalism. Among earlier European immigrants, transnational ties had a fairly short life: continued day-to-day involvement in the communal life of the sending societies fell off sharply after the first generation. To be sure, "Some hyphenated Americans," as Mary Waters and her colleagues note, "continued to play an important role in sending society politics or international political movements, such as

Zionism and the struggles for Irish independence. But by and large they did so as ethnic *Americans*, not as 'transmigrants.' "[49] Many second- and third-generation Jews have identified with and given financial support to Israel, but most do not have close relatives in Israel or ongoing contact with people there.

Connections with their parents' homelands became extremely attenuated among the children of Jewish and Italian immigrants. Consider the Jewish *landsmanshaftn* which, as I mentioned in Chapter 6, sent large sums of money to their home communities after World War I. They were, as Daniel Soyer observes, a one-generation phenomenon, and had "little attraction for most of their members' American children, who had developed their own sense of Jewish-American identity and to whom their parents' parochial loyalties seemed irrelevant at best. The fact that the aging societies continued to utilize Yiddish and Yiddish-accented English as their official languages made them seem all the more old-worldly."[50] I don't think I'm unusual, as a third-generation descendant of eastern European immigrants, in not even knowing the name of the places in Poland and Russia my maternal or paternal grandparents came from.

Jews of course were exceptional in their low rates of return migration— and in having most of their number wiped out in eastern Europe by the Holocaust. But transnational ties appear to have atrophied among Italians, too. Among Irvin Child's second-generation Italian informants in New Haven in the late 1930s, only one mentioned even wanting to return to Italy. As Robert Smith comments: "Given the series of questions Child asks about the informants' opinions about Italy and things Italian, and a chapter devoted entirely to 'in group' Italian Americans, it seems likely that if return to Italy was an important part of the second generation's experience it would have been mentioned."[51] In East Harlem in the 1920s and 1930s, according to Robert Orsi, Italian immigrant parents created an idealized version of southern Italy "into which they demanded their children gaze while making it clear that their children could never enter it. . . . They were Americani."[52] In the 1990s, an Italian-based tourist agency was tapping into a growing market of affluent Italian Americans as it offered tours to ancestral villages as part of its "Progetto Ritorno," since, as the brochure states, "only a fraction have ever visited Italy."

What happened to undercut transnationalism among second generation Jews and Italians? There were, for a start, the processes of assimilation that went on in the schools and other institutions, as those born and bred in America learned English and American ways and became engaged with life in this country. Schools, settlement houses, and Progressive reformers put pressure on immigrants and their children to abandon old-fashioned customs and languages and attachments to the Old World. Many Jews and Italian Americans in the second generation also managed to climb the socioeconomic ladder, if only in small steps. Also critical: their ethnic communities received few fresh recruits after the 1920s in the wake of legislated immigration restrictions and the back-to-back cataclysms of the Great Depression and World War II. Without replenishment, the number of Italians and Jews with fresh memories of and connections to the homeland became steadily smaller. The economies in Italy and eastern Europe, moreover, had little to offer the children of immigrant parents. And political events—World War II and the Holocaust—cut off connections there and heightened their patriotic embrace of America.

What about today? Some of the same factors still operate to undermine second-generation transnationalism. Most of the current second generation do not function within transnational social fields in the sense of moving back and forth between this country and their parents' homelands and retaining close personal ties there. As members of the second generation enter the labor force, a good number will do well and carve out successful careers here. The forces of assimilation are still strong. English, as Rubén Rumbaut observes, is triumphing with "breathtaking rapidity" among today's immigrant children.[53] Surveys in southern California and Florida show that by the time children of immigrants are high school seniors, the vast majority prefer English to their parents' native language. By then, only about a third of the seniors surveyed said that they spoke their parents' language very well and only a quarter said they read it very well.[54] English may have become the global language of money, but the loss of the parental language surely has implications for the second generation's ability to maintain ongoing ties with their parents' homelands.

But if members of the present second generation, like their predecessors, are becoming more and more American, a number of new developments suggest that transnationalism will have a longer life than it did in the past. Different circumstances today and in the years ahead may well support and sustain transnational connections for at least some of the current second generation. Let's hope there is no World War III—because if there is, no one will be left in any generation. One hopes, too, that no Holocaust will wipe out all the relatives of any one immigrant group. Even if there is some move toward restrictionism, the United States is likely to remain an immigration country for the foreseeable future, allowing five or six hundred thousand persons to enter a year; New York can expect to receive a disproportionate share, if only because of the networks that link newcomers to settlers.[55] Continued inflows will bring new arrivals who will enrich and replenish ethnic communities—and include substantial numbers of people, of all ages, with close ties to the homeland. Moreover, as I discussed in Chapter 6, transnational ties are more visible and more acceptable in today's multicultural America, so that the second generation often feel pride—not shame—in connections to their parents' homelands.

Where dual nationality provisions extend to the second generation—as is now the case for Dominican New Yorkers—this may foster continued political involvement in the home country among the second generation. When recent electoral reforms in the Dominican Republic go into effect, U.S.-born adult children of Dominican parents will have the right to vote abroad in Dominican elections. Some are bound to exercise this privilege.

Then there's the fact that a number of second-generation New Yorkers will have spent significant chunks of their childhood and teenage years in their parents' homeland, thereby creating and strengthening ties to relatives and friends there. Some immigrants send their children home to grandparents because they need day care. Others ship teenagers home for high school to protect them from drugs, gangs, and sexual precociousness in New York.[56] Dominican educators and government officials estimate that as many as ten thousand students from schools in the United States, mainly from the New York area, are enrolled in the country's schools. Many Mexican parents send their children back to their villages during summer vacations so that they will not get into trouble in New York.[57] At the other end of the life course, parental retirement patterns may also strengthen transnational ties. Some of the first generation will end up retiring to their birthplaces, assuring that their children will make regular trips to see them and keeping children and grandchildren connected, however tenuously, to the sending country. Language may play a role, too, particularly among Hispanics who, studies show, are most likely to be bilingual in the second generation.[58] In the context of a huge Spanish-speaking community in New York, including Spanish-language newspapers and radio and television programs, many children of Latino immigrants will speak and understand Spanish, thereby facilitating the maintenance of ties to the homeland. This was unlike their Italian and Jewish predecessors who, by and large, were English-only groups.

If economic restructuring and the declining demand for less educated labor threaten the ability of many members of the second generation to advance, then some may try their hand at ventures (including illegal ones) that involve transnational connections. In today's global economy, this is a tack the more successful may take up as well. That some sending nations today have robust and growing economies means that they may attract a number of educated and well-trained descendants of the current immigrants, who will find it profitable to invest in their parents' homeland, return there for a time to work, or end up commuting back and forth. In *Accidental Asian,* Eric Liu describes a friend—an American-born Chinese (or ABC) like himself—who spent little time thinking about China as a child but as an adult joined some friends to start a new investment bank focusing on Asian business and China-related deals.[59]

Cheap air travel and widespread global tourism in the modern era will also increase the firsthand contact that members of the second generation have with their homelands, although caution is needed in evaluating whether short vacations or special tours to the homeland are evidence of, or lead to, significant transnationalism. Listen to Eric Liu again, describing his two trips to China: "I never felt the transcendence the child of immigrants is supposed to experience upon going *back.* . . . Part of it was that I have no family left on the mainland. Part of it too was that I was with my redheaded wife . . . and this often made us a minor spectacle. . . . Mostly, I was unsure what it was I should have been searching for."[60]

The verdict is not yet in on how important transnational ties really are—or will be—in the lives of today's second generation, particularly as they grow up, move into the workforce, and establish families of their own. Research is needed to explore some key questions: How much contact do members of the second generation actually have with their parents' country of origin? How much circular migration is there? Are members of the second generation sending back remittances to their parents' country of origin? Are there political ties or organizations that unite communities of second-generation youth in the United States and their parents' home villages or cities?[61] Remember, too, that becoming American and maintaining transnational links are not mutually exclusive. One of the great insights of the recent transnational literature is that individuals can keep up ties to their own (or their parents') home countries at the very same time as they are committed to, and influenced by, involvements in activities, institutions, and relationships in this country. To the extent that members of the second generation do maintain transnational ties, we need to know just what the consequences are for their opportunities, relationships, and engagements here, from their occupational prospects to their family relations and political behavior.

From a comparative perspective, it seems clear that connections to their parents' homelands will be more important for the present second generation than they were last time. Yet a note of caution is in order. Although researchers need to be sensitive to transnational ties among the second generation, there is a risk of seeing transnationalism everywhere and over-emphasizing its centrality. Some members of the second generation will maintain ongoing and close connections to their parents' countries of origin, but they are likely to be a minority. The vast majority, born and raised here, will be primarily oriented to people, institutions, and places in this country—and it is the implications of growing up in America, not ties to their parents' homelands, that should be our primary object of study.

It is a long journey from Ellis Island's piers to the terminals at John F. Kennedy International Airport. Manhattan's Little Italy has shrunk to a couple of blocks, and the gentrified parts of the Lower East Side are now styled the East Village.[62] Ellis Island, in fact, is now mostly in New Jersey. The immigrant communities of the past are gone forever, but the people who came of age in them have left an indelible imprint on the city. Among many other contributions, they shaped the very culture, and the institutions, that the newest immigrants confront as they, in turn, make the metropolis their home. New York is constantly invigorated as new groups plant their roots here, and the newcomers themselves are—and will be—irrevocably changed by their own journeys through New York.

# Notes

## Introduction

1. According to figures from the Immigration and Naturalization Service, the annual rate of immigration into New York City was 78,477 in the 1970s, 85,602 in the 1980s, and 112,598 in the early 1990s (Lobo, Salvo, and Virgin 1996: 10).

2. Puzo 1969; Di Donato 1937; Cahan 1917; Roth 1969; Howe 1976; Weinberg 1988.

3. Hobsbawm and Ranger 1983. A recent analysis of national public opinion polls concludes that Americans tend to look at immigration through rose-colored glasses turned backwards: "The American public expresses positive and approving attitudes towards immigrants who came 'earlier,' but expresses negative sentiments about those who are coming at whatever time a survey is being conducted" (Simon and Lynch 1999: 458).

4. Nadell 1981: 274–75.

5. Brimelow 1995.

6. Bendix 1964: 17. On comparisons in historical sociology, see Bonnell 1980; Skocpol and Somers 1980; and Kiser and Hechter 1991.

7. Morawska 1990: 188.

8. Kennedy 1996: 68.

9. My research on Jamaicans and immigrant health-care workers is reported in Foner 1985, 1986, 1987, 1994. *New Immigrants in New York* (Foner 1987) brings together ethnographic accounts on several immigrant groups.

10. On politics, see Michael Jones-Correa's study of Latin American immigrants in Queens, which makes some interesting comparisons with the past with regard to the role of the Democratic political machine and naturalization rates (1998b: 69–90, 96–97). The essays in the volume being prepared by Gary Gerstle and John Mollenkopf analyze modes of political incorporation and civic culture among immigrants today and in the past.

11. In 1997, 26 percent of the 20.1 million people in the New York Consolidated Metropolitan Statistical Area were foreign born (Farley 1998).

12. Other groups such as Syrians, Greeks, Chinese, and West Indians made up a relatively small proportion of the city's arrivals in this period. As late as 1920, for example, only about five thousand Chinese and thirty-five thousand black, mostly West Indian, immigrants lived in New York (Kasinitz 1992: 41; Wong 1982: 7). See Binder and Reimers 1995 for an account of the diversity among New York immigrants between 1880 and World War I.

13. Binder and Reimers 1995: 136; Kraly and Hirschman 1994: 22; Moore 1981: 21.

14. Riis 1971 [1890]: 43, 47, 85–86.

## Chapter 1: Who They Are and Why They Have Come

1. Glazer and Moynihan 1970: 8. By 1855, the Irish-born made up 28 percent of the city, the German-born 16 percent, and they remained the dominant foreign-born groups until the end of the century. In 1890, the Irish-born and German-born and their children made up 52 percent of the population of New York and Brooklyn (Glazer and Moynihan 1970; Rosenwaike 1972). By 1920, after several decades of enormous Jewish and Italian immigration, foreign-born Jews and Italians and their children made up about 43 percent of the city's population.

2. For figures on the Russian Jewish and Italian immigrant populations, see Kessner 1977; Rosenwaike 1972; and Watkins and Robles 1993. The category "Russian Jews" for 1880 combines the census figures for natives of Russia and Poland. Prior to 1890 it is likely that most Jews who came from the Russian empire reported Poland as their birthplace (Rosenwaike 1972: 69).

3. This was a marked increase from 1880, when New York City's population was 1.2 million, with about another 570,000 in Brooklyn, which was then a separate city (Rosenwaike 1972).

4. Because the U.S. census did not ask respondents' religion, researchers customarily rely on Russian birthplace as a proxy for eastern European Jews (see, e.g., Kessner 1977; Lieberson and Waters 1988; Model 1993; Perlmann 1988). One exception, a study of the foreign-born population in the United States based on the 1910 Census Public Use Sample, uses Yiddish as the mother tongue to identify immigrant Jews. In this analysis, New York City had an even higher concentration of the nation's foreign-born eastern European Jews (54 percent); Philadelphia came in second, with 9 percent; Chicago third, with 6 percent (Watkins and Robles 1994: 373–75).

5. Waldinger 1996a: 52; Waldinger 1996c: 1079–80.

6. Flores and Salvo 1997.

7. Waldinger 1996a: 50.

8. Lobo, Salvo, and Virgin 1996: 13.

9. Kasinitz and Vickerman 1995. These include Antigua, Bahamas, Barbados, Belize, British Virgin Islands, Dominica, Grenada, Guyana, Jamaica, Montserrat, St. Kitts–Nevis, St. Lucia, St. Vincent, and Trinidad and Tobago.

10. Flores and Salvo 1997.

11. Salvo, Ortiz, and Lobo 1994: vi. These figures on the nationality distribution of New York City's Hispanics refer to people of Hispanic ancestry, including those born in the United States. In 1990, two-fifths of the city's Puerto Rican population was born in Puerto Rico (21).

12. When Chinese settlements in broader metropolitan areas are compared, however, New York came second to the San Francisco Bay metropolitan area (Lin 1998: 28).

13. Lessinger 1995: 80.

14. Mahler 1995b: 41–43.

15. Joseph 1967: 189–90.

16. Kessner 1977: 37–38.

17. Ibid., 36–37; Bodner 1985.

18. Rumbaut 1991: 230.

19. Lobo, Salvo, and Virgin 1996: 27–29. INS data on occupational background are not without problems. The "current" occupation category on the immigrant visa does not always refer to the occupation a person held before immigrating. If the prospective immigrant, for example, has already been in the U.S. on a temporary visa and is seeking to "adjust" his or her status, occupational information could refer to the last job held back home or to a job held in the U.S. For those entering under occupational preferences, occupational information is taken from the Labor Department form and refers to the occupation in the U.S. for which certification was sought (see Lobo, Salvo and Virgin 1996).

20. Data on the educational attainment of working-age immigrants, which includes island-born Puerto Ricans, were calculated by Hector Cordero-Guzman, New School for Social Research. The figures on post-1965 Chinese immigrants are from Cordero-Guzman and Grosfoguel 1998. See table 6, this vol.

21. Mollenkopf, Kasinitz, and Lindholm 1995; Salvo and Ortiz 1992: 189–90.

22. These figures refer to persons twenty-five years of age or older. Mollenkopf, Kasinitz, and Lindholm 1995; Hernandez et al. 1995. For New Yorkers as a whole, 30 percent were college graduates (Hernandez et al. 1995).

23. Mollenkopf, Kasinitz, and Lindholm 1995.

24. Aleinikoff 1997. The immigration law of 1903 forbade the admission of foreign proponents of anarchism; in 1917, the anarchist clause was expanded to exclude from the United States advocates of violent revolution and those who advocated sabotage or belonged to revolutionary organizations (Higham 1955: 112, 202).

25. The literacy test was enacted by Congress in 1917 over President Wilson's veto. Two earlier attempts to pass such legislation were stymied by presidential vetoes—by President Cleveland in 1897 and President Taft in 1912. According to the 1917 law, immigrants in the United States could bring in or send for certain close family members—e.g., wives, mothers, and grandmothers—who were exempt from exclusion by literacy (Ueda 1997).

26. La Sorte 1985: 32.

27. Ibid., 33.

28. Siu, for example, cites newspaper stories about Chinese immigrants in Chicago in the pre–World War I period who had been smuggled into the country through Texas and Canada (1987: 201–2).

29. Yu 1992: 21–22; see also Siu 1987: 196–200.

30. Schmitt 1997. Although additional immigrants continue to enter the city without proper documents, the number of unauthorized immigrants is not cumulative. Some die or leave the city, and others eventually legalize their status.

31. Schmitt 1997.

32. Portes and Rumbaut 1996: 10.

33. Grasmuck and Pessar 1991: 171–72; see also Georges 1990.

34. Papademetriou and DiMarzio 1986.

35. See Georges 1990; Grasmuck and Pessar 1991; Margolis 1994; Pessar 1995a.

36. Massey et al. 1994: 741.

37. For an analysis of the incorporation of the "eastern European periphery into the Atlantic world economy" at the "long turn of the century" (1880–1914), with a focus on Poland, see Morawska 1989. Also see the comparison of the mechanisms, forms, and patterns of European migration in the turn of the twentieth century (1870–1914) and recent periods (1955–94) (Morawska and Spohn 1997).

38. Cf. Massey et al. 1994.

39. Ibid.

40. Portes and Rumbaut 1990: 231.

41. Massey et al. 1993, 1994.

42. Archdeacon 1983: 117–18.

43. Tomasi 1975: 16–19. The analysis of causes of Italian emigration draws on Alba 1985, Archdeacon 1983, Barton 1975, Bodner 1985, and Briggs 1978.

44. Alba 1985: 38.

45. Ibid., 39.

46. Bodner 1985; Briggs 1978.

47. Cinel 1982a.

48. On the causes of eastern European Jewish emigration, see Ewen 1985; Joseph 1967; Kuznets 1985; and Rischin 1962.

49. Ewen 1975: 52.

50. Joseph 1967: 67–68.

51. Ibid., 68.

52. Rischin 1962: 30.

53. Jewish artisans, displaced by large manufacturers, often found it hard to get work in new workshops and factories. Both Jewish and gentile owners preferred Christians, who worked on the Saturday Sabbath and were thought to be less wedded to old production methods than Jewish artisans and less likely to be involved in labor unrest (Glenn 1990: 32).

54. Quoted in Glenn 1990: 44.

55. Interview in Kramer and Masur 1976: 92.

56. Joseph 1967: 68.

57. Kuznets 1975.

58. Interview in Kramer and Masur 1976: 10.

59. Archdeacon 1983: 117.

60. Wyman 1993: 24.

61. Mangione and Morreale 1992: 98.

62. Cited in Morawska 1989: 261.

63. Antin quoted in Takaki 1993: 280.

64. Briggs 1985: 69; Ewen 1985: 56.

65. See Massey et al. 1993.

66. Quoted in Howe 1976: 27.

67. Cinel 1982b: 37.

68. Wyman 1993: 15.

69. Georges 1990.

70. Koslovsky 1981.

71. Aleinikoff 1997; see also Zolberg 1995, 1999.

72. The Great Depression and the suppression of emigration in postrevolutionary Russia also played a role in stemming the flow (see Massey 1995). The Johnson-Reed Act reduced the number of European immigrants allowed yearly to 2 percent of the foreign-born residents of each nationality in the United States, according to the 1890 census, a time when few southern and eastern European immigrants were present. Family exemptions from the quotas were permitted for the spouses and minor children of American citizens. After 1929, a yearly ceiling of 150,000 immigrants was parceled out in proportion to the distribution of national origins in the population of the United States in 1920. Canada and Latin American countries were exempt from the quota, and special laws barred Asian immigration. For a short summary of major legislative milestones in U.S. immigration history, see Fix and Passel 1994.

73. The system established by the 1965 reforms essentially remains in place, with some modifications and changes. The 1965 law established an annual ceiling of 170,000 visas for the Eastern hemisphere and 120,000 for the Western hemisphere, although spouses, children, and parents of U.S. citizens could enter without numerical limit. A single worldwide ceiling of 290,000 was created in 1976, replacing the hemispheric quotas. The Immigration Reform and Control Act of 1986 (IRCA) enabled undocumented aliens living in the country continuously since 1982 to apply for legal status (until 1988). The result was all-time highs of 1.5 million and 1.8 million immigrants officially admitted in 1990 and 1991, respectively; the 1990 total included 885,000 formerly undocumented aliens who had been legalized; the 1991 total, 1.1 million.

The Immigration Act of 1990 created a new flexible cap of 700,000 visas for all categories of immigrants, falling to 675,000 in 1995 (excluding refugees). This represented an increase over previous levels, which had been averaging about 600,000 annually during the 1980s (not including aliens granted legal status under the provisions of IRCA). Immediate relatives of adult U.S. citizens could still enter without numerical restrictions. Among other things, the 1990 law increased the number of visas for spouses and children of permanent residents and the number of employment visas aimed at immigrants with higher skills. It also established a diversity program intended for immigrants from countries thought to be under-represented in immigration. For details of immigration legislation in the past few decades, see Fix and Passel 1994; Kraly 1987; Reimers 1992; Ueda 1994. Chapter 3 of *The Newest New Yorkers, 1990–1994* (Lobo, Salvo and Virgin 1996) discusses the implications of the 1990 act for New York City.

74. U.S. foreign policy concerns also played a role. Fearing political instability and gains by left-wing factions in the wake of Rafael Trujillo's assassination, the U.S. government sought to reduce political tensions by using emigration as a safety valve. The U.S. provided new facilities and expanded its consular staff in the Dominican Republic to speed up the visa process (Georges 1990; Grasmuck and Pessar 1991).

75. In 1992, the average wait for a spouse or minor child of a permanent resident alien (for a family second-preference visa) was about two years. It was much longer for brothers and sisters of adult U.S. citizens (family fourth preference); most of the 65,000 people who entered under the fourth-preference category in 1992 had waited about nine years; those from the Philippines in this category had waited over fifteen years (Center for Immigration Studies 1992).

76. See Reimers 1992.

77. Stone 1982.

78. See Stafford 1987.

79. Grasmuck and Pessar 1991.

80. Portes and Rumbaut 1990: 13.

81. Chen 1992: 64; Lessinger 1995; cf. Yoon 1997, on Korea.

82. Margolis 1994, 1997.

83. Basch et al. 1994: 231–32.

84. Lynn Trentacoste, interview with Haitian immigrants in Queens, November 20, 1996, Urban Anthropology course, Purchase College.

85. F. Markowitz 1993: 51.

86. Mahler 1995b.

87. Zhou 1992: 61–62.

88. Min 1996: 30.

89. Grasmuck and Pessar 1991: 46; Pessar 1987, 1995. The minimum monthly salary in the U.S. represents the salary received for a forty-hour week, four weeks a month, based on the federal minimum wage rate (Grasmuck and Pessar 1991: 47).

90. Margolis 1994: 77.

91. Ibid., 79.

92. Georges 1990: 225–27.

93. On the role of family ties in recent immigration, see Rumbaut 1997b.

94. Jasso and Rosenzweig, cited in Massey et al. 1994.

95. Arnold et al., cited in Massey et al. 1994.

96. Georges 1990: 81.

97. Tilly 1990: 90; Foner 1987: 198.

98. Bryce-Laporte 1987.

99. Portes and Stepick 1993: 207.

100. Ibid., 206.

101. See Carino 1996; Espiritu 1996; Rumbaut 1996.

102. Daniels 1990: 225.

103. Antin, quoted in Nadell 1981: 272.

104. Cohen 1949: 60.

105. La Sorte 1985: 12.

106. Ibid., 14.

107. Cohen 1995 [1918]: 57–62.

108. Daniels 1990: 187.

109. La Sorte 1985: 29. Trachoma was an especially frequent cause of rejection in Italy; in 1906, of the more than twenty-five thousand intending emigrants turned away for medical reasons by Italian examiners, eight thousand had trachoma, and another seven thousand were suspected carriers.

110. On the journey from eastern Europe to America, including crossing in steerage, see Nadell 1981.

111. Daniels 1990: 187.

112. Nadell 1981: 278.

113. Chotzinoff 1955: 58.

114. Cohen 1949: 61.

115. Nadell 1981: 278.

116. For a detailed account of the process of obtaining a visa and arriving in New York, see Margolis 1994, on Brazilian immigrants.

117. Center for Immigration Studies 1997.

118. Margolis 1994: 31.

119. Georges 1990: 82.

120. Margolis 1994: 39.

121. Pessar 1995a: 10.

122. In 1990, buying a false visitor's visa cost Salvadorans about five thousand dollars (Mahler 1995b: 48). For a fascinating account of the various legal and illegal mechanisms, including purchased passports, that members of one Dominican extended family used to come to the United States, see Garrison and Weiss 1987.

123. Rohter 1997.

124. In July and August 1996 alone, the U.S. Coast Guard apprehended close to nine hundred Dominicans who were trying to enter the U.S. by boat without the proper documents; the 1996 fiscal year total was a little over six thousand (Migration World Dateline 1996; MacSwain 1996). As a result of intensive Coast Guard enforcement operations in 1997, the number of Dominicans attempting the voyage dropped dramatically, and only twelve hundred Dominicans were interdicted that

fiscal year (CISNEWS 1998). U.S. authorities reported a rise in the traffic in 1998, with a growing number of arrests logged that year (Fineman 1998).

125. Fineman 1998.

126. Mahler 1995b: 48.

127. Dillon 1996; Dunn 1994; Kwong 1997; Sengupta 1998a.

128. Kwong 1997: 80.

129. Mahler 1995b: 49.

## Chapter 2: Where They Live

1. The television movie is called "Mrs. Santa Claus" (1996). See also Wenger (1997), who argues that by the 1920s and 1930s second-generation Jews were already reimagining the Lower East Side in terms that transformed poverty, crime, and poor living conditions into a narrative of Jewish struggle, perseverance, and self-congratulation.

2. "Rats and Squalor, at $800 a Month" 1996; Giordano and Rivera 1990: 16.

3. Hood 1993: 169.

4. Ibid., 25.

5. Kessner 1977: 136.

6. Gabaccia 1984: 67; Kessner 1977: 130.

7. Gabaccia 1992: 235.

8. Rischin 1962: 93.

9. Cahan 1960: 92.

10. The 1990 figure is from a table produced by the New York Department of City Planning, Population Division, "1990 Census: Total Population, Total Housing Units and Density, New York City and Boroughs by Census Tract," March 1991.

11. On the Lower East Side during this period, see Hood 1993; Kessner 1977; Plunz 1990; Rischin 1962; Sorin 1992.

12. Rischin 1962: 76.

13. Riis 1971 [1890]: 85.

14. Kessner 1977: 46.

15. Hapgood 1967 [1902]: 113.

16. Rischin 1962: 55.

17. Odencrantz 1919: 12.

18. Gabaccia 1984: 67.

19. Odencrantz 1919: 12.

20. For a thoughtful analysis of the origins of the festa of the Madonna of 115th Street in East Harlem and the role it played among Italian immigrants, see Orsi 1985.

21. Mangione and Morreale 1992: 170–71.

22. Logan 1997b; White, Dymowski, and Wang 1994.

23. Cohen 1992: 208–9. Cohen's study used the New York State Manuscript Census for 1905 and 1925.

24. Kessner 1977: 155.

25. Gurock 1979: 49–50.

26. Gurock 1979; Kessner 1977; Moore 1992.

27. Kessner 1977: 158.

28. Gabaccia 1992: 246.

29. Gurock 1979: 42.

30. Orsi 1985.

31. Kessner 1977: 145.

32. Gurock 1979: 52. Henry Roth's autobiographical novel, *Mercy of a Rude Stream* (1994), gives a wonderful picture of growing up in Harlem in this period.

33. Hood 1993: 136.

34. Kessner 1977: 146.

35. Moore 1992: 257–58.

36. Landesman 1969.

37. Kazin 1946: 12.

38. Plunz 1990: 50–87.

39. Hammack 1982: 97; Kessner 1977: 132. Strictly speaking, tenements were residential buildings constructed for use by three or more families—until the Multiple Dwelling Law of 1929 revised building standards. The key change was that all windows providing light and ventilation had to be at least thirty feet from any wall or other obstruction (Oser 1999). By 1865, as Richard Plunz (1990: 13) notes, the word *tenement* was a well-established term in the technical vocabulary of housing for the urban poor.

40. Gabaccia 1984: 68.

41. Fee and Corey 1994: 31.

42. Plunz 1990: 33.

43. Chotzinoff 1955: 123.

44. Quoted in Joselit 1986: 40.

45. Ewen 1985: 150.

46. Chotzinoff 1955: 122–23.

47. Plunz 1990: 47. As late as 1915–16, only 9 percent of the approximately eleven thousand tenements in Manhattan below 14th Street were new-law tenements (Lubove 1962: 265).

48. Gabaccia 1984: 71.

49. Odencrantz 1919: 14.

50. Ewen 1985: 155.

51. According to Elizabeth Ewen, the rent for a steam-fitted apartment in New York City was $360 a year. Only those with annual incomes of $1,500 could afford such an apartment—and they were few (1985: 152).

52. Howe 1976: 148.

53. Lower East Side Tenement Museum 1995: appendix 8, 5.

54. Gabaccia 1984: 75–77.

55. The Immigration Commission's 1911 study reported that 56 percent of the

Russian Jewish households in New York and 20 percent of southern Italian families had boarders living with them (Glenn 1990: 74).

56. See Glenn 1990: 61; Gabaccia 1984: 80–82; Kessner 1977: 99–103.

57. Borgenicht 1942: 192.

58. Howe 1976: 178.

59. Kessner 1977: 145.

60. Weisser 1985: 76.

61. Schoenebaum cited in Zukin and Zwerman 1985: 8. The Brownsville tenements housed, on average, five families each.

62. Kazin 1946: 12.

63. Borgenicht 1942.

64. Gurock 1979: 162.

65. Roth 1994: 16.

66. Orsi 1985: 29.

67. Moore 1992: 252–61.

68. According to historian Beth Wenger, the Lower East Side emerged as a nostalgia center for New York Jews who no longer lived there during the Great Depression; it became "a living reminder of an idealized immigrant world as well as a mirror of the past that reflected the extent of Jewish progress" (1996: 84).

69. Flores and Salvo 1997; Rosenwaike 1972: 133. The New York urban region, as defined by the Regional Plan Association, includes, in addition to the city's five boroughs, Dutchess, Nassau, Orange, Putnam, Rockland, Suffolk, Ulster, and Westchester counties in New York; Bergen, Essex, Hudson, Hunterdon, Mercer, Middlesex, Monmouth, Morris, Ocean, Passaic, Somerset, Sussex, Union, and Warren counties in New Jersey; and Fairfield, Litchfield, and New Haven counties in Connecticut (see Armstrong 1998).

70. An analysis of 1990 census data shows that when immigrant workers journey to work, the largest proportion in each of the New York urban region's counties, with the exception of Queens, travel to a job in their own county. In Queens, slightly more immigrant workers travel to Manhattan to work (unpublished tables on county-to-county journey-to-work trips, calculated by Regina Armstrong, 1996).

71. Lin 1998; Zhou 1994; Zhou and Logan 1991.

72. Ruf 1994.

73. Min 1996: 38–39.

74. Portes and Sensenbrenner 1993.

75. Massing, quoted in Guarnizo 1992.

76. Orleck 1987; Sexton 1995.

77. Lobo, Salvo, and Virgin 1996: 108–11.

78. Quoted in Kasinitz 1987: 61; see also Kasinitz 1992: 69.

79. Waldinger 1987: 8.

80. Ibid., 3.

81. Mollenkopf 1993: 27. Although the vast majority of Hispanic and West Indian New Yorkers do not live in the old slum neighborhoods, some of course do. West

Indians have begun to branch out from central Brooklyn to Bedford-Stuyvesant and Brownsville; some Dominicans have been moving to Williamsburg; and Mexicans are a growing presence in East Harlem (see Lobo, Salvo, and Virgin 1996).

82. Waldinger 1987: 3.

83. On figures for the inner cities, see Flores and Salvo 1997; on New York City, see Mollenkopf 1993: 93.

84. Flores and Salvo 1987; see also Frey 1996.

85. Orlean 1992: 97; Waldinger 1987: 4. In 1990, 53 percent of the population of Community District 3, which encompasses the Jackson Heights neighborhood, was foreign born, up from 41 percent ten years earlier. The largest Latino groups in the district were Dominicans, Colombians, and Ecuadorians (Sanchez 1997). On the history of Jackson Heights, see Hood 1993: 173–78.

86. Smith 1995. The Asian presence in Flushing increased from 2,571 in 1970 to 19,508 in 1990, or from 6 percent to 36 percent of the population. (Non-Hispanic whites were 29 percent of the population, down from 76 percent in 1970.) Together the Koreans and Chinese represent three quarters of all Asians in the neighborhood, with Indians making up about 20 percent (Smith and Zhou n.d.).

87. Lobo, Salvo, and Virgin 1996: 159–60.

88. Orleck 1987.

89. Winnick 1990: 62; see Smith 1995, on Flushing.

90. Millman 1997: 89–98.

91. These figures are from the 1910 Census (U.S. Bureau of the Census 1913).

92. Vecoli 1965: 214–15.

93. Friedman 1984.

94. LaGumina 1988: 82, 87.

95. See Shargel and Drimmer 1994.

96. Flores and Salvo 1997.

97. Mahler 1995a: 196–97.

98. The conventional definition of the word suburb—the entire territory of the metropolitan area beyond the statistically designated central city—is extremely broad; it includes inner suburbs, large suburban cities, office parks, retail centers, manufacturing communities, and even low-density rural territory as well as stereotypic bedroom communities (Frey 1995).

99. The 1910 figure is based on census data for that year (U.S. Bureau of the Census 1913); the 1990 figure is from Flores and Salvo 1997.

100. Flores and Salvo 1997; see also Alba et al. 1999.

101. Nationwide, according to a study based on data from the 1980 and 1990 censuses, there is a marked income gradient in suburbanization for immigrant populations. Indeed, for many immigrant groups, households in the highest quintile of household income generally draw close to the suburbanization rates of comparable whites (Alba et al. 1999).

102. These figures, based on 1990 census data, are from Flores and Salvo 1997.

103. Foderaro 1991.

104. Berger 1993. According to INS figures, another 1,238 legal immigrants moved to Port Chester between 1991 and 1994, mostly from Hispanic countries. A five-part series, "New Immigrants Change the Face of the Suburbs," in the Westchester Gannett newspapers, looks at the impact of recent immigrants in the county (Sheingold 1995).

105. Alba et al. 1995: 634.

106. See Mahler 1995b.

107. See Khandelwal 1995; Lessinger 1995.

108. The Queens Council of the Arts has put together a guide to ethnic communities along the number 7 train. Entitled "The International Express," it gives information about restaurants, churches, stores, and festivals (Harlow 1995).

109. Winnick 1990: 68–69.

110. Lobo, Salvo, and Virgin 1996; Page 1997.

111. Smith 1995.

112. Lobo, Salvo, and Virgin 1996: 81.

113. Alba et al. 1995.

114. Ibid., 642.

115. Alba et al. 1995; Smith 1995.

116. Alba et al. 1995: 634.

117. Winnick 1990: 66–67.

118. Alvarez 1996; Giordano and Rivera 1990; Kinkead 1992.

119. Sontag 1996.

120. Wolff 1994.

121. Sontag 1996: 1, 44.

122. Mahler 1995b: 86.

123. Bruni and Sontag 1996.

124. Bruni 1997; Holloway 1997.

125. Schill, Friedman, and Rosenbaum 1998.

126. In his study of Elmhurst, Queens, Roger Sanjek argues that illegal building alterations—e.g., putting up plywood room partitions or installing water and electrical connections oneself—are the more serious problems, as distinct from the practice of tenants and homeowners renting rooms to lodgers (1998: 189).

127. Bruni and Sontag 1996.

128. Margolis 1994: 63–71.

129. Pessar 1987.

130. Jackson 1985: 118; Blackburn 1995: 17.

131. Nationally, after ten to twenty years in the U.S., immigrants from China and Taiwan who were between the ages of thirty-five and forty-four in 1990 surpassed native whites of the same age in levels of home ownership (McArdle 1997: 364).

132. Ibid., 363.

133. Grasmuck and Grosfoguel 1997.

134. Abramsky 1997; Millman 1996.

135. Kasinitz 1987: 64–65.

136. Nossiter 1995.

137. Smith 1995; Smith and Zhou n.d. An analysis of Chinese-owned businesses in two zip codes in the Flushing area in 1990 shows twenty-two banks and bank branches and fifty-four real estate agencies (Smith 1995).

138. McArdle 1997: 362.

139. Logan and Spitze 1994.

140. Ewen 1985: 162. For a contemporary case study of interethnic relations in a rundown polyethnic Chicago tenement, see Conquergood 1992. Breakdowns and emergencies created a sense of community among the residents from different ethnic groups, friendships developed among neighbors, and the "free-for-all mixing of ethnicities" was most intense among young children who played in the building's courtyard.

141. Portes and Rumbaut 1996: 86.

142. Alba et al. 1997: 885.

143. See Massey and Denton 1993.

144. Min 1998: 67.

145. Zhou and Logan 1991.

146. Moore 1981: 38.

147. Alba et al. 1997.


## Chapter 3: The Work They Do

1. Figures on the occupational background of Jews and Italians are based on statistics collected for immigrants to the United States generally, not just those who settled in New York.

2. See Kessner 1977: 33-38.

3. Foerster 1919: 333.

4. Ibid., 331.

5. Perlmann 1996a.

6. Gambino 1974: 78.

7. The percentages of less than fifty dollars are from Lieberson (1980: 28); the annual household-income figures are from the 1909 U.S. Immigration Commission's reports (cited in Cohen 1992: 43-44).

8. Data calculated by Hector Cordero-Guzman, New School for Social Research; they include island-born Puerto Ricans.

9. The occupational data on immigrants entering New York City in the early 1990s are from Lobo, Salvo, and Virgin 1996: 27-30; they refer to legal immigrants sixteen to sixty-four years old. The category "operators, fabricators, and laborers" includes lower-skilled blue-collar occupations such as sewing machine operators, factory workers, and construction laborers (ibid., 24-25). The figures for the New York urban region are from an unpublished report on the Regional Plan Association's project, "The Region's Immigrant Population and Work Force Preparedness," directed by Regina Armstrong and Emanuel Tobier.

10. Data calculated by Hector Cordero-Guzman, New School for Social Research.

11. Portes and Rumbaut 1996: 210.

12. See Kim 1987: 224; Park 1997: 58; and Yoon 1997: 125.

13. Cited in Yoon 1997: 246.

14. See Lin (1998), chap. 3, for a discussion of the inflow of overseas Chinese investment capital into New York City, particularly into Manhattan's core Chinatown and the Flushing satellite Chinatown. According to one estimate, between 1985 and 1990 $1.7 billion of venture capital from Asia was invested in new high-technology start-up firms in California's Silicon Valley region (Fong 1998).

15. Kessner 1977: 24.

16. The discussion of New York's economic growth in this period draws on Drennan and Matson 1995; Hammock 1982; Kessner 1977. On the garment industry, see Rischin 1962; Waldinger 1986.

17. Waldinger 1986: 50–51.

18. Sorin 1992: 74.

19. See Phelps-Stokes 1918, chap. 8, for a discussion of the building projects in New York City between 1880 and 1910.

20. Model 1993: 172–73.

21. The discussion of New York's current economy is drawn from a variety of sources: Armstrong 1998; Drennan 1991; Drennan and Matson 1995; Foderaro 1998; O'Cleireacain 1997; Torres 1995; and Waldinger 1996a.

22. Drennan and Matson 1995. The combined "services" category includes financial services (FIRE, meaning finance, insurance, and real estate) and professional and business services.

23. The figures refer to employed New Yorkers between the ages of twenty-five and sixty-four (Waldinger 1996a: 38–41).

24. New York City local government employment was about fifty-four thousand in 1900 (Erie 1988: 85). The 1995 figure is from O'Cleireacain 1997: 25.

25. McMahon et al. 1997: 16–17.

26. Perez-Pena 1997; Eaton 1998. In March 1999, the city's unemployment rate had dropped to 6.4 percent, its lowest in a decade, but still higher than the national rate of 4.1 percent (Eaton 1999).

27. Armstrong 1998.

28. Sassen 1988, 1991.

29. This analysis is based on census data for persons who reported working in New York City in 1980 and 1990 (Mollenkopf 1997).

30. Cf. Kasinitz and Vickerman 1995. For an analysis of immigrant dominance of the domestic service employment sector in New York City and its repercussions, see Kaufman (2000).

31. Waldinger 1996a.

32. Between 1900 and 1920, 223,000 native whites of foreign or mixed parentage left the city, while 73,000 native whites of native parentage moved in. From

1900 to 1940, the number of white residents of New York City born outside of New York State almost tripled, climbing from 225,000 to 641,000 (Rosenwaike 1972: 100–103).

33. Wright and Ellis 1996: 326. As Wright and Ellis (1996: 348) note, future analyses should place New York City in the context of the metropolitan labor market and account for commuters into the city as well as out-migration from the five boroughs to the suburbs and beyond.

34. On eastern European Jews in New York's garment industry, see Glenn 1990; Green 1997; Howe 1976; Kessner 1977; Rischin 1962; Sorin 1992; and Waldinger 1986.

35. On the size of the German Jewish population, see Binder and Reimers 1995: 81; on German Jewish ownership in the clothing industry, see Gold and Phillips 1996: 189.

36. Rischin 1962: 61.

37. Sorin 1992: 74. These figures include women as well as men. In 1910, more than a third of Russian-born Jewish men in metropolitan New York City were in the garment industry (Model 1993: 173).

38. Waldinger 1996a; Model 1993.

39. Fenton 1975: 71–94; Baily 1999: 98.

40. Gambino 1974: 86.

41. Model 1993: 178.

42. Kessner 1977: 58.

43. Quoted in Kessner 1977: 57.

44. Foerster 1919: 347.

45. See Friedman-Kasaba 1996: 167; Kessner 1977: 56; Green 1997: 194.

46. Odencrantz 1919: 63.

47. Industrial Commission 1901, quoted in Friedman-Kasaba 1996: 125.

48. See Glenn 1990; Friedman-Kasaba 1996; Cohen 1992.

49. Figures on barbers are from Model 1993: 179; on Italian shoemakers, see Fenton 1975.

50. Kraut 1983: 71.

51. Perlmann 1996b: 16.

52. Lestchinsky 1942.

53. Joseph 1967; Kraut 1983.

54. Kraut 1983: 76.

55. Morawska 1996: 41.

56. Roskolenko 1971: 93.

57. Heinze 1990: 196.

58. Kraut 1983: 73.

59. Borgenicht 1942: 198–99.

60. Kraut 1983: 75. According to Andrew Heinze (1990: 196), in 1906 pushcart vendors in New York averaged between fifteen and eighteen dollars a week; this figure was comparable to what many skilled garment workers earned at the time.

61. Rischin 1962: 56.

62. Kraut 1983: 76.

63. Rischin 1962: 57–58; Sorin 1992: 77.

64. Rischin 1962: 59–60.

65. Ibid., 73; see also Kessner 1977: 87–88.

66. Foerster 1919: 339.

67. Gabaccia 1984: 63.

68. Howe 1976: 78.

69. Basch 1990: 33. Other demands were weekly pay; the abolition of the sub-contracting system and of fines; an equal distribution of work during the slack season; and union recognition. When the strike was settled, most shops reduced the hours of work, and inside subcontracting was abolished (Glenn 1990). On organizing drives and the establishment of garment workers' unions at the beginning of the twentieth century see, for example, Basch 1990; Ewen 1985; Glenn 1990; Howe 1976; Orleck 1995; and Rischin 1962. On the role of Italians in New York unions, see Fenton 1975.

70. Quoted in Orleck 1995: 33.

71. Sorin 1992: 115; Tentler 1979: 18; Glenn 1990: 121.

72. Friedman-Kasaba 1996: 124.

73. The concept of an ethnic enclave economy was originally put forward by Wilson and Portes (1980) in an analysis of Cubans in Miami. More recently, Portes (1995) has defined ethnic enclaves as spatially clustered networks of businesses owned by members of the same minority.

74. Glenn 1990: 134–35.

75. Cf. Bailey and Waldinger 1991.

76. Glenn 1990: 136.

77. See Alba 1985; DeConde 1971; Fenton 1975.

78. Kessner 1981: 228.

79. Model 1993. A group's average occupational status was measured by an index based on the income, education, and prestige of occupations (see Model 1993: 170–71 on methods used in the study). In 1910, native-born Irishmen's occupational status was 87 percent that of native-born white men of native parents.

80. Higgs 1971.

81. Logan 1997a.

82. Hatton and Williamson 1998: 173. In New York City in the first decade of the twentieth century, individuals between the ages of twenty-five and forty-four—that is, those in their prime working years—accounted for the largest net outflow of native whites (Rosenwaike 1972: 100).

83. Carter and Sutch 1998: 338. Economist Claudia Goldin found that a 1 percentage point increase in a city's foreign-born population reduced unskilled wage rates by about 1 to 1.5 percent (1994c: 250).

84. Waldinger 1996a: 97–98.

85. Kessner 1977: 58; La Sorte 1985: 65. On occasion, the competition between Italian and Irish workers erupted in open conflict. At a work site in Mamaroneck (Westchester County), about two hundred Irishmen attacked a group of Italian workers who were receiving their monthly pay, injuring several Italians and forcing them and their families to abandon their homes and flee south to the Bronx (La Sorte 1985: 151).

86. Kessner 1977: 56–58; see also Model 1993: 181–82.

87. Fenton 1975: 263–64.

88. McKivigan and Robertson 1996: 311–12; Model 1993: 172.

89. Fenton 1975: 255.

90. McKivigan and Robertson 1996: 312.

91. See Model 1993: 182; Waldinger 1996a: 62, 141.

92. Hatton and Williamson 1998: 174.

93. Carter and Sutch 1998: 337.

94. Kessner 1977: 51–65.

95. Kwong 1994: 26.

96. Ruf 1994.

97. Waldinger 1996a: 260. In Pyong Gap Min's 1988 survey of married Korean women in New York City, nearly half of Korean wives and 61 percent of their husbands were self-employed (1996: 47).

98. Yoon 1997: 246.

99. Waldinger 1996a: 121.

100. Foner 1994.

101. The campaign to unionize the city's huge nonprofit ("voluntary") hospital system took place between the late 1950s and early 1970s. Before unionization, in 1958, starting wages at the city's voluntary hospitals ranged from $28 to $34 per week; in 1983, minimum wages under the union contract began at $294 a week (Fink and Greenberg 1989: 193–94).

102. Between 1971 and 1990, blacks gained 44,000 jobs in municipal employment, the sharpest proportional growth occurring in the agencies that the mayor directly controlled (Waldinger 1996a: 229). These gains were due partly to the expansion of the city's payrolls but also to political changes that opened up civil service structures to African Americans and to ethnic succession, as native whites opted for better positions in the private sector or retired (Waldinger 1996a: chap. 7).

103. Fink and Greenberg 1989.

104. Waldinger 1996a: 119–21; Palmer 1995: 33. The four countries are Jamaica, Trinidad and Tobago, Barbados, and Guyana.

105. Ong and Azores 1994: 180.

106. Lobo, Salvo, and Virgin 1996: 29.

107. Goetz 1997.

108. See Kasinitz and Vickerman 1995.

109. Waldinger 1986: 111; Waldinger 1996a: 151–53.

110. See Waldinger (1986) for a detailed account of the structural changes in New York's garment industry in the post–World War II years and the entry of recent immigrants.

111. Hendricks cited in Waldinger 1986: 115.

112. Waldinger 1986: 117.

113. Rios n.d.

114. This is the estimated number of Korean garment shops as of December 1991 (Min 1998: 54).

115. Korean greengrocers also increasingly hire Mexican and Ecuadorian workers as a way to keep wages down; there is also the fear, in saturated markets, that Korean workers will become competitors by learning the business and opening up stores in the neighborhood (see Kim 1999; Lee 1999).

116. Chin 1997; Kim 1999; Min 1996: 60.

117. Waldinger 1996a: 263.

118. Zhou 1992: 96.

119. Ibid., 172–73; Torres 1995: 126.

120. Waldinger 1996a: 125–27.

121. Zhou 1992: 175–77.

122. Tuchman and Levine 1996.

123. Waldinger 1996a: 123.

124. Zhou 1992: 96.

125. Goetz 1997.

126. MacDonald 1995.

127. Many Korean-owned stores are both greengroceries and general groceries. In 1991 the number of stores in the New York metropolitan area engaged in produce or grocery retail was about three thousand (Min 1996: 53–54).

128. Lee 1999; Min 1996: 54–63. On the reasons for the high rates of Korean self-employment and their success in small business, see Kim 1987; Min 1996; Park 1997; Yoon 1997; Waldinger et al. 1990.

129. Waldinger 1996a: 258.

130. Waldinger et al. 1990: 108–9.

131. Zhou 1992: 97–99.

132. Guarnizo 1992; Mahler, cited in Daykin et al. 1994.

133. Pessar 1995a: 25.

134. See Husock 1996; Kasinitz and Vickerman 1995.

135. In 1990, 2.5 percent of working-age Guyanese immigrants in New York City, 3.8 percent of Trinidadians, and 3.9 percent of Jamaicans were self-employed. This compares to 17.7 percent of Korean immigrants, who had the highest self-employment rate of all New York City immigrant groups (Kasinitz and Vickerman 1995). It is worth noting that, contrary to stereotypes about West Indians' "genius for business" in the early part of the century, a recent analysis of 1925 New York census data shows that West Indian men had extremely low self-employment rates

then as well (under 2 percent)—lower than rates for African American men and far lower than those for all New York men at the time (Model 1999).

136. See Waldinger 1986: 44–45.

137. Kasinitz and Vickerman 1995; see also Waldinger 1996a, chap. 8.

138. This was the rate as of 1998. See also Foner 1994: 17–19.

139. Chin 1997.

140. See Kwong 1997; Lii 1995; Zhou 1992.

141. Mitchell 1992; Smith 1996.

142. Colen 1989, 1990; Foner 1986.

143. Passel and Clark 1998: 7.

144. The other three post-1965 foreign-born groups that had a higher proportion of professionals than native whites were Germans, British, and Japanese (Cordero-Guzman and Grosfoguel 1998).

145. As table 8 shows, the disparity in earnings between immigrants and native whites is much more pronounced among college graduates (native whites earn about thirteen thousand dollars more) than among those with less than a high school degree (native whites earn about seven hundred dollars more). As I have noted, the skills, training, and professional credentials of college graduates educated in their home countries are often not applicable in the United States, and many arrive in middle-age, when it is especially hard to get a start in well-paying professional jobs. Another problem is the lack of networks to the mainstream economy—and to well-paid private-sector jobs—that come with advanced educational training in the United States. On top of this, many foreign-born college graduates are not fluent in English; racial and ethnic discrimination can also hinder their economic progress into the upper reaches of the occupational hierarchy.

146. It is unclear, however, whether or when immigrants' earnings will catch up to those of native whites. A recent study shows that in 1995 immigrants in New York State who had been in the United States for fifteen years or more had average incomes that exceeded those of natives, but the study did not separate native whites from native minorities (Passel and Clark 1998). As I discuss below, native minorities have lower earnings than the foreign-born. Also, because the study used cross-sectional rather than longitudinal data, it did not directly address what will happen to recent-entry cohorts as they live longer in the United States.

147. In 1990, according to census data calculated by Hector Cordero-Guzman, of the 4.8 million New Yorkers between the ages of sixteen and sixty-four, 17.7 percent were U.S.-born blacks and 6.7 percent U.S.-born Hispanics. Another 3.5 percent were island-born Puerto Ricans who entered before 1965.

148. An intriguing analysis of the earnings of white, Asian, black, and Hispanic foreign-born workers, aged nineteen to thirty-nine, in low-skilled and low-wage jobs in New York City also shows immigrants generally doing better than native minorities. Using census data, the analysis shows that immigrant women's wages were close to or above native black and Hispanic women's. Among men, all the foreign-

born earned substantially more than native blacks; black and white immigrants earned more than native-Hispanic men, while Asian and Hispanic immigrant men did about as well as native Hispanics (Howell and Mueller 1996).

149. Howell and Mueller 1997.

150. Waldinger 1996a: 314.

151. Wilson 1996: 141.

152. Island-born Puerto Ricans also have slightly higher unemployment rates than Russians (see table 8).

153. Smith and Edmonston 1997: 236.

154. Howell and Mueller 1997: 22.

155. Kasinitz and Rosenberg 1996.

156. Lee 1998.

157. Newman 1999: 62, 242–46. See also Kirschenman and Neckerman 1991 and Wilson 1996 on preferences for immigrant Hispanics over native blacks in Chicago.

158. Waldinger 1997: 374–75.

159. See Lee 1998; Kasinitz and Rosenberg 1996; Newman 1999; Waldinger 1997.

160. Kasinitz and Rosenberg 1996: 191.

161. Ibid.

162. See Waldinger 1997.

163. Ibid.

164. Kasinitz and Rosenberg (1996: 189–90) argue, in their study of Red Hook, Brooklyn, that native minorities in the neighborhood lack networks that connect them to low-skilled jobs. Because few local African American men are employed in blue-collar industries, there are few opportunities to sponsor young people. In the public-sector jobs where African American women are concentrated, sponsorship is limited by bureaucratic regulations and requirements. The pervasive fear of violence in the community and the decline in organizational life have also limited local people's ability to build effective job networks.

165. See Waldinger n.d.

166. Waldinger 1996a: 315. By 1990, more than one-third of African Americans in New York City worked in the public sector, where blacks held around 35 percent of all city jobs. As Waldinger has argued, the declining white presence in municipal employment in the last few decades provided opportunities for blacks. Blacks were also treated more equitably in government jobs than in the private sector, partly because of African American political influence and partly because the buildup of black employment created networks that supported entry and upward movement (Waldinger 1996a: 109–11; Waldinger 1995: 273–75).

167. Waldinger 1996a.

168. In 1910, according to Suzanne Model's analysis of census data, Russian-born men (27.9), Italian-born men (23.8), and African American men (southern born, 23.7; northern born, 22.6) all had low occupational scores, though African American men did least well (1993: 175–82).

169. Waldinger 1996a: 316.

## Chapter 4: Immigrant Women and Work

1. Spain and Bianchi 1996: 56–59.

2. Epstein 1970; Lindsey 1997.

3. Weiner 1985: 85.

4. Among the factors that explain this shift are the growth of the clerical and sales sectors and the rising demand for white-collar office workers; declining fertility rates and the proliferation of labor-saving devices in the household that made mothers more available for work outside the home; and the expansion of high school education and the rise in age at which teenage girls left school, which kept them out of the labor market (see Goldin 1990, 1994b; Lamphere 1987; Weiner 1985).

5. Spain and Bianchi 1996: 85.

6. See, for example, Espiritu 1997; Morokvasic 1984; Pessar 1999.

7. The percentage of women in the Italian immigration increased over time: from 21.1 percent during the period 1881–90 to 22.9 percent during 1901–10 and 30.6 percent during 1911–1920 (Tomasi 1975: 22).

8. Joseph 1967: 176.

9. Glenn 1990: 48.

10. Quoted in Cohen 1992: 39–41.

11. Cohen 1995 [1918].

12. Ibid., 84.

13. Glenn 1990: 89.

14. Ibid., 80.

15. Cohen 1992: 51–53, 59; see also Odencrantz 1919.

16. Glenn 1990:79.

17. Kessner and Caroli 1978.

18. Glenn 1990: 84.

19. Cohen 1992: 65–66; Odencrantz 1919; Glenn 1990: 118–19.

20. Ewen 1985: 194.

21. Glenn 1990: 84. According to one account, some single Russian Jewish women before the 1920s withheld part of their income from the common fund, although this often led to generational conflict (Friedman-Kasaba 1996: 172; Weinberg 1988: 187). In a few cases, when family income permitted, parents allowed Italian daughters to keep a portion of their income for personal expenses, because they feared that otherwise daughters would and could secretly withhold wages if conflicts arose (Cohen 1992: 71).

22. Odencrantz 1919: 176.

23. Peiss 1986: 68.

24. See Jacobs and Greene (1994) and Perlmann (1988). The reports of the U.S. Immigration Commission (1911) on high school attendance in New York City also show Russian Jewish males more likely to attend than females.

25. Quoted in Ewen 1985: 194.

26. Cohen 1992: 118. Analyzing census data for Italians in Providence, Rhode Island, Joel Perlmann (1988: 93) writes that "however low the chances for extended schooling among the Italian boys, they were lower still among the girls. In 1915 . . . about half as many Italian girls as boys entered or graduated from high school." See also the reports of the U.S. Immigration Commission on the children of immigrants in schools (1911).

27. Cohen 1995 [1918]: 125.

28. Odencrantz 1919: 100.

29. Ibid., 158.

30. Basch 1990; Baum et al. 1976: 130–31; Odencrantz 1919: 159.

31. Odencrantz 1919: 158.

32. Glenn 1990: 154–59; Cohen 1992: 69.

33. Hyman 1995: 100.

34. Baum et al. 1976: 221.

35. Cohen 1992: 72–73.

36. Weinberg 1988: 205.

37. Ibid., 187–88.

38. Cohen 1995 [1918]: 74.

39. Goldin 1990: 119.

40. The average age of marriage for the first generation of Italian immigrant women was around twenty, most having come to America specifically to join fiancés or husbands (Cohen 1992: 86–87). Most Jewish immigrant women had married and had stopped working outside the home by the age of twenty- two (Ewen 1985: 230).

41. Tentler 1979: 176–79.

42. Roth 1991 [1934]: 158, 169.

43. Friedman-Kasaba 1996: 184.

44. Interview in Kramer and Masur 1976: 125.

45. Weinberg 1988: 12.

46. Glenn 1990: 12, 14.

47. Baum et al. 1976: 68.

48. Ewen 1985: 39–40.

49. Glenn 1990: 78.

50. Cahan 1960 [1917]: 97.

51. Glenn 1990: 6, 68–79.

52. Kessner and Caroli 1978: 25–26.

53. Glenn 1990: 67.

54. Kessner and Caroli 1978: 26.

55. Glenn 1990: 74.

56. Weinberg 1988: 135.

57. Ewen 1985: 120.

58. Glenn 1990: 76.

59. Kazin 1946: 66–67. See also Hyman 1983.

60. Heinze 1990: 111.

61. Weinberg 1988: 105.

62. Baum et al. 1976: 214.

63. Most first-generation Jewish women attending evening school in New York City were single working women or women preparing for the job market. Married immigrant women may have been overwhelmed by the pressures of homework, household tasks, and family life. Many would have felt uncomfortable in alien surroundings or had to remain at home with their children, since Jewish men were reluctant to stay home with the children (Baum et al. 1976: 128–29).

64. Glenn 1990: 71.

65. Ewen 1985: 149.

66. Glenn 1990: 89.

67. Cohen 1992: 15–36; Gabaccia 1984, chap. 3.

68. Navarro della Miraglia, cited in Gabaccia 1984: 44.

69. Gabaccia 1984: 38, 44.

70. Kessner and Caroli 1978: 20–21.

71. Odencrantz 1919: 20.

72. Cohen 1992: 93.

73. Friedman-Kasaba 1996: 126.

74. Glenn 1990: 69.

75. Willett, quoted in Friedman-Kasaba 1996: 125–26.

76. Ewen 1985: 124–25.

77. Van Kleeck 1913: 94–95.

78. Ibid., 98.

79. Cohen 1992: 101.

80. Van Kleeck 1913: 105–8.

81. Quoted in Van Kleeck 1913: 95. In general, far fewer female factory workers had children of preschool age than did homeworkers (Cohen 1992: 96; see also Boris 1994: 107).

82. Sartorio, quoted in Mangione and Morreale 1992: 160.

83. Peiss 1986: 25.

84. Gabaccia 1984: 95.

85. Breckenridge 1994 [1921]: 104–5.

86. Gabaccia 1984: 99.

87. Quoted in Ewen 1985:149.

88. Gabaccia 1984: 92.

89. Donato 1992; Houston et al. 1984.

90. Salvo and Ortiz 1992: 75; Lobo, Salvo and Virgin 1996: 19–20.

91. Salvo and Ortiz 1992: 73.

92. Stafford 1987: 135.

93. See Foner 1973.

94. See Kim 1987; Lessinger 1995.

95. See chapter 1, n. 19, on the limitations of INS data on occupational background.

96. Lobo, Salvo, and Virgin 1996: 29.

97. Goldin 1994a.

98. See Boris 1994.

99. These same factors, according to Grasmuck and Grosfoguel (1997), also account for the fact that Dominican female householders have a poverty rate almost twice that of Jamaican female heads.

100. Mollenkopf, Kasinitz, and Lindholm 1995: 156.

101. Margolis 1994; see also Colen 1990.

102. Zhou 1992: 173.

103. Pessar 1995b: 44. Pessar has developed her analysis of Dominican women in a number of publications. See Pessar 1982, 1984, 1986, 1987, 1995a, 1995b, as well as Grasmuck and Pessar 1991.

104. Pessar 1987: 121.

105. Grasmuck and Pessar 1991: 147.

106. Pessar 1995a: 79–80.

107. Zhou and Nordquist 1994: 201; Mahler 1996; Burgess and Gray 1981: 104.

108. Pessar 1995a: 60.

109. Espiritu 1997: 70.

110. Chen 1992: 77–78. In his study of one hundred Taiwanese households in Queens, Chen found that men were most likely to help with garbage disposal and vacuuming, jobs seen as requiring physical strength. Taiwanese professional men helped out slightly more around the house than men in the working and business-owner classes. Chen links this to the work schedules of the different classes of men. He suggests that because professional men had shorter working hours, usually from nine to five, they could spend more time at home than business owners, who put in long hours in their stores, or working-class men, who worked long hours at restaurant jobs. On the distribution of housework in Korean immigrant households in New York City, see Min (1998) and Park (1997).

111. Min 1998; Park 1997; see also Lim 1997, on Korean women in Texas.

112. Cf. Lamphere 1987.

113. Burgess and Gray 1981: 102.

114. Ibid.

115. Pessar 1984.

116. See Foner 1997a.

117. Pessar and Grasmuck 1991: 152.

118. Pessar 1995a; Foner 1994.

119. Foner 1986: 145.

120. Foner 1994.

121. Zhou 1992: 178.

122. Pessar 1995b: 45.

123. See Foner 1994: chap. 7.

124. Lessinger 1995: 113–14; see also Gibson 1988: 111–12, on Punjabi Sikhs in California.

125. Mollenkopf et al. 1997.

126. Min 1998: 73–74. Zhou and Bankston (1998: 175- 180) report a similar kind of change among the Vietnamese in New Orleans, where fathers now supported their daughters' educational pursuits in order to ensure that the daughters would have the potential to earn a high salary, find relatively high-status mates, and increase their birth families' status. Vietnamese mothers also emphasized that education would improve their daughters' bargaining position with their husbands within the context of traditional gender roles.

127. Chen 1992: 254.

128. As Elizabeth Bogen notes, immigrants of the late nineteenth and early twentieth century had no food stamps or Medicaid, no housing subsidies or government-sponsored job-training programs. The help that existed for the poor and otherwise disadvantaged was provided by private charity (Bogen 1987: 110).

129. Cf. Kibria 1993; Repak 1995.

130. F. Markowitz 1993: 190.

131. Gurak and Kritz 1996.

132. F. Markowitz 1993; see also Orleck 1987.

133. Margolis 1994: 237.

134. Foner 1986.

135. Pessar 1995a: 81–82.

136. Cf. Hondagneu-Sotelo 1994; Jones-Correa 1998a; Kibria 1993.

137. Hondagneu-Sotelo 1999: 569.

138. Min 1998:38.

139. Gilbertson 1995; Zhou and Logan 1989.

140. Min 1998: 45–46. A 1988 survey, based on telephone interviews with a randomly selected sample of Korean married women in New York City, found that 38 percent of the women in the labor force worked together with their husbands in the same business; 12 percent ran their own businesses independently of their husbands; and 36 percent were employed in co-ethnic businesses (Min 1998: 39).

141. See Finder 1995.

142. Colen 1989.

143. It is not uncommon for Korean immigrant couples to ask their mothers or mothers-in-law to come to New York to live with them to help out with child care (Min 1998).

144. Day-care centers are in short supply, and they are often more expensive than babysitters in the immigrant community. Zhou notes that in 1988 there was only one subsidized day-care center for garment workers in Chinatown and no more than a few home day-care services sponsored by the city government and some quasi-governmental organizations. The New York City Chinatown Daycare Center had space for only eighty children, chosen by lottery from among the fami-

lies of the approximately twenty thousand members of the International Ladies Garment Workers Union who worked in Chinatown's garment industry. The fee for subsidized day care in the late 1980s ranged from eight to ten dollars a week for each child from a low-income family (Zhou 1992: 178–79).

145. Zhou 1992: 178.

146. Colen 1989; Soto 1987.

147. These figures are from Min's 1988 telephone survey (Min 1998: 43).

148. Kim 1996: 128.

149. Pessar 1982.

150. Pessar 1995b: 41–44.

151. Jones-Correa 1998b: 171.

152. Menjivar (1999) reports that among recent Guatemalan and Salvadoran immigrants in California, women who were the sole household wage earners, because of men's inability to earn an income, often ended up doing all the household chores to avoid making their spouses feel inadequate and to assure the men that they still held authority.

153. Kim 1996: 170.

154. See Margolis 1998; Min 1998; Pessar 1995a.

155. Lessinger 1995; Mahler 1996.

156. Hagan suggests a link between domestic violence among the Maya in Houston and the absence of the "watchful eyes of parents and other elderly kin" (1994: 58–59). Also see Ong's (1995) account of marital abuse experienced by two migrant Chinese women in San Francisco, one from an elite Beijing family, the other from a working-class Hong Kong background.

157. Weiner 1985: 84–85; Tentler 1979: 139–42.

158. See Lamphere 1987.

159. Ibid., 288.

160. Prieto 1992: 190.

161. Espiritu 1997: 117; see also Brettell and Simon 1986 and Morokvasic 1984.

162. Min 1998: 38.

163. Laslett 1965.

## Chapter 5: The Sting of Prejudice

1. For the 1900 figures, see Haslip-Viera (1996) and Kraly and Hirschman (1994); for 1960, Glazer and Moynihan (1970: 318). The 1998 figure is from the March 1998 Current Population Survey Annual Demographic Supplement, John Mollenkopf, Center for Urban Research, CUNY Graduate Center. Native stock refers here to native born to native parents. In 1998, New York City's black and Hispanic population was 37 percent foreign born, 22 percent second generation, and 42 percent native stock.

2. Jacobson 1998: 10.

3. See Cartmill 1999; Goodman 1997.

4. Kasinitz 1992: 4.

5. Following Stephen Cornell and Douglas Hartmann, I use the term *race* to refer to a group of human beings "defined by itself or others as distinct by virtue of perceived common physical characteristics that are held to be inherent"; *ethnicity* refers to perceived common ancestry, the perception of a shared history of some sort, and shared symbols of peoplehood (1998: 24, 32).

6. Barrett and Roediger (1997) use the phrase "inbetween peoples," Jacobson (1998), "probationary whites." On the ambiguous racial status of Jewish and Italian immigrants, see Barrett and Roediger 1997; Gerstle 1997a; Jacobson 1995, 1998; and Roediger 1994.

7. Barrett and Roediger 1997.

8. Sacks (1994). Noel Ignatiev (1995) strikes a similar note when he titles his recent book on another, earlier immigrant group *How the Irish Became White.*

9. Jacobson 1998: 10.

10. Higham 1955: 271.

11. Grant 1916: 14, 18, 16.

12. Ibid., 228.

13. Ross 1914: 113, 114, 95.

14. Ibid., 287, 119, 154.

15. Quoted in Higham 1955: 273.

16. Quoted in Lubove 1962: 54.

17. *New York: A Collection from Harper's Magazine* 1991: 304.

18. Quoted in Jacobson 1998: 178.

19. Riis 1971 [1890]: 44–47, 86.

20. Barrett and Roediger 1997; Higham 1955: 190.

21. Quoted in Ludmerer 1972: 70.

22. Higham 1984: 45.

23. Ludmerer 1972.

24. See Higham (1955: 316–24) on the attraction of the principle of national origins, which seemed to maintain America's racial status quo—since there were relatively few southern and eastern Europeans in the U.S. in 1890—at the same time as it gave "comfort to the democratic conscience" by treating all Europeans according to a principle of equality.

25. Barrett and Roediger 1997: 7.

26. Barrett and Roediger 1997: 8–9; see also Alba 1985: 68; Alba 1999: 14–15.

27. DeConde 1971: 102.

28. Higham 1955: 173.

29. Child 1943: 112, 81.

30. Barrett and Roediger 1997: 9.

31. See Jacobson 1998: 171–99.

32. Lieberson 1980: 32.

33. Goldstein 1997a. Eric Goldstein offers an interesting account of the changing use of racial language among Jews themselves in response to the mass eastern

European immigration and racial attacks against Jews. In the 1870s and 1880s, Jewish community leaders used the language of race as a way to capture pride in their Jewish heritage; by the turn of the century, they opposed, or became more guarded in, the use of racial language (Goldstein 1997b).

34. Barker, Dodd, and Commager, cited in Fitzgerald 1979: 79–80.

35. Higham 1984: 128–40.

36. Dinnerstein 1994: 93; see also Daniels 1997a: 104–5.

37. Gambino 1974: 71.

38. Dinnerstein 1994: 75, 88.

39. Ibid., 86, 159.

40. Cf. Jacobson 1998.

41. On the role of race and ethnicity in the lives of West Indian New Yorkers, see Bryce-Laporte 1972; Foner 1985, 1987; Kasinitz 1992; Stafford 1987; Sutton and Makiesky 1975; and Vickerman 1999. My own comparative research on West Indians in London and New York also explores why being black is very different in London, where there is no large native-born black population (see Foner 1985, 1998b, 1998c).

42. Kasinitz 1992; Waters 1992.

43. Waters 1992.

44. E.g., Skogan 1995.

45. This is a point Andrew Hacker (1998) makes in discussing the disparity between polling data that show low levels of prejudice among white Americans and continued racial divisions, including low levels of toleration for more than a small number of blacks in their neighborhoods.

46. Kasinitz 1992; Vickerman 1999.

47. Hacker 1992: 21; on West Indian experiences with racial slurs, insults, and slights, see Vickerman 1999: chap. 3.

48. Feagin 1991.

49. Vickerman 1999: 104.

50. Waters 1995.

51. Bashi 1996.

52. Feagin 1991.

53. Crowder 1999. The category West Indian in Crowder's study refers to West Indian ancestry. Waldinger (1987) found similar levels of segregation on the basis of 1980 census data for New York City.

54. Quoted in Waldman 1998: 6.

55. Mollenkopf 1993; Waldman 1998.

56. Crowder 1999: 94.

57. Cf. Logan and Alba 1996.

58. Massey and Denton 1993.

59. Harrison and Bennett 1995: 165–66; Yetman 1999: 253.

60. Farley 1996: 264–65.

61. In a recent account, Donald Robotham shows that the negative associations

with blackness continue. The current informal Jamaican popular culture, he argues, accepts the "hegemony of brownness," identifying blackness as "slackness" or "X-rated." "The black DJ from the ghetto sings: '. . . Me love me money and thing, But most of all me love me browning [brown girl]' " (1998: 320).

62. See Foner 1987.

63. Vickerman 1999: 42.

64. Sutton and Makiesky 1975: 130.

65. On the dynamics of West Indian ethnic identity and distancing from American blacks, see Foner 1987; Stafford 1987; and Vickerman 1999.

66. Coombs 1970: 31.

67. Foner 1987: 205–6.

68. Wright 1994.

69. Massey 1993.

70. Portes and MacLeod 1996.

71. Fox 1996.

72. Cf. Farley 1996; Hollinger 1995.

73. Sanjek 1994: 109.

74. Fox 1996: 33.

75. Mahler 1995b: 113.

76. Cf. Fox 1996: 33.

77. Samantha Lyman interview with Cuban immigrant, Urban Anthropology class, Purchase College, SUNY, December 1997.

78. Smith 1996, 1997b, 1998c. See also Mahler 1995a: 229 on Salvadorans.

79. Margolis 1994, 1998.

80. Grasmuck and Pessar 1996: 284.

81. Quoted in Rodriguez 1994: 136.

82. Grosfoguel and Georas 1996: 195.

83. Pessar 1995a: 42–43; Grasmuck and Pessar 1996.

84. Denton and Massey 1989; see also Alba and Nee 1997. In the 1980 census, Hispanics who wrote entries such as Cuban, Puerto Rican, or some other Spanish identification in response to the race question were coded as "Spanish race" (Denton and Massey 1989: 793).

85. Harrison and Bennett 1995: 165.

86. Grasmuck and Pessar 1996: 284.

87. Rodriguez 1994: 141.

88. Pessar 1995a: 43.

89. Grasmuck and Pessar 1996: 289–90; Pessar 1995a: 43.

90. Fox 1996: 24; Rodriguez 1996.

91. Grasmuck and Pessar 1996: 284.

92. Cf. Rodriguez 1994.

93. Denton and Massey 1989.

94. Mahler 1993; Mahler 1995b: 119.

95. Quoted in Lopez 1996: 55–56.

96. For a history of the immigration and naturalization laws that discriminated against Asians see Daniels 1997b; Lee 1989; Min 1995; United States Commission on Civil Rights 1992; Ueda 1997.

97. Wollenberg 1995: 8–9.

98. Espiritu 1997: 109.

99. Brimelow 1995: 189, 215.

100. Alba et al. 1995.

101. Slyomovics 1995.

102. Scott 1997; see also Sanjek 1994.

103. McCarthy 1995.

104. Goldberg 1995.

105. Harold Isaacs, quoted in Mazumdar 1989: 34. In terms of color prejudice, "'brown,' even a non-American born as in Indonesians and Filipinos—is a good deal less mild; but it is 'black'—wherever it comes from—that sets the racial-color counters clicking the most violently. The Indian, shading along a wide spectrum from fair to brown to black, arouses these reactions in varying measures."

106. Lessinger 1997.

107. Harrison and Bennett 1995: 174.

108. Indeed, a number of Asian-American scholars note that a downside of the model minority stereotype is that it diverts attention away from the existence of continued racism against Asians. Other damaging consequences that have been mentioned are that it leads people to ignore the pressing needs of the significant number of poorer, less successful Asian immigrants; it may result in undue pressure on young Asians to do well in school and their careers; and it may be used to discredit blacks and Hispanics by implying that if only they worked and studied hard, they, too, would be as successful as Asians (see Kwong 1987; Takaki 1993; and United States Commission on Civil Rights 1992).

109. Dublin 1996: 146.

110. Espiritu 1994.

111. United States Commission on Civil Rights 1992.

112. Holloway 1995.

113. Lessinger 1995: 139–42.

114. Min 1996: 119–25.

115. Quoted in Lind 1995: 108.

116. McNickle 1993: 48. The term "dago" was used freely in print, even in leading newspapers, according to Michael La Sorte. Indeed, its use was so widespread that the Italian consul in New York received a letter one day with the salutation: "Dear consul of Dagoland" (1985: 139).

117. Fuchs 1990: 397.

118. Brimelow 1995: 116–17.

119. Brimelow 1995: 9–11. As David Reimers (1998: 112) notes, of the restrictionists published by major houses, Brimelow is clearly the most outspoken about cultural and racial issues.

120. See Glazer 1997; Reimers 1998. What Reimers calls "the new restrictionists" include Beck 1996; Briggs 1996; and Lamm and Imhoff 1985. For a full account of the new restrictionists' arguments see Reimers 1998.

121. Purnick 1995.

122. Hernstein and Murray 1994.

123. A recent study based on the 1996 New York City Housing and Vacancy Survey shows that blacks and Latinos are more likely than whites or Asians to live in lower-quality neighborhoods in terms of crime rates, percentage of neighborhood population receiving public assistance, percentage of subsidized housing units, and percentage of buildings with safety violations (Rosenbaum et al. 1998).

124. Raab 1997.

125. March 1998 CPS (Current Population Survey) Annual Demographic Supplement, John Mollenkopf, Center for Urban Research, CUNY Graduate Center.

126. Farley 1996: 160.

127. See, for example, Alba and Nee 1997 and Sanjek 1994 on the expansion of the category white; see Rose 1985 for a more pessimistic view.

## Chapter 6: Transnational Ties

1. Speranza 1974 [1906]: 310.

2. Basch et al. 1994: 7.

3. Glick Schiller 1996: 4.

4. Glick Schiller et al. 1992: 1; Basch et al. 1994: 7; see also Sutton 1992.

5. Portes 1997: 813.

6. Goldberg 1992: 205; Jones 1992: 219.

7. Glick Schiller 1996. See Glick Schiller 1999 for a revised version of this paper.

8. Guarnizo 1997, 1998; see also Smith 1997a, 1998a.

9. E.g., Topp 1997.

10. Pessar 1995a: 76.

11. Cahan 1970: 27; Wyman 1993: 61.

12. Speranza 1974 [1906]: 309. According to the Italian Bureau of Emigration, in 1903 23 million lire arrived in Italy from abroad (about $7.75 million) 18 million of which came from the United States. Except for 1906 and 1907, the remittances from overseas increased every year, passing 150 million lire in 1916 and reaching one billion lire in 1920 (Cinel 1982a: 75).

13. Soyer 1997: 172, 177.

14. Cinel 1982a: 71.

15. Wyman 1993: 130–31.

16. Jones-Correa 1998b: 96.

17. Glick Schiller 1996.

18. Sarna 1981.

19. Ibid., 264.

20. Wyman 1993.

21. Joseph 1967: 139.

22. Wyman 1993: 79.

23. La Sorte 1985: 218.

24. Wyman 1993: 131, 23–24.

25. Speranza 1974 [1906].

26. On Italian "birds of passage" and return migration, see Archdeacon 1983; Cinel 1982a, 1982b; Foerster 1919; Tomasi 1975; and Wyman 1993. For a general discussion of return migration to Europe, see also Morawska 1991.

27. Wyman 1993: 79.

28. Sarna 1981: 266.

29. Kramer and Masur 1976: 2.

30. Glick Schiller 1996.

31. Jacobson 1995: 2, 62.

32. Topp 1997.

33. Doyle 1996; McNickle 1996.

34. For an interesting comparison of the involvement of the Italian and Mexican states in their emigrant populations, see R. Smith 1998a.

35. Wyman 1993: 93–94, 199.

36. Glick Schiller et al. 1995; Rouse 1995.

37. See Portes 1996.

38. Pessar 1995a: 69.

39. Foner 1994.

40. Lessinger 1992.

41. Lessinger 1995: 42.

42. R. Smith 1998c.

43. It was not possible to make a transatlantic phone call until 1927, and then it was prohibitively expensive—two hundred dollars in present-day currency for a three-minute call to London. These days, phone parlors and card businesses buy telephone minutes in bulk from long-distance carriers and sell them at sharply discounted rates (see Sontag and Dugger 1998).

44. Basch et al. 1994: 237.

45. Lessinger 1992: 61; see Min 1998 on Koreans' phone contact with family members back home.

46. Margolis 1998: 115 .

47. Margolis 1995b.

48. Lessinger 1995: 41.

49. Mathieu 1998: 140.

50. Sontag and Dugger 1998.

51. Portes 1996.

52. Pessar 1995a: 77.

53. Lessinger 1995: 91; see also Lessinger 1992.

54. Lessinger 1995: 89.

55. See Wong 1998.

56. Min 1998: 113–18.

57. Pessar 1995a: 75.

58. Gabaccia 1998.

59. Aristide's successor, René Préval, distanced himself from Aristide on many points, including the use of the term "Tenth Department," although he retained the Ministry of Haitians Living Abroad (Glick Schiller and Fouron 1998: 148–49).

60. DeSipio 1998; Guarnizo 1998; Smith 1998a.

61. Sengupta 1996.

62. J. Smith 1998.

63. Sontag and Rohter 1997.

64. Guarnizo 1997.

65. For a fascinating analysis of the contexts and conditions influencing immigrants' views and decisions about naturalization, based on a case study of an extended family of Dominican immigrants in the late 1990s, see Gilbertson and Singer (2000). Nationwide, in 1997 alone, 1.4 million applications for naturalization were filed with the Immigration and Naturalization Service, a threefold increase over those filed in 1994.

66. Rohter 1996.

67. Guarnizo 1998: 79.

68. On the politics of dual nationality legislation in the Colombian and Dominican cases, see Sanchez 1997; Graham 1997; and Guarnizo 1997. Also see Jones-Correa (1998b: 160–68) on lobbying efforts for dual citizenship among Colombians, Ecuadorians, and Dominicans in New York.

69. Geyer 1996.

70. Nugent 1992: 159.

71. Shumsky, quoted in Nugent 1992: 159; see Shumsky 1992.

72. Quoted in Goldberg 1992: 212.

73. Schwartz 1995.

74. Brumberg 1986: 71.

75. Glick Schiller 1996.

76. Guarnizo 1997.

77. Nagourney 1996.

78. Guarnizo 1997.

79. Basch et al. 1994.

80. Rosenblatt 1993.

81. Hollinger 1995: 154.

82. Hondagneu-Sotelo and Avila 1997.

83. Hollinger 1995: 153.

84. Levitt 1998; see also Levitt (2000).

85. Glick Schiller et al. 1995: 54.

86. Basch 1987.

87. See Mahler 1995a.

88. Hondagneu-Sotelo and Avila 1997.

89. Jones-Correa 1998a. According to Jones-Correa, it is Latin American women activists who are able to combine loyalty to the home country with an engagement in American politics. Having gained independence and power in New York with their income, they have a greater desire than men to stay in this country. They also have more experience dealing with public institutions through their children. The result is that migrant women activists are more likely than men to involve themselves in New York City politics and the problems of the immigrant community there.

## Chapter 7: Going to School

1. Glazer and Moynihan 1970: 155.

2. Greer 1972.

3. Glazer 1997.

4. Berrol 1974, 1976, 1981. It also became harder to obtain working papers; in 1903, documentary proof of age and, in 1913, completion of the sixth grade were now required. In 1908, there were 7,860 fourteen-year-old Russian Jewish students in New York's schools but only 3,511 fifteen-year-olds, a decline of 55 percent.

5. In the Immigration Commission's study, students are broken down into nationality groups according to the "nativity and race of the father of the pupil," so that, for example, Russian Jewish children are those with a Russian Jewish father. Native whites are native born with a native-born white father. Unfortunately, these and other data available for the turn of the century period do not allow us to distinguish between children born abroad and those born in the United States to immigrant parents.

6. Van Denberg 1911.

7. Perlmann 1988: 123.

8. Gorelick 1982: 123.

9. Of course, as Berrol (1976) herself admits, establishing origins from surnames is far from exact.

10. Berrol 1976, 1994; Gorelick 1982: 123; Howe 1976: 270.

11. Gorelick 1982: 123.

12. Berrol 1976.: 262.

13. Hillquit 1934: 40.

14. Berrol 1994: 72.

15. Brumberg 1986: 181–82.

16. Berrol 1978: 293.

17. This figure is based on the ratio of New York City's public high school students to the number of fifth, sixth, seventh, and eighth graders in 1908. In that year, about 40 percent of eighth graders entered the first year of high school, but less than a fifth of the freshmen made it to the senior year. These figures, like others in

this section that refer to 1908, are from the U.S. Immigration Commission's report (1911) on the children of immigrants in New York City's schools.

18. Combined enrollment at the eight colleges and six law and medical schools surveyed by the Immigration Commission in 1908 was about six thousand.

19. Gorelick 1982.

20. Spewack 1995: 86.

21. Hillquit 1934: 31.

22. This is not to deny the importance of school reforms in this period. Under Superintendent Maxwell's progressive administration in the beginning of the century, there were important innovations like summer-vacation schools, evening schools for advanced and trade education, libraries in every school building, and higher standards for teachers' licenses. On the reforms of this period and the role of Superintendent Maxwell see Berrol 1978 and Ravitch 1974.

23. Berrol 1978: 86.

24. Ibid., 42.

25. Tyack 1974: 230.

26. Berrol 1978: 93.

27. Ibid., 217–25.

28. Ibid., 228.

29. With few exceptions, Jewish day schools were not established in this period (Berrol 1976; Brumberg 1986: 60–61). Some Jewish children went to afternoon Hebrew classes, but the important school was the public one and *cheder* took second place. In 1908, the city's Catholic schools had about seventy-three thousand students, of which the Irish (with about twenty-six thousand) were the largest group. Almost half of the city's Irish school children were in parochial school, compared to about 10 percent of Italian school children.

30. Olneck and Lazerson 1974: 459; Ayres 1909.

31. Berrol 1974: 33.

32. Covello 1967: 294.

33. Berrol 1974: 33.

34. In 1908, when the age for working papers was fourteen, the Immigration Commission report shows a 40 percent drop in enrollment for southern Italians between the ages of thirteen and fourteen, compared to a 23 percent decline for Russian Jews. For those between the ages of fourteen and fifteen, the declines were much steeper: 55 percent for Russian Jews, 65 percent for southern Italians (U.S. Immigration Commission 1911).

35. Berrol 1974: 33.

36. Cohen 1982.

37. Van Denberg 1911. The other percentages comparing Russian Jews, Italians, and native whites are derived from the Immigration Commission's figures on the composition of different elementary and high school grades in 1908.

38. These figures refer to all Jews, whatever their national origin. According to

the Immigration Commission study, Russian and Polish Jews made up three-fifths of the Jewish students at the eight colleges.

39. According to the Immigration Commission's report, of the 4,230 students in the eight colleges surveyed in 1908, 939 were Jewish, 2,074 native white, and 37 Italian. The breakdown: Adelphi (115 students: 68 percent native white, 6 percent Jewish, no Italians); Barnard (455 students: 67 percent native white, 5 percent Jewish, no Italians); City College (676 students: 12 percent native white; 74 percent Jewish, 1 percent Italian); Columbia University (1,283 students: 57 percent native white, 11 percent Jewish, 1 percent Italian); Fordham (104 students: 52 percent native white, no Jews, 2 percent Italian); Columbia University Teachers College (544 students: 69 percent native white, 3 percent Jewish, less than 1 percent Italian); Hunter College (703 students: 41 percent native white, 27 percent Jewish, 1 percent Italian); Polytechnic Institute of Brooklyn (344 students: 45 percent native white, 16 percent Jewish, 1 percent Italian). The several law schools and medical schools in the report enrolled about another 1,700 students: 23 percent were Jewish, 52 percent native white, and 2 percent Italian (U.S. Immigration Commission 1911). The two colleges of pharmacy surveyed by the Immigration Commission were heavily Jewish: nearly half of the 370 students were Jewish, almost all of Russian and Polish origin; 8 percent of the pharmacy students were Italian.

40. This proportion is based on the eight colleges in the Immigration Commission's 1908 survey.

41. DeWind 1997: 135.

42. In 1997–98, 37.5 percent of New York City's nearly 1.1 million public school students were Hispanic, and 35.9 percent non-Hispanic black; 10.3 percent were Asian and 15.7 percent white. New York City Board of Education figures on ethnicity do not distinguish between the native and foreign-born (Board of Education 1998).

43. This figure is based on 1990 census data on the educational attainment of New York City's population aged twenty-five and older (Rivera-Batiz 1994). As Claudia Goldin (1994a) argues, the rapid rise of the high school in America took place from around 1910 to 1940 as the economy began producing white-collar jobs that demanded more formal education than was provided at the elementary level. The reduced demand for juvenile labor in manufacturing, in response to the availability of immigrant labor and increased mechanization and capital intensity, is also, according to Goldin, a factor in explaining the increase in high school enrollments and graduation rates.

44. Mare 1995: 202.

45. The big growth in college enrollments was a post–World War II phenomenon. By the coming of World War II, not even 15 percent of the nation's eighteen- to twenty-one-year-old population attended college; thirty years later, the proportion had approached 50 percent (Nasaw 1979). By 1990, nearly a quarter of the nation's twenty-five- to twenty-nine-year-olds had spent four or more years in college (Mare 1995).

46. Rivera-Batiz 1994: 48.

47. Ibid., 57. Nationwide, the mean annual income earned by high school dropouts in 1990 was $11,045, compared to $17,072 for high school graduates, $31,256 for college graduates, and $42,800 for those who had finished five or more years of higher education (Roberts 1994: 232; see Mare 1995).

48. Rivera-Batiz 1994: 57.

49. See Gorelick 1982: 67, 195.

50. Not surprisingly, the open-admissions policy sparked heated debates. Supporters argued that it provided opportunities that students used well: large numbers who would have been denied entrance under earlier standards received bachelor's degrees and got better-paying jobs as a result. In their study of members of the first three freshman classes admitted to CUNY after the adoption of open admissions, David Lavin and David Hyllegard (1996) found that more than half who were let in only because of the looser admissions criteria ended up graduating. However, critics say that academic standards plummeted because so many students were unprepared and that remediation swallowed up scarce resources (MacDonald 1994; Traub 1994). In response to these criticisms, the university approved a proposal in 1998 to bar students who are unable to pass proficiency exams from the senior colleges.

51. The new plan, to be phased in over several years, allows some special exemptions—for example, for students with certain SAT exam scores. According to CUNY figures, about fourteen hundred of the approximately fourteen thousand freshman who typically enter the senior colleges will be kept out. Each senior college specifies the grade-point average students must have and standing in high school graduating classes, and some are requiring S.A.T. scores (Arenson 1998, 1999).

52. See Freedman 1990: chap. 15.

53. Rivera-Batiz 1996.

54. Bellock 1995.

55. McDonnell and Hill 1993: 77.

56. Starting in 1997, enrollment in the New York City public school system began to slow down; it grew by only eighty-three hundred in 1997–98. Fewer babies are being born as baby boomers reach the end of their childbearing years. Also, more children are leaving the city schools, some in favor of nearby suburbs, others returning to their home countries. There has also been a slight falloff in the number of newly admitted students who are foreign born: 42,245 in the 1996–97 school year, compared to 45,750 in 1994–95 (Sengupta 1998b).

57. Rivera-Batiz 1996.

58. Edry 1998.

59. Rivera-Batiz 1996.

60. Personal communication, Pedro Mateu-Gelabert.

61. Van Gelder 1996.

62. Berne 1993; Rivera Batiz 1995.

63. These are the results for the students who took the tests in English. Students designated Limited English Proficient (LEP) and who had been in an English-language school system for less than twenty months were exempt from the reading test. The math test was translated into Spanish, Chinese, and Haitian Creole and given to about twenty-six thousand LEP students. The overall performance of those who took the translated version of the math test was much worse than among those who took the English version (Board of Education of the City of New York 1995).

64. These figures are from *The Class of 1996: Four Year Longitudinal Report and 1995–96 Event Dropout Rates,* published by the Division of Assessment and Accountability (Board of Education of the City of New York 1996).

65. Freedman 1990.

66. Board of Education of the City of New York 1999.

67. Jones 1994.

68. Richards et al. 1994.

69. In 1997–98, enrollment in bilingual programs in the New York City public schools was as follows: 67,806 students were enrolled in Spanish; 7,075 in Chinese; 2,079 in Haitian-Creole; 1,119 in Russian; 636 in Korean; 339 in Bengali; 228 in Polish; 145 in Arabic; 115 in French; 63 in Urdu; and 49 in Punjabi (Board of Education of the City of New York 1999).

70. Board of Education of the City of New York 1994a.

71. Hohn 1995.

72. The Board of Education data refer to the class of 1996. The graduation rate for students who were recent immigrants to New York City's public schools in middle school was 51 percent, compared to 48 percent for nonimmigrants; the dropout rate for the recent immigrants was 13 percent, and for nonimmigrants 17 percent (Board of Education of the City of New York 1996).

73. The improvements in test scores are based on an analysis of standardized scores among students in grades three to twelve (DeWind 1997).

74. The figures on the immigrant profile of CUNY and its colleges are drawn from a study conducted by CUNY, *Immigration/Migration and the CUNY Student of the Future* (Edwards and Ishikawa 1995). Of the foreign-born CUNY freshmen in 1990, about half had diplomas from New York high schools; the other half either had a GED or a foreign or out-of-state diploma.

75. Kao and Tienda 1995: 9.

76. Vernez and Abrahamse 1996: 27–40. The only exception was that Asian natives were slightly more likely than Asian immigrants to stay continuously through four years of college.

77. For national figures on the high levels of Asian American educational achievement—higher than among whites as well as blacks and Hispanics—see Barringer et al. (1993) and Mare (1995).

78. DeWind 1997.

79. These results refer to students entering the city schools in kindergarten or grades one through three (Board of Education of the City of New York 1994a).

80. Board of Education of the City of New York 1996.

81. Other groups in these schools were represented as follows (Newman 1995): Stuyvesant (41 percent white, 5 percent black, 4.3 Hispanic); Bronx High School of Science (40 percent white, 11 percent black, 9 percent Hispanic); and Brooklyn Technical High School (15 percent white, 39 percent black, and 14 percent Hispanic).

82. Hacker 1992: 139, 142. Among students with family incomes over seventy thousand dollars, Asians averaged 68 points higher than whites (143).

83. Vernez and Abrahamse 1996: 38.

84. Ross [Rosten] 1937: 79.

85. Glazer 1997: 166.

86. Brumberg 1986: 208.

87. Glazer 1997: 42.

88. Quoted in Brumberg 1986: 71.

89. Quoted in Tyack 1974: 237.

90. Howe 1976: 275. On German-English bilingual schools, see Kamphoefner 1994; Tyack 1997; Tyack 1994: 107–9. Tyack (1997) suggests that German immigrants' success in achieving bilingual schools and/or German instruction in a number of cities, such as Indianapolis and Cincinnati, was related to their prosperity and political clout. Indeed, in Wisconsin, where state laws decreed teaching in English, a county superintendent said in his annual report that it was better to look the other way when he found that schools were conducted in German, for fear that the Germans would abandon the public schools. Interestingly, in New York City, a brief experiment with two German schools in the 1830s, staffed by teachers who understood German, ended when the trustees found that the attendance rule (students were allowed to attend only for one year) was being violated (Berrol 1982: 33).

91. Berrol 1982; Moore 1981: 90.

92. Moore 1981: 100. See also Howe 1976: 278.

93. Brumberg 1986: 134.

94. Covello 1958: 43–44.

95. Fitzgerald 1979.

96. By 1939, more than fifteen thousand students were studying Italian in the junior and senior high schools of the New York City school system, the largest number—more than fourteen hundred students—at New Utrecht High School in the largely Italian Bensonhurst section of Brooklyn. By 1937, there were fourteen hundred students studying Hebrew in six public high schools in the city (Montalto 1981).

97. Tyack 1997.

98. Brumberg 1986: 132.

99. Berrol 1981.

100. Berrol 1982.

101. Kraut 1994: 232.

102. The term Americanization lost ground, according to Nathan Glazer (1997: 109–10), in part because of the excesses of the 1920s, when it became associated with laws that restricted immigration, limited the rights of aliens, and banned teaching in foreign languages and with administrative actions that expelled aliens.

103. Tyack 1997.

104. Nieves 1991.

105. McDonnell and Hill 1993: 77.

106. Carmen Iris-Rivera, "The Education of Immigrants in New York City Public Schools," roundtable discussion, New York University, December 1996.

107. See Rumbaut 1997a.

108. Glazer 1997: 79.

109. Ibid., 13. For criticisms of multicultural curricula in the public schools, see Salins 1997.

110. Board of Education of the City of New York 1994b.

111. Ibid., 1994c.

112. Sanjek 1992. In a later publication, Sanjek (1998: 332–34) uses the term "rituals of inclusion" to describe events like "International Day" and "Cultural Sharing Day," which celebrated the Chinese New Year, Dominican Republic Independence Day, and Brotherhood Week.

113. Dao 1992.

114. Min 1998: 81.

115. In 1974, the Supreme Court interpreted civil rights laws that guaranteed equality for those speaking a foreign language as meaning that school districts could not discriminate against students with limited English proficiency by denying them special instructional programs that would ease their full participation in school while learning English.

116. Portes and Rumbaut 1996: 210–15; Portes and Schauffler 1994.

117. Alba 1999: 10–11.

118. Steinberg 1996: 99.

119. Rumbaut 1997b: 33.

120. Mateu-Gelabert 1997: 151–52.

121. Portes and Zhou 1993.

122. See Fordham 1996; Fordham and Ogbu 1986; Olsen 1997; Stepick 1998.

123. Mateu-Gelabert 1997.

124. The overwhelming majority of New York City's immigrants attend the public schools. A sprinkling of immigrant children attend the city's elite private schools (where annual tuition runs more than fifteen thousand dollars ), typically on scholarships meant to add diversity to the student body. The Catholic schools do not collect data on the birthplaces of their students, but presumably a significant chunk of the forty-three thousand Hispanics, twenty-four thousand blacks, and nine thousand Asians in the city's Catholic elementary and high schools in the

five boroughs in 1995–96 were immigrants or children of immigrants. A significant number of Russian Jewish children attend a Hebrew day school or yeshiva, often for the elementary school years, before gaining admission to a special high school program or one of the selective New York city high schools (R. Markowitz 1993). There are also a number of private and religious academies that are predominantly West Indian (see Kasinitz 1992).

125. Portes 1995; see also Zhou and Bankston 1998.

126. Waters 1994.

127. Mollenkopf et al. 1997; Zhou and Bankston 1998.

128. Perlmann 1988: 115; see also Alba 1985: 59–62.

129. Covello 1967: 287.

130. Perlmann 1988: 216–17.

131. Kao and Tienda 1995; Vernez and Abrahamse 1996.

132. Vernez and Abrahamse 1996.

133. See Steinberg 1996: 83–87; Vernez and Abrahamse 1996.

134. MacDonald 1995: 15.

135. Min 1998: 32.

136. Zhou 1997: 93.

137. Kim 1996: 114–15.

138. Zhou 1997: 198–99.

139. Ibid., 194.

140. Ibid., 193–94; see Min 1998: 32, 66, 80 on Koreans.

141. Sung 1987: 76–78.

142. Berrol 1974. It is unclear how much having Jewish teachers made a difference. By 1908, 11 percent of the city's public school teachers were Jewish, about a third of whom had a Russian background (U.S. Immigration Commission 1911). Since most were assigned to Jewish immigrant neighborhoods, a significant minority of Jewish children had co-ethnic teachers. Less than 1 percent of the city's teachers were Italian; the few Italian teachers and the lone Italian principal licensed in the first decade of the century were assigned to Little Italy (Berrol 1974).

143. Zhou 1997: 202.

144. Dunn 1995a; Min 1995.

145. MacDonald 1995: 20.

146. See Goldscheider and Zuckerman 1984 and Steinberg 1981, who argue for the primary role of social-class factors in the educational and economic success of the Jews.

147. Cohen 1982.

148. Ibid.

149. Mollenkopf, Kasinitz, and Lindholm 1995: 154. The figures refer to immigrants aged twenty-five and older in 1990.

150. Mare 1995: 177.

151. Bennet 1997.

152. Goldberg 1995. The assistant district attorney grew up in South Korea; the

Brown University student was born in the United States not long after her parents arrived.

153. Kim 1996: 61; Kwong 1987: 73. The Korean woman's children, born in Korea, came here at a very young age.

154. These figures are for people of Asian ancestry and include those born in the United States as well as abroad. The average household income for Hispanics was $30,726, and for blacks $36,558. Within the Asian population, Filipinos ($64,847) and Japanese ($73,283) stood out at the high end, with Koreans ($41,600) and Vietnamese ($39,558) at the bottom (Rivera-Batiz 1994: 44).

155. Goldberg 1995.

156. Min 1998: 66–67.

157. By comparison, as table 6 shows, 7 percent of post-1965 working-age Korean immigrants, 9 percent of Indians, and 2 percent of Filipinos had less than a ninth-grade education (Cordero-Guzman and Grosfoguel 1998).

158. Foner 1973: 68.

159. See Min 1998: chap. 5, on Koreans.

160. Rivera-Batiz 1994: 44.

161. These figures refer to those twenty-five years of age and older at the time of the 1990 census (Mollenkopf, Kasinitz, and Lindholm 1995: 154.)

162. Waters 1997b, 1994; Neckerman et al. 1999.

163. Waters 1997b: 19–20.

164. Waters 1997b. See Mateu-Gelabert (1997) for a detailed account of the chaotic and dangerous environment of another, predominantly Hispanic Brooklyn high school, where teachers also lacked control over their classrooms and had low expectations of students.

165. Waters 1994, 1997a.

166. Bromsen 1935: 458.

167. Portes and Rumbaut 1996, chap. 7; cf. Gibson 1988 on the concept of additive acculturation.

## Chapter 8: Looking Backward—and Forward

1. Jacobson 1998: 6.

2. Cf. Perlmann and Waldinger 1997: 902.

3. See Gleason 1980; Higham 1984; Jacobson 1998.

4. See Sacks 1994; Jacobson 1998: chap. 3.

5. Jacobson 1998: 104.

6. Goldstein 1997a.

7. Jacobson 1998: 246–73.

8. Alba and Nee 1997: 846.

9. Barrett and Roediger 1997: 11.

10. Lieberson 1980: 30.

11. Ibid., 34–35.

12. Cf. Lieberson 1980: 31–32.

13. Child 1943: 81.

14. Lieberson 1980: 32–34.

15. Cited in Alba 1999: 18.

16. Alba 1999: 19.

17. For racial forecasts for the future, including what are often called optimistic and pessimistic scenarios, see Alba 1999; Alba and Nee 1997; Lind 1998; Perlmann and Waldinger 1997; and Sanjek 1994.

18. Perlmann and Waldinger 1997: 905.

19. Lind 1998.

20. Yetman 1999: 253.

21. Wong 1995: 55.

22. Cornell and Hartmann 1998: 244.

23. Crouch 1996: 170.

24. Alba 1999: 20.

25. Cf. Model 1988: 376.

26. See Cohen (1992) for tables, based on 1950 census data for the New York–New Jersey metropolitan area, that compare the occupations of first- and second-generation Italians and first- and second-generation Jews, breaking down the figures by gender and by age group. Logan's (1997a) analysis of the average occupational standing of white ethnic groups, by nativity, based on 1960 data for New York central cities shows U.S.- born Russians, with a score of 53, ranking ahead of foreign-born Russians (39) and U.S.-born Italians, with a score of 36, ahead of their foreign-born counterparts (26).

27. Cf. Waldinger and Perlmann (1998: 12), who use the term "gendered pathways."

28. Gambino 1974: 235.

29. Cohen 1992: 170, 173.

30. Ibid., 162.

31. Ibid., 172–73.

32. In 1960, only 6 percent of the graduates of City College and 11 percent at Hunter had Italian surnames (Glazer and Moynihan 1970: 201). By 1972, after the open-admissions policy of the City University of New York went into effect, 34,000 of the system's 169,000 matriculated undergraduates were Italian American. By the mid-1970s, at Fordham University, a private Catholic university once heavily Irish, a significant proportion of the students were of Italian background (Binder and Reimers 1995: 200).

33. R. Markowitz 1993: 2, 16.

34. Cohen 1992: 169, 174.

35. See Wenger 1996: 22–24.

36. See Waldinger 1996a: chap. 7.

37. Ibid., 105, 96–101.

38. Gans 1992; Waldinger and Perlmann 1998: 6.

39. Gans 1992: 182.

40. Mollenkopf et al. 1997.

41. Ibid.

42. Waldinger and Perlmann 1998: 18.

43. Mollenkopf et al. 1997.

44. Waldinger and Perlmann 1998: 13.

45. Ibid., 6.

46. Perlmann and Waldinger 1997.

47. Rumbaut 1997a: 507.

48. This is the study being conducted by Philip Kasinitz, John Mollenkopf, and Mary Waters. Mollenkopf et al. (1997) and Waters et al. (1998) report on preliminary findings from the first phase of this study.

49. Waters, Kasinitz, and Mollenkopf 1998.

50. Soyer 1997: 204.

51. R. Smith 1998a: 202.

52. Orsi 1990: 141.

53. Quoted in Dugger 1998: A11.

54. Rumbaut 1998.

55. Cf. Waldinger 1996b: 470.

56. Sontag and Dugger 1998.

57. Rohter 1998; R. Smith 1998b.

58. Portes and Hao 1997; Rumbaut 1998.

59. Liu 1998: 121.

60. Ibid., 131–32.

61. Waters, Kasinitz, and Mollenkopf 1998.

62. See Janet Abu-Lughod's edited collection, *From Urban Village to East Village* (1994).

# References

Abramsky, Sasha. 1997. "Do-It-Yourself Bank." *Brooklyn Bridge* 2: 56–58.

Abu-Lughod, Janet (ed.). 1994. *From Urban Village to East Village*. Oxford: Blackwell.

Alba, Richard. 1985. *Italian-Americans: Into the Twilight of Ethnicity*. Englewood Cliffs: Prentice-Hall.

———. 1990. *Ethnic Identity: The Transformation of White America*. New Haven: Yale University Press.

———. 1999. "Immigration and the American Realities of Assimilation and Multiculturalism." *Sociological Forum* 14: 3–25.

Alba, Richard, Nancy Denton, Shu-yin Leung, and John R. Logan. 1995. "Neighborhood Change under Conditions of Mass Immigration: The New York City Region, 1970–1990." *International Migration Review* 29: 625–56.

Alba, Richard, John R. Logan, and Kyle Crowder. 1997. "White Ethnic Neighborhoods and Assimilation: The Greater New York Region, 1980–1990." *Social Forces* 75: 883–909.

Alba, Richard, John R. Logan, Brian Stults, Gilbert Marzan, and Wenquan Zhang. 1999. "Immigrant Groups and Suburbs: A Reexamination of Suburbanization and Spatial Assimilation." *American Sociological Review* 64: 446–60.

Alba, Richard, and Victor Nee. 1996. "The Relevance of Assimilation for Post-1965 Immigrant Groups." Paper presented at a conference of the Social Science Research Council, Becoming American/America Becoming, Sanibel Island, Fla.

———. 1997. "Rethinking Assimilation Theory for a New Era of Immigration." *International Migration Review* 31: 826–74.

Aleinikoff, T. Alexander. 1997. "Policing Boundaries: Migration, Citizenship and the State." Paper presented to Social Science Research Council Workshop on Immigrants, Civic Culture, and Modes of Political Incorporation, Santa Fe, N. Mex.

Alvarez, Lizette. 1996. "Down from Poverty: Mexico to Manhattan." *New York Times*, October 9.

Antin, Mary. 1969 [1911]. *The Promised Land*. Boston: Houghton Mifflin.

Archdeacon, Thomas. 1983. *Becoming American*. New York: Free Press.

Arenson, Karen. 1997. "CUNY Calls Class of 2000 Best Prepared since 1970." *New York Times*, May 21.

——. 1998. "CUNY to Tighten Admissions Policy at Four-Year Schools." *New York Times*, May 27.

——. 1999. "Plan to Exclude Remedial Students Approved at CUNY," *New York Times*, November 23.

Armstrong, Regina. 1998. "The Economy of the New York Urban Region." Paper prepared for the Regional Plan Association, New York.

Ayres, Leonard. 1909. *Laggards in Our Schools*. New York: Russell Sage.

Baily, Samuel L. 1999. *Immigrants in the Land of Promise: Italians in Buenos Aires and New York City, 1870-1914*. Ithaca: Cornell University Press.

Bailey, Thomas, and Roger Waldinger. 1991. "Primary, Secondary and Enclave Labor Markets: A Training Systems Approach." *American Sociological Review* 56: 432-45.

Barrett, James, and David Roediger. 1997. "Inbetween Peoples: Race, Nationality, and the 'New Immigrant' Working Class." *Journal of American Ethnic History* 16: 3-44.

Barringer, Herbert, Robert Gardner, and Michael Levin. 1993. *Asians and Pacific Islanders in the United States*. New York: Russell Sage Foundation.

Barton, Josef. 1975. *Peasants and Strangers*. Cambridge: Harvard University Press.

Basch, Françoise. 1990. "The Shirtwaist Strike in History and Myth." Introduction to Theresa Malkiel, *The Diary of a Shirtwaist Striker*. Ithaca: ILR Press.

Basch, Linda. 1987. "The Vincentians and Grenadians: The Role of Voluntary Associations in Immigrant Adaptation to New York City." In Nancy Foner (ed.), *New Immigrants in New York*. New York: Columbia University Press.

Basch, Linda, Nina Glick Schiller, and Cristina Szanton Blanc. 1994. *Nations Unbound: Transnational Projects, Postcolonial Predicaments, and Deterritorialized Nation-States*. Langhorne, Penn.: Gordon and Breach.

Bashi, Vilna. 1996. " 'We Don't Have That Back Home': Race, Racism and the Social Networks of West Indian Immigrants." Paper presented at the American Sociological Association, New York.

Baum, Charlotte, Paula Hyman, and Sonya Michel. 1976. *Jewish Women in America*. New York: Dial.

Bayor, Ronald. 1988. *Neighbors in Conflict: The Irish, Germans, Jews, and Italians of New York City, 1929-1941*. Urbana: University of Illinois Press.

Beck, Roy. 1996. *The Case Against Immigration: The Moral, Economic, Social, and Environmental Reasons for Reducing U.S. Immigration Back to Traditional Levels*. New York: Norton.

Bellock, Pam. 1995. "Experiment in Teaching Immigrants Gets Rolling." *New York Times*, September 7.

Bendix, Reinhard. 1964. *Nation-Building and Citizenship*. New York: John Wiley.

Bennet, James. 1997. "Fourth Graders Successful, Study Shows." *New York Times*, June 11.

Berger, Joseph. 1993. "Bienvenidos a Los Suburbios." *New York Times*, July 29.

Berne, Robert. 1993. "School Finance and Governance in New York City: Can It Change?" Paper presented at the conference New York/London: Schools and Communities Through the Prism of Race, Class, and Ethnicity, Queens College, City University of New York.

Berrol, Selma. 1974. "Turning Little Aliens into Little Citizens: Italians and Jews in New York City Public Schools, 1900-1914." *Proceedings of the Seventh Annual Conference of the American Italian Historical Association*, Towson State College, Md.

———. 1976. "Education and Economic Mobility: The Jewish Experience in New York City, 1880-1920." *American Jewish Historical Quarterly* 65: 257-71.

———. 1978. *Immigrants at School, New York City, 1898-1914*. New York: Arno.

———. 1981. "The Open City: Jews, Jobs, and Schools in New York City, 1880-1915." In Diane Ravitch and Ronald Goodenow (eds.), *Educating an Urban People: The New York City Experience*. New York: Teachers College Press.

———. 1982. "Public Schools and Immigrants: The New York Experience." In Bernard Weiss (ed.), *American Education and the European Immigrant, 1840-1940*. Urbana: University of Illinois Press.

———. 1994. *East Side/East End: Eastern European Jews in London and New York, 1870-1920*. Westport: Praeger.

———. 1996. *Growing Up American: Immigrant Children in America Then and Now*. New York: Twayne.

Binder, Frederick, and David Reimers. 1995. *All the Nations under Heaven: An Ethnic and Racial History of New York City*. New York: Columbia University Press.

Blackburn, Anthony J. 1995. *Housing New York City*. New York: Department of Housing Preservation and Development.

Board of Education of the City of New York. 1994a. "Educational Progress of Students in Bilingual and ESL Programs: A Longitudinal Study, 1990-1994." Report of the Board of Education of the City of New York.

———. 1994b. *Getting Started in the New York City Public Schools: A Manual for New Teachers*. New York: Board of Education of the City of New York.

———. 1994c. *Grade 8 United States and New York State History: A Multicultural Perspective*. New York: Board of Education of the City of New York.

———. 1995. "Citywide Test Results in Reading and Mathematics." Report of the Board of Education of the City of New York.

———. 1996. *The Class of 1996: Four Year Longitudinal Report and 1995-96 Event Dropout Rates*. Division of Assessment and Accountability. New York: Board of Education of the City of New York.

———. 1998. *Facts and Figures, 1997-1998*. New York: Board of Education of the City of New York.

———. 1999. *Facts and Figures: Answers to Frequently Asked Questions about Limited English Proficient Students and Bilingual/ESL Programs, 1997-1998*. New York: Office of Bilingual Education.

Bodner, John. 1985. *The Transplanted*. Bloomington: Indiana University Press.

Bogen, Elizabeth. 1987. *Immigration in New York*. New York: Praeger.

Bonnell, Victoria. 1980. "The Uses of Theory, Concepts and Comparison in Historical Sociology." *Comparative Studies in Society and History* 22: 156–73.

Borgenicht, Louis. 1942. *The Happiest Man*. New York: Putnam's.

Boris, Ellen. 1994. *Home to Work*. New York: Cambridge University Press.

Bourgois, Philippe. 1996. "Confronting Anthropology, Education, and Inner-City Apartheid." *American Anthropologist* 98: 249–65.

Breckenridge, Sophonisba. 1994 [1921]. "The Duties of the Housewife Remain Manifold and Various." In Maxine Seller (ed.), *Immigrant Women*. 2d ed. Albany: State University of New York Press.

Brettell, Caroline, and Rita Simon. 1986. "Immigrant Women: An Introduction." In Rita Simon and Caroline Brettell (eds.), *International Migration: The Female Experience*. Totowa, N.J.: Rowman and Allenheld.

Briggs, John. 1978. *An Italian Passage*. New Haven: Yale University Press.

Briggs, Vernon. 1996. *Mass Immigration and the National Interest*. Armonk, N.Y.: M. E. Sharpe.

Brimelow, Peter. 1995. *Alien Nation: Common Sense about America's Immigration Disaster*. New York: Random House.

Bromsen, Archie. 1935. "The Public School's Contribution to the Maladaptation of the Italian Boy." Appendix E in Caroline Ware, *Greenwich Village, 1920–1930*. New York: Harper and Row.

Brumberg, Stephan. 1986. *Going to America, Going to School: The Jewish Immigrant Public School Encounter in Turn-of-the-Century New York City*. New York: Praeger.

Bruni, Frank. 1997. "Beckoned by Promise, Felled by a Short Cut." *New York Times*, May 5.

Bruni, Frank, and Deborah Sontag. 1996. "Behind a Suburban Facade in Queens, a Teeming Angry Urban Arithmetic." *New York Times*, October 8.

Bryce-Laporte, Roy S. 1972. "Black Immigrants: The Experience of Invisibility and Inequality." *Journal of Black Studies* 3: 29–56.

———. 1987. "New York City and the New Caribbean Immigration: A Contextual Statement." In Constance Sutton and Elsa Chaney (eds.), *Caribbean Life in New York City*. New York: Center for Migration Studies.

Burgess, Judith, and Meryl Gray. 1981. "Migration and Sex Roles: A Comparison of Black and Indian Trinidadians in New York City." In Delores Mortimer and Roy Bryce-Laporte (eds.), *Female Immigrants to the United States: Caribbean, Latin American, and African Experiences*. Washington, D.C.: Research Institute on Immigration and Ethnic Studies.

Cahan, Abraham. 1960 [1917]. *The Rise of David Levinsky*. New York: Harper and Row.

———. 1970 [1896]. *Yekl and Other Stories of Yiddish New York*. New York: Dover.

Camarota, Steven. 1999. "Immigrants in the United States, 1998." *Backgrounder* (January): 1–11. Washington, D.C.: Center for Immigration Studies.

Carino, Benjamin. 1996. "Filipino Americans: Many and Varied." In Silvia Pedraza and Rubén Rumbaut (eds.), *Origins and Destinies.* Belmont, Calif.: Wadsworth.

Carter, Susan, and Richard Sutch. 1998. "Historical Background to Current Immigration Issues." In James Smith and Barry Edmonston (eds.), *The Immigration Debate: Studies on the Economic, Demographic, and Fiscal Effects of Immigration.* Washington, D.C.: National Research Council.

Cartmill, Matt. 1999. "The Status of the Race Concept in Physical Anthropology." *American Anthropologist* 100: 651–60.

Center for Immigration Studies. 1992. "Visa List Swells to Almost Three Million." *Scope* (Summer): 6–9.

———. 1997. "Immigrant Visa Waiting List at 3.6 Million." *Immigration Review* (Spring): 5–6.

Chaney, Elsa. 1979. "The World Economy and Contemporary Migration." *International Migration Review* 13: 204–12.

Chen, Hsiang-Shui. 1992. *Chinatown No More: Taiwan Immigrants in Contemporary New York.* Ithaca: Cornell University Press.

Child, Irvin. 1943. *Italian or American? The Second Generation in Conflict.* New Haven: Yale University Press.

Chin, Margaret. 1997. "When Coethnic Assets Become Liabilities: Mexican, Ecuadorian, and Chinese Workers in New York City." Paper presented at the conference Transnational Communities and the Political Economy of New York in the 1990s, New School for Social Research, New York.

Chotzinoff, Samuel. 1955. *A Lost Paradise.* New York: Knopf.

Cinel, Dino. 1982a. *From Italy to San Francisco: The Immigrant Experience.* Stanford: Stanford University Press.

———. 1982b. "The Seasonal Emigration of Italians in the Nineteenth Century: From Internal to International Migration." *Journal of Ethnic Studies* 10: 43–68.

CISNEWS. 1998. "U.S. Coast Guard Migration Year in Review for Fiscal Year 1997," March 31, Center for Immigration Studies, Washington, D.C.

Cohen, David. 1970. "Immigrants and the Schools." *Review of Educational Research* 40: 13–27.

Cohen, Miriam. 1982. "Changing Education Strategies among Immigrant Generations: New York Italians in Comparative Perspective." *Journal of Social History* 5: 443–66.

———. 1992. *Workshop to Office: Two Generations of Italian Women in New York, 1900–1950.* Ithaca: Cornell University Press.

Cohen, Morris. 1949. *A Dreamer's Journey.* Boston: Beacon Press.

Cohen, Rose. 1995 [1918]. *Out of the Shadow: A Russian Jewish Girlhood on the Lower East Side.* Ithaca: Cornell University Press.

Colen, Shellee. 1989. "Just a Little Respect: West Indian Domestic Workers in New York City." In Elsa Chaney and Mary Garcia Castro (eds.), *Muchachas No More: Household Workers in Latin America and the Caribbean.* Philadelphia: Temple University Press.

———. 1990. "Housekeeping for the Green Card: West Indian Household Workers, the State, and Stratified Reproduction in New York." In Roger Sanjek and Shellee Colen (eds.), *At Work in Homes.* Monograph 3. Washington, D.C.: American Ethnological Society.

Conquergood, Dwight. 1992. "Life in Big Red: Struggles and Accommodations in a Chicago Polyethnic Tenement." In Louise Lamphere (ed.), *Structuring Diversity.* Chicago: University of Chicago Press.

Coombs, Orde. 1970. "West Indians in New York: Moving Beyond the Limbo Pole." *New York,* July, 28–32.

Cordero-Guzman, Hector, and Ramón Grosfoguel. 1998. "The Demographic and Socio-Economic Characteristics of Post-1965 Foreign Born Immigrants to New York City: What Does Data from the 1990 Census Suggest about National Origin Differences in Immigrant Selectivity and Immigrant Incorporation?" Paper presented at the Paul Lazarsfeld Center for Social Sciences, Columbia University.

Cornell, Stephen, and Douglas Hartmann. 1998. *Ethnicity and Race.* Thousand Oaks, Calif.: Pine Forge Press.

Covello, Leonard. 1958. *The Heart Is the Teacher.* New York: McGraw-Hill.

———. 1967. *The Social Background of the Italo-American School Child.* Leiden: Brill.

Crouch, Stanley. 1996. "Race Is Over." *New York Times Magazine,* September 26, 170–71.

Crowder, Kyle. 1999. "Residential Segregation of West Indians in the New York/ New Jersey Metropolitan Area: The Roles of Race and Ethnicity." *International Migration Review* 33: 79–113.

Daniels, Roger. 1990. *Coming to America.* New York: HarperCollins.

———. 1997a. *Not Like Us: Immigrants and Minorities in America, 1890–1924.* Chicago: Ivan Dee.

———. 1997b. "United States Policy Towards Asian Immigrants: Contemporary Developments in Historical Perspective." In Darrell Hamamoto and Rodolfo Torres (eds.), *New American Destinies.* New York: Routledge.

Dao, James. 1992. "At P.S. 19, Bilingual Is Not Enough." *New York Times,* May 25.

Daykin, David, Hongsook Eu, and Emily Zimmerman. 1994. "Neighborhood Profile No. 5: Washington Heights/Inwood." New York: United Way of New York City.

DeConde, Alexander. 1971. *Half Bitter, Half Sweet: An Excursion into Italian-American History.* New York: Scribner's.

Denton, Nancy, and Douglas Massey. 1989. "Racial Identity among Caribbean Hispanics: The Effect of Double Minority Status on Residential Segregation." *American Sociological Review* 54: 790–808.

DeSipio, Louis. 1998. "Building a New Foreign Policy among Friends: National Efforts to Construct Long-Term Relationships with Latin American Emigres in the United States." Paper presented at the conference States and Diasporas, Casa Italiana, Columbia University.

DeWind, Josh. 1997. "Educating the Children of Immigrants in New York's Restructured Economy." In Margaret Crahan and Alberto Vourvoulias-Bush (eds.), *The City and the World: New York's Global Future.* New York: Council on Foreign Relations.

DeWind, Josh, and Philip Kasinitz. 1997. "Everything Old Is New Again? Processes and Theories of Immigrant Incorporation." *International Migration Review* 31: 1096–111.

Di Donato, Pietro. 1937. *Christ in Concrete.* New York: Bobbs-Merrill.

Dillon, Sam. 1996. "Asian Aliens Now Smuggled from Mexico." *New York Times,* May 30.

Dinnerstein, Leonard. 1982. "Education and the Advancement of American Jews." In Bernard Weiss (ed.), *American Education and the European Immigrant, 1840–1940.* Urbana: University of Illinois Press.

———. 1994. *Anti-Semitism in America.* New York: Oxford University Press.

Dinnerstein, Leonard, and David Reimers. 1988. *Ethnic Americans.* Englewood Cliffs, N.J.: Prentice-Hall.

Donato, Katherine. 1992. "Understanding U.S. Immigration: Why Some Countries Send Women and Others Send Men." In Donna Gabaccia (ed.), *Seeking Common Ground.* Westport, Conn.: Praeger.

Doyle, Joe. 1996. "Striking for Ireland on the New York Docks." In Ronald Bayor and Thomas Meagher (eds.), *The New York Irish.* Baltimore: Johns Hopkins University Press.

Drennan, Matthew. 1991. "The Decline and Rise of the New York Economy." In John Mollenkopf and Manuel Castells (eds.), *Dual City.* New York: Russell Sage Foundation.

Drennan, Matthew, and Cathy Matson. 1995. "Economy." In Kenneth Jackson (ed.), *Encyclopedia of New York City.* New Haven: Yale University Press.

Duany, Jorge. 1998. "Reconstructing Racial Identity, Ethnicity, Color and Class among Dominicans in the United States and Puerto Rico." *Latin American Perspectives* 25: 147–72.

Dublin, Thomas (ed.). 1996. *Becoming American, Becoming Ethnic: College Students Explore Their Roots.* Philadelphia: Temple University Press.

Dugger, Celia. 1998. "Among Young of Immigrants, Outlook Rises." *New York Times,* March 21.

Dunn, Ashley. 1994. "After Crackdown, Smugglers of Chinese Find New Routes." *New York Times,* November 1.

———. 1995a. "Cram Schools: Immigrants' Tools for Success." *New York Times,* January 28.

———. 1995b. "Starting Over Without Fear: A Newark Neighborhood Has Been Transformed by Illegal Immigrants." *New York Times,* January 16.

Eaton, Leslie. 1998. "City's Jobless Rate Sinks to 7.3%, Lowest since 1990." *New York Times,* September 18.

———. 1999. "City's Unemployment Rate Stays at Its Lowest, Reassuring Wary Economists." *New York Times,* May 21.

Edry, Sandy. 1998. "Less Congestion, But . . ." *New York Times,* September 10.

Edwards, Linda, and Caroline Ishikawa. 1995. "The Changing Profile of CUNY Students." In *Immigration/Migration and the CUNY Student of the Future.* New York: City University of New York.

Epstein, Cynthia. 1970. *A Woman's Place.* Berkeley: University of California Press.

Erie, Stephen. 1988. *Rainbow's End: Irish-Americans and the Dilemmas of Urban Machine Politics, 1840-1985.* Berkeley: University of California Press.

Espiritu, Yen Le. 1994. "The Intersection of Race, Ethnicity and Class: The Multiple Identities of Second-Generation Filipinos." *Diaspora* 1: 249-73.

———. 1996. "Colonial Oppression, Labour Importation and Group Formation: Filipinos in the United States." *Ethnic and Racial Studies* 19: 29-48.

———. 1997. *Asian American Women and Men.* Thousand Oaks, Calif.: Sage Publications.

Ewen, Phyllis. 1985. *Immigrant Women in the Land of Dollars: Life and Culture on the Lower East Side, 1890-1925.* New York: Monthly Review Press.

Fainstein, Norman. 1995. "Black Ghettoization and Social Mobility." In Michael Peter Smith and Joe Feagin (eds.), *The Bubbling Cauldron.* Minneapolis: University of Minnesota Press.

Farley, Reynolds. 1996. *The New American Reality.* New York: Russell Sage Foundation.

———. 1998. "First and Second Generation Immigrants in New York: Their Numbers and Characteristics." Paper delivered at a meeting of the Eastern Sociological Society, Philadelphia.

Feagin, Joe. 1991. "The Continuing Significance of Race: Antiblack Discrimination in Public Places." *American Sociological Review* 56: 101-16.

Fee, Elizabeth, and Steven Corey. 1994. *Garbage: The History and Politics of Trash in New York City.* New York: New York Public Library.

Fenton, Edward. 1975. *Immigrants and Unions, A Case Study: Italians and American Labor, 1870-1920.* New York: Arno Press.

Finder, Alan. 1995. "Despite Tough Laws, Sweatshops Flourish." *New York Times,* February 6.

Fineman, Mark. 1998. "Dominican Bones Line Pathway to States." *Los Angeles Times,* March 9.

Fink, Leon, and Brian Greenberg. 1989. *Upheaval in the Quiet Zone: A History of Hospital Workers' Union 1199.* Urbana: University of Illinois Press.

Fisher, Ian. 1997. "Love of Country, if Not Each Other." *New York Times,* March 9.

Fitzgerald, Frances. 1979. *America Revised.* New York: Vintage.

Fix, Michael, and Jeffrey Passel. 1994. *Immigration and Immigrants: Setting the Record Straight.* Washington, D.C.: The Urban Institute.

Flores, Ronald, and Joseph Salvo. 1997. "Foreign-for-Native Replacement Patterns in the New York Urban Region." Paper prepared for the Regional Plan Association, New York.

Foderaro, Lisa. 1991. "Wider Mosaic: Suburbs Jobs Lure Immigrants." *New York Times,* December 7.

———. 1998. " 'Made in New York' Is Coming Back into Fashion." *New York Times,* January 13.

Foerster, Robert. 1919. *The Italian Emigration of Our Times.* Harvard: Harvard University Press.

Foner, Nancy. 1973. *Status and Power in Rural Jamaica.* New York: Teachers College Press.

———. 1985. "Race and Color: Jamaican Migrants in London and New York City." *International Migration Review* 19: 708-27.

———. 1986. "Sex Roles and Sensibilities: Jamaican Women in New York and London." In Rita Simon and Caroline Brettell (eds.), *International Migration: The Female Experience.* Totowa, N.J.: Rowman and Allenheld.

———. 1987. "The Jamaicans: Race and Ethnicity among Migrants in New York City." In Foner (ed.), *New Immigrants in New York.* New York: Columbia University Press.

———. 1994. *The Caregiving Dilemma: Work in an American Nursing Home.* Berkeley: University of California Press.

———. 1997a. "The Immigrant Family: Cultural Legacies and Cultural Changes." *International Migration Review* 31: 961-74.

———. 1997b. "What's New about Transnationalism?: New York Immigrants Today and at the Turn of the Century." *Diaspora* 6: 355-76.

———. 1998a. "Benefits and Burdens: Immigrant Women and Work in New York City." *Gender Issues* 16: 5-24.

———. 1998b. "Towards a Comparative Perspective on West Indian Migration." In Mary Chamberlain (ed.), *Caribbean Migration.* London: Routledge.

———. 1998c. "West Indian Identity in the Diaspora: Comparative and Historical Perspectives." *Latin American Perspectives* 25: 173-88.

———. 1999. "Immigrant Women and Work in New York, Then and Now." *Journal of American Ethnic History* 18: 95-113.

Fong, Timothy. 1998. *The Contemporary Asian American Experience.* Upper Saddle River, N.J.: Prentice-Hall.

Fordham, Signithia. 1996. *Blacked Out: Dilemmas of Race, Identity, and Success at Capital High.* Chicago: University of Chicago Press.

Fordham, Signithia, and John Ogbu. 1986. "Black Students' School Success: Coping with the Burden of Acting White." *Urban Review* 18: 176-206.

Fox, Geoffrey. 1996. *Hispanic Nation.* New York: Birch Lane Press.

Freedman, Samuel. 1990. *Small Victories.* New York: HarperCollins.

Frey, William. 1995. "The New Geography of Population Shifts." In Reynolds Farley (ed.), *State of the Union: Volume II, Social Trends.* New York: Russell Sage Foundation.

———. 1996. "Immigration, Domestic Migration, and Demographic Balkanization in America: New Evidence for the 1990s." *Population and Development Review* 22: 741–63.

Friedman, Stephen. 1984. "Industrialization, Immigration and Transportation to 1900." In Marilyn Weigold (ed.), *Westchester County: The Past Hundred Years, 1883–1983.* Valhalla, N.Y.: Westchester County Historical Society.

Friedman-Kasaba, Kathie. 1996. *Memories of Migration: Gender, Ethnicity, and Work in the Lives of Jewish and Italian Women in New York, 1870–1924.* Albany: SUNY Press.

Fuchs, Lawrence. 1990. *The American Kaleidoscope.* Hanover: University Press of New England.

Gabaccia, Donna. 1984. *From Sicily to Elizabeth Street.* Albany: SUNY Press.

———. 1992. "Little Italy's Decline: Immigrant Renters and Investors in a Changing City." In David Ward and Oliver Zunz (eds.), *The Landscape of Modernity.* New York: Russell Sage Foundation.

———. 1994. *From the Other Side: Women, Gender, and Immigrant Life in the U.S., 1820–1990.* Bloomington: Indiana University Press.

———. 1998. "Italians and Their Diasporas: Cosmopolitans, Exiles and Workers of the World." Paper presented at the conference States and Diasporas, Casa Italiana, Columbia University.

Gambino, Richard. 1974. *Blood of My Blood: The Dilemma of Italian-Americans.* New York: Doubleday.

Gans, Herbert. 1992. "Second Generation Decline: Scenarios for the Economic and Ethnic Futures of Post-1965 American Immigrants." *Ethnic and Racial Studies* 15: 173–92.

Garrison, Vivian, and Carol Weiss. 1987. "Dominican Family Networks and United States Immigration Policy." In Constance Sutton and Elsa Chaney (eds.), *Caribbean Life in New York City.* New York: Center for Migration Studies.

Georges, Eugenia. 1990. *The Making of a Transnational Community.* New York: Columbia University Press.

Gerstle, Gary. 1997a. "Liberty, Coercion and the Making of Americans." *Journal of American History* 84: 524–58.

———. 1997b. "The Power of Nations." *Journal of American History* 84: 576–80.

Geyer, Georgie Anne. 1996. *Americans No More: The Death of American Citizenship.* New York: Atlantic Monthly Press.

Gibson, Margaret. 1988. *Accommodation without Assimilation.* Ithaca: Cornell University Press.

Gilbertson, Greta. 1995. "Women's Labor and Enclave Employment: The Case of Dominican and Colombian Women in New York City." *International Migration Review* 19: 657–71.

Gilbertson, Greta, and Douglas Gurak. 1993. "Broadening the Enclave Debate: The Labor Market Experiences of Dominican and Colombian Men in New York City." *Sociological Forum* 8: 205–20.

Gilbertson, Greta, and Audrey Singer. 2000. "Naturalization under Changing Conditions of Membership: Dominican Immigrants in New York City." In Nancy Foner, Rubén Rumbaut, and Steven Gold (eds.), *Immigration Research for a New Century.* New York: Russell Sage Foundation.

Giordano, Rita, and Elaine Rivera. 1990. "The Welcome Mat Wears Thin: Many Find City Housing Substandard." *New York Newsday,* June 26.

Giuliani, Rudolph. 1997. "Keep America's Door Open." *Wall Street Journal,* January 9.

Glazer, Nathan. 1997. *We Are All Multiculturalists Now.* Cambridge: Harvard University Press.

Glazer, Nathan, and Daniel Moynihan. 1970. 2d ed. *Beyond the Melting Pot.* Cambridge: MIT Press.

Gleason, Philip. 1980. "American Identity and Americanization." In Stephen Thernstrom (ed.), *Harvard Encyclopedia of American Ethnic Groups.* Cambridge: Harvard University Press.

Glenn, Susan. 1990. *Daughters of the Shtetl: Life and Labor in the Immigrant Generation.* Ithaca: Cornell University Press.

Glick Schiller, Nina. 1996. "Who Are Those Guys? A Transnational Reading of the U.S. Immigrant Experience." Paper presented at a conference of the Social Science Research Council, Becoming American/America Becoming, Sanibel Island, Fla.

———. 1999. "Transmigrants and Nation-States: Something Old and Something New in the U.S. Immigrant Experience." In Charles Hirschman, Philip Kasinitz, and Josh DeWind (eds.), *The Handbook of International Migration.* New York: Russell Sage Foundation.

Glick Schiller, Nina, Linda Basch, and Cristina Blanc-Szanton. 1992. "Transnationalism: A New Analytic Framework for Understanding Migration." In Nina Glick Schiller, Linda Basch, and Cristina Blanc-Szanton (eds.), *Towards a Transnational Perspective on Migration.* New York: New York Academy of Sciences.

———. 1995. "From Immigrant to Transmigrant: Theorizing Transnational Migration." *Anthropological Quarterly* 68: 48–63.

Glick Schiller, Nina, and Georges Fouron. 1998. "Transnational Lives and National Identities: The Identity Politics of Haitian Immigrants." In Michael P. Smith and Luis Guarnizo (eds.), *Transnationalism from Below.* New Brunswick, N.J.: Transaction.

Goetz, Thomas 1997. "Why New York Taco Stands Are Chinese." *New York Times Magazine,* October 19, 59.

Gold, Steven, and Bruce Phillips. 1996. "Mobility and Continuity among Eastern European Jews." In Silvia Pedraza and Rubén Rumbaut (eds.), *Origins and Destinies.* Belmont, Calif.: Wadsworth.

Goldberg, Barry. 1992. "Historical Reflections on Transnationalism, Race, and the American Immigrant Saga." In Nina Glick Schiller, Linda Basch, and Cristina

Blanc-Szanton (eds.), *Towards a Transnational Perspective on Migration.* New York: New York Academy of Sciences.

Goldberg, Jeffrey. 1995. "The Overachievers." *New York Magazine,* April 10.

Goldin, Claudia. 1990. *Understanding the Gender Gap.* New York: Oxford University Press.

———. 1994a. "How America Graduated From High School: 1910 to 1960." Working Paper no. 4762. Cambridge, Mass.: National Bureau of Economic Research.

———. 1994b. "Labor Markets in the Twentieth Century." Working Paper Series on Historical Factors in Long Run Growth, no. 58. Cambridge, Mass.: National Bureau of Economic Research.

———. 1994c. "The Political Economy of Immigration Restriction in the United States, 1890 to 1921." In Claudia Goldin and Gary Libecap (eds.), *The Regulated Economy.* Chicago: University of Chicago Press.

Goldscheider, Calvin, and Alan Zuckerman. 1984. *The Transformation of the Jews.* Chicago: University of Chicago Press.

Goldstein, Eric. 1997a. "A White Race of Another Kind: Immigrant Jews and Whiteness in the Urban North, 1914–1945." Paper presented at a meeting of the Organization of American Historians, San Francisco.

———. 1997b. "Different Blood Flows in Our Veins: Race and Jewish Self-Definition in Late Nineteenth Century America." *American Jewish History* 85: 29–55.

Goodman, Alan. 1997. "Bred in the Bone?" *The Sciences* 37: 20–25.

Gorelick, Sherry. 1982. *City College and the Jewish Poor: Education in New York, 1880–1914.* New York: Schocken.

Graham, Pamela. 1997. "Political Incorporation and Re-Incorporation: Simultaneity in the Dominican Migrant Experience." Paper presented at the conference Transnational Communities and the Political Economy of New York City in the 1990s, New School for Social Research, New York.

Grant, Madison. 1916. *The Passing of the Great Race.* New York: Scribner's.

Grasmuck, Sherri, and Ramón Grosfoguel. 1997. "Geopolitics, Economic Niches and Gendered Social Capital among Recent Caribbean Immigrants in New York City." *Sociological Perspectives* 40: 339–64.

Grasmuck, Sherri, and Patricia Pessar. 1991. *Between Two Islands.* Berkeley: University of California Press.

———. 1996. "Dominicans in the United States: First- and Second-Generation Settlement, 1960–1990." In Silvia Pedraza and Rubén Rumbaut (eds.), *Origins and Destinies.* Belmont, Calif.: Wadsworth.

Green, Nancy. 1997. *Ready-to-Wear and Ready-to-Work.* Durham: Duke University Press.

Greer, Colin. 1972. *The Great School Legend.* New York: Basic.

Grosfoguel, Ramón, and Chloe Georas. 1996. "The Racialization of Latino Caribbean Migrants in the New York Metropolitan Area." *Centro* 8: 191–201.

Guarnizo, Luis. 1992. "One Country in Two: Dominican-Owned Firms in New York and in the Dominican Republic." Ph.D. diss., Johns Hopkins University.

———. 1997. "On the Political Participation of Transnational Migrants: Old Practices and New Trends." Paper presented at a Social Science Research Council workshop, Immigrants, Civic Culture, and Modes of Political Incorporation: A Contemporary and Historical Comparison, Santa Fe, N. Mex.

———. 1998. "The Rise of Transnational Social Formations: Mexican and Dominican State Responses to Transnational Migration." *Political Power and Social Theory* 12: 45–94.

Gurak, Douglas, and Mary Kritz. 1996. "Social Context, Household Composition and Employment among Migrant and Nonmigrant Dominican Women." *International Migration Review* 30: 399–422.

Gurock, Jeffrey. 1979. *When Harlem Was Jewish, 1870–1930*. New York: Columbia University Press.

Hacker, Andrew. 1992. *Two Nations*. New York: Scribner's.

———. 1998. "Grand Illusion." *New York Review of Books* 45: 26–29.

Hagan, Jacqueline. 1994. *Deciding to Be Legal: A Maya Community in Houston*. Philadelphia: Temple University Press.

Hammack, David. 1982. *Power and Society: Greater New York at the Turn of the Century*. New York: Russell Sage Foundation.

Hapgood, Hutchins. 1967 [1902]. *The Spirit of the Ghetto*. Harvard: Cambridge University Press.

Harlow, Ilana. 1995. "The International Express: A Guide to Ethnic Communities along the 7 Train." New York: Queens Council on the Arts.

Harrison, Roderick, and Claudette Bennett. 1995. "Racial and Ethnic Diversity." In Reynolds Farley (ed.), *State of the Union: Volume Two, Social Trends*. New York: Russell Sage Foundation.

Hartmann, Edward. 1948. *The Movement to Americanize the Immigrant*. New York: Columbia University Press.

Haslip-Viera, Gabriel. 1996. "The Evolution of the Latino Community in New York City: Early Nineteenth Century to the Present." In Gabriel Haslip-Viera and Sherrie Baver (eds.), *Latinos in New York*. Notre Dame: University of Notre Dame Press.

Hatton, Timothy, and Jeffrey Williamson. 1998. *The Age of Mass Migration: Causes and Economic Impact*. New York: Oxford University Press.

Heilman, Samuel. 1995. *Portrait of American Jews: The Last Half of the Twentieth Century*. Seattle: University of Washington Press.

Heinze, Andrew. 1990. *A Search for Abundance: Jewish Immigrants, Mass Consumption, and the Search for an American Identity*. New York: Columbia University Press.

Hernandez, Ramona, and Francisco Rivera-Batiz. 1997. *Dominican New Yorkers: A Socioeconomic Profile*. New York: CUNY Dominican Studies Institute.

Hernandez, Ramona, Francisco Rivera-Batiz, and Roberto Agodini. 1995. *Dominican New Yorkers: A Socioeconomic Profile*. New York: CUNY Dominican Studies Institute.

Hernstein, Richard, and Charles Murray. 1994. *The Bell Curve: Intelligence and Class Structure in American Life*. New York: Free Press.

Higgs, Robert. 1971. "Race, Skills and Earnings: American Immigrants in 1901." *Journal of Economic History* 31: 420–28.

Higham, John. 1955. *Strangers in the Land*. New Brunswick: Rutgers University Press.

———. 1984. *Send These to Me*. Baltimore: Johns Hopkins University Press.

Hillquit, Morris. 1934. *Loose Leaves from a Busy Life*. New York: Macmillan.

Hobsbawm, Eric, and Terence Ranger (eds.). 1983. *The Invention of Tradition*. Cambridge: Cambridge University Press.

Hohn, Gabriela. 1995. "Creole Students Need Help to Succeed." *Carib News*, June 6.

Hollinger, David. 1995. *Postethnic America*. New York: Basic.

Holloway, Lynette. 1995. "Brokers Said to Exploit Fear to Stir Queens Home Sales." *New York Times*, May 5.

———. 1997. "Faulty Wiring Is Cited in Fire That Killed 4." *New York Times*, April 23.

Hondagneu-Sotelo, Pierrette. 1999. "Introduction: Gender and Post-1965 U.S. Immigration." *American Behavioral Scientist* 42: 565–76.

Hondagneu-Sotelo, Pierrette, and Ernestine Avila. 1994. *Gendered Transitions*. Berkeley: University of California Press.

———. 1997. "I'm Here, but I'm There: The Meanings of Latina Transnational Motherhood." *Gender and Society* 11: 548–71.

Hood, Clifton. 1993. *722 Miles: The Building of the Subways and How They Transformed New York*. New York: Simon and Schuster.

Houston, Marion, Roger Kramer, and Joan Mackin Barrett. 1984. "Female Predominance of Immigration to the United States since 1930: A First Look." *International Migration Review* 18: 908–63.

Howe, Irving. 1976. *World of Our Fathers*. New York: Simon and Schuster.

Howell, David, and Elizabeth Mueller. 1996. "Skill Mismatch, Labor Market Restructuring and the Changing Economic Status of Foreign-Born Workers in New York City and Los Angeles." Paper presented at a conference of the Social Science Research Council, Becoming American/America Becoming, Sanibel Island, Fla.

———. 1997. "The Effects on African-American Earnings: A Jobs-Level Analysis of the New York City Labor Market, 1979–1989." Working Paper no. 210. The Jerome Levy Economics Institute, Bard College.

Husock, Howard. 1996. "Enterprising Van Drivers Collide with Regulation." *City Journal* 6: 60–68.

Hyman, Paula. 1983. "Culture and Gender: Women in the Immigrant Jewish Community." In David Berger (ed.), *The Legacy of Jewish Immigration: 1881 and Its Impact*. New York: Brooklyn College Press.

———. 1995. *Gender and Assimilation in Modern Jewish History*. Seattle: University of Washington Press.

Ignatiev, Noel. 1995. *How the Irish Became White*. New York: Routledge.

Jackson, Kenneth. 1985. *The Crabgrass Frontier*. New York: Oxford University Press.

Jacobs, Jerry, and Margaret Greene. 1994. "Race and Ethnicity: Social Class and Schooling." In Susan Cott Watkins (ed.), *After Ellis Island*. New York: Russell Sage Foundation.

Jacobson, Matthew. 1995. *Special Sorrows*. Cambridge: Harvard University Press.

———. 1998. *Whiteness of a Different Color: European Immigrants and the Alchemy of Race*. Cambridge: Harvard University Press.

Jones, Charisse. 1994. "Melting Pot Still Bubbles at P.S. 327." *New York Times*, June 12.

Jones, Delmos. 1992. "Which Migrant? Permanent or Temporary?" In Nina Glick Schiller, Linda Basch, and Cristina Blanc Szanton (eds.), *Towards a Transnational Perspective on Migration*. New York: New York Academy of Sciences.

Jones-Correa, Michael. 1998a. "Different Paths: Gender, Immigration and Political Participation." *International Migration Review* 32: 326–49.

———. 1998b. *Between Two Nations: The Political Predicament of Latinos in New York*. Ithaca: Cornell University Press.

Joselit, Jenna. 1986. "The Landlord as Czar: Pre-World War I Tenant Activity." In Ronald Lawson (ed.), *The Tenant Movement in New York City, 1904–1984*. New Brunswick: Rutgers University Press.

Joseph, Samuel. 1967. *Jewish Immigration to the United States: From 1881–1910*. New York: AMS Press.

Kamphoefner, Walter. 1994. "German-American Bilingualism: *Cui Malo?* Mother Tongue and Socioeconomic Status among the Second Generation in 1940." *International Migration Review* 28: 846–65.

Kao, Grace, and Marta Tienda. 1995. "Optimism and Achievement: The Educational Performance of Immigrant Youth." *Social Science Quarterly* 76: 1–19.

Kasinitz, Philip. 1987. "The Minority Within: The New Black Immigrants." *New York Affairs* 10: 44–58.

———. 1992. *Caribbean New York*. Ithaca: Cornell University Press.

Kasinitz, Philip, and Jan Rosenberg. 1996. "Missing the Connection: Social Isolation and Employment on the Brooklyn Waterfront." *Social Problems* 43: 180–96.

Kasinitz, Philip, and Milton Vickerman. 1995. "Ethnic Niches and Racial Traps: Jamaicans in the New York Regional Economy." Paper presented to the Social Science History Association, Chicago.

Kaufman, Kathy. 2000. "Outsourcing the Hearth: The Impact of Immigration on Labor Allocation in American Families." In Nancy Foner, Rubén Rumbaut, and Steven Gold (eds.), *Immigration Research for a New Century*. New York: Russell Sage Foundation.

Kazin, Alfred. 1946. *A Walker in the City*. New York: Harcourt Brace and Jovanovich.

Kennedy, David. 1996. "Can We Still Afford to be a Nation of Immigrants?" *Atlantic Monthly*, November, 51–68.

Kessner, Thomas. 1977. *The Golden Door: Italian and Jewish Immigrant Mobility in New York City, 1880–1915*. New York: Oxford University Press.

————. 1981. "Jobs, Ghettoes and the Urban Economy, 1880–1915." *American Jewish History* 21: 219–38.

Kessner, Thomas, and Betty Boyd Caroli. 1978. "New Immigrant Women at Work: Italians and Jews in New York City, 1880–1905." *Journal of Ethnic Studies* 5: 19–31.

Khandelwal, Madhulika. 1995. "Indian Immigrants in Queens, New York City: Patterns of Spatial Concentration and Distribution, 1965–1990." In Peter van der Veer (ed.), *Nation and Migration: The Politics of Space in the South Asian Diaspora.* Philadelphia: University of Pennsylvania Press.

Kibria, Nazli. 1993. *Family Tightrope: The Changing Lives of Vietnamese Americans.* Princeton: Princeton University Press.

Kim, Ai Ra. 1996. *Women Struggling for a New Life: The Role of Religion in the Cultural Passage from Korea to America.* Albany: State University of New York Press.

Kim, Dae Young. 1999. "Beyond Coethnic Solidarity: Mexican and Ecuadorian Employment in Korean-Owned Businesses in New York City." *Ethnic and Racial Studies* 22: 581–605.

Kim, Illsoo. 1987. "The Koreans: Ethnic Business in an Urban Frontier." In Nancy Foner (ed.), *New Immigrants in New York.* New York: Columbia University Press.

Kinkead, Gwen. 1992. *Chinatown.* New York: HarperCollins.

Kirschenman, Joleen, and Kathryn Neckerman. 1991. "We'd Love to Hire Them, But—: The Meaning of Race for Employers." In Christopher Jencks and Paul Peterson (eds.), *The Urban Underclass.* Washington, D.C.: Brookings Institution.

Kiser, Edgar, and Michael Hechter. 1991. "The Role of General Comparative-Historical Sociology." *American Journal of Sociology* 97: 1–30.

Koslovsky, Joanne. 1981. "Going Foreign: Causes of Jamaican Migration." *NACLA Report on the Americas* 15: 1–31.

Kraly, Ellen. 1987. "U.S. Immigration Policy and the Immigrant Populations of New York City." In Nancy Foner (ed.), *New Immigrants in New York.* New York: Columbia University Press.

Kraly, Ellen, and Charles Hirschman. 1994. "Immigrants, Cities and Opportunities: Some Historical Insights from Social Demography." In Mary Powers and John Macisco (eds.), *The Immigration Experience in the United States.* New York: Center for Migration Studies.

Kramer, Sydelle, and Jenny Masur (eds.). 1976. *Jewish Grandmothers.* Boston: Beacon Press.

Kraut, Alan. 1983. "The Butcher, the Baker, the Pushcart Peddler: Jewish Foodways and Entrepreneurial Opportunity in the East European Immigrant Community, 1880–1940." *Journal of American Culture:* 71–83.

————. 1986. "Silent Strangers: Germs, Genes and Nativism in John Higham's *Strangers in the Land.*" *American Jewish History* 76: 142–58.

————. 1994. *Silent Travelers: Germs, Genes and the "Immigrant Menace."* New York: Basic.

Kuznets, Simon. 1975. "Immigration of Russian Jews to the United States: Background and Structure." *Perspectives in American History* 9: 33–124.

Kwong, Peter. 1987. *The New Chinatown.* New York: Hill and Wang.

———. 1994. "The Wages of Fear." *Village Voice,* April 26, 25–29.

———. 1997. *Forbidden Workers: Illegal Chinese Immigrants and American Labor.* New York: New Press.

LaGumina, Salvatore. 1982. "American Education and the Italian Immigrant Response." In Bernard Weiss (ed.), *American Education and the European Immigrant, 1840–1940.* Urbana: University of Illinois Press.

———. 1988. *From Steerage to Suburbia: Long Island Italians.* New York: Center for Migration Studies.

Lamm, Richard, and Gary Imhoff. 1985. *The Immigration Time Bomb.* New York: Truman Talley.

Lamphere, Louise. 1987. *From Working Daughters to Working Mothers: Immigrant Women in a New England Industrial Community.* Ithaca: Cornell University Press.

Landesman, Alter F. 1969. *Brownsville: The Birth, Development and Passing of a Jewish Community.* New York: Bloch.

Laslett, Peter. 1965. *The World We Have Lost.* New York: Scribners.

La Sorte, Michael. 1985. *La Merica: Images of Italian Greenhorn Experience.* Philadelphia: Temple University Press.

Lavin, David, and David Hyllegard. 1996. *Changing the Odds: Open Admissions and the Life Chances of the Disadvantaged.* New Haven: Yale University Press.

Lee, Chang-Rae. 1995. *Native Speaker.* New York: Riverhead.

Lee, Jennifer. 1998. "Cultural Brokers: Race-Based Hiring in Inner City Neighborhoods." *American Behavioral Scientist* 41: 927–37.

———. 1999. "Retail Niche Domination among African American, Jewish, and Korean Entrepreneurs: Competition, Coethnic Advantage, and Coethnic Disadvantage." *American Behavioral Scientist* 42: 1398–1416.

Lee, Sharon. 1989. "Asian Immigration and American Race Relations: From Exclusion to Acceptance?" *Ethnic and Racial Studies* 12: 368–90.

Lessinger, Johanna. 1992. "Investing or Going Home? A Transnational Strategy among Indian Immigrants in the United States." In Nina Glick Schiller, Linda Basch, and Cristina Blanc Szanton (eds.), *Towards a Transnational Perspective on Migration.* New York: New York Academy of Sciences.

———. 1995. *From the Ganges to the Hudson.* Boston: Allyn and Bacon.

———. 1997. "A Dialogue with Johanna Lessinger." *Anthropology Newsletter* 38 (November–December): 42.

Lestchinsky, Jacob. 1942. "The Position of the Jews in the Economic Life of America." In Isacque Graeber and Stuart Britt (eds.), *Jews in a Gentile World.* New York: Macmillan.

Levitt, Peggy. 2000. "Migrants Participate across Borders: Towards an Understanding of Forms and Consequences." In Nancy Foner, Rubén Rumbaut, and Steven Gold (eds.), *Immigration Research for a New Century.* New York: Russell Sage Foundation.

———. 1998. "Forms of Transnational Community and Their Impact on the Second Generation: Preliminary Findings." Paper presented at the conference Transnationalism and the Second Generation, Harvard University.

Lieberson, Stanley. 1963. *Ethnic Patterns in American Cities*. New York: Free Press of Glencoe.

———. 1980. *A Piece of the Pie*. Berkeley: University of California Press.

Lieberson, Stanley, and Mary Waters. 1988. *From Many Strands*. New York: Russell Sage Foundation.

Lii, Jane. 1995. "Week in Sweatshop Reveals Grim Conspiracy of the Poor." *New York Times*, March 12.

Lim, In-Sook. 1997. "Korean Immigrant Women's Challenge to Gender Inequality at Home." *Gender and Society* 11: 31–51.

Lin, Jan. 1998. *Reconstructing Chinatown: Ethnic Enclave, Global Change*. Minneapolis: University of Minnesota Press.

Lind, Michael. 1995. "American by Invitation." *New Yorker*, April 24, 107–13.

———. 1998. "The Beige and the Black." *New York Times Magazine*, August 16, 38–39.

Lindsey, Linda. 1997. *Gender Roles: A Sociological Perspective*. Upper Saddle River, N.J.: Prentice-Hall.

Liu, Eric. 1998. *Accidental Asian*. New York: Random House.

Lobo, Arun Peter, Joseph Salvo, and Vicky Virgin. 1996. *The Newest New Yorkers, 1990-1994*. New York: Department of City Planning.

Logan, John. 1997a. "White Ethnics in the New York Economy, 1920-1960." Working Paper no. 113. New York: Russell Sage Foundation.

———. 1997b. "The Ethnic Neighborhood, 1920-1970." Working Paper no. 112. New York: Russell Sage Foundation.

Logan, John, and Richard Alba. 1996. "Does Race Matter Less for the Truly Advantaged? Residential Patterns in the New York Metropolis." Paper presented at the 1996 W. E. B. Du Bois Conference, Conservatism, Affirmative Action, and Other Public Policy Issues, Wright State University.

Logan, John, and Glenna Spitze. 1994. "Family Neighbors." *American Journal of Sociology* 100: 453–76.

Lopez, Ian Haney. 1996. *White by Law: The Legal Construction of Race*. New York: New York University Press.

Lower East Side Tenement Museum. 1995. *Lower East Side Tenement Museum: A Special Resource Study*. Boston: National Park Service.

Lubove, Roy. 1962. *The Progressives and the Slums: Tenement House Reform in New York City, 1890-1917*. Pittsburgh: University of Pittsburgh Press.

Ludmerer, Kenneth. 1972. "Genetics, Eugenics, and the Immigration Restriction Act of 1924." *Bulletin of the History of Medicine* 46: 59–81.

MacDonald, Heather. 1994. "Downward Mobility: The Failure of Open Admissions at City University." *City Journal* 4: 10–20.

———. 1995. "Why Koreans Succeed." *City Journal* 5: 12–29.

MacSwain, Angus. 1996. "Dominicans Smuggled into Puerto Rico." CISNEWS, October 18.

Mahler, Sarah. 1992. "Tres Veces Mojado: Undocumented Central and South American Migration to Suburban Long Island." Ph.D. diss., Columbia University.

———. 1993. "No Harmony in the Suburbs: White Suburbanites and Latino Immigrants on Long Island." Paper presented at a meeting of the American Anthropological Association, Washington, D.C.

———. 1995a. *American Dreaming: Immigrant Life on the Margins.* Princeton: Princeton University Press.

———. 1995b. *Salvadorans in Suburbia.* Boston: Allyn and Bacon.

———. 1996. "Bringing Gender to a Transnational Focus: Theoretical and Empirical Ideas." Manuscript.

Mangione, Jerre, and Ben Morreale. 1992. *La Storia: Five Centuries of the Italian American Experience.* New York: HarperCollins.

Mare, Robert. 1995. "Changes in Educational Attainment and School Enrollment." In Reynolds Farley (ed.), *State of the Union: America in the 1990s*, vol. 1, *Economic Trends.* New York: Russell Sage Foundation.

Margolis, Maxine. 1994. *Little Brazil: An Ethnography of Brazilian Immigrants in New York.* Princeton: Princeton University Press.

———. 1995. "Transnationalism and Popular Culture: The Case of Brazilian Immigrants in the United States." *Journal of Popular Culture* 29: 29–41.

———. 1998. *An Invisible Minority: Brazilians in New York City.* Boston: Allyn and Bacon.

Markowitz, Fran. 1993. *A Community in Spite of Itself: Soviet Jewish Emigrés in New York.* Washington, D.C.: Smithsonian Institution Press.

Markowitz, Ruth Jacknow. 1993. *My Daughter, the Teacher: Jewish Teachers in the New York Schools.* New Brunswick: Rutgers University Press.

Massey, Douglas. 1993. "Latinos, Poverty and the Underclass: A New Agenda for Research." *Hispanic Journal of Behavioral Sciences* 15: 449–75.

———. 1995. "The New Immigration and Ethnicity in the United States." *Population and Development Review* 21: 631–52.

Massey, Douglas, and Nancy Denton. 1993. *American Apartheid.* Cambridge: Harvard University Press.

Massey, Douglas, et al. 1993. "Theories of International Migration: A Review and Appraisal." *Population and Development Review* 19: 431–66.

———. 1994. "An Evaluation of International Migration Theory: The North American Case." *Population and Development Review* 20: 699–751.

Mateu-Gelabert, Pedro. 1997. "Street Ethos: Surviving High School." Ph.D. diss., New York University.

Mathieu, Joan. 1998. *Zulu: An Irish Journey.* New York: Farrar, Straus and Giroux.

Mazumdar, Sucheta. 1989. "Race and Racism: South Asians in the United States." In Gail Nomura, Russell Endo, Stephen Sumida, and Russell Leong (eds.), *Frontiers of Asian American Studies.* Pullman, Wash.: Washington State University Press.

McArdle, Nancy. 1997. "Home Ownership Attainment of New Jersey Immigrants."

In Thomas J. Espenshade (ed.), *Keys to Successful Immigration: Implications of the New Jersey Experience*. Washington, D.C.: Urban Institute Press.

McCarthy, Sheryl. 1995. "Getting to Know the Minority." *New York Newsday,* April 3.

McDonnell, Lorraine, and Paul Hill. 1993. *Newcomers in American Schools: Meeting the Educational Needs of Immigrant Youth*. Santa Monica, Calif.: Rand.

McKivigan, John, and Thomas Robertson. 1996. "The Irish American Worker in Transition, 1877-1914: New York as a Test Case." In Ronald Bayor and Timothy Meagher (eds.), *The New York Irish*. Baltimore: Johns Hopkins University Press.

McMahon, Thomas, Larian Angelo, and John Mollenkopf. 1997. "Hollow in the Middle: The Rise and Fall of New York City's Middle Class." Report of the New York City Council Finance Division, The City of New York.

McNickle, Chris. 1993. *To Be Mayor of New York*. New York: Columbia University Press.

———. 1996. "When New York Was Irish, and After." In Ronald Bayor and Timothy Meagher (eds.), *The New York Irish*. Baltimore: Johns Hopkins University Press.

Menjivar, Cecilia. 1999. "The Intersection of Work and Gender: Central American Immigrant Women and Employment in California." *American Behavioral Scientist* 42: 601-27.

Migration World Dateline. 1996. "Backdoor Immigration Flows via Puerto Rico." *Migration World* 24: 13.

Millman, Joel. 1996. "Ghetto Blasters." *Forbes* 157: 76-82.

———. 1997. *The Other Americans*. New York: Viking.

Min, Pyong Gap. 1995. "Korean Americans." In Min (ed.), *Asian Americans*. Thousand Oaks, Calif.: Sage Publications.

———. 1996. *Caught in the Middle: Korean Communities in New York and Los Angeles*. Berkeley: University of California Press.

———. 1998. *Changes and Conflicts: Korean Immigrant Families in New York*. Boston: Allyn and Bacon.

Mitchell, Alison. 1992. "Wary Recruits: Immigrants Vie for Day Jobs." *New York Times,* May 26.

Model, Suzanne. 1988. "The Economic Progress of European and East Asian Americans." *Annual Review of Sociology* 14: 363-80.

———. 1993. "The Ethnic Niche and the Structure of Opportunity: Immigrants and Minorities in New York City." In Michael Katz (ed.), *The "Underclass" Debate*. Princeton: Princeton University Press.

———. 1999. "Where New York's West Indians Work." Paper presented at the conference West Indian Migration to New York: Historical, Comparative, and Transnational Perspectives, Research Institute for the Study of Man, New York.

Mollenkopf, John. 1993. *New York City in the 1980s: A Social, Economic and Political Atlas*. New York: Simon and Schuster.

———. 1994. *A Phoenix in the Ashes*. Princeton: Princeton University Press.

———. 1997. "Economic Restructuring and Labor Market Outcomes." In "Hollow in the Middle: The Rise and Fall of New York City's Middle Class," prepared by

Thomas McMahon, Larian Angelo, and John Mollenkopf. Report of the New York City Council Finance Division, The City of New York.

Mollenkopf, John, Philip Kasinitz, and Matthew Lindholm. 1995. "Profiles of Nine Immigrant Categories and Their Sub-Groups and of Island-Born Puerto Ricans." In *Immigration/Migration and the CUNY Student of the Future.* New York: City University of New York.

Mollenkopf, John, Philip Kasinitz, Mary Waters, Nancy Lopez, and Dae Young Kim. 1997. "The School to Work Transition of Second Generation Immigrants in Metropolitan New York: Some Preliminary Findings." Paper presented at the conference, The Second Generation, The Jerome Levy Economics Institute, Bard College.

Montalto, Nicholas. 1981. "Multicultural Education in the New York City Public Schools, 1919-1941." In Diane Ravitch and Ronald Goodenow (eds.), *Educating an Urban People: The New York City Experience.* New York: Teachers College Press.

Moore, Deborah Dash. 1981. *At Home in America: Second Generation New York Jews.* New York: Columbia University Press.

———. 1992. "On the Fringes of the City: Jewish Neighborhoods in Three Boroughs." In David Ward and Oliver Zunz (eds.), *The Landscape of Modernity.* New York: Russell Sage Foundation.

Morawska, Ewa. 1989. "Labor Migrations of Poles in the Atlantic World Economy, 1880-1914." *Comparative Studies in Society and History* 31: 237-72.

———. 1990. "The Sociology and Historiography of Immigration." In Virginia Yans-McLaughlin (ed.), *Immigration Reconsidered.* New York: Oxford University Press.

———. 1991. "Return Migrations: Theoretical and Research Agenda." In Rudolph Vecoli and Suzanne Sinke (eds.), *A Century of European Migrations, 1830-1930.* Urbana: University of Illinois Press.

———. 1996. *Insecure Prosperity.* Princeton: Princeton University Press.

Morawska, Ewa, and Willfried Spohn. 1997. "Moving Europeans in the Globalizing World: Contemporary Migrations in a Historical-Comparative Perspective, 1955-1994 v. 1870-1914." In Wang Gungwu (ed.), *Global History and Migration.* Boulder: Westview.

Morokvasic, Mirjana. 1984. "Birds of Passage Are Also Women." *International Migration Review* 18: 886-907.

Moss, Mitchell, Anthony Townsend, and Emanuel Tobier. 1997. "Immigration Is Transforming New York City." New York: Taub Urban Research Center, New York University.

Mueller, Elizabeth, and David Howell. 1996. "Immigrants as Workers in New York City: A Review of Current Debates and Evidence." Immigrants in New York Series, Working Paper no. 3. New York: New School for Social Research.

Muller, Thomas. 1993. *Immigrants and the American City.* New York: New York University Press.

Nadell, Pamela. 1981. "The Journey to America by Steam: The Jews of Eastern Europe in Transition." *American Jewish History* 71: 269–84.

Nagourney, Adam. 1996. "Long Roads to City Hall Get Longer." *New York Times,* December 4.

Nasaw, David. 1979. *Schooled to Order.* New York: Oxford University Press.

Neckerman, Kathryn, Prudence Carter, and Jennifer Lee. 1999. "Segmented Assimilation and Minority Cultures of Mobility." *Ethnic and Racial Studies* 22: 945–65.

*New York: A Collection from Harper's Magazine.* 1991. New York: Gallery Books.

Newman, Katherine. 1995. "The Employer Consortium: Improving Job Mobility among Low-Wage Workers in the Inner City." Working Paper no. 69. New York: Russell Sage Foundation.

———. 1999. *No Shame in My Game: The Working Poor in the Inner City.* New York: Alfred Knopf and the Russell Sage Foundation.

Newman, Maria. 1995. "Cortines Has Plan to Coach Minorities into Top Schools." *New York Times,* March 21.

———. 1996. "In New York City High Schools, Paths to Diplomas Grow Longer for Many." *New York Times,* June 3.

Nieves, Evelyn. 1991. "Big Classes, Little Space in Elmhurst." *New York Times,* March 30.

Nossiter, Adam. 1995. "Jamaican Way Station in the Bronx." *New York Times,* October 25.

Nugent, Walter. 1992. *Crossings: The Great Transatlantic Migrations, 1870-1914.* Bloomington: Indiana University Press.

O'Cleireacain, Carol. 1997. "The Private Economy and Public Budget of New York City." In Margaret Crahan and Alberto Vourvoulias-Bush (eds.), *The City and the World: New York's Global Future.* New York: Council of Foreign Relations.

Odencrantz, Louise. 1919. *Italian Women in Industry: A Study of Conditions in New York City.* New York: Russell Sage Foundation.

Olneck, Michael, and Marvin Lazerson. 1974. "The School Achievement of Immigrant Children, 1900-1930." *History of Education Quarterly* 14: 453–82.

Olsen, Laurie. 1997. "Public Education, Immigrants and Racialization: The Contemporary Americanization Project." Paper presented to the conference Immigrants, Civic Culture, and Modes of Political Incorporation: A Contemporary and Historical Comparison, Sante Fe, N. Mex.

Ong, Aihwa. 1995. "Women out of China: Traveling Tables and Traveling Theories in Postcolonial Feminism." In Ruth Behar and Deborah Gordon (eds.), *Women Writing Culture.* Berkeley: University of California Press.

Ong, Paul, and Tania Azores. 1994. "Migration and Incorporation of Filipino Nurses." In Paul Ong, Edna Bonacich, and Lucie Cheng (eds.), *The New Asian Immigration in Los Angeles and Global Restructuring.* Philadelphia: Temple University Press.

Orlean, Susan. 1992. "All Mixed Up." *New Yorker,* June 22, 90–104.

Orleck, Annelise. 1987. "The Soviet Jews: Life in Brighton Beach, Brooklyn." In

Nancy Foner (ed.), *New Immigrants in New York*. New York: Columbia University Press.

———. 1995. *Common Sense and a Little Fire: Women and Working Class Politics in the United States, 1900-1965*. Chapel Hill: University of North Carolina Press.

Orsi, Robert A. 1985. *The Madonna of 115th Street: Faith and Community in Italian Harlem, 1880-1950*. New Haven: Yale University Press.

———. 1990. "The Fault of Memory: 'Southern Italy' in the Imagination of Immigrants and the Lives of Their Children in Italian Harlem, 1920-1945." *Journal of Family History* 15: 133-47.

Oser, Alan. 1999. "Making Tenements Modern." *New York Times* (Real Estate Section), April 4.

Page, Susan. 1997. "Exploring the Challenges of Immigration." *USA Today*, October 13.

Palmer, Ransford. 1995. *Pilgrims from the Sun: West Indian Migration to America*. New York: Twayne.

Papademetriou, Demetrios, and Nicholas DiMarzio. 1986. *Undocumented Aliens in the New York Metropolitan Area*. New York: Center for Migration Studies.

Park, Kyeyoung. 1997. *The Korean American Dream*. Ithaca: Cornell University Press.

Passel, Jeffrey, and Rebecca Clark. 1998. "Immigrants in New York: Their Legal Status, Income and Taxes." Washington, D.C.: The Urban Institute.

Pedraza, Silvia. 1991. "Women and Migration: The Social Consequences of Gender." *Annual Review of Sociology* 17: 303-25.

Peiss, Kathy. 1986. *Cheap Amusements: Working Women and Leisure in Turn-of-the-Century New York*. Temple: Temple University Press.

Perez-Pena, Richard. 1997. "Study Shows New York Has the Greatest Income Gap." *New York Times*, December 17.

Perlmann, Joel. 1988. *Ethnic Differences*. New York: Cambridge University Press.

———. 1996a. "Literacy among the Jews of Russia in 1897: A Reanalysis of Census Data." Working Paper no. 182, The Jerome Levy Economics Institute, Bard College.

———. 1996b. "Which Immigrant Occupational Skills? Explanations of Jewish Economic Mobility in the United States and New Evidence, 1910-1920." Working Paper no. 181, The Jerome Levy Economics Institute, Bard College.

Perlmann, Joel, and Roger Waldinger. 1997. "Second Generation Decline? Children of Immigrants, Past and Present: A Reconsideration." *International Migration Review* 31: 893-922.

Pessar, Patricia. 1982. "Kinship Relations of Production in the Migration Process: The Case of Dominican Emigration to the United States." Occasional Paper no. 32. New York: Center for Latin American and Caribbean Studies, New York University.

———. 1984. "The Linkage Between the Household and the Workplace of Dominican Women in the United States." *International Migration Review* 18: 1188-211.

———. 1986. "The Role of Gender in Dominican Settlement in the United States."

In June Nash and Helen Safa (eds.), *Women and Change in Latin America*. South Hadley, Mass.: Bergin and Garvey.

———. 1987. "The Dominicans: Women in the Household and the Garment Industry." In Nancy Foner (ed.), *New Immigrants in New York*. New York: Columbia University Press.

———. 1995a. *A Visa for a Dream*. Boston: Allyn and Bacon.

———. 1995b. "On the Homefront and in the Workplace: Integrating Women into Feminine Discourse." *Anthropological Quarterly* 68: 37–47.

———. 1999. "The Role of Gender, Households and Social Networks in the Migration Process: A Review and Appraisal." In Charles Hirschman, Philip Kasinitz, and Josh DeWind (eds.), *The Handbook of International Migration*. New York: Russell Sage Foundation.

Phelps-Stokes, I. N. 1967 [1918]. *The Iconography of Manhattan Island*, vol. 3. New York: Arno Press.

Plunz, Richard. 1990. *A History of Housing in New York City*. New York: Columbia University Press.

Portes, Alejandro. 1995. "Children of Immigrants: Segmented Assimilation and Its Determinants." In Alejandro Portes (ed.), *The Economic Sociology of Immigration*. New York: Russell Sage Foundation.

———. 1996. "Global Villagers: The Rise of Transnational Communities." *The American Prospect* (March–April): 74–78.

———. 1997. "Immigration Theory for a New Century: Some Problems and Opportunities." *International Migration Review* 31: 799–825.

Portes, Alejandro, and Lingxin Hao. 1997. "English First or English Only? Bilingualism and Parental Language Loss in the Second Generation." Paper presented at the conference The Second Generation, The Jerome Levy Economics Institute, Bard College.

Portes, Alejandro, and Dag MacLeod. 1996. "What Shall I Call Myself?: Hispanic Identity Formation in the Second Generation." *Ethnic and Racial Studies* 19: 523–47.

Portes, Alejandro, and Rubén Rumbaut. 1990. *Immigrant America*. Berkeley: University of California Press.

———. 1996. *Immigrant America*. 2d ed. Berkeley: University of California Press.

Portes, Alejandro, and Richard Schauffler. 1994. "Language and the Second Generation: Bilingualism Yesterday and Today." *International Migration Review* 28: 640–61.

Portes, Alejandro, and Julia Sensenbrenner. 1993. "Embeddedness and Immigration: Notes on the Social Determinants of Economic Action." *American Journal of Sociology* 98: 1320–50.

Portes, Alejandro, and Alex Stepick. 1993. *City on the Edge*. Berkeley: University of California Press.

Portes, Alejandro, and Min Zhou. 1993. "The New Second Generation: Segmented

Assimilation and Its Variants among Post-1965 Immigrant Youth." *Annals of the American Academy of Political and Social Science* 530: 74–98.

Prieto, Yolanda. 1992. "Cuban Women in New Jersey: Gender Relations and Change." In Donna Gabaccia (ed.), *Seeking Common Ground.* Westport, Conn.: Praeger.

Purnick, Joyce. 1995. "Metro Matters: A So-Sorry Situation, Politicians' Apologies." *New York Times,* April 17.

Puzo, Mario. 1969. *The Godfather.* New York: G. P. Putnam's.

Raab, Selwyn. 1997. "City's Police Brutality Report Card." *New York Times,* August 17.

"Rats and Squalor, at $800 a Month." 1996. *New York Times,* editorial, October 14.

Ravage, Marcus. 1917. *An American in the Making: The Life Story of an Immigrant.* New York: Harper and Brothers.

Ravitch, Diane. 1974. *The Great School Wars: A History of the New York City Public Schools.* New York: Basic.

Reimers, David. 1992. *Still the Golden Door.* 2d ed. New York: Columbia University Press.

———. 1998. *Unwelcome Strangers: American Identity and the Turn Against Immigration.* New York: Columbia University Press.

Repak, Terry. 1995. *Waiting on Washington: Central American Workers in the Nation's Capital.* Philadelphia: Temple University Press.

Richards, Craig, Donna Merritt, and Tian Ming Sheu. 1994. "Strategic Environmental Factors Constraining Fiscal Resources in Urban Schools: The Case of New York City." In Francisco Rivera-Batiz (ed.), *Reinventing Urban Education.* New York: IUME Press, Teachers College, Columbia University.

Riis, Jacob. 1971 [1890]. *How the Other Half Lives.* New York: Dover.

Rios, Palmira. n.d. "Dominicans in the New York Region." Paper prepared for the Regional Plan Association, New York.

———. 1992. "Comments on Rethinking Migration: A Transnational Perspective." In Nina Glick Schiller, Linda Basch, and Cristina Blanc-Szanton (eds.), *Towards a Transnational Perspective on Migration.* New York: New York Academy of Sciences.

Rischin, Moses. 1962. *The Promised City.* Cambridge: Harvard University Press.

Rivera-Batiz, Francisco. 1994. "The Multicultural Population of New York City: A Socioeconomic Profile of the Mosaic." In Francisco Rivera-Batiz (ed.), *Reinventing Urban Education.* New York: IUME Press, Teachers College, Columbia University.

———. 1995. "Immigrants and Schools: The Case of the Big Apple." *Forum for Applied Research and Public Policy* (Fall): 84–89.

———. 1996. "The Education of Immigrant Children: The Case of New York City." The Immigrant New York Series, Working Paper no. 1. New York: New School for Social Research.

Rivera-Batiz, Francisco, and Lillian Marti. 1995. "A School System at Risk: A Study

of the Consequences of Overcrowding in the New York City Public Schools."
IUME Research Report no. 95-I, Teachers College, Columbia University.

Roberts, Sam. 1994. *Who We Are: A Portrait of America Based on the Latest U.S. Census.*
New York: Times Books.

Robotham, Donald. 1998. "Transnationalism in the Caribbean: Formal and Informal." *American Ethnologist* 25: 307–21.

Rodriguez, Clara. 1994. "Challenging Racial Hegemony: Puerto Ricans in the
United States." In Steven Gregory and Roger Sanjek (eds.), *Race.* New Brunswick, N.J.: Rutgers University Press.

———. 1996. "Racial Themes in the Literature: Puerto Ricans and Other Latinos." In Gabriel Haslip-Viera and Sherrie Baver (eds.), *Latinos in New York.* Notre
Dame: University of Notre Dame Press.

Rodriguez, Clara, and Hector Cordero-Guzman. 1992. "Placing Race in Context."
*Ethnic and Racial Studies* 15: 523–42.

Roediger, David. 1994. *Toward the Abolition of Whiteness.* London: Verso.

Rohter, Larry. 1996. "U.S. Benefits Go: Allure to Dominicans Doesn't." *New York
Times,* October 12.

———. 1997. "Flood of Dominicans Lets Some Enter U.S. by Fraud." *New York
Times,* February 19.

———. 1998. "Island Life Not Idyllic for Youths from U.S." *New York Times,* February 20.

Rose, Frederick. 1995. "The Growing Backlash Against Immigration Includes Many
Myths." *Wall Street Journal,* April 26.

Rose, Peter. 1985. "Asian Americans: From Pariahs to Paragons." In Nathan Glazer
(ed.), *Clamor at the Gates.* San Francisco: Institute for Contemporary Studies.

Rosenbaum, Emily, Samantha Friedman, Michael Schill, and Hielke Buddelmeyer.
1998. "Nativity Differences in Neighborhood Quality among New York City
Households, 1996." Working Paper no. 98–4. Center for Real Estate and Urban
Policy, New York University School of Law.

Rosenblatt, Roger. 1993. "Sunset, Sunrise." *New Republic,* December 27, 20–23.

Rosenwaike, Ira. 1972. *Population History of New York City.* Syracuse: Syracuse University Press.

Roskolenko, Harry. 1971. *The Time That Was Then.* New York: Dial Press.

Ross, Edward A. 1914. *The Old World in the New.* New York: Century.

Ross, Leonard Q. [Leo Rosten]. 1937. *The Education of H\*Y\*M\*A\*N  K\*A\*P\*L\*A\*N.*
New York: Harcourt Brace.

Roth, Henry. 1991 [1934]. *Call It Sleep.* New York: Noonday Press.

———. 1994. *Mercy of a Rude Stream.* New York: St. Martin's.

Roth, Philip. 1969. *Portnoy's Complaint.* New York: Random House.

Rouse, Roger. 1992. "Making Sense of Settlement: Class Transformation, Cultural
Struggle, and Transnationalism among Mexican Migrants in the United States."
In Nina Glick Schiller, Linda Basch, and Cristina Blanc-Szanton (eds.), *Towards*

*a Transnational Perspective on Migration.* New York: New York Academy of Sciences.

―――. 1995. "Thinking Through Transnationalism: Notes on the Cultural Politics of Class Relations in a Contemporary United States." *Public Culture* 7: 353–402.

Ruf, Gregory. 1994. "Ba Da Dao: Avenue of Prosperity." Report prepared for a Community History/Exhibition Planning Project, Brooklyn Historical Society and Chinatown History Museum.

Rumbaut, Rubén. 1991. "Passages to America: Perspectives on the New Immigration." In Alan Wolfe (ed.), *America at Century's End.* Berkeley: University of California Press.

―――. 1996. "Origins and Destinies: Immigration, Race, and Ethnicity in Contemporary America." In Silvia Pedraza and Rubén Rumbaut (eds.), *Origins and Destinies.* Belmont, Calif.: Wadsworth.

―――. 1997a. "Paradoxes (and Orthodoxies) of Assimilation." *Sociological Perspectives* 40: 481–511.

―――. 1997b. "Ties That Bind: Immigration and Immigrant Families in the United States." In Alan Booth, Ann Crouter, and Nancy Landale (eds.), *Immigration and the Family.* Mahwah, N.J.: Lawrence Erlbaum.

―――. 1998. "Transformations: The Post-Immigrant Generation in an Age of Diversity." Paper presented at the annual meeting of the Eastern Sociological Society, Philadelphia.

Sacks, Karen Brodkin. 1994. "How Did Jews Become White Folks?" In Steven Gregory and Roger Sanjek (eds.), *Race.* New Brunswick: Rutgers University Press.

Salins, Peter. 1997. *Assimilation American Style.* New York: Basic.

Salvo, Joseph, and Ronald Ortiz. 1992. *The Newest New Yorkers: An Analysis of Immigration into New York City during the 1980s.* New York: Department of City Planning.

Salvo, Joseph, Ronald Ortiz, and Arun Peter Lobo. 1994. *Puerto Rican New Yorkers in 1990.* New York: Department of City Planning.

Sanchez, Arturo. 1997. "Transnational Political Agency and Identity Formation among Colombian Immigrants." Paper presented at the conference Transnational Communities and the Political Economy of New York in the 1990s, New School for Social Research, New York.

Sanjek, Roger. 1992. "The Organization of Festivals and Ceremonies among Americans and Immigrants in Queens, New York." In Ake Daun, Billy Ehn, and Barbro Klein (eds.), *To Make the World Safe for Diversity.* Stockholm: Swedish Immigration Institute and Museum.

―――. 1994. "Intermarriage and the Future of Races in the United States." In Steven Gregory and Roger Sanjek (eds.), *Race.* New Brunswick: Rutgers University Press.

―――. 1998. *The Future of Us All: Race and Neighborhood Politics in New York City.* Ithaca: Cornell University Press.

Sarna, Jonathan. 1981. "The Myth of No Return: Jewish Return Migration to Eastern Europe, 1881–1914." *American Jewish History* 71: 256–68.

Sassen, Saskia. 1988. *The Mobility of Labor and Capital.* New York: Cambridge University Press.

———. 1991. *The Global City.* Princeton: Princeton University Press.

Schill, Michael, Samantha Friedman, and Emily Rosenbaum. 1998. "The Housing Conditions of Immigrants in New York City." Working Paper no. 98-2. Center for Real Estate and Urban Policy, New York University School of Law.

Schmitt, Eric. 1997. "Illegal Immigrants Rose to 5 Million in '96." *New York Times,* February 8.

Schwartz, Benjamin. 1995. "The Diversity Myth: America's Leading Export." *Atlantic Monthly,* May, 57–67.

Scott, Jenny. 1997. "Orphan Girls of China at Home in New York." *New York Times,* August 19.

Sengupta, Somini. 1996. "Immigrants in New York Pressing for Drive for Dual Nationality." *New York Times,* December 30.

———. 1998a. "Crackdowns Have Smugglers Trying New Routes, Officials Say." *New York Times,* June 1.

———. 1998b. "Public Schools See Enrollment Slowing Down." *New York Times,* August 2.

Sexton, Joe. 1995. "The Cold War in Brighton Beach." *New York Times,* January 17.

Shargel, Baila, and Harold Drimmer. 1994. *The Jews of Westchester: A Social History.* Fleischmanns, N.Y.: Purple Mountain Press.

Sheingold, Dave. 1995. "The Next Wave: New Immigrants Change the Face of the Suburbs." *Daily Item* (Gannett Suburban Newspapers, Westchester), 5-pt. series, December 3–7.

Shumsky, Neil. 1992. "Let No Man Stop to Plunder: American Hostility to Return Migration, 1880–1924." *Journal of American Ethnic History* 11: 56–75.

Simon, Rita, and James Lynch. 1999. "A Comparative Assessment of Public Opinion Toward Immigrants and Immigration Policies." *International Migration Review* 33: 455–67.

Siu, Paul. 1987. *The Chinese Laundryman.* New York: New York University Press.

Skocpol, Theda, and Margaret Somers. 1980. "The Uses of Comparative History in Macrosocial Inquiry." *Comparative Studies in Society and History* 22: 174–97.

Skogan, Wesley. 1995. "Crime and Racial Fears of White Americans." *Annals of the American Academy of Political and Social Science* 539: 59–69.

Slyomovics, Susan. 1995. "The Muslim World Day Parade." In Peter van der Veer (ed.), *Nation and Migration: The Politics of Space in the South Asian Diaspora.* Philadelphia: University of Pennsylvania Press.

Smith, Christopher. 1995. "Asian New York: The Geography and Politics of Diversity." *International Migration Review* 29: 59–84.

Smith, Christopher, and Min Zhou. n.d. "Flushing: Capital and Community in a Transitional Neighborhood." Manuscript.

Smith, James. 1998. "Mexico's Dual Nationality Opens Doors." *Los Angeles Times,* March 20.

Smith, James, and Barry Edmonston (eds.). 1997. *The New Americans: Economic, Demographic, and Fiscal Effects of Immigration.* Washington, D.C.: National Academy Press.

Smith, Robert. 1996. "Mexicans in New York: Membership and Incorporation in a New Immigrant Community." In Gabriel Haslip-Viera and Sherrie Baver (eds.), *Latinos in New York.* Notre Dame: University of Notre Dame Press.

———. 1997a. "Transnational Migration, Assimilation, and Political Community." In Margaret Crahan and Alberto Vourvoulias Bush (eds.), *The City and the World: New York's Global Future.* New York: Council on Foreign Relations.

———. 1997b. "Racial and Ethnic Hierarchies and the Incorporation of Mexicans in New York City: Transnational Communities and Labor Market Niches." Paper presented at the conference Transnational Communities and the Political Economy of New York City in the 1990s, New School for Social Research, New York.

———. 1998a. "Reflections on Migration, the State and the Construction, Durability and Newness of Transnational Life." *Soziale Welt* 12: 197-217.

———. 1998b. "Notes for a Paper on Transnationalism in the Second Generation among Mexican Americans in Brooklyn." Paper presented at the conference Transnationalism and the Second Generation, Harvard University.

———. 1998c. "Transnational Localities: Community, Technology and the Politics of Membership within the Context of Mexico and US Migration." In Michael Peter Smith and Luis Guarnizo (eds.), *Transnationalism from Below.* New Brunswick: Transaction.

Sontag, Deborah. 1996. "For Poor, Life 'Trapped in a Cage.'" *New York Times,* October 6.

Sontag, Deborah, and Celia Dugger. 1998. "The New Immigrant Tide: A Shuttle Between Worlds." *New York Times,* July 19.

Sontag, Deborah, and Larry Rohter. 1997. "Dominicans May Allow Voting Abroad." *New York Times,* November 15.

Sorin, Gerald. 1992. *A Time for Building: The Third Migration, 1880-1920.* Baltimore: Johns Hopkins University Press.

Soto, Isa Maria. 1987. "West Indian Child Fostering: Its Role in Migrant Exchanges." In Constance Sutton and Elsa Chaney (eds.), *Caribbean Life in New York City.* New York: Center for Migration Studies.

Soyer, Daniel. 1997. *Jewish Immigrant Associations and American Identity in New York, 1880-1939.* Cambridge: Harvard University Press.

Spain, Daphne, and Suzanne Bianchi. 1996. *Balancing Act: Motherhood, Marriage, and Employment among American Women.* New York: Russell Sage Foundation.

Speranza, Gino. 1974 [1906]. "Political Representation of Italo-American Colonies in the Italian Parliament." In Francisco Cordasco and Eugene Bucchioni (eds.),

*The Italians: Social Backgrounds of an American Group.* Clifton, N.J.: Augustus M. Kelley.

Spewack, Bella. 1995. *Streets: A Memoir of the Lower East Side.* New York: Feminist Press.

Stafford, Susan Buchanan. 1987. "The Haitians: The Cultural Meaning of Race and Ethnicity." In Nancy Foner (ed.), *New Immigrants in New York.* New York: Columbia University Press.

Steinberg, Laurence. 1996. *Beyond the Classroom.* New York: Simon and Schuster.

Steinberg, Stephen. 1981. *The Ethnic Myth.* New York: Atheneum.

———. 1986. "The Rise of the Jewish Professional: Case Studies of Jewish Intergenerational Mobility." *Ethnic and Racial Studies* 9: 280–91.

Stepick, Alex. 1998. *Pride against Prejudice: Haitians in the United States.* Boston: Allyn and Bacon.

Stone, Carl. 1982. *The Political Opinions of the Jamaican People, 1976-1981.* Kingston: Blackett.

Sung, Betty Lee. 1987. *The Adjustment of Chinese Immigrant Children in New York City.* New York: Center for Migration Studies.

Sutton, Constance. 1992. "Transnational Identities and Cultures: Caribbean Immigrants in the United States." In Michael D'Innocenzo and Josef Sirefman (eds.), *Immigration and Ethnicity.* Westport, Conn.: Greenwood.

Sutton, Constance, and Susan Makiesky. 1975. "Migration and West Indian Racial and Ethnic Consciousness." In Helen Safa and Brian duToit (eds.), *Migration and Development.* The Hague: Mouton.

Takaki, Ronald. 1993. *A Different Mirror.* Boston: Little Brown.

Tentler, Leslie Woodcock. 1979. *Wage-Earning Women.* New York: Oxford University Press.

Thistlewaite, Frank. 1960. "Migration from Europe Overseas in the Nineteenth and Twentieth Centuries." Reprinted in Rudolph Vecoli and Suzanne Sinke (eds.), *A Century of European Migrations, 1830-1930.* Urbana: University of Illinois Press, 1991.

Tilly, Charles. 1990. "Transplanted Networks." In Virginia Yans-McLaughlin (ed.), *Immigration Reconsidered.* New York: Oxford University Press.

Tomasi, Silvano. 1975. *Piety and Power.* New York: Center for Migration Studies.

Topp, Michael Miller. 1997. "The Transnationalism of the Italian American Left: The Lawrence Strike of 1912 and the Italian Chamber of Commerce of New York City." *Journal of American Ethnic History* 17: 39–63.

Torres, Andres. 1995. *Between Melting Pot and Mosaic.* Philadelphia: Temple University Press.

Traub, James. 1994. *City on a Hill: Testing the American Dream at City College.* Reading, Mass.: Addison-Wesley.

Tuchman, Gaye, and Harry Levine. 1996. "Safe Trayf." *Brandeis Review* 16: 24–31.

Tyack, David. 1974. *The One Best System: A History of American Urban Education.* Cambridge: Harvard University Press.

———. 1997. "School for Citizens: The Politics of Civic Education, 1790-1990." Paper presented at the Social Science Research Council Workshop on Immigrants, Political Incorporation, and Civic Culture, Santa Fe, N. Mex.

Ueda, Reed. 1994. *Postwar Immigrant America: A Social History.* New York: St. Martin's Press.

———. 1997. "Historical Patterns of Immigrant Status and Incorporation in the United States." Paper presented at the Social Science Research Council Workshop on Immigrants, Political Incorporation and Civic Culture, Santa Fe, New Mexico.

U.S. Bureau of the Census. *Population 1910: Thirteenth Census of the United States, 1910,* vol. 1. Washington, D.C.: Government Printing Office.

U.S. Commission on Civil Rights. 1992. *Civil Rights Issues Facing Asian Americans in the 1990s.* Washington, D.C.: U.S. Commission on Civil Rights.

U.S. Immigration Commission. 1911. *The Children of Immigrants in Schools.* Washington, D.C.: Government Printing Office.

Van Denberg, Joseph. 1972 [1911]. *Causes of the Elimination of Students from the Secondary Schools of New York City, 1906-1910.* New York: AMS Press.

Van Gelder, Lawrence. 1996. "One in Eight Students Attend Fewer Class Hours Than Required, a Report Finds." *New York Times,* March 13.

Van Kleeck, Mary. 1913. *Artificial Flower Makers.* New York: Russell Sage Foundation.

Vecoli, Rudolph. 1965. *The People of New Jersey.* Princeton: Van Nostrand.

Vernez, Georges, and Allan Abrahamse. 1996. *How Immigrants Fare in U.S. Education.* Santa Monica, Calif.: Rand.

Vickerman, Milton. 1999. *Crosscurrents: West Indians and Race in America.* New York: Oxford University Press.

Waldinger, Roger. n.d. "Social Capital or Social Closure? Immigrant Networks in the Labor Market." Manuscript.

———. 1986. *Through the Eye of the Needle.* New York: New York University Press.

———. 1987. "Beyond Nostalgia: The Old Neighborhood Revisited." *New York Affairs* 10: 1-12.

———. 1989. "Structural Opportunity or Ethnic Advantage? Immigrant Business Development in New York." *International Migration Review* 23: 48-72.

———. 1995. "When the Melting Pot Boils Over: The Irish, Jews, Blacks and Koreans of New York." In Michael Peter Smith and Joe Feagin (eds.), *The Bubbling Cauldron.* Minneapolis: University of Minnesota Press.

———. 1996a. *Still the Promised City?: African Americans and New Immigrants in Postindustrial New York.* Cambridge: Harvard University Press.

———. 1996b. "Ethnicity and Opportunity in the Plural City." In Roger Waldinger and Mehdi Bozorgmehr (eds.), *Ethnic Los Angeles.* New York: Russell Sage Foundation.

———. 1996c. "From Ellis Island to LAX: Immigrant Prospects in the American City." *International Migration Review* 30: 1078-86.

————. 1997. "Black/Immigrant Competition Re-assessed: New Evidence from Los Angeles." *Sociological Perspectives* 40: 365–86.

Waldinger, Roger, Howard Aldrich, Robin Ward and Associates. 1990. *Ethnic Entrepreneurs*. Newbury Park, Calif.: Sage.

Waldinger, Roger, and Joel Perlmann. 1998. "Second Generations: Past, Present, Future." *Journal of Ethnic and Migration Studies* 24: 5–24.

Waldman, Amy. 1998. "Old Places, New Faces: In Southern Brooklyn, Coexistence but Not Quite Community." *New York Times* (city section), April 12.

Waters, Mary. 1992. "Ethnic and Racial Groups in the USA: Conflict and Cooperation." Paper presented at the International Conference on Ethnic Conflicts, Autonomy, and the Devolution of Power in Multiethnic States, Moscow.

————. 1994. "Ethnic and Racial Identities of Second Generation Black Immigrants in New York City." *International Migration Review* 28: 795–820.

————. 1995. "The Intersection of Gender, Race and Ethnicity in Identity Development of Caribbean American Teens." In Bonnie Leadbeater and Niobe Way (eds.), *Urban Adolescent Girls: Resisting Stereotypes*. New York: New York University Press.

————. 1997a. "Immigrant Families at Risk: Factors That Undermine Chances for Success." In Alan Booth, Ann Crouter, and Nancy Landale (eds.), *Immigration and the Family*. Mahwah, N.J.: Lawrence Erlbaum.

————. 1997b. "The Impact of Racial Segregation on the Education and Work Outcomes of Second Generation West Indians in New York City." Paper presented at the conference The Second Generation, The Jerome Levy Institute, Bard College.

Waters, Mary, Philip Kasinitz, and John Mollenkopf. 1998. "Transnationalism and the Children of Immigrants in the United States: What Are the Issues?" Paper presented at the conference Transnationalism and the Second Generation, Harvard University.

Watkins, Susan Cotts, and Arodys Robles. 1994. "A Tabular Presentation of Immigrant Characteristics, by Ethnic Group." In Susan Cotts Watkins (ed.), *After Ellis Island: Newcomers and Natives in the 1910 Census*. New York: Russell Sage Foundation.

Weinberg, Sydney Stahl. 1988. *The World of Our Mothers*. Chapel Hill: University of North Carolina Press.

Weiner, Lynn. 1985. *From Working Girl to Working Mother: The Female Labor Force in the United States, 1820–1980*. Chapel Hill: University of North Carolina Press.

Weisser, Michael. 1985. *A Brotherhood of Memory*. New York: Basic.

Wenger, Beth. 1996. *New York Jews and the Great Depression*. New Haven: Yale University Press.

————. 1997. "Memory as Identity: The Invention of the Lower East Side." *American Jewish History* 85: 3–27.

White, Michael, Robert Dymowski, and Shilian Wang. 1994. "Ethnic Neighbors and Ethnic Myths: An Examination of Residential Segregation in 1910." In Susan Cotts Watkins (ed.), *After Ellis Island*. New York: Russell Sage Foundation.

Wilson, William Julius. 1996. *When Work Disappears*. New York: Knopf.

Wilson, Kenneth, and Alejandro Portes. 1980. "Immigrant Enclaves: An Analysis of the Labor Market Experiences of Cubans in Miami." *American Journal of Sociology* 86: 296–319.

Winnick, Louis. 1990. *New People in Old Neighborhoods*. New York: Russell Sage Foundation.

Wolff, Craig. 1994. "Immigrants to Life Underground." *New York Times*, March 13.

Wollenberg, Charles. 1995. " 'Yellow Peril' in the Schools." In Don Nakanishi and Tina Yamano Nishida (eds.), *The Asian American Educational Experience*. New York: Routledge.

Wong, Bernard. 1982. *Chinatown*. New York: Holt, Rinehart and Winston.

———. 1998. *Ethnicity and Entrepreneurship: The New Chinese Immigrants in the San Francisco Bay Area*. Boston: Allyn and Bacon.

Wong, Shawn. 1995. *American Knees*. New York: Simon and Schuster.

Wright, Lawrence. 1994. "One Drop of Blood." *New Yorker*, July 25, 46–55.

Wright, Richard, and Mark Ellis. 1996. "Immigrants and the Changing Racial/Ethnic Division of Labor in New York City, 1970–1990." *Urban Geography* 17: 317–53.

Wyman, Mark. 1993. *Round-Trip America: The Immigrants Return to Europe, 1880–1930*. Ithaca: Cornell University Press.

Yamada, Ken, and Ji-Yeon Yuh. 1990. "Singled Out for Success." *New York Newsday*, June 29.

Yetman, Norman. 1999. "Patterns of Ethnic Integration in America." In Norman Yetman (ed.), *Majority and Minority: The Dynamics of Race and Ethnicity in American Life*. Boston: Allyn and Bacon.

Yezierska, Anzia. 1975 [1925]. *The Bread Givers*. New York: Persea.

Yoon, In-Jin. 1997. *On My Own: Korean Businesses and Race Relations in America*. Chicago: University of Chicago Press.

Yu, Renqui. 1992. *To Save China, To Save Ourselves: The Chinese Hand Laundry Alliance of New York*. Philadelphia: Temple University Press.

Zhou, Min. 1992. *Chinatown: The Socioeconomic Profile of an Urban Enclave*. Philadelphia: Temple University Press.

———. 1994. "Chinatown Revisited: Community-Based Organizations, Immigrant Families, and the Younger Generation." Working Paper no. 67. New York: Russell Sage Foundation.

———. 1995. "Chinatowns: Continued Renewal of Immigrant Communities." Paper presented at the conference Immigrant and Minority Entrepreneurship, University of Texas, Austin.

———. 1997. "Social Capital in Chinatown: The Role of Community-Based Organizations and Families in the Adaptation of the Younger Generation." In Maxine

Seller and Lois Weis (eds.), *Beyond Black and White: New Faces and Voices in U.S. Schools.* Albany: State University of New York Press.

Zhou, Min, and Carl Bankston III. 1998. *Growing Up American.* New York: Russell Sage Foundation.

Zhou, Min, and John Logan. 1989. "Returns on Human Capital in Ethnic Enclaves: New York City's Chinatown." *American Journal of Sociology* 86: 295–319.

———. 1991. "In and Out of Chinatown: Residential Mobility and Segregation of New York's Chinese." *Social Forces* 70: 387–407.

Zhou, Min, and Regina Nordquist. 1994. "Work and Its Place in the Lives of Immigrant Women: Garment Workers in New York City's Chinatown." *Applied Behavioral Science Review* 2: 187–211.

Zolberg, Aristide. 1995. "From Invitation to Interdiction: U.S. Foreign Policy and Immigration since 1945." In Michael Teitelbaum and Myron Weiner (eds.), *Threatened Peoples, Threatened Borders.* New York: Norton.

———. 1999. "Matters of State: Theorizing Immigration Policy." In Charles Hirschman, Philip Kasinitz, and Josh DeWind (eds.), *The Handbook of International Migration.* New York: Russell Sage Foundation.

Zukin, Sharon, and Gilda Zwerman. 1985. "Housing for the Working Poor: A Historical View of Jews and Blacks in Brownsville." *New York Affairs* 9: 3–18.

# Index